Artificial Intelligence of Things (AIoT) for Retail and Services Management

Joaquim Monteiro Pratas
Porto Accounting and Business School, CEOS, Polytechnic Institute of Porto, Portugal

Maria Antónia Rodrigues
Porto Accounting and Business School, CEOS, Polytechnic Institute of Porto, Portugal & SIIS Porto, Portugal

Maria Amélia Carvalho
Porto Accounting and Business School, CEOS, Polytechnic Institute of Porto, Portugal

IGI Global
Scientific Publishing
Publishing Tomorrow's Research Today

Published in the United States of America by
IGI Global Scientific Publishing
701 East Chocolate Avenue
Hershey, PA, 17033, USA
Tel: 717-533-8845 | Fax: 717-533-7115
Website: https://www.igi-global.com E-mail: cust@igi-global.com

Library of Congress Cataloging-in-Publication Data

Names: Pratas, Joaquim Monteiro, 1980- editor. | Rodrigues, Maria Antonia, 1977- editor. | Carvalho, Maria Amélia Machado, 1989- editor.

Title: Artificial intelligence of things (AIOT) for retail and services management / edited by: Joaquim Pratas, Maria Rodrigues, Maria Amélia Machado Carvalho.

Description: Hershey, PA : IGI Global Scientific Publishing, [2026] | Includes bibliographical references and index. | Summary: "This book aims to expand the knowledge and empirical research about the fusion of Artificial Intelligence and Internet of Things (AIoT), in the context of retail and services management, both public and private"-- Provided by publisher.

Identifiers: LCCN 2024055469 (print) | LCCN 2024055470 (ebook) | ISBN 9798369385128 (hardcover) | ISBN 9798369385135 (paperback) | ISBN 9798369385142 (ebook)

Subjects: LCSH: Retail trade--Data processing. | Artificial intelligence--Marketing applications. | Internet of things.

Classification: LCC HF5429.15 .A78 2025 (print) | LCC HF5429.15 (ebook) | DDC 381/.14--dc23/eng/20250214

LC record available at https://lccn.loc.gov/2024055469

LC ebook record available at https://lccn.loc.gov/2024055470

British Cataloguing in Publication Data

A Cataloguing in Publication record for this book is available from the British Library.

Table of Contents

Detailed Table of Contents

This study analyzes current knowledge on Artificial Intelligence of Things (AIoT) and identifies key research trends using bibliometric methods. The analyzed documents were published in the Business and Management categories of the Web of Science database. Findings reveal AIoT as an emerging topic, with most publications post-2019. The most cited documents focus on AIoT's role in digital transformation and Industry 4.0, implementation challenges, and technological components. They also explore transformative effects on retail, marketing, customer experiences, service innovations, and deepfakes. The co-citation analysis differentiates principally between consumer experience effects and company efficiency due to AIoT. The bibliographic coupling map identifies eight research clusters: AIoT technologies and equipment, sustainability, privacy and cybersecurity, entrepreneurship, servitization and co-creation, supply chain and Industry 4.0, organizational culture, and Lean Six Sigma. The study also highlights contributions, limitations, and future research directions.

This study explores AIoT solutions to spark innovative retail management concepts. It begins with a review of technology evolution in retail, from barcodes to big data analytics, covering smart retailing, digital transformation, and the integration of IoT, AI, and AIoT. The methodology includes a bibliometric study and qualitative

benefits, including improved demand forecasting, dynamic pricing, and reduced shrinkage, justify the investment. The paper also discusses the challenges of technical integration, data security, and regulatory compliance that retailers must consider. Ultimately, a careful cost-benefit analysis can help retailers assess the potential of smart shelf systems to improve competitiveness and optimize stock management in an increasingly dynamic retail environment.

The ever-growing presence of fake reviews on e-commerce platforms poses a significant challenge for online shoppers. These deceptive reviews, often generated by businesses to inflate sales or by competitors to sabotage reputations, can mislead customers and undermine trust in online retailers. To address this issue, researchers are developing various techniques for fake review detection. This chapter explores four key approaches to combating fraudulent reviews. The proposed model identifies characteristic patterns in reviewer behavior, linguistic features, and sentiment analysis. By analyzing these elements, machine learning algorithms trained on vast datasets can distinguish between genuine and fabricated reviews. Building on this, deep learning models utilize artificial neural networks to capture more complex patterns from larger review datasets, potentially improving detection accuracy.

The convergence of evolving consumer profiles, digital access, and ease of online product discovery in the mid-2010s created a virtuous cycle. This gave rise to first-generation entrepreneurs who launched D2C brands with minimal capital, relying on consumer insights and identifying gaps in a competitive market. D2C websites acted as consumer labs, offering insights into consumer behavior. As these brands faced distribution bottlenecks, they began diversifying their channels. Savings from streamlined inventory and distribution were reinvested into customer acquisition via aggressive search engine and social media campaigns. D2C brands adopted various technologies—such as voice search, AI-driven conversations, augmented reality, recommender systems, image recognition, and blockchain—to enhance customer experiences. These technologies not only simplified website navigation but also boosted engagement and conversions. The future of D2C brands lies in vertical integration and the digital transformation of offline businesses.

Automated customer support systems have become essential in enhancing the efficiency and responsiveness of service industries. This paper presents a proposed automated customer support tool designed to overcome the limitations of traditional support models by leveraging advanced data processing techniques. The system utilizes Data Extraction, Data Transformation, and Data Import using Business Intelligence (BI) tools to create a dynamic, adaptive framework for real-time, personalized customer assistance. By extracting relevant data from various sources, transforming it into usable formats, and integrating it into BI tools for enhanced visualization and analysis, the tool enables a proactive, data-driven approach to customer support. The system also incorporates AI-powered analytics to predict customer issues and adapt to ongoing interactions, ensuring that responses remain relevant and timely. Moreover, the tool ensures seamless integration with human agents for escalation, providing a hybrid solution that combines automation with human expertise.

The integration of Artificial Intelligence (AI) technologies, such as chatbots and virtual assistants, has profoundly transformed customer experiences across various industries. This chapter explores the enhancement of customer experiences through AI in retail, finance, and healthcare sectors. It investigates the key factors necessary for the successful implementation of human-AI collaboration and examines real-world applications to draw valuable lessons. Furthermore, it outlines best practices for integrating AI to anticipate customer needs and improve decision-making

Preface

The global marketplace is being reshaped by the convergence of Artificial Intelligence (AI) and the Internet of Things (IoT), forming the Artificial Intelligence of Things (AIoT), which drives smarter consumer engagement and operational efficiency (Rodrigues & Proença, 2022a; Rosário & Raimundo, 2025). Especially in retail and services, AIoT augments IoT systems with intelligent capabilities, enabling more efficient operations and improved user experiences. And IoT collects more data needed to train AI models and algorithms.

IoT enables continuous data collection through millions of interconnected sensors embedded in vehicles, buildings, machines, drones, robots, smartphones, and smart retail infrastructure (Mohamed, 2023). AI processes this data in real time via intelligent systems that increasingly emulate human characteristics (Nozari et al., 2024).

Smart Retailing, fueled by disruptive technologies, enables retailers to innovate, strengthen market performance, and enhance brand leadership (Pratas et al., 2022). Initially reliant on RFID and basic sensors, IoT now integrates and complements AI, robotics, and AR/VR across retail environments (Ajayi et al., 2023). Devices equipped with sensors generally support demand-side activities, while RFID, Bluetooth, Wi-Fi, and GPS generally enhance operational control (Hossain et al., 2021). IoT has transformed retail by enabling cost-effective platforms, fraud detection, demand forecasting, inventory control, cybersecurity, and customer service optimization (Khan et al., 2023). AI further boosts customer satisfaction and competitiveness through data-driven insights and operational efficiency (Oosthuizen et al., 2021).

Smart services are revolutionizing various sectors by blending physical components with intelligent and connected technologies (Gotz et al., 2018). Built upon big data and powered by innovations like IoT and AI, these services foster digital transformation and usher in new business models (Rodrigues & Proença, 2022b). AI enhances service delivery through personalization, cost reduction, and real-time data exchange between consumers, providers, and devices via sensors (Kim, 2023). It also reshapes customer relationships by enabling personalized interactions, convenience, and even anthropomorphic interfaces, fostering co-created value. Yet, challenges persist—users may face technological anxiety, privacy risks, diminished human contact, and a sense of lost control (Chaturvedi & Verma, 2023).

Public service and management are similarly impacted, notably through Smart Cities—urban ecosystems where AI integrates with IoT to gather and manage data from people, sensors, and infrastructure. These systems optimize traffic, energy usage, and public assets while promoting sustainability, environmental stewardship, and efficient waste management (Bedi et al., 2022; Bibri et al., 2023; Fang et al., 2023).

Thus, AIoT presents significant opportunities for retail and service management, while simultaneously posing complex challenges for businesses, governments, individuals, and regulatory bodies.

More than a guide, this book *"Artificial Intelligence of Things (AIoT) for Retail and Services Management"* offers a forward-looking exploration of AIoT's transformative role in retail and services management. Aimed at professionals, researchers, and students, it examines advanced applications across public and private sectors, balancing practical benefits with key challenges. It provides actionable insights for innovation leaders and is essential reading for those seeking expertise in AIoT-driven industries such as retail and services.

ORGANIZATION OF THE BOOK

This book comprises twelve chapters, each examining core applications of Artificial Intelligence of Things (AIoT) in retail and services management.

The book begins with the first chapter that has an overview of AIoT's current state-of-the-art and emerging research directions, followed by an analysis of AIoT's role in retail transformation and future possibilities in the second chapter. The subsequent chapters (third and fourth) address AIoT-driven marketing practices, including recommendation systems, augmented reality integration, and social media analysis. Then the focus shifts to supply chain optimization through RFID and related technologies with respective measurement and business analysis in fifth and sixth chapters. The seventh and eight chapters focus on Fake Review Detection Techniques in E-Commerce and Direct Business to Consumer brands using AI and IoT. The next chapters (ninth, tenth and eleventh) focus on services management, namely the Customer Support Business powered by Automated Models, Human-AI fusion in services and Smart city management with AIoT-driven solutions. Finally, the last chapter focuses of the legal and ethical aspects of AIoT, AI and IoT utilization.

In a more detailed way, the first chapter, *"Artificial Intelligence of Things (AIoT): Current Knowledge and Emerging Research Trends"* by Joaquim Pratas from the Polytechnic Institute of Porto and research centers CEOS.PP and GOVCOPP – University of Aveiro, offers a comprehensive overview of AIoT, outlining key research areas, industry applications, and emerging trends. A bibliometric study reveals influential research clusters and recent academic advances, illustrating AIoT's evolution and significance.

The second chapter, *"Retail Evolution Using Artificial Intelligence of Things (AIoT): An exploratory analysis and innovative ideas using literature review and creativity techniques"*, by Joaquim Pratas (Polytechnic Institute of Porto; CEOS. PP and GOVCOPP – University of Aveiro), Paulo Gonçalves (Polytechnic Institute of Porto; CEOS.PP), and Joseph Kaswengi (University of Orléans; VALLOREM), explores AIoT's impact on retail through a bibliographic coupling study. It also develops new creative ideas based on focus groups that used techniques to generate new ideas such as mind mapping and morphological analysis. It details how device-generated data is processed by algorithms to improve customer experience and operations, and presents a practical framework for developing innovative AIoT applications using structured idea-generation techniques.

The third chapter, *"Exploring Personalized Recommendations and AIoT in Retail Enhancing Consumer Engagement with AR Technology"* by Usha Rani (from Koneru Lakshmaiah Education Foundation), investigates how AI-driven personalized recommendations and AR technology impact consumer behavior in online cosmetics retail. The study shows that AIoT enhances engagement and product confidence, significantly influencing purchasing decisions.

The fourth chapter, *"Leveraging RFID Technology for Smart Shelf Inventory Management in Retail"* by Usha Rani (from Koneru Lakshmaiah Education Foundation), explores how RFID-enabled smart shelves enhance inventory accuracy, reduce stock misplacement, and improve operational efficiency and customer satisfaction. The chapter also presents a cost-benefit analysis to help retailers assess the strategic value and competitive advantage of adopting this technology.

Chapter five *"Improving Online Trust Through Comparative Analysis of Fake Review Detection Techniques in E-Commerce"* by Monica Bhutani (from Bharati Vidyapeeth College of Engineering), investigates how fake reviews (whether promotional or defamatory) erode consumer trust and presents machine learning and deep learning methods to detect deceptive content. Using natural language processing to identify linguistic anomalies, the chapter offers a thorough evaluation of detection techniques, equipping readers to assess reviews more critically and make informed purchasing decisions.

In the chapter six, *"Direct to Consumer Brands (D2C) – Business Model Innovation using Artificial Intelligence"* by Rahul Gupta (from the Center of Management Sciences and School of Management of Jain University), Rupesh Kumar (from Alliance University), and Bharathi Gopal (from the ICFAI Business School), explores how D2C brands disrupt traditional retail through consumer insights, outsourced supply chains, and digital platforms. Initially web-based and supported by social media advertising and venture capital, these brands now invest in AI and other technologies (such as voice search, AR, recommendation systems and blockchain) to enhance personalization and conversion. The chapter envisions vertical integration and digital transformation of offline commerce as the next evolution in D2C business models.

The chapter seven, *"Revolutionizing Customer Support Business Impact Analysis of Automated Models"* by Usha Rani (from Koneru Lakshmaiah Education Foundation), introduces a data-driven approach to enhancing customer support through Business Intelligence tools and AI analytics. By enabling context-aware, adaptive interactions, the model anticipates customer needs and delivers timely, personalized responses, overcoming the limitations of traditional support systems based on high-capacity data processing technologies.

The chapter eight, *"Human-AI Fusion: Elevating Customer Experience Across Selected Service Industries"* by Razia Nagina (from Lovely Professional University, India), examines how blending AI technologies with human expertise enhances service delivery in retail, finance, and healthcare. This synergy enables personalized, real-time interactions, improves efficiency, and strengthens customer loyalty. The chapter presents best practices and sector-specific examples, offering a compelling analysis of this evolving collaborative model.

Chapter nine, *"Innovative Ideas for Smart City Management using AIoT-driven Solutions"* by Joaquim Pratas (from Polytechnic Institute of Porto; CEOS.PP and GOVCOPP – University of Aveiro) and Ana Isabel Melo (from Águeda School of Technology and Management – University of Aveiro and CIPES), explores how AIoT technologies can optimize smart city management. They identify key data-collection devices, the actors involved, and how the gathered information is used and accessed by stakeholders. Building on this analysis, they propose AIoT-based solutions through an extensive literature review, a bibliometric study using bibliographic coupling, and focus group sessions. Techniques like mind mapping and morphological analysis were used to spark innovative ideas, also offering readers a practical method to generate their own creative solutions.

In the tenth and final chapter *"Legal and Ethical Challenges in the Integration of AIoT in Retail"* by David Jiménez (from EAE Business School and UNIE University of Madrid), Eduardo Dittmar (from Rey Juan Carlos University), and Jenny Portillo (from University of Sevilla), explores how legal frameworks and ethical principles influence marketing strategies and consumer behavior in AIoT-driven retail. Through literature review and case studies, the chapter addresses issues such as data privacy and personal data use, highlighting the tension between consumer protection and technological optimization, and outlining the challenges and opportunities these innovations present.

Joaquim Pratas
Porto Accounting and Business School, CEOS, Polytechnic Institute of Porto, Portugal

Maria Antónia Rodrigues
Porto Accounting and Business School, CEOS, Polytechnic Institute of Porto, Portugal & SIIS Porto, Portugal

Maria Amélia Carvalho
Porto Accounting and Business School, CEOS, Polytechnic Institute of Porto, Portugal

REFERENCES

Ajayi, S., Loureiro, S. M. C., & Langaro, D. (2023). Internet of things and consumer engagement on retail: State-of-the-art and future directions. *EuroMed Journal of Business, 18*(3), 397–423. DOI: 10.1108/EMJB-10-2021-0164

Bedi, P., Goyal, S. B., Rajawat, A. S., Shaw, R. N., & Ghosh, A. (2022). Application of AI/IoT for Smart Renewable Energy Management in Smart Cities. In: Piuri, V., Shaw, R.N., Ghosh, A., Islam, R. (eds) *AI and IoT for Smart City Applications*. Studies in Computational Intelligence, 1002. Springer, Singapore. https://doi.org/ DOI: 10.1007/978-981-16-7498-3_8

Bibri, S. E., Alexandre, A., Sharifi, A., & Krogstie, J. (2023). Environmentally sustainable smart cities and their converging AI, IoT, and big data technologies and solutions: An integrated approach to an extensive literature review. *Energy Informatics, 6*(9), 9. Advance online publication. DOI: 10.1186/s42162-023-00259-2 PMID: 37032812

Chaturvedi, R., & Verma, S. (2023). Opportunities and Challenges of AI-Driven Customer Service. In Sheth, J. N., Jain, V., Mogaji, E., & Ambika, A. (Eds.), *Artificial Intelligence in Customer Service*. Palgrave Macmillan., DOI: 10.1007/978-3-031-33898-4_3

Fang, B., Yu, J., Chen, Z., Osman, A. I., Farghali, M., Ihara, I., Hamza, E. H., Rooney, D. W., & Yap, P.-S. (2023). Artificial intelligence for waste management in smart cities: A review. *Environmental Chemistry Letters, 21*(4), 1959–1989. DOI: 10.1007/s10311-023-01604-3 PMID: 37362015

Götz, C., Hohler, S., & Benz, C. (2018). Towards Managing Smart Service Innovation: A Literature Review. In: Satzger, G., Patrício, L., Zaki, M., Kühl, N., Hottum, P. (eds) *Exploring Service Science. IESS 2018*. Lecture Notes in Business Information Processing, 331. Springer, Cham. https://doi.org/DOI: 10.1007/978-3-030-00713-3_8

Hossain, M. S., Chisty, N. M. A., Hargrove, D. L., & Amin, R. (2021). Role of Internet of Things (IoT) in Retail Business and Enabling Smart Retailing Experiences. *Asian Business Review, 11*(2), 75–80. DOI: 10.18034/abr.v11i2.579

Khan, S., Khari, M., & Azrour, M. (2023). IoT in retail and e-commerce. *Electronic Commerce Research*. Advance online publication. DOI: 10.1007/s10660-023-09785-3

Kim, M. (2023). Connecting artificial intelligence to value creation in services: Mechanism and implications. *Service Business, 17*(4), 851–878. DOI: 10.1007/s11628-023-00547-7

Mohamed, K. S. (2023). Deep Learning for IoT "Artificial Intelligence of Things (AIoT)". In *Deep Learning-Powered Technologies. Synthesis Lectures on Engineering, Science, and Technology*. Springer., DOI: 10.1007/978-3-031-35737-4_3

Nozari, H., Szmelter-Jarosz, A., & Rahmaty, M. (2024). Smart Marketing Based on Artificial Intelligence of Things (AIoT) and Blockchain and Evaluating Critical Success Factors. In Irani, H., & Nozari, H. (Eds.), *Smart and Sustainable Interactive Marketing* (pp. 68–82). IGI Global., DOI: 10.4018/979-8-3693-1339-8.ch005

Oosthuizen, K., Botha, E., Robertson, J., & Montecchi, M. (2021). Artificial intelligence in retail: The AI-enabled value chain. *Australasian Marketing Journal, 29*(3), 264–273. DOI: 10.1016/j.ausmj.2020.07.007

Pratas, J., Amorim, C., & Reis, J. L. (2022). Smart Retailing Technologies Impact in Brand Leadership and Market Performance: A Conceptual Model. In Reis, J. L., Peter, M. K., Cayolla, R., & Bogdanović, Z. (Eds.), *Marketing and Smart Technologies. Smart Innovation, Systems and Technologies* (Vol. 280). Springer., DOI: 10.1007/978-981-16-9272-7_26

Rodrigues, M., & Proença, J. (2022b). *Preface, Impact of Digital Transformation on the Development of New Business Models and Consumer Experience* (Global Ed.). IGI., https://www.igi-global.com/book/impact-digital-transformation-development-new/276093, DOI: 10.4018/978-1-7998-9179-6

Rodrigues, M. A., & Proença, J. F. (2022a). *Impact of Digital Transformation on the Development of New Business Models and Consumer Experience*, IGI Global eds, USA. DOI: , ISBN13: 9781799891796. https://www.igi-global.com/book/impact-digital-transformation-development-new/276093DOI: 10.4018/978-1-7998-9179-6

Rosário, A. T., & Raimundo, R. J. (2025). The Integration of AI and IoT in Marketing: A Systematic Literature Review. *Electronics (Basel), 14*(9), 1854. DOI: 10.3390/electronics14091854

Acknowledgment

The editors would like to acknowledge the support of the researchers and the IGI Global editorial team involved in this project. Among the editors, authors, and reviewers, more than twenty researchers participated and committed to the book.

Fifteen authors from diverse countries and continents, namely France, India, Portugal, Spain and United Kingdom, contributed to the book. The editors would like to thank each of the authors for their contributions.

All chapters were reviewed by several reviewers, whose valuable work helped enrich and improve the final result of the book. Therefore, we are grateful for the support of the researchers who contributed to the review process of each chapter, including the collaboration of Carla Amorim (Polytechnic Institute of Maia), Elói Jorge (Higher Institute of Business and Tourism; and ISCAP, Polytechnic of Porto), Jorge Pacheco (Polytechnic Institute of Cávado and Ave; and ISCAP, Polytechnic of Porto), José Duarte Santos (ISCAP, Polytechnic of Porto), Kamalendu Pal (University of London), Paulo Pires (ISCAP, Polytechnic of Porto), Rahul Gupta (Center of Management Sciences and School of Management of Jain University), Razia Nagina (Lovely Professional University), Sara Teixeira (ISCAP, Polytechnic of Porto), Usharani Bhimavarapu (Koneru Lakshmaiah Education Foundation), and Zaíla Oliveira (University of Maia and ISCAP, Polytechnic of Porto).

The editors also appreciate IGI Global's support throughout the process.

This work is financed by portuguese national funds through FCT - Fundação para a Ciência e Tecnologia, under the project UID/05422: Centre for Organisational and Social Studies of Polytechnic of Porto.

Joaquim Pratas
Porto Accounting and Business School, CEOS, Polytechnic Institute of Porto, Portugal

Maria Antónia Rodrigues
Porto Accounting and Business School, CEOS, Polytechnic Institute of Porto, Portugal & SIIS Porto, Portugal

Maria Amélia Carvalho
Porto Accounting and Business School, CEOS, Polytechnic Institute of Porto, Portugal

Chapter 1
Artificial Intelligence of Things (AIoT): Current Knowledge and Emerging Research Trends

Joaquim Monteiro Pratas
https://orcid.org/0000-0002-7432-9242
Instituto Superior de Contabilidade e Administração, Instituto Politécnico do Porto, Portugal

ABSTRACT

This study analyzes current knowledge on Artificial Intelligence of Things (AIoT) and identifies key research trends using bibliometric methods. The analyzed documents were published in the Business and Management categories of the Web of Science database. Findings reveal AIoT as an emerging topic, with most publications post-2019. The most cited documents focus on AIoT's role in digital transformation and Industry 4.0, implementation challenges, and technological components. They also explore transformative effects on retail, marketing, customer experiences, service innovations, and deepfakes. The co-citation analysis differentiates principally between consumer experience effects and company efficiency due to AIoT. The bibliographic coupling map identifies eight research clusters: AIoT technologies and equipment, sustainability, privacy and cybersecurity, entrepreneurship, servitization and co-creation, supply chain and Industry 4.0, organizational culture, and Lean Six Sigma. The study also highlights contributions, limitations, and future research directions.

DOI: 10.4018/979-8-3693-8512-8.ch001

INTRODUCTION

Artificial Intelligence of Things (AIoT) is a technological convergence that integrates artificial intelligence (AI) within the internet of things (IoT) infrastructure. The primary goal of AIoT is to enhance the efficiency of IoT operations, improve human-machine interactions, and facilitate more advanced data management and analytics (Yasar et al., 2023).

The evolution of AIoT has been shaped by significant advancements in both AI and IoT technologies over the years. Initially, IoT devices were primarily deployed for basic automation and data collection tasks. However, with the integration of AI, these devices have evolved into sophisticated systems capable of conducting complex data analysis and autonomous decision-making processes. This transformation has been fueled by the emergence of low-power AIoT chips, advancements in edge computing, and the development of highly efficient machine learning algorithms (Burrows, 2021). The convergence of these technologies is reshaping data processing and analysis, offering greater intelligence and efficiency in various sectors.

AIoT chips are specialized processors designed to execute AI tasks directly within IoT devices, enabling real-time data processing and decision-making at the source. This innovation addresses the growing need for faster, more efficient data handling by reducing latency and bandwidth consumption. Edge computing further enhances AIoT capabilities by bringing computational processes closer to data sources, eliminating the necessity for extensive data transfers to centralized cloud servers. This approach significantly improves response times, making it particularly valuable in applications demanding immediate processing, such as autonomous vehicles and smart city infrastructures (Deng et al., 2020; Gill et al., 2024).

Simultaneously, advanced machine learning algorithms have been optimized to function efficiently on these edge devices, leveraging the computational power of AIoT chips for tasks such as predictive maintenance, image recognition, and real-time anomaly detection (Bourechak et al., 2023). Collectively, these technologies are driving innovation across multiple industries, paving the way for more intelligent, responsive, and adaptive systems.

Within the retail sector, AIoT technologies contribute to a wide range of applications, including smart shelves, automated checkout systems, and personalized shopping experiences. AIoT chips embedded within retail environments facilitate real-time inventory monitoring, while edge computing processes data locally, enabling instant alerts and updates to prevent stock shortages and optimize inventory management. Machine learning algorithms further refine retail operations by analyzing customer behavior and preferences, allowing for personalized recommendations and targeted marketing strategies that enhance sales performance and customer satisfaction. Additionally, AIoT-driven security systems analyze video footage in real time to identify potential security threats and mitigate theft risks (Heins, 2023). AIoT-powered self-checkout systems and smart shopping carts streamline the purchasing process, significantly reducing wait times and improving the overall shopping experience (Hunt & Rolf, 2022).

In the service industry, AIoT plays a transformative role by revolutionizing customer service and operational efficiency across several domains. AI-powered chatbots and virtual assistants handle customer inquiries with real-time responsiveness, ensuring swift and accurate interactions. Edge computing minimizes processing delays, enhancing the quality of customer service experiences. Predictive maintenance, powered by machine learning, helps businesses anticipate potential equipment failures before they occur, thereby reducing downtime and maintenance expenditures. This is particularly beneficial in industries such as hospitality, transportation, healthcare, and banking, where service reliability is crucial.

In hospitality, AIoT also improves guest experiences through personalized offerings, including automated check-ins, customized room settings, and smart concierge services. In transportation, AIoT facilitates traffic management optimization, vehicle maintenance forecasting, and real-time commuter updates, leading to improved transportation efficiency. Healthcare applications leverage AIoT systems to monitor patients' vital signs, predict health complications, and generate personalized treatment plans, thereby enhancing patient outcomes and reducing medical costs. Meanwhile, in banking, AIoT strengthens security through biometric authentication, detects fraudulent transactions in real-time, and provides personalized financial guidance to customers (Dini et al., 2024; Khadam et al., 2024; Villar et al., 2024).

The significance of AIoT today is evident in its broad spectrum of applications, spanning smart homes, healthcare, industrial automation, and urban development. AIoT technologies optimize efficiency, lower operational costs, and enhance user experiences by delivering real-time insights and proactive solutions (Rawas, 2024). As research continues to address critical challenges surrounding security, privacy, and ethical considerations, AIoT is positioned to become a cornerstone of future technological advancements. Given its promising trajectory, AIoT remains an emerging research area with vast opportunities for exploration.

Thus, this study seeks to identify and analyze existing research surrounding AIoT, highlighting the primary themes and applications of AIoT-based investigations. Additionally, it aims to delineate key research clusters, evaluate the impact of significant scientific contributions, and examine emerging trends likely to shape the future of AIoT development using a bibliometric study methodology.

BACKGROUND

Applications and Benefits of AIoT in Business and Society

AIoT solutions are permeating various sectors of both business and society, demonstrating their vast applicability and transformative benefits.

In the realm of retail, AIoT systems are revolutionizing the business as well as related activities such as warehousing, inventory management and supply chain logistics.

This adoption of AIoT systems also extends to the service industries, where AIoT enhances banking operations, refines advertisement strategies and business model, and improves healthcare delivery through advanced monitoring and predictive analytics, among other sectors. AIoT's influence is also evident in smart home technologies and domotics, transportation sector, smart parking, waste management, and in services provided in agriculture and food industry.

Retailing

The integration of AIoT within the retail industry is revolutionizing several key areas, including security, shopping experience enhancement, customer insights, marketing, inventory management, and equipment maintenance.

AIoT-enabled security cameras are transforming store security by detecting and deterring shoplifters through the recognition of suspicious activities, promptly alerting store personnel. Intelligent shopping carts, equipped with image recognition and sensors, can track items placed in the cart and provide real-time updates on promotions, thereby enhancing the shopping experience. Smart sensors within the store monitor customer footfall and behavior, offering valuable insights into popular areas and potential bottlenecks, which assist retailers in optimizing store layouts and staffing strategies.

Additionally, smart mirrors integrated with AIoT technology can suggest fashion items based on customers' preferences and past purchases, creating a personalized shopping experience. AIoT's analytical capabilities allow for the delivery of customized marketing messages and promotions by analyzing customer data, ensuring targeted and effective marketing strategies.

Moreover, AIoT systems are pivotal in inventory management by monitoring stock levels in real-time through the use of smart shelves and digital price tags. This real-time monitoring ensures efficient inventory management, reduces stockouts, and optimizes replenishment processes.

Predictive maintenance capabilities of AIoT further enhance retail operations by anticipating maintenance needs for essential equipment such as refrigeration units and HVAC systems, thus minimizing downtime and ensuring smooth operations (Matthews, 2020; Thomas, 2022; Velosiot, 2024).

Warehousing and Inventory Management

The application of AIoT within warehousing and inventory management has ushered in a transformative era characterized by advanced automated inventory tracking, intelligent warehousing, streamlined picking and sorting processes, real-time monitoring, sophisticated demand forecasting, and predictive maintenance.

AIoT systems employ sensors and RFID tags to provide real-time, precise tracking of inventory, ensuring that information on stock levels and locations is consistently accurate and up-to-date. This technological precision extends to the optimization of warehouse layouts and workflows, informed by data analysis on product movement and storage patterns, thereby enhancing operational efficiency. The automation of picking and sorting is significantly enhanced through AIoT-powered robots and automated systems, which meticulously manage these tasks to reduce errors and boost productivity. Furthermore, AIoT systems continuously monitor environmental conditions, such as temperature and humidity, within storage areas, thereby ensuring product quality and regulatory compliance. Predictive analytics, facilitated by AIoT, enables the analysis of historical sales data and real-time market trends to forecast future demand accurately. This predictive capability allows businesses to manage inventory levels with heightened efficacy. Additionally, AIoT's capacity to predict maintenance needs for warehouse equipment, including conveyor belts and forklifts, through sensor data analysis, markedly reduces downtime and associated maintenance costs (10 DS Team, 2023; Albayrak et al., 2023; Armenta, 2024).

Supply Chain Management

The application of AIoT within supply chain management introduces groundbreaking innovations across several critical dimensions, including real-time tracking, inventory management, demand forecasting, automated warehousing, risk management, sustainable practices, and predictive maintenance.

AIoT leverages IoT sensors and GPS technology to enable real-time tracking of goods, providing comprehensive visibility into the entire supply chain. This end-to-end visibility allows for proactive decision-making, ensuring that potential issues are addressed promptly. Moreover, AIoT optimizes inventory levels by continuously analyzing real-time data on stock levels, demand patterns, and supply chain disruptions. Such analysis guarantees efficient inventory management and minimizes the risks of overstocking or stockouts. By scrutinizing historical sales data alongside real-time market trends, AIoT can accurately predict future demand, allowing businesses to prepare adequately. The incorporation of AIoT-powered robots and automated systems in warehouses streamlines tasks such as picking, packing, and sorting, thereby enhancing efficiency and reducing errors.

Furthermore, AIoT is instrumental in monitoring and analyzing potential risks, including natural disasters and supply chain disruptions. This capability enables businesses to devise effective contingency plans and mitigate risks proactively. AIoT also contributes to sustainable supply chain practices by optimizing routes and reducing energy consumption, thus enhancing environmental sustainability. Predictive maintenance, facilitated by AIoT, involves analyzing sensor data to anticipate maintenance needs for supply chain equipment, such as trucks and warehouse machinery. This predictive approach minimizes downtime and maintenance costs, ensuring smooth and uninterrupted operations (Nozari et al., 2022; Dhaduk, 2024; Nozari, 2024).

Banking

The implementation of AIoT within the banking sector is heralding a new era of personalized services, automated customer support, smart automated teller machines (ATMs), branch automation, and robust fraud detection and prevention mechanisms.

AIoT systems are instrumental in crafting personalized banking experiences by meticulously analyzing customer data and preferences. This technological advancement facilitates the provision of bespoke financial advice, tailored product recommendations, and targeted marketing campaigns. Additionally, AIoT enhances customer support through the deployment of chatbots and virtual assistants, which efficiently manage customer inquiries, provide support, and execute routine tasks. This technological prowess extends to ATMs, incorporating features such as biometric authentication and personalized greetings, thereby elevating the user experience. The automation of various processes within bank branches is another notable application of AIoT. It streamlines operations such as check processing, document management, and customer queue management, thereby enhancing operational efficiency and significantly reducing wait times. Furthermore, AIoT's ability to analyze transaction data in real-time is pivotal in detecting and preventing fraudulent activities. By integrating sophisticated AI algorithms with IoT devices, banks can swiftly identify unusual patterns and promptly alert customers and authorities (Fares et al., 2023; Manta et al., 2024).

Advertisement Industry

The integration of AIoT within the advertisement industry is catalyzing advancements across several domains, including personalized advertising, in-store advertising, interactive advertising, automated campaign optimization, and real-time analytics.

AIoT systems possess the capability to scrutinize real-time data from various IoT devices, enabling the delivery of personalized advertisements tailored to consumers' preferences, behaviors, and locations. This personalization elevates the relevance of advertisements and enhances consumer engagement. Moreover, in the context of in-store advertising, AIoT leverages beacons and sensors to detect when customers are near specific products, subsequently sending targeted ads to their smartphones. This approach not only encourages purchases but also streamlines the shopping experience.

Furthermore, AIoT facilitates interactive advertising by enabling real-time engagement through quizzes, polls, and games. Such interactive elements foster a deeper connection between consumers and brands, enhancing the overall marketing impact. The automation of campaign optimization is another remarkable application of AIoT. By continuously monitoring and analyzing performance data, AIoT systems make real-time adjustments to advertising campaigns, thereby improving their effectiveness and efficiency. Finally, AIoT provides real-time analytics on advertisement performance, empowering advertisers to make informed, data-driven decisions to refine their strategies (Cogniteq, 2023; Wakefield, 2024).

Healthcare Industry

The deployment of AIoT within the healthcare industry is catalyzing significant advancements across various domains, including remote patient monitoring, predictive analytics for disease management, virtual health assistants, wearable devices for remote health monitoring, smart hospital systems, AI-driven medical imaging and diagnostics, and AI-assisted drug discovery and development.

AIoT systems are transforming patient monitoring by leveraging wearable sensors and smart home devices to continuously track vital signs and health conditions. These devices transmit real-time data to healthcare providers, enhancing the ability to monitor patients remotely and ensure timely interventions.

Furthermore, AIoT is proficient in analyzing extensive datasets from electronic health records and wearable devices. This analytical capability predicts disease outbreaks and identifies patient health trends, facilitating proactive healthcare measures. Virtual health assistants powered by AIoT provide personalized health advice, medication reminders, and support for chronic condition management, thereby improving patient engagement and health outcomes. Wearable devices play a crucial role in remote health monitoring by tracking physical activity, sleep patterns, and other health metrics. This real-time data is invaluable for creating tailored healthcare plans.

Within hospital environments, AIoT optimizes operations by automating routine tasks, managing inventory, and ensuring the proper maintenance of medical equipment. This optimization streamlines hospital workflows and enhances efficiency. AIoT's impact extends to medical imaging technologies, where it provides advanced image analysis and diagnostics. This technology aids radiologists in detecting abnormalities with greater accuracy and speed. Moreover, AIoT accelerates the drug discovery process by analyzing vast amounts of biological data. Its capability to identify potential drug candidates more efficiently accelerates the development of new medications (IoT World Magazine, 2024; Medwave, 2024; Ordr, 2024).

Smart Homes and Domotics

The integration of AIoT is revolutionizing the concept of smart homes and domotics, significantly advancing various facets of home automation. This paradigm shift is particularly evident in smart security systems, energy management, intelligent lighting, voice assistants, and health monitoring. AIoT enhances home security by deploying smart cameras, motion sensors, and sophisticated AI algorithms. These technologies collaborate to detect and notify homeowners of any suspicious activities, thereby bolstering security measures. Furthermore, AIoT optimizes energy consumption through the analysis of data from smart meters, thermostats, and appliances. This analysis offers real-time insights and facilitates the automation of energy-saving strategies, thus promoting efficient energy use. Intelligent lighting systems, governed by AIoT, are capable of adjusting based on occupancy, natural light levels, and user preferences. This dynamic control ensures optimal lighting conditions while concurrently reducing energy consumption (Guo et al., 2019; Sepasgozar et al., 2020). These systems can be seamlessly controlled via smartphones, smart speakers, or voice assistants, such as Amazon Alexa and Google Home, through voice commands. Moreover, AIoT integrates wearable devices and sensors to monitor the health and well-being of residents. These advanced systems are equipped to track vital signs, detect falls, and issue real-time alerts to caregivers or emergency services, significantly enhancing healthcare delivery and resident safety (Joyia et al., 2017).

Transportation

AIoT is transforming the transportation industry, with significant applications in smart traffic management, parking systems, fleet management, ride-sharing optimization, autonomous vehicles, predictive maintenance, and environmental monitoring.

In the realm of smart traffic management, AIoT systems analyze traffic data in real-time to optimize traffic flow, reduce congestion, and enhance road safety. These systems also assist drivers in locating available parking spots promptly thereby reducing the time spent searching for parking and alleviating traffic congestion. Fleet management benefits immensely from AIoT through route optimization for delivery vehicles, fuel usage monitoring, and vehicle performance tracking, all of which contribute to heightened efficiency and reduced operational costs. Similarly, ride-sharing services are enhanced by AIoT's capability to predict demand, optimize routes, and offer personalized travel recommendations. The development of autonomous vehicles is significantly propelled by AIoT. It enables self-driving cars and trucks to utilize sensors, cameras, and AI algorithms to navigate roads, detect obstacles, and make real-time decisions. Predictive maintenance is another critical area where AIoT excels. By analyzing data from sensors, it predicts maintenance needs for vehicles and infrastructure, thereby reducing downtime and maintenance costs.

Lastly, AIoT plays a crucial role in environmental monitoring by overseeing air quality and noise levels around transportation hubs. This monitoring ensures compliance with environmental regulations and contributes to improved public health (Rizzoli, 2021; Shah, 2024; Flatirons, 2024; Intuz, 2024). Overall, AIoT's integration into the transportation sector signifies a paradigm shift towards more efficient, safe, and environmentally conscious mobility solutions.

Smart Parking

The incorporation of AIoT into smart parking systems is yielding transformative advancements in several key areas, including the analysis of real-time parking availability and guidance, automated license plate recognition (ALPR), predictive analytics, and payment and reservation systems.

AIoT systems offer real-time updates on parking space availability through the deployment of sensors and cameras. This technology enables drivers to swiftly locate parking spots, thereby reducing traffic congestion and emissions. Moreover, AIoT facilitates the guidance of drivers to available parking spaces via digital signage and mobile applications, significantly enhancing the overall parking experience. ALPR technology, powered by AIoT, allows for the seamless identification and tracking of vehicles as they enter and exit parking facilities. This automation not only streamlines the parking process but also increases efficiency. Additionally, AIoT can analyze historical parking data to predict future parking demand. This predictive capability enables parking operators to optimize space utilization and pricing strategies effectively. Finally, AIoT empowers the integration of online payment and reservation systems. This functionality allows drivers to book and pay for parking spots in advance, promoting convenience and efficiency (Alaba et al, 2024; Intuz, 2022; Parking Telecom, 2022).

Waste Management Industry

AIoT is significantly enhancing the waste management industry through its diverse applications, including smart waste bins, waste sorting robots, waste generation prediction, environmental monitoring, and predictive analytics for collection routes.

In the realm of smart waste bins, AIoT systems monitor fill levels in real-time and notify waste management services when emptying is required. This innovation ensures timely and efficient waste collection, minimizing the risks of overflow and associated health hazards. Moreover, waste sorting robots, powered by AIoT, can accurately identify and separate different types of waste. This capability markedly improves recycling efficiency and reduces contamination, thus contributing to more sustainable waste management practices. AIoT also aids in predicting future waste generation by analyzing historical data alongside real-time inputs. This predictive power enables waste management companies to plan more effectively and allocate resources optimally. Furthermore, AIoT systems monitor environmental conditions, such as air quality and temperature, around waste management facilities, ensuring compliance with environmental regulations and mitigating potential hazards. In addition, AIoT employs data from various sensors to predict waste generation patterns and optimize collection routes. This analytical capability reduces fuel consumption and enhances the efficiency of waste collection operations, fostering a more sustainable and cost-effective approach to waste management (Fang et al., 2023; Sharma, 2023; Mulé, 2024).

Agriculture

AIoT is revolutionizing agriculture through its diverse applications, including precision farming, pest and disease detection, crop yield predictions, automated irrigation, and supply chain management. AIoT systems possess the capability to continuously monitor soil conditions, crop health, and weather patterns in real-time. This real-time data empowers farmers to make informed, data-driven decisions, optimizing crop management practices. Furthermore, AIoT can analyze imagery from drones or cameras, enabling the early detection of pests and diseases. This early detection facilitates timely intervention, significantly mitigating crop losses.

AIoT's predictive analytics can also forecast crop yields by integrating data from various sensors and historical records. Automated irrigation systems, governed by AIoT, utilize real-time data from soil moisture sensors to ensure efficient water usage and minimize waste. This precise control over irrigation contributes to sustainable agricultural practices. Additionally, AIoT enhances supply chain management by tracking the movement of agricultural products from farm to consumer. This tracking ensures transparency, efficiency, and the maintenance of optimal conditions during transport and warehousing (Adli et al., 2023). Overall, AIoT stands as a transformative force in agriculture, promoting sustainability, efficiency, and enhanced productivity.

Food Industry

The integration of AIoT within the food industry is revolutionizing numerous facets, encompassing food safety compliance, personalized nutrition, smart packaging, supply chain optimization and predictive maintenance.

AIoT systems monitor food processing environments in real-time, detecting potential contamination and ensuring strict adherence to safety standards. This real-time surveillance is paramount in maintaining the integrity of food safety protocols. Furthermore, AIoT's capability to analyze consumer data facilitates the provision of personalized dietary recommendations and meal plans, meticulously tailored to individual health needs and preferences. In the realm of smart packaging, AIoT plays a critical role by monitoring the freshness of food products and delivering real-time information to consumers. This technological advancement not only reduces food waste but also enhances quality control measures. Additionally, AIoT systems are integral to tracking food products from farm to table, ensuring transparency and efficiency throughout the supply chain. This comprehensive oversight is instrumental in reducing waste and bolstering food safety within supply chains. Finally, AIoT's predictive maintenance capabilities for food processing equipment are transformative. By accurately predicting machinery maintenance needs, AIoT significantly reduces downtime and ensures continuous production (Ding et al., 2023; Mavani et al., 2022; Mittal, 2024).

Challenges and Barriers of AIoT Adoption

The adoption of AIoT by businesses presents several significant challenges and barriers that must be addressed by businesses, organizations, and consumers.

The foremost challenge pertains to the high initial costs associated with AIoT implementation, which involve substantial investments in IoT devices, AI software, and the requisite infrastructure upgrades (Kulkarni et al., 2022; Pratas et al., 2024).

This financial burden can deter organizations from pursuing AIoT solutions, particularly smaller enterprises with limited resources.

Another critical challenge involves the integration of AIoT systems with pre-existing business systems and processes. This integration is often complex and time-consuming, requiring significant investments in technology and employee training. Furthermore, as businesses expand, scalability issues may arise. Scaling AIoT solutions to accommodate increased data volumes and more intricate operations can prove daunting (Dijkman et al., 2015). Moreover, there is often a shortage of skilled professionals capable of developing, implementing, and managing AIoT systems, particularly in certain regions. This scarcity of expertise can hinder the timely adoption and effective utilization of AIoT technologies (Awaisi et al., 2024).

Data privacy and security also pose substantial concerns for AIoT adoption. The data collected by IoT devices is highly sensitive, necessitating robust security measures to protect against cyber-attacks and data breaches. Additionally, businesses must navigate complex regulatory and compliance issues, adhering to industry-specific standards and international trade laws to ensure lawful operations (Alenizi & Al-Karawi, 2022).

Addressing these challenges requires a concerted effort by businesses, policymakers, and educational institutions to develop comprehensive strategies, foster innovation, and build a skilled workforce capable of harnessing the full potential of AIoT.

METHODOLOGY

Research Questions

The objectives of this research are centered on identifying the current state of knowledge concerning the topic of AIoT and discerning the prevailing research trends within this domain. These goals will be attained through a rigorous analysis of the most pertinent and influential literature on the subject. Specifically, this study aims to address the following research questions:

- Research question 1: Which scientific documents about AIoT had the greatest impact in terms of their citations?
- Research question 2: What are the main research topics and trends about AIoT topic?
- Research question 3: What was the evolution over time of the publication of scientific documents about AIoT topic research clusters?

Methodology Based on Bibliometric Study

The methodology employed to address the formulated research questions is based in bibliometric studies, which are very important to academic research (Pratas & Oliveira, 2023). These studies provide a quantitative analysis of scientific literature, enabling the identification of patterns, trends, and impacts within a specific field. Utilizing a range of metrics such as citation counts, h-index, and impact factors, bibliometric studies evaluate the influence and dissemination of research outputs. These methods are bifurcated into two primary categories: evaluative, which assesses the impact of research, and relational, which explores the relationships between different research entities (Ninkov et al., 2022). The application of bibliometric analysis has burgeoned with the advent of digital databases and tools such as Web of Science, Scopus, and Google Scholar, facilitating comprehensive data collection and analysis (Passas, 2024). This methodology not only enhances our understanding of the development and dynamics of scientific fields but also underpins strategic decision-making in research funding and policy.

The research strategy in this work, was to collect data from the Web of Science Core Collection (WoSCC), searching for topics with the keywords related with Artificial Intelligence of Things (AIoT), such as "AIoT", or "artificial intelligence internet of things", or "Artificial intelligence*of Things", or "artificial intelligence internet of things aiot", or "artificial intelligence of things", or "artificial intelligence of things aiot", or "artificial intelligence over the internet of things aiot", or "artificial intelligence-of-things", or "artificial internet of things", or "autonomous internet of things", or "industrial aiot", in the Web of Science categories of Business and Management. The WoSCC was chosen because is the database with stricter journal selection, meaning it includes highly reputable journals. It also includes Impact Factor metrics and extensive citation connections, making it ideal for assessing research influence. The data was retrieved in 18th November 2024, and the data analysis was performed using VOS Viewer software.

A comprehensive suite of analyses was conducted, including citation analysis, keyword co-occurrence mapping, co-citation mapping, and bibliographic coupling mapping. These methodological approaches facilitate the identification of current knowledge within the realm of AIoT research. By employing these techniques, the study aims to elucidate the predominant research trends and propose prospective avenues for future research.

FINDINGS

Top 10 Most Cited Documents: Citations Analysis

To address the first research question, “Which scientific documents about AIoT had the greatest impact in terms of their citations?”, a thorough citation analysis was conducted. This analysis aimed to trace the influence and impact of pivotal papers over time. Given the impracticality of listing all the relevant documents, the paper includes a table that enumerates the top ten most-cited documents. The results of this analysis are presented in table 1, offering valuable insights into the most influential contributions in the field of AIoT.

Table 1. Top 10 most cited documents

Title	Authors and date	Source	Number of citations
Building dynamic capabilities for digital transformation: An ongoing process of strategic renewal	Warner & Wager (2019)	Long Range Planning (Q1)	1074
Siri, Siri, in my hand: Who’s the fairest in the land? On the interpretations, illustrations, and implications of artificial intelligence	Kaplan & Haenlein (2019)	Business Horizons (Q1)	859
The Future of Retailing	Grewal et al (2017)	Journal of Retailing (Q1)	556
Technological disruptions in services: lessons from tourism and hospitality	Buhalis et al (2019)	Journal of Service Management (Q1)	351
A strategic framework for artificial intelligence in marketing	Huang & Rust (2021)	Journal of the Academy of Marketing Science (Q1)	350
Transforming the Customer Experience through New Technologies	Hoyer et al (2020)	Journal of Interactive Marketing (Q1)	336
Industry 4.0: Opportunities and Challenges for Operations Management	Olsen & Tomlin (2020)	Manufacturing & Service Operations Management (Q1)	332
The emergence of deepfake: A review	Westerlund (2019)	Technology Innovation Management Review (Q2)	299
An agile co-creation process for digital servitization: A micro-service innovation approach	Sjodin et al (2020)	Journal of Business Research (Q1)	264
Artificial intelligence: a survey on evolution, models, applications and future trends	Lu (2019)	Journal of Management Analytics (Q1)	258

The most frequently cited article by Warner & Wager (2019) explores the digital transformation associated with AIoT. Digital transformation is defined as the utilization of emerging digital technologies, such as mobile, AI, cloud, blockchain, and IoT, in order to drive significant business improvements, enhance customer experiences, streamline operations, and create new business models. The dynamic capabilities of organizations to incorpore digital transformation are categorized into different dimensions, including digital sensing (scouting, scenario planning, digital mindset crafting), digital seizing (rapid prototyping, balancing digital portfolios, strategic agility), and digital transforming (navigating innovation systems, redesigning internal structures, improving digital maturity). These dimensions, along with contextual factors such as external triggers and internal enablers or barriers, are crucial for strategically renewing business models and fostering collaborative approaches and organizational culture (Warner & Wager, 2019). AI demands substantial organizational change, more so than other technologies (Pratas et al., 2024).

Kaplan & Haenlein (2019), the second most cited article, define AI as a system's capability to accurately interpret external data, learn from it, and utilize these learnings to achieve specific goals through flexible adaptation, exemplified by Siri. They propose the 3Cs model of Organizational Implications of AI, encompassing Confidence, Change, and Control. Confidence requires managers to demonstrate assurance to their employees in a rapidly evolving environment, and consumers to trust the abilities and recommendations of AI systems. Change necessitates employees to continually adapt their roles and skills through lifelong learning, while competitors must be perpetually outperformed through superior hardware or data. Control involves regulating machines to prevent autonomous decisions and implicit biases, as well as managing the ecosystem of managers, employees, machines, consumers, and competitors.

The third most cited article by Grewal et al. (2017) reveals that retailers have adopted various technologies to engage customers, focusing on five key areas: decision-making tools, visual display and merchandise offerings, consumption and engagement, big data collection and usage, and analytics for profitability.

Buhalis et al. (2019), the fourth most cited article, discuss how technological disruptions are creating smart environments that transform industry structures, processes, and practices, particularly through a value co-creation lens in the tourism and hospitality sector.

In the fifth most cited article, Huang & Rust (2021) argue that AI can be harnessed for marketing research, strategy (segmentation, targeting, positioning), and actions that progressively enhance efficiency. They delineate the roles of mechanical AI, thinking AI, and feeling AI at different stages of marketing: research, strategy (STP), and action.

Hoyer et al. (2020), the sixth most cited article, examine how emerging technologies like IoT, AR, VR, MR, virtual assistants, chatbots, and AI-powered robots are transforming the customer experience across the shopping journey, in the phases of pre-transaction, transaction, and post-transaction.

Olsen & Tomlin (2020), the seventh most cited article, highlight Industry 4.0 as a new industrial revolution driven by cyber-physical systems. It underscores the real-time integration of physical and digital systems and the transformative potential of enabling technologies such as AI, IoT, blockchain, additive manufacturing, and advanced robotics.

The eighth most cited article by Westerlund (2019) discusses the challenges posed by novel digital technologies in distinguishing between real and fake media. The rise of deepfakes (hyper-realistic videos created using AI) presents significant societal threats, including misinformation, national security risks, and undermining public trust in information.

Sjodin et al. (2020), the ninth most cited article, explore how manufacturing firms and their customers co-create digital service innovations to address the digitalization paradox. Their empirical study suggests that value co-creation in digital servitization is best managed through an agile micro-service innovation approach, emphasizing incremental investments and learning by doing.

The tenth most cited article by Lu (2019) predicts that breakthroughs in platforms, algorithms, and interfaces will further advance AI development. AI, as the cornerstone of Industry 4.0, IoT, and big data, is poised to revolutionize various fields, promoting automation and intelligent systems, and facilitating human-machine collaboration—a concept encapsulated by transhumanism (Mijwil & Abttan, 2021).

In resume, the ten most cited papers encompass pivotal themes, such as AIoT's role in digital transformation and Industry 4.0, AI implementation challenges, and the technological components of platforms, algorithms, and interfaces. They also examine the transformative effects of AI on retail, marketing, customer experiences, service innovations, and the implications of deepfakes.

Regarding source analysis, all top-cited documents originate from academic journals, primarily within the first quartile (Q1) of publications, with the exception of "The emergence of deepfake: A review" published in Technology Innovation Management Review, which is classified in the second quartile (Q2). The journals featuring these top-cited articles include Long Range Planning, Business Horizons, Journal of Retailing, Journal of Service Management, Journal of the Academy of Marketing Science, Journal of Interactive Marketing, Manufacturing & Service Operations Management, Technology Innovation Management Review, Journal of Business Research, and Journal of Marketing Analytics. Each journal is represented by a single highly-cited paper.

Main Researched Topics About AIoT

To address the second research question, "What are the main research topics and trends concerning the AIoT topic?", an array of bibliometric study techniques, including keyword co-occurrence, co-citation, and bibliographic coupling, was employed. The essence of a keyword co-occurrence map lies in unveiling the relationships among frequently occurring keywords within the selected document sample, thereby facilitating the exploration of prevalent themes and topics in the research domain. In our investigation, VOS Viewer software was utilized to create a keyword co-occurrence map. The analysis was conducted with the unit of "All keywords", employing the "Full counting" method, and setting a minimum occurrence threshold of 20. Out of the initial 2101 keywords, 31 met the threshold, allowing for the identification of four distinct clusters.

The first cluster appears to revolve around major trends and processes in management adoption of AIoT and new technologies, indicated by keywords such as digitalization, digital transformations, and Industry 4.0. The second cluster seems focused on the operationalization, impacts, and functioning of technology, highlighted by keywords like machine learning, AI, IoT, and model. The third cluster pertains to the strategic management of organizations and associated concerns, with keywords including management, system, sustainability, and blockchain. Lastly, the fourth cluster is linked to the operational and tactical management of organizations and projects, with keywords such as supply chain and design.

Figure 1. Keyword co-occurrence map

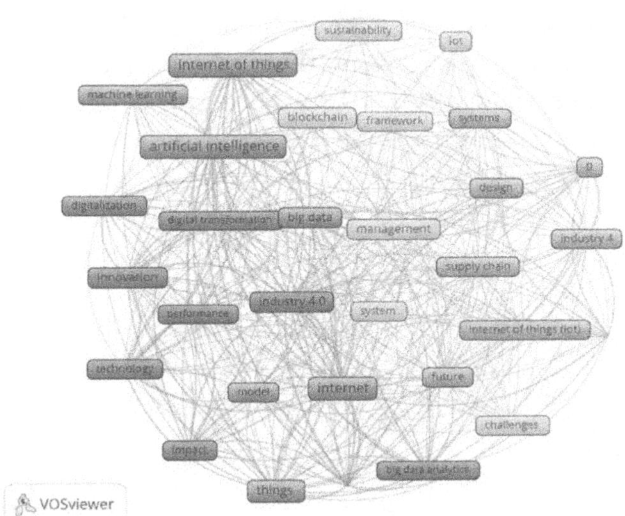

Simultaneously, a co-citation map was developed. The co-citation maps reveals how often pairs of documents are cited together. It allows a good understanding of the structure of the research field. The co-citation analysis that was performed in this research had as unit of analysis the cited references, the counting method of full counting, and the chosen minimum number of citations of a cited reference was 10. Of the 24628 cited references, 33 meet the threshold.

Four clusters were identified. In Figure 2, the co-citation map is meticulously illustrated. Cluster 1, distinguished by its red hue, primarily delves into the exposition of the Fourth Industrial Revolution. It presents groundbreaking technologies such as service robots, smart connected products, chatbots, and virtual assistants, along with the explanation of their profound implications for businesses and markets. Cluster 2, depicted in green, concentrates on the significant impacts of new technologies on supply chain management, logistics, and sustainable practices. Cluster 3, marked in blue, focuses on the consumer experience with these technologies, particularly through the interaction between consumers and smart objects. Lastly, Cluster 4, highlighted in yellow, examines the implications of new technologies and computerization on the job market and the functions of workers.

The horizontal axis of the map appears to demarcate the customer experience in the left, from company efficiency in relation to new technologies in the right side. The vertical axis seems to distinguish the analysis of technology itself from its interface with users.

Therefore, it is feasible to delineate four distinct quadrants: the first encompassing the customer experience as it pertains to the inherent characteristics of the new technology; the second focusing on the customer experience in relation to the interface with said technology.

The third quadrant addresses the company's operational efficiency derived directly from the new technology itself, while the fourth examines the efficiency gains associated with the interaction between the technology and the consumer interface.

Figure 2. Co-citation map

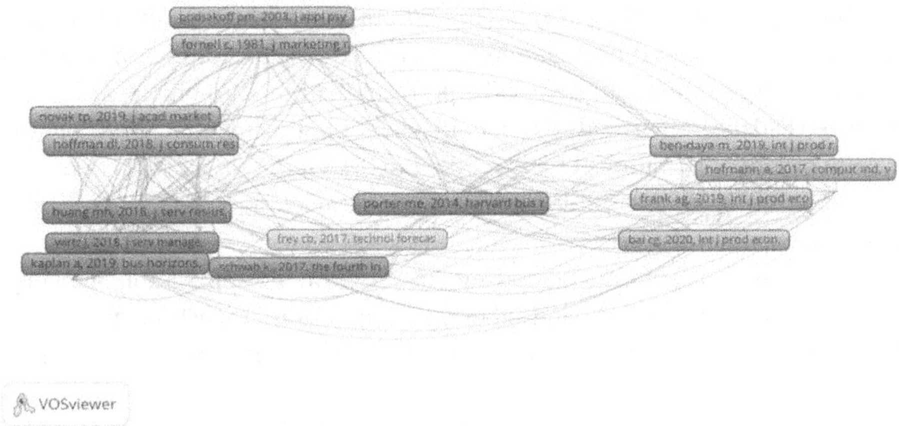

The average year of publication of the cluster 2 is 2016,55, so this cluster is the most recent, followed by cluster 2 and 4 respectively. The oldest cluster is the 3, possibly because the topic of interaction of consumer with new technologies, and consumer experience is a topic that is related with technologies beyond AIoT.

Table 2. Co-citations analysis clusters

Cluster	References
Cluster 1	Barney, J. 1991; Brynjolfsson, E., 2014; Davenport 2020; Haenlein, 2019; Huang, 2018; Kaplan, 2019; Ng ICL, 2017; Porter, 2014; Schwab, 2017; Teece, 2010; Wirtz, 2018. Number = 11 Average year = 2014,27
Cluster 2	Bai, C.G. 2020; Ben-Daya, 2019; Dalenogare, 2018; Frank, 2019; Frederico, 2020; Hofmann, 2017; Lasi, 2014; Tranfield, 2003; Vaidya Saurabh, 2018; Wang, 2016; Xu, 2018. Number = 11 Average year = 2016,55
Cluster 3	Davis, F.D. 1989; Fornell, 1981; Hair, 2017; Hoffman, D.L. 2018; Novak, 2019; Podsakoff, 2003; Puntoni, 2021; Venkatesh, 2003. Number = 8 Average year = 2006,38
Cluster 4	Atzori 2010; Frey C.B. 2017; Gubbi, 2013. Number = 3 Average year = 2013,3(3)

Bibliographic Coupling Map

The bibliographic coupling analysis has the purpose of showing the relationships between documents based on shared references. It is useful for identifying related works and emerging research trends. To perform the bibliographic coupling map, we analyzed had the unit of analysis "documents", counting method "Full counting", Minimum number of citations of a document of 30. Of the total of 435 documents, 81 meet the threshold, and 78 documents were connected to each other. Eight research clusters were identified.

The first cluster, represented in red, concentrates on the application of emerging technologies, such as AI, IoT, and others, within various industries and services. This research stream emphasizes personalization, customer experience, wearables, chatbots, and robots.

The second cluster, highlighted in green, primarily explores the intersection of new technologies with sustainability, environmental concerns, and the circular economy.

The third cluster, depicted in dark blue, focuses on the adoption of new technologies, examining the challenges, opportunities, and barriers, particularly in terms of privacy and cybersecurity of data.

The fourth cluster, marked in yellow, predominantly addresses the implications of disruptive technologies in analyzing phenomena like the Covid-19 pandemic and entrepreneurship.

The fifth cluster, shaded in purple, delves into the research stream of servitization, digital offerings, and co-creation within the paradigm of new technologies.

The sixth cluster, illustrated in light blue, examines the role of new technologies in the supply chain, logistics, and operations related to Industry 4.0.

The seventh cluster, shown in orange, investigates the integration of new technologies with organizational culture, focusing on total quality, circular economy, team creativity, total inspection, and evaluation. This research underscores the need for collaboration between quality experts and data scientists to prepare for the Fourth Industrial Revolution.

The eighth cluster, represented in grey, encompasses studies on Lean Six Sigma and quality management processes within Industry 4.0, highlighting Lean Six Sigma as a methodology for enhancing productivity, increasing customer satisfaction, and reducing operational costs.

In resume, in the bibliographical coupling map, the horizontal axis contrasts a generic approach to AIoT and new technologies, which does not concentrate on specific industries or applications, against a more targeted approach focusing on specific industries and applications. Meanwhile, the vertical axis distinguishes the strategic nature of AIoT and other emerging technologies at the upper end from their tactical nature at the lower end.

The documents that belong to each cluster are identified in table 3.

Table 3. Clusters highlighted in the Bibliographic coupling analysis

Cluster	
1	22 items: - Beverungen et al (2019). Conceptualizing Smart service systems; Electronic Markets. - Buhalis et al (2019). Technological disruption in services: lessons from tourism and hospitality; Journal of Service Management. - Chandra et al (2022). Personalization in personalized marketing: trends and ways forward; Psychology and Marketing. - Chatterjee et al (2021). Understanding AI adoption in manufacturing and production firms using an integrated TAM-TOE model; Technological forecasting and Social change. - Chouk & Mani (2019). Factors for and against resistance to smart services: role of consumer lifestyle and ecosystem related variables; Journal of Services Marketing. - Ehret & Wirtz (2017). Unlocking value from machines: Business models and the industrial internet-of-things; Journal of Marketing Management. - Grewal et al (2017). The future of retailing; Journal of Retailing. - Gupta et al (2020). Digital Analytics: modeling for insights and new methods; Journal of Interactive Marketing. - Hoyer et al (2020). Transforming the customer experience through new technologies; Journal of Interactive Marketing. - Huang & Rust (2021). A strategic framework for artificial intelligence in Marketing; Journal of the Academy of Marketing Science. - Huarng et al (2022). Adoption model of healthcare wearable devices; Technological forecasting and Social change. - Jimenez-Barreto et al (2021). "Find a flight for me, Oscar!" Motivational customer experiences with chatbots; International Journal of Contemporary Hospitality Management. - Kim et al (2017). What makes tourists feel negatively about tourism destinations? Application of hybrid text mining methodology to smart destination management; Technological forecasting and Social change. - Mercan et al (2021). Improving the service industry with hyper-connectivity: IoT in Hospitality; International Journal of Contemporary Hospitality Management. - Mustak et al (2021). Artificial intelligence in Marketing: topic modeling, scientometric analysis, and research agenda; Journal of Business Research. - Quach et al (2022). Digital technologies: Tensions in privacy and data; Journal of the Academy of Marketing Science. - Rosete et al (2020). Service robots in the Hospitality Industry: an exploratory literature review; Exploring service science (IESS 2020) - Rust (2020). The future of marketing; International Journal of Research in Marketing. - Sjodin et (2018). Smart factory implementation and process innovation: a preliminary maturity model for leveraging digitalization in manufacturing; Research – Technology management. - Wu et al (2017). The internet of things and interaction style: the effect of smart interaction on brand attachment; Journal of Marketing Management. - Xing et al (2021). Socio-technical barriers affecting large-scale deployment of AI-enabled wearable medical devices among the ageing population in China; Technological forecasting and Social change. - Zhang et al (2023). AIoT-enabled smart surveillance for personal data digitalization: contextual personalization-privacy paradox in smart home; Information & Management.

continued on following page

Table 3. Continued

Cluster	
2	**19 items:** - Agrawal & Narain (2023). Analysis of enablers for the digitalization of supply chain using an interpretive structural modelling approach; International Journal of Productivity and Performance Management. - Ahi et al (2022). Advanced technologies and international business: a multidisciplinary analysis of the literature; International Business Review. - Akbari & Hopkins (2022). Digital technologies as enablers of supply chain sustainability in an emerging economy; Operations Management Research. - Asokan et al (2022). Socially responsible operations in the industry 4.0 era: Post-covid-19 technology adoption and perspectives on future research; International Journal of Operations and Production Management. - Bhattacharya & Chatterjee (2022). Digital project driven Supply Chains: A new paradigm; Supply Chain Management – An International Journal. - Chauhan et al (2022). Linking circular economy and digitalisation technologies: a systematic literature review of past achievements and future promises; Technological forecasting and Social change. - Deng et al (2021). A systematic review of a digital twin city: a new pattern of urban governance toward smart cities; Journal of Management Science and Engineering. - Dhamija & Bag (2020). Role of Artificial Intelligence in operations environment: a review and bibliometric analysis; Total Quality Management journal - Ding Yangke et al (2021). Smart logistics based on the internet-of-things technology: an overview; International Journal of Logistics – Research and Applications. - Dong et al (2021). The impact of emerging and disruptive technologies on freight transportation in the digital era: current state and and future trends; International Journal of Logistics Management. - Ertz et al (2022). How transitioning to industry 4.0 promotes circular product lifetimes; Industrial Marketing Management. - Haji et al (2020). Roles of technology in improving perishable food supply chains; Logistics – Basel. - Hopkins & Hawking (2018). Big data analytics and IoT in logistics: a case study; International Journal of Logistics Management. - Jagtap et al (2021). Food logistics 4.0: opportunities and challenges; Logistics – Basel. - Kamble et al (2022). Digital twin for sustainable manufacturing supply chains: current trends, future perspectives, and an implementation framework; Technological forecasting and Social change. - Lu & Ning (2020). A vision of 6G – 5G's sucessor; Journal of Management Analytics - Miskiewicz (2020). Internet of Things in Marketing: Bibliometric Analysis; Marketing and Management of Innovations. - Rane & Narvel (2021). Re-designing the business organization using disruptive innovations based on blockchain-IoT integrated architecture for improving agility in future industry 4.0; Benchmarking – An International Journal. - Rusch et al (2023). Application of Digital technologies for sustainable Product management in a circular economy: a review; Business Strategy and the Environment.

continued on following page

Table 3. Continued

Cluster	
3	**12 items:** - Cho et al (2023). What's driving the diffusion of next-generation digital technologies?; Technovation. - Correia Loureiro et al (2021). Artificial Intelligence in business: state of the art and future research agenda; Journal of Business Research. - Haenlein & Kaplan (2021). Artificial Intelligence and Robotics: Shaking up the business world and society at large. Journal of Business Research. - Kaczorowska-Spychalska (2019). How chatbots influence marketing; Management – Poland. - Kaplan & Haenlein (2019). Siri, Siri, in my hand: Who's the fairest in the land? On the interpretations, illustrations, and implications of Artificial Intelligence; Business Horizons. - Kaplan & Haenlein (2020). Rulers of the world, unite! The challenges and opportunities of Artificial Intelligence; Business Horizons. - Krafft et al (2020). Challenges and opportunities for marketing scholars in times of the fourth industrial revolution; Journal of Interactive Marketing. - Lee (2021). Cybersecurity: Risk management framework and investment cost analysis; Business Horizons. - Lowry et al (2017). Why security and privacy research lies at the centre of the information systems (is) artefact: proposing a bold research agenda; European Journal of Information Systems. - Martinelli et al (2021). The enabling technologies of industry 4.0: examining the seeds of the fourth industrial revolution; Industrial and corporate change. - Ransbotham et al (2016). Special section introduction – Ubiquitous it and digital vulnerabilities; Information systems research. - Sousa & Wilks (2018). Sustainable skills for the world of work in the digital age; Systems Research and Behavioral Science.
4	**8 items:** - Abdel-Basset et al (2021). An intelligent framework using disruptive technologies for Covid-19 analysis; Technological forecasting and social change. - Giuggioli & Pellegrini (2023). Artificial intelligence as an enabler for entrepreneurs: a systematic literature review and an agenda for future research; International Journal of Entrepreneurial Behavior and Research. - Haleem & Javaid (2020). Medical 4.0 and its role in healthcare during Covid-19 pandemic: a review; Journal of Industrial Integration and Management, Innovation and Entrepreneurship. - Javaid et al (2020). Industry 5.0: Potential applications in Covid-19; Journal of Industrial Integration and Management, Innovation and Entrepreneurship. - Javaid et al (2021). Significant applications of Big Data in industry 4.0; Journal of Industrial Integration and Management, Innovation and Entrepreneurship. - Javaid et al (2022). Artificial intelligence applications for industry 4.0: a literature-based study. Journal of Industrial Integration and Management, Innovation and Entrepreneurship. - Khan & Javaid (2022). Role of internet of things (IoT) in adoption of industry 4.0; Journal of Industrial Integration and Management, Innovation and Entrepreneurship. - Zeba et al (2021). Technology mining: Artificial intelligence in Manufacturing. Technological forecasting and social change.

continued on following page

Table 3. Continued

Cluster	
5	**8 items:** - Ardito et al (2022). Industry 4.0 transition: a systematic literature review combining the absorptive capacity theory and the data-information-knowledge hierarchy; Journal of Knowledge Management. - Chen et al (2021). On the road to digital servitization: the (dis)continuous interplay between business model and digital technology. International Journal of Operations and Production Management. - Gebauer et al (2020). How to convert digital offerings into revenue enhancement – conceptualizing business model dynamics through explorative case studies; Industrial Marketing Management. - Mahmood & Mubarik (2020). Balancing innovation and exploitation in the fourth industrial revolution: role of intellectual capital and technology absorptive capacity. Technological forecasting and social change. - Si et al (2023). Technology, entrepreneurship, innovation and social change in digital economics. Technovation. - Sjodin et al (2020). An agile co-creation process for digital servitization: a micro-service innovation approach. Journal of Business Research. - Volberda et al (2021). Strategizing in a digital world: overcoming cognitive barriers, reconfiguring routines and introducing new organizational forms. Long Range Planning. - Warner & Waeger (2019). Building dynamic capabilities for digital transformation: an ongoing process of strategic renewal. Long Range Planning.
6	**4 items:** - Calatayud et al (2019). The self-thinking supply chain; Supply Chain Management – An international journal. - Klumpp & Zijm (2019). Logistics innovation and social sustainability: how to prevent and artificial divide in human-computer interaction; Journal of Business Logistics. - Lu (2019). Artificial intelligence: a survey on evolution, models, applications and future trends; Journal of Management Analytics. - Olsen & Tomlin (2020). Industry 4.0: Opportunities and challenges for Operations Management; Manufacturing and Service Operations Management.
7	**3 items:** - Kumar et al (2021). Influence of new-age technologies on marketing: a research agenda; Journal of Business Research - Park et al (2017). Building a new culture for quality management in the era of the fourth industrial revolution; Total Quality Management & Business Excellence - Ramakrishna et al (2020). Emerging industrial revolution: symbiosis of industry 4.0 and circular economy: the role of universities. Science Technology and Society.
8	**2 items:** - Yadav et al (2020). Impact of Industry4.0/ICTs, Lean Six Sigma and quality management systems on organisational performance; Total Quality Management - Yadav et al (2021). Critical success factors for lean six sigma in quality 4.0; International Journal of Quality and Service Sciences

The bibliographical coupling map is represented in the figure 3.

Figure 3. Bibliographic coupling map

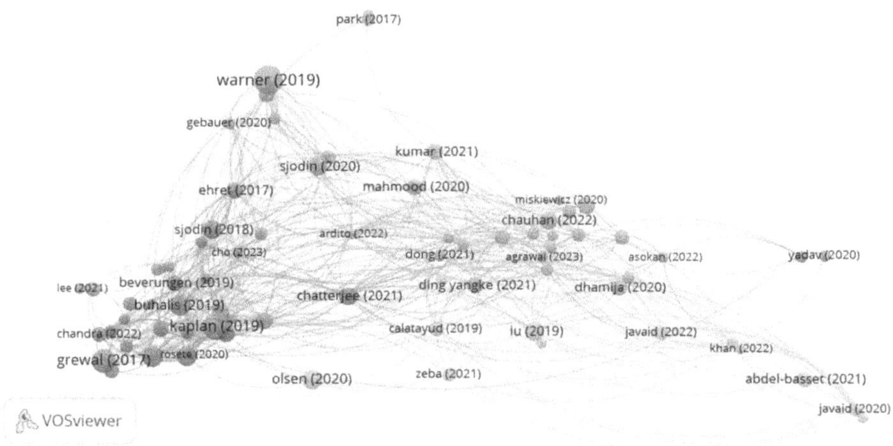

Evolution Over Time of the Publication of Scientific Documents About AIoT Topic: Research Clusters Trends Per Year

The AIoT topic is recognized as an emerging area of research, with the primary documents examining it being relatively recent. The average publication year of the papers within each cluster is detailed in Table 4, revealing that all clusters consist of papers published predominantly after the beginning of 2019. Notably, the most recent papers belong to cluster 2 and cluster 4, with their average publication year being post-2021. Cluster 2 predominantly explores the interplay between new technologies and aspects of sustainability, environmental concerns, and the circular economy. Conversely, cluster 4 delves into the effects of the Covid-19 pandemic and the domain of entrepreneurship, highlighting the significant recent scholarly attention these areas have received.

Table 4. Clusters highlighted in the Bibliographic coupling analysis, by age of articles

Cluster	Average year of publication of articles
1	2019,91
2	2021,21
3	2019,6(6)
4	2021,25

continued on following page

Table 4. Continued

Cluster	Average year of publication of articles
5	2020,75
6	2019,25
7	2019,3(3)
8	2020,50

CONCLUSION

Theoretical Contributions

This work delves into the current knowledge and emerging research trends regarding AIoT, focusing on the various existing equipment and their functionalities, the key industries employing them, and the applications and benefits they provide to businesses, public and private organizations, and society at large. It also addresses the challenges and barriers to AIoT adoption.

The most frequently cited literature in this area highlights the digital transformation process, recognizing AIoT as a pivotal technology. This comprehensive approach aligns with the integration of AIoT within the Industry 4.0 framework. The adoption of AIoT is closely associated with the organizational changes necessitated by AI and the collaborative processes between humans and machines. Notably, several top-cited works emphasize the transformative impact of technology adoption and co-creation processes in industries such as Retail and Tourism, as well as in digital service innovations. Changes in marketing practices related to AIoT are also significant, particularly in the evolving nature of Segmentation, Targeting, and Positioning (STP) strategies, enhanced personalization and customization, and the altered customer shopping journey due to new technologies like AIoT.

The main research topics identified through keyword co-occurrence analysis include Digitalization, Digital Transformation, and Industry 4.0. Additionally, it encompasses the functionality of new technologies (with keywords such as Machine Learning, AI, IoT, and Model), the strategic management of companies integrating AIoT (featuring keywords like Management, System, and Sustainability), and operational management activities related to AIoT applications (highlighted by keywords such as Supply Chain and design).

The co-citation analysis identified four clusters:

- The 4th industrial revolution and its technologies;

- The supply chain and logistics associated with sustainability effects;
- The consumer experience with new technologies;
- The effects of computerisation in jobs.

The emerging cluster, as it is the most recent, in this co-citation analysis is centered on the impact of sustainability on supply chain and logistics, which marks the latest frontier of research. Conversely, the examination of consumer experiences with new technologies represents the most established cluster. This analysis reveals two primary dimensions: one focuses on evaluating customer experience versus company efficiency driven by AIoT, while the other contrasts the intrinsic analysis of the technology with its interface and interaction with consumers.

By understanding these dimensions, we can appreciate how AIoT not only enhances operational efficiency but also transforms consumer interactions, balancing technological advancement with user-centric design. This dual perspective is crucial for comprehensively assessing the multifaceted effects of AIoT in both corporate and consumer spheres.

Finally in the bibliographic coupling map analysis, eight clusters were identified:

- Application of AIoT in several industries and services;
- AIoT (and related technologies) relationship with sustainability, environmental concerns and circular economy;
- Challenges and barriers in the adoption of technologies, namely data privacy and cybersecurity;
- Relationship between technology, COVID-19 and entrepreneurship;
- Servitization, digital offerings and co-creation;
- AIoT in Supply chain, logistics and operations in Industry 4.0;
- Organizational culture and new technologies;
- Lean Six Sigma and quality management.

Two primary dimensions have emerged in the examination of AIoT literature. The first dimension highlights the dichotomy between a generic approach and the focus on specific industries and topics related to AIoT.

The second dimension contrasts the strategic versus the tactical nature of AIoT in management contexts. Given the nascent nature of AIoT, it is noteworthy that most clusters identified in the literature have papers published only after 2019. The clusters pertaining to the relationship between AIoT and sustainability, environmental concerns, and the circular economy, as well as the intersection of technology, COVID-19, and entrepreneurship, are particularly recent, with the average publication year being 2021.

Hence, AIoT technologies represent a vibrant and emerging area of research. Their application spans across numerous sectors and industries, linking them to a wide array of contemporary topics, making AIoT a compelling subject for further exploration and study.

Managerial Contributions

This study on AIoT provides invaluable insights for managers of both public and private organizations, enabling them to make informed decisions, stimulate innovation, and maintain a competitive edge in the evolving AIoT landscape. By identifying the most cited documents, the study highlights the most impactful and influential research areas within AIoT. This recognition aids managers in deciding where to focus their attention and resources, thus enhancing the understanding of AIoT subcomponents. Furthermore, identifying the most referenced authors and institutions involved in AIoT can facilitate potential collaborations, driving innovation and ensuring the organization remains at the forefront of the field.

Moreover, comprehending the research clusters allows managers to discern emerging trends and patterns in AIoT. This foresight aids in anticipating future developments and equipping the organization to adapt to new technological advancements.

Ultimately, the insights derived from this study enable managers to formulate long-term goals and objectives, positioning their company to effectively leverage AIoT technologies for sustained growth and success.

Limitations and Future Research Directions

This study acknowledges several limitations inherent in bibliometric analyses. Firstly, these analyses depend significantly on the quality and comprehensiveness of the databases utilized. Incomplete or biased datasets can lead to skewed results. Our analysis exclusively considered research documents available in the Web of Science database. While other research databases could provide a broader spectrum of research documents, the Web of Science database remains the world's leading scientific citation search and analytical information platform. It serves both as a research tool supporting a diverse array of scientific endeavors and as a dataset for large-scale, data-intensive studies.

Additionally, alternative bibliometric techniques could have been employed. Bibliometric studies tend to favor more established research, as newer publications have had less opportunity to accumulate citations.

The focus of this study was on disciplines within Business and Management. Given that AIoT is examined across various other disciplines, this bibliometric study may be considered somewhat incomplete. However, this decision was made to concentrate the analysis effectively.

Lastly, the rapidly evolving nature of AIoT signifies that this bibliometric analysis may quickly become outdated, underscoring the necessity for continuous updates to maintain its relevance.

Future research directions, based on this bibliometric study, can enhance the understanding of the emergent AIoT technology. The study of AIoT equipment and technologies in retailing and services can be approached both generally and within specific industries, examining the customer (or citizen) experience as well as the increased efficiency in processes for companies, organizations, and society as a whole. Personalized and customized processes and offers based on AIoT, and new marketing-mix possibilities can also be interlinked with these aspects.

The interface between machines and humans, along with the concept of trans-humanism, warrants further exploration. Additionally, research could focus on the global measures required by AIoT for strategic management changes within companies, organizations, and society, necessitating new governance structures. Investigating specific AIoT applications in tactical management, aimed at short-term improvements in areas such as quality management, Six Sigma, supply chain, logistics, and operations, could yield valuable insights.

The challenges and barriers to AIoT adoption, particularly legal aspects related to data privacy and cybersecurity, present another crucial area for investigation. Furthermore, examining the relationship between AIoT, sustainability, environmental protection, the circular economy, and entrepreneurship (through the development of new companies or the application of AIoT technologies in existing enterprises) is essential.

Finally, the role of AIoT in digitalization, digital transformation, and Industry 4.0 should be continuously analyzed due to the ongoing advancements in these areas. Comparative studies of AIoT development and adoption across different countries in these contexts can provide valuable insights.

Given the exploratory and emergent nature of AIoT, a morphological analysis is suggested to explore the various possibilities for research and creativity, focusing on the components highlighted in this bibliometric study (Jordanous & Keller, 2016; Farina et al, 2024; Yin et al, 2024).

REFERENCES

Adli, H. K., Remli, M. A., Wan Salihin Wong, K. N. S., Ismail, N. A., González-Briones, A., Corchado, J. M., & Mohamad, M. S. (2023). Recent Advancements and Challenges of AIoT Application in Smart Agriculture: A Review. *Sensors (Basel), 23*(7), 3752. DOI: 10.3390/s23073752 PMID: 37050812

Alaba, F. A., Oluwadare, A., Sani, U., Oriyomi, A. A., Lucy, A. O., & Najeem, O. (2024). Enabling Sustainable Transportation Through IoT and AIoT Innovations. In Misra, S., Siakas, K., & Lampropoulos, G. (Eds.), *Artificial Intelligence of Things for Achieving Sustainable Development Goals. Lecture Notes on Data Engineering and Communications Technologies* (Vol. 192). Springer., DOI: 10.1007/978-3-031-53433-1_14

Albayrak, Ö., Erkayman, B., & Usanmaz, B. (2023). Applications of Artificial Intelligence in Inventory Management: A Systematic Review of the Literature. *Archives of Computational Methods in Engineering, 30*, 2605–2625. DOI: 10.1007/s11831-022-09879-5

Alenizi, A. S., & Al-Karawi, K. A. (2022). Internet of Things (IoT) Adoption: Challenges and Barriers. In: Yang, XS., Sherratt, S., Dey, N., Joshi, A. (eds) *Proceedings of Seventh International Congress on Information and Communication Technology. Lecture Notes in Networks and Systems,* 464. Springer. https://doi.org/ DOI: 10.1007/978-981-19-2394-4_20

Armenta, A. (2024). AI Applications in Warehouse and Inventory Management. 16th September 2024. Control. Retrieved 25th November 2024 from https://control .com/technical-articles/ai-applications-in-warehouse-and-inventory-management/

Awaisi, K. S., Ye, Q., & Sampalli, S. (2024). A Survey of Industrial AIoT: Opportunities, Challenges, and Directions. *IEEE Access : Practical Innovations, Open Solutions, 12*, 96946–96996. DOI: 10.1109/ACCESS.2024.3426279

Bourechak, A., Zedadra, O., Kouahla, M. N., Guerrieri, A., Seridi, H., & Fortino, G. (2023). At the Confluence of Artificial Intelligence and Edge Computing in IoT-Based Applications: A Review and New Perspectives. *Sensors (Basel), 23*(3), 1639. DOI: 10.3390/s23031639 PMID: 36772680

Buhalis, D., Harwood, T., Bogicevic, V., Viglia, G., Beldona, S., & Hofacker, C. (2019). Technological disruptions in services: Lessons from tourism and hospitality. *Journal of Service Management, 30*(4), 484–506. DOI: 10.1108/JOSM-12-2018-0398

Burrows, L. (2021). *The present and future of AI. Finale Doshi-Velez on how AI is shaping our lives and how we can shape AI.* October, 19. Retrieved 23th November 2024 from https://seas.harvard.edu/news/2021/10/present-and-future-ai

Cogniteq (2023). *How IoT is Changing Advertising: Benefits and Use-Cases.* Retrieved 25th November 2024 from https://www.cogniteq.com/blog/how-iot-changing-advertising-new-possibilities-and-top-use-cases

Deng, S., Zhao, H., Fang, W., Yin, J., Dustdar, S., & Zomaya, A. Y. (2020). Edge Intelligence: The confluence of Edge Computing and Artificial Intelligence. arXiv:1909.00560v2. https://arxiv.org/html/2407.04053v1

Dhaduk, H. (2024). *AI in Supply Chain: Top Use Cases and Applications With Examples.* 22th July 2024. Simform. Retrieved 25th November 2024 from https://www.simform.com/blog/ai-in-supply-chain/

Dijkman, R. M., Sprenkels, B., Peeters, T., & Janssen, A. (2015). Business models for the Internet of things. *International Journal of Information Management, 35*(6), 672–678. DOI: 10.1016/j.ijinfomgt.2015.07.008

Ding, H., Tian, J., Yu, W., Wilson, D. I., Young, B. R., Cui, X., Xin, X., Wang, Z., & Li, W. (2023). The Application of Artificial Intelligence and Big Data in the Food Industry. *Foods, 12*(24), 4511. DOI: 10.3390/foods12244511 PMID: 38137314

Dini, P., Diana, L., Elhanashi, A., & Saponara, S. (2024). Overview of AI-Models and Tools in Embedded IIoT Applications. *Electronics (Basel), 13*(12), 2322. DOI: 10.3390/electronics13122322

Fang, B., Yu, J., Chen, Z., Osman, A. I., Farghali, M., Ihara, I., Hamza, E. H., Rooney, D. W., & Yap, P.-S. (2023). Artificial intelligence for waste management in smart cities: A review. *Environmental Chemistry Letters, 21*(4), 1959–1989. DOI: 10.1007/s10311-023-01604-3 PMID: 37362015

Fares, O. H., Butt, I., & Lee, S. H. M. (2023). Utilization of artificial intelligence in the banking sector: A systematic literature review. *Journal of Financial Services Marketing, 28*(2), 835–852. DOI: 10.1057/s41264-022-00176-7

Farina, M., Pedrycz, W., & Lavazza, A. (2024). Towards a mixed human-machine creativity. *Journal of Cultural Cognitive Science, 8*(2), 151–165. DOI: 10.1007/s41809-024-00146-6

Flatirons (2024). AI in Transportation Industries: Use Cases and Benefits. 28th January. Flatirons. Retrieved 25th November 2024 from https://flatirons.com/blog/ai-in-transportation-industries/

Gill, S. S., Golec, M., Hu, J., Xu, M., Du, J., Wu, H., Walia, G. K., Murugesan, S. S., Ali, B., Kumar, M., Ye, K., Verma, P., Kumar, S., Cuadrado, F., & Uhlig, S. (2024). *Edge AI: A Taxonomy, Systematic Review and Future Directions*. arXiv:2407.04053v1 04 Jul 2024. https://arxiv.org/html/2407.04053v1

Grewal, D., Roggeveen, A. L., & Nordfalt, J. (2017). The Future of Retailing. *Journal of Retailing*, *93*(1), 1–6. DOI: 10.1016/j.jretai.2016.12.008

Guo, X., Shen, Z., Zhang, Y., & Wu, T. (2019). Review on the Application of Artificial Intelligence in Smart Homes. *Smart Cities*, *2*(3), 402–420. DOI: 10.3390/smartcities2030025

Heins, C. (2023). Artificial intelligence in retail – a systematic literature review. *Foresight*, *25*(2), 264–286. DOI: 10.1108/FS-10-2021-0210

Hoyer, H. D., Kroschke, M., Schmitt, B., Kraume, K., & Shankar, V. (2020). Transforming the Customer Experience Through New Technologies. *Journal of Interactive Marketing*, *51*(1), 57–71. DOI: 10.1016/j.intmar.2020.04.001

Huang, M. H., & Rust, R. T. (2021). A strategic framework for artificial intelligence in marketing. *Journal of the Academy of Marketing Science*, *49*(1), 30–50. DOI: 10.1007/s11747-020-00749-9

Hunt, W., & Rolf, S. (2022). *Artificial Intelligence and automation in Retail: benefits, challenges and applications (a union perspective)*. UNI Global Union. Friedrich Ebert Stiftung. Retieved 24 th November from https://library.fes.de/pdf-files/bueros/bruessel/19054.pdf

Intuz (2022). *AI-enabled IoT Smart Parking Management System*. Intuz. Retrieved 24th November 2024 from https://www.intuz.com/blog/iot-in-smart-parking-management-benefits-challenges

Intuz (2024). 9 Most Practical Applications of AI in Transportation. Intuz. Retrieved 25th November 2024 from https://www.intuz.com/blog/use-cases-of-ai-in-transportation

IoT World Magazine. (2024). *15 Examples of Digital Healthcare Solutions with AI, IoT, and Blockchain in 2024*. Retrieved 25th November 2024 from https://iotworldmagazine.com/2024/03/29/2198/15-examples-of-digital-healthcare-solutions-with-ai-iot-and-blockchain-in-2024

Jordanous, A., & Keller, B. (2016). Modelling Creativity: Identifying Key Components through a Corpus-Based Approach. *PLoS One*, *11*(10), e0162959. DOI: 10.1371/journal.pone.0162959 PMID: 27706185

Joyia, G. J., Liaqat, R. M., Farooq, A., & Rehman, S. (2017). Internet of Medical Things (IOMT): Applications benefits and future challenges in healthcare domain. *Journal of Communication*, *12*(4), 240–247.

Kaplan, A., & Haenlein, M. (2019). Siri, Siri, in my hand: Who's the fairest in the land? On the interpretations, illustrations, and implications of artificial intelligence. *Business Horizons*, *62*(1), 15–25. DOI: 10.1016/j.bushor.2018.08.004

Khadam, U., Davidsson, P., & Spalazzese, R. (2024). Exploring the Role of Artificial Intelligence in Internet of Things Systems: A Systematic Mapping Study. *Sensors (Basel)*, *24*(20), 6511. DOI: 10.3390/s24206511 PMID: 39459993

Kulkarni, P. M., Gokhale, P. P., & Dandannavar, P. (2022). Internet of Things (IoT) Adoption: Challenges among small and medium scale enterprises (SMEs). In: Haldorai, A., Ramu, A., Mohanram, S. & Zgheib, R. (eds) *4th EAI International Conference on Big Data Innovation for Sustainable Cognitive Computing*. EAI/ Springer. https://doi.org/DOI: 10.1007/978-3-031-07654-1_9

Lu, Y. (2019). Artificial intelligence: A survey on evolution, models, applications and future trends. *Journal of Management Analytics*, *6*(1), 1–29. DOI: 10.1080/23270012.2019.1570365

Manta, A. G., Bădîrcea, R. M., Doran, N. M., Badareu, G., Gher escu, C., & Popescu, J. (2024). Industry 4.0 Transformation: Analysing the Impact of Artificial Intelligence on the Banking Sector through Bibliometric Trends. *Electronics (Basel)*, *13*(9), 1693. DOI: 10.3390/electronics13091693

Matthews, K. (2020). *5 applications of AIoT in the retail industry*. 19th February. IoT Times. Retrieved 24th November 2024 from https://iot.eetimes.com/5-applications-of-aiot-in-the-retail-industry/

Mavani, N. R., Ali, J. M., Othman, S., Hussain, M. A., Hashim, H., & Rahman, N. (2022). Application of Artificial Intelligence in Food Industry - A Guideline. *Food Engineering Reviews*, *14*(1), 134–175. DOI: 10.1007/s12393-021-09290-z PMID: 40477643

Medwave (2024). *How AI is Transforming Healthcare: 12 Real-World Use Cases.* Retrieved 24th November 2024 from https://medwave.io/2024/01/how-ai-is-transforming-healthcare-12-real-world-use-cases/

Mijwil, M. M., & Abttan, R. A. (2021). Artificial Intelligence: A Survey on Evolution and Future Trends. *Asian Journal of Applied Sciences*, *9*(2). Advance online publication. DOI: 10.24203/ajas.v9i2.6589

Mittal, A. (2024). *AI in Food Industry: Benefits, Use Cases, and Trends in 2025.* Rerieved 25th November 2024 from https://www.ongraph.com/ai-in-food-industry/

Mulè, L. (2024). *Revolutionizing waste management: the role of AI in building sustainable practices.* Retrieved 25th November from https://aiforgood.itu.int/revolutionizing-waste-management-the-role-of-ai-in-building-sustainable-practices/

Ninkov, A., Frank, J. R., & Maggio, L. A. (2022). Bibliometrics: Methods for studying academic publishing. *Perspectives on Medical Education, 11*(3), 173–176. DOI: 10.1007/S40037-021-00695-4 PMID: 34914027

Nozari, H. (2024). Investigating Key Dimensions and Key Indicators of AIoT-Based Supply Chain in Sustainable Business Development. In Misra, S., Siakas, K., & Lampropoulos, G. (Eds.), *Artificial Intelligence of Things for Achieving Sustainable Development Goals. Lecture Notes on Data Engineering and Communications Technologies* (Vol. 192). Springer., DOI: 10.1007/978-3-031-53433-1_15

Nozari, H., Szmelter-Jarosz, A., & Ghahremani-Nahr, J. (2022). *Analysis of the Challenges of Artificial Intelligence of Things (AIoT) for the Smart Supply Chain (Case Study: FMCG Industries). Sensors (Basel), 22*(8), 2931–2945. DOI: 10.3390/s22082931 PMID: 35458916

Olsen, T. L., & Tomlin, B. (2020). Industry 4.0: Opportunities and Challenges for Operations Management. *Manufacturing & Service Operations Management, 22*(1), 113–122. Advance online publication. DOI: 10.1287/msom.2019.0796

Ordr (2024). *10 Internet of Things (IoT) Healthcare Examples.* Retrieved 24th November 2024 from https://ordr.net/article/iot-healthcare-examples

Parking Telecom. (2022). AI-based Smart Parking Solutions. Retrieved 24th November 2024 from https://parkingtelecom.com/en/ai-based-smart-parking-solutions/

Passas, I. (2024). Bibliometric Analysis: The Main Steps. *Encyclopedia, 4*(2), 1014–1025. DOI: 10.3390/encyclopedia4020065

Pratas, J., & Oliveira, Z. (2023). QR Codes Research in Marketing: A Bibliometric and Content Analysis. In Reis, J. L., Peter, M. K., Varela González, J. A., & Bogdanović, Z. (Eds.), *Marketing and Smart Technologies. Smart Innovation, Systems and Technologies* (Vol. 337). Springer., DOI: 10.1007/978-981-19-9099-1_19

Pratas, J., Rodrigues, M. A., & Carvalho, M. A. (2024). *Unraveling Managerial Resistance: An Analysis of the reasons of Non-Investment in Cutting-Edge Digital Technologies.* ISPGAYA International Congress 2024 – Business and Sustainability. Vila Nova de Gaia, Portugal.

Rawas, S. (2024). AI: The future of humanity. *Discover Artificial Intelligence*, *4*(1), 25. DOI: 10.1007/s44163-024-00118-3

Rizzoli, A. (2021). *AI in Transportation: 9 Disruptive Use Cases [2024 Update].* V7 Labs. Retrieved 23th November 2024 from https://www.v7labs.com/blog/ai-in-transportation

Sepasgozar, S., Karimi, R., Farahzadi, L., Moezzi, F., Shirowzhan, S. M., Ebrahimzadeh, S., Hui, F., & Aye, L. (2020). A Systematic Content Review of Artificial Intelligence and the Internet of Things Applications in Smart Home. *Applied Sciences (Basel, Switzerland)*, *10*(9), 3074. DOI: 10.3390/app10093074

Shah, H. (2024). *AI in Transportation Industry: Use Cases, Benefits, Applications and Real World Examples.* 9th October 2024. Prismetric. Retrieved 25th november 2024 from https://www.prismetric.com/ai-in-transportation/

Sharma, R. (2023). Leveraging AI and IoT for Sustainable Waste Management. In Whig, P., Silva, N., Elngar, A. A., Aneja, N., & Sharma, P. (Eds.), *Sustainable Development through Machine Learning, AI and IoT. ICSD 2023. Communications in Computer and Information Science* (Vol. 1939). Springer., DOI: 10.1007/978-3-031-47055-4_12

Sjodin, D., Parida, V., Kohtamaki, M., & Wincent, J. (2020). An agile co-creation process for digital servitization: A micro-service innovation approach. *Journal of Business Research*, *112*, 478–491. DOI: 10.1016/j.jbusres.2020.01.009

Thomas, M. (2022). *14 Key IoT In Retail Examples You Need to Know.* 28th September. Built In. Retrieved 24th November from https://builtin.com/articles/iot-in-retail-tech-applications

Velosiot (2024). *Top IoT Use Cases in Retail with Real-Life Examples.* 20th February. Retrieved 25th November 2024 from https://blog.velosiot.com/top-iot-use-cases-in-retail-with-real-life-examples

Villar, E., Martín Toral, I., Calvo, I., Barambones, O., & Fernández-Bustamante, P. (2024). Architectures for Industrial AIoT Applications. *Sensors (Basel)*, *24*(15), 4929. DOI: 10.3390/s24154929 PMID: 39123976

Wakefield, L. (2024). *Understanding the adoption and application of AI in Digital Advertising.* IAB Europe and Microsoft, 30th April 2024. Retrieved 25th November 2024 from https://iabeurope.eu/knowledge_hub/iab-europe-and-microsofts-understanding-the-adoption-and-application-of-ai-in-digital-advertising-report/

Warner, K. S. R., & Wäger, M. (2019). Building dynamic capabilities for digital transformation: An ongoing process of strategic renewal. *Long Range Planning, 52*(3), 326–349. DOI: 10.1016/j.lrp.2018.12.001

Westerlund, M. (2019). The Emergence of Deepfake Technology: A Review. *Technology Innovation Management Review, 9*(11), 39–52. DOI: 10.22215/timreview/1282

10. xDS Team (2023). *The Intelligent Warehouse: AI's Impact on Modern Inventory Strategies*. 13th December. 10xDS. Retrieved 25th November 2024 from https://10xds.com/blog/ai-impact-on-modern-inventory-strategies/

Yasar, K., Gillis, A. S., & Christensen, G. (2023). *Artificial intelligence of things (AIoT)*. Retrieved 22th November 2024 from https://www.techtarget.com/iotagenda/definition/Artificial-Intelligence-of-Things-AIoT

Yin, H., Zhang, Z. P., & Liu, Y. Y. (2024). The Exploration of Integrating the Midjourney Artificial Intelligence Generated Content Tool into Design Systems to Direct Designers towards Future-Oriented Innovation. *Systems, 11*(12), 566. Advance online publication. DOI: 10.3390/systems11120566

ADDITIONAL READING

Ahvar, E., Ahvar, S., & Lee, G. M. (2024). Artificial Intelligence of Things: Architectures, Applications, and Challenges. In: Ziegler, S., Radócz, R., Quesada Rodriguez, A., Matheu Garcia, S.N. (eds) *Springer Handbook of Internet of Things*. Springer Handbooks. Springer. https://doi.org/DOI: 10.1007/978-3-031-39650-2_19

Bibri, S. E., Krogstie, J., Kaboli, A., & Alahi, A. (2024). Smarter eco-cities and their leading-edge artificial intelligence of things solutions for environmental sustainability: A comprehensive systematic review. *Environmental Science and Ecotechnology, 19*, 100330. Advance online publication. DOI: 10.1016/j.ese.2023.100330 PMID: 38021367

Garcia, C. G., Nunez-Valdez, E. R., García-Díaz, V., Bustelo, C. P. G., & Lovelle, J. M. C. (2018). A Review of Artificial Intelligence in the Internet of Things. *International Journal of Interactive Multimedia and Artificial Intelligence, 5*(4), 9–20. DOI: 10.9781/ijimai.2018.03.004

Ghosh, A., Chakraborty, D., & Law, A. (2018). Artificial intelligence in Internet of things. *CAAI Transactions on Intelligence Technology, 3*(4), 208–218. DOI: 10.1049/trit.2018.1008

Perwej, Y., Akhtar, N., & Agarwal, D. (2024). The emerging technologies of Artificial Intelligence of Things (AIoT) current scenario, challenges, and opportunities. In: Mishra, D., Verma, A.K., Sharma, S. (eds) *Convergence of Artificial Intelligence and Internet of Things for Industrial Automation.* CRC Press. Taylor & Francis Group. DOI: 10.1201/9781003509240

Siam, S. I., Ahn, H., Liu, L., Alam, S., Shen, H., Cao, Z., Shroff, N., Krishnamachari, B., Srivastava, M. & Zhang, M. (2024). *Artificial Intelligence of Things: A Survey.* ACM Transactions on Sensor Networks. Article Pre-Print (August 2024), 70 pages. https://doi.org/DOI: 10.1145/3690639

Sung, T. W., Tsai, P. W., Gaber, T., & Lee, C. Y. (2021). Artificial Intelligence of Things (AIoT) Technologies and Applications. *Wireless Communications and Mobile Computing*, *2021*(1), 9781271. Advance online publication. DOI: 10.1155/2021/9781271

Zhang, J., & Tao, D. (2020). *Empowering Things with Intelligence: A Survey of the Progress, Challenges, and Opportunities in Artificial Intelligence of Things*. IEEE Internet of Things Journal. https://doi.org//arXiv.2011.08612DOI: 10.48550

KEY TERMS AND DEFINITIONS

Artificial Intelligence (AI): refers to the simulation of human intelligence in machines that are programmed to think, learn, and make decisions. AI systems use algorithms and models to process data, recognize patterns, and perform tasks that typically require human intelligence, such as visual perception, speech recognition, decision-making, and language translation.

Artificial Intelligence of Things (AIoT): refers to the convergence of Artificial Intelligence (AI) and the Internet of Things (IoT). It involves integrating AI technologies with IoT devices to enhance their capabilities. AIoT enables smarter, more efficient systems that can analyze data, make decisions, and act autonomously. This combination allows for advanced automation, predictive maintenance, and improved user experiences across various industries.

Customer Experience: refers to the overall perception and feelings a customer has about their interactions with a company or brand throughout their entire journey. This includes all touchpoints, from initial awareness and engagement to purchasing and post-purchase support. A positive customer experience is crucial for building loyalty, satisfaction, and long-term relationships.

Digitalization: refers to the process of converting analog information into digital formats and integrating digital technologies into everyday activities and business processes. It involves the use of digital tools and systems (for communication and collaboration, project management, data analytics and visualization, customer relationship management, cloud services, document management and storage, e-commerce and marketing automation tools, among others) to transform and optimize operations, enhance efficiency, improve data management, and enable new ways of interacting and conducting business. Digitalization impacts various sectors driving innovation and growth in the digital age.

Industry 4.0: refers to the fourth industrial revolution, characterized by the integration of digital technologies into manufacturing and industry. It involves the use of Internet of Things (IoT), Artificial Intelligence (AI), robotics, big data, and advanced analytics to create smart factories where machines and systems are interconnected and can communicate with each other. This leads to increased automation, improved efficiency, and real-time data-driven decision-making in industrial processes.

Internet-of-Things (IoT): refers to the network of physical objects or "things" embedded with sensors, software, and other technologies, which connect and exchange data with other devices and systems over the internet. This connectivity enables these objects to collect and share data, making them "smart" and capable of interacting with the environment and each other to provide improved services and functionalities.

Smart Retailing: refers to the integration of advanced technologies, such as Internet of Things (IoT), Artificial Intelligence (AI), and data analytics, into the retail environment. This approach enhances the shopping experience by personalizing customer interactions, optimizing inventory management, and streamlining operations. Smart Retailing leverages real-time data to make informed decisions, improve customer satisfaction, and increase overall efficiency in the retail sector.

Smart Service Systems: is an integrated network of technologies, including Internet of Things (IoT) and Artificial Intelligence (AI), designed to deliver intelligent, responsive, and personalized services. These systems enable real-time data collection, analysis, and decision-making, enhancing the efficiency and effectiveness of various services across different sectors, such as healthcare (with remote patient monitoring and telemedicine platforms), transportation (with smart traffic management and autonomous vehicles), retail (with personalized shopping experiences and smart inventory management), energy management (with smart grids and smart home energy systems), and customer support (with chatbots and predictive maintenaince).

Chapter 2
Retail Evolution Using Artificial Intelligence of Things (AIoT):
An Exploratory Analysis and Innovative Ideas Using Literature Review and Creativity Techniques

Joaquim Monteiro Pratas
https://orcid.org/0000-0002-7432-9242
Instituto Superior de Contabilidade e Administração, Instituto Politécnico do Porto, Portugal

Paulo Jorge Gonçalves
https://orcid.org/0000-0002-1195-5027
Instituto Superior de Contabilidade e Administração, Instituto Politécnico do Porto, Portugal

Joseph Kaswengi
University of Orléans, France

ABSTRACT

This study explores AIoT solutions to spark innovative retail management concepts. It begins with a review of technology evolution in retail, from barcodes to big data analytics, covering smart retailing, digital transformation, and the integration of IoT, AI, and AIoT. The methodology includes a bibliometric study and qualitative analysis via focus groups, using mind maps and morphological analysis. The bibliometric study identifies eleven research clusters. Focus groups generate ideas highlighting AIoT actions to enhance customer experience and boost operational

DOI: 10.4018/979-8-3693-8512-8.ch002

efficiency. The process suggests parameters for morphological analysis, illustrated with five novel ideas. This tool inspires innovative AIoT-driven retail management ideas. The study also discusses theoretical and managerial contributions, limitations, and future research directions.

INTRODUCTION

In recent years, retail has evolved rapidly, driven by digital technologies. These innovations introduced new sales channels, such as transactional websites, mobile apps and social media, among others. They also brought advanced retail analytics and operational changes, enhancing retailers' efficiency. Emerging technologies like the Internet of Things (IoT) and Artificial Intelligence (AI) are also gaining traction in retail managers' agendas, transforming the industry (Grewal et al., 2018). As these technologies become more accessible and widely adopted, their utilization by retailers increases (Pratas & Brito, 2019).

IoT is a transformative force in retail, enhancing business models and enabling continuous data collection through millions of interconnected sensors in various devices and locations. AI, another significant technology, has two primary applications: value chain optimization and consumer experience enhancement (Heins, 2023). AI strengthens the retail value chain by offering insights into inventory management, operations optimization, and customer engagement. It improves demand forecasts, enhances operational efficiency, generates deeper insights, and fosters trust with consumers (Oosthuizen et al., 2020). Noble & Mende (2023) highlight AI and robotics' transformative power in consumer experience through exoskeletons, smart mirrors, and grab-and-go checkouts. Ogunbiyi et al. (2023) mention chatbots, in-store assistants, virtual fitting rooms, and visual and voice search systems as AI technologies in retail. Cao (2021) identifies AI strategies for data management, process improvement, and value creation, categorized into automation, hyper-personalization, complementarity, and innovation. Jayakrishnan (2022) provides a comprehensive overview of AI's adoption in retail, and in e-commerce, AI applications include recommendation systems, sentiment analysis, trust, personalization, and optimization (Bawack et al., 2022).

The integration of AI with IoT, known as Artificial Intelligence of Things (AIoT), is also revolutionizing retail. Post-COVID-19, retailers are adopting data-driven models, leveraging cloud technologies and agile innovations to enhance digitalization, social networks, adaptive supply chains, omnichannel models, and sustainability (Rao et al., 2021). AI analyzes IoT-collected data in real-time, providing valuable insights. Retailers use AI tools to boost customer satisfaction, create seamless experiences, and increase sales, profitability, and competitiveness based on the data that IoT devices collect.

Despite AIoT's growing integration in retail, comprehensive studies on its impact and effectiveness remain lacking. There's also a need for a clearer understanding of the opportunities AIoT offers retailers, as this technology is still in its infancy (Singh, 2020; Hunt & Rolf, 2022).

This research aims to identify the main data IoT collection devices in retail, ways AI algorithms can use this data, main AIoT applications for customer experience and operations improvement, and finally, create a methodology to generate innovative ideas for using AIoT in retail through creativity and idea-generation techniques. Our methodology involves a comprehensive literature review, a bibliometric study using bibliographic coupling analysis, followed by focus group sessions that utilize idea-generation techniques like mind maps and morphological analysis to develop innovative AIoT-driven solutions for retailing.

The text is structured as follows: it begins with an introductory section, followed by a background section highlighting the evolution of technologies applied in retail, emergent technologies, smart retailing, and digital transformation in retail, AIoT applications in retail, and the conceptual framework and research questions. The methodology section details the research design and explains the innovative approach of bibliographic coupling combined with focus groups. The Findings section presents insights from the bibliographic coupling analysis (in terms of research clusters and topics) and the focus groups, using a morphological analysis matrix to identify main parameters and options for generating innovative ideas in retail management using AIoT. Finally, the Conclusions section highlights the theoretical and managerial contributions, limitations, and future research directions.

BACKGROUND

Evolution of Technologies Applied in Retail in the Last Forty Years: From Barcodes to Extensive Big Data Analysis

Constant Innovation and Evolution in Retail Industry

Retail has consistently been a sector marked by incessant innovation and evolution. Retail evolution over time is explicable through retailers' adaptive responses to consumer dynamics, competitive pressures, shifts in value propositions, the perpetual transformation of business models, and the incorporation of emerging technologies.

Gauri et al. (2021) articulate a framework for novel retail formats, grounded in two principal strategies: reducing friction in the purchasing process by augmenting convenience and minimizing wait times, and enhancing consumer experiences through personalization and remote interactions. Technologies tend to offer either of these benefits or both simultaneously.

Barcodes and scanning technologies

Rivera et al. (2021) conduct an extensive review of the principal technologies documented in grocery retail literature over time. Foundational technologies, such as barcodes and scanning technologies emerged in the 1980s.

Barcodes, typically imprinted on products, encapsulate detailed information, including price, manufacturer, and stock levels. Upon scanning at the point of sale (POS), these barcodes facilitate real-time inventory updates, enabling retailers to monitor stock levels with augmented accuracy and efficiency. Additionally, scanning barcodes at checkout significantly accelerates the process, reducing customer wait times. Barcodes extend their utility by storing promotional information and discounts, thereby enhancing marketing efforts. Furthermore, barcodes facilitate comprehensive tracking of products throughout the supply chain, ensuring transparency and operational efficiency. Some retail stores employ handheld barcode scanners to assist customers directly on the sales floor, enhancing overall shopper satisfaction.

Electronic Price Labels (EPL) and Electronic Invoicing

The advent of electronic devices, such as electronic price labels (EPL) and electronic invoicing in grocery retail, can be traced back to the mid-1990s. EPL technology represents substantial innovation in price management, replacing traditional paper price labels with a system that ensures real-time communication between a central computer database and the EPLs. This facilitates instantaneous updates on shelf prices, mitigating human errors and ensuring price accuracy at the checkout counter. Additionally, this technology reduces manual labor associated with updating paper labels and expedites the pace at which price changes can be implemented in the store. The implementation of electronic invoicing in grocery retail promotes a more collaborative supply chain between suppliers and retailers, streamlining the invoicing process and resulting in considerable cost savings and a reduction in administrative overhead.

Internet and E-Commerce

Entering the 21st century, the internet and e-commerce revolutionized retail by transforming business operations and customer interactions. The internet enabled retailers to establish an online presence, reach a global audience, and offer products and services beyond physical locations. E-commerce platforms facilitated seamless transactions, allowing customers to shop from home or anywhere in the world. This shift expanded market reach, streamlined operations, reduced costs, and provided valuable data insights for better decision-making. It introduced new business models for retailers but increased logistical complexity, as deliveries needed to be made to customers' chosen locations, typically residences. Each transaction mapping facilitated customer relationship management, tracking individual customer purchases in e-commerce.

Radio Frequency Identification (RFID)

Radio Frequency Identification (RFID) also revolutionized retail operations in the early 21st century, using radio waves to facilitate communication between a tag and a reader. An RFID system comprises three primary components: the RFID tag, the RFID reader, and the antenna. Each tag contains a microchip and an antenna, enabling the reader to communicate with it through radio waves. There are two types of RFID tags: passive and active. Passive tags, lacking their power source, are energized by the reader's signal. Active tags possess their power source, such as a battery, and can transmit signals over longer distances. When an RFID tag enters the range of a reader, the reader emits a radio signal. For passive tags, this signal provides the necessary energy to activate the tag, which then responds by transmitting its stored data back to the reader. The reader captures this response and converts the radio waves into digital data, which can be processed and utilized by various applications, including inventory management and point-of-sale systems. RFID technology allows retailers to achieve real-time, accurate inventory tracking, enhancing stock management by reducing both overstock and out-of-stock situations. RFID also streamlines processes such as receiving, restocking, and shipping goods, reducing manual labor, expediting operations, and improving overall efficiency. Additionally, RFID helps mitigate theft and loss by tracking the movement of goods within the store and during transportation. Furthermore, RFID technology enhances the customer shopping experience by facilitating quicker checkouts, personalized promotions, and efficient product location within the store, boosting overall customer satisfaction. The data collected through RFID tags provides valuable insights into consumer behavior, sales trends, and inventory patterns, enabling retailers to make data-driven decisions and optimize their strategies.

Self-Service Technology (SST) and Self-Service Checkout Systems

The advent of self-service technology (SST) and self-service checkout systems marked a significant transformation within the retail sector. These innovations revolutionized the shopping experience by enabling customers to manage their transactions independently, eliminating the need for cashier assistance. The implementation of self-service checkouts significantly reduced waiting times for customers, facilitating quicker transactions and ensuring smoother store flow. Retailers benefited from reduced labor costs, as fewer staff were required to oversee checkout lines. This cost-saving measure allowed for a more effective allocation of resources within stores. Additionally, many customers appreciated the autonomy and convenience provided by self-service systems, allowing them to scan, bag, and pay for their items at their own pace, ultimately enhancing their overall shopping experience.

Omnichannel Retailing and Mobile Applications

With the launch of smartphones with greater capabilities, such as the first iPhone in 2007, mobile applications revolutionized retail by enabling omnichannel retailing. Consumers could access retailers' transactional websites 24/7, allowing seamless interactions through multiple channels, be it in-store, online, or via mobile devices. This technological leap introduced the concept of omnichannel retailing. Sagar (2024) identifies omnichannel retailing, data-driven decision-making, and the integration of emerging technologies as pivotal concepts shaping the discourse on digital transformation in the retail sector. Omnichannel retailing allowed consumers to compare prices, read reviews, and access product information on the go. Retailers could send targeted promotions and offers directly to consumers' mobile devices. Moreover, mobile apps facilitated easier and quicker purchasing processes, ultimately boosting sales (Lazaris & Vrechopoulos, 2014; Strom et al., 2014).

Customization and personalization Through Mobile Apps and SMS Marketing

Wireless networks in smartphones further enhanced the shopping experience, making it more convenient, personalized, and efficient for consumers. Retailers could engage with customers in real-time through mobile apps and SMS marketing, providing personalized offers and promotions. With the integration of GPS technology, location-specific deals could be sent to customers, enriching their shopping experience. The introduction of mobile payment systems streamlined transactions, reducing the need for physical wallets. Additionally, retailers could gather valuable customer data through mobile interactions, allowing for more informed business decisions and targeted marketing strategies (Shankar & Balasubramanian, 2009).

Cloud Computing and Massive Data Storage

In 2012, the advent of mobile cloud computing profoundly transformed the retail industry by offering unparalleled flexibility, scalability, and efficiency. Retailers gained the ability to store, process, and manage vast volumes of data on remote servers, enabling real-time access to inventory, sales, and customer information. This technological leap allowed retailers to deliver personalized shopping experiences through data analytics and machine learning, tailoring recommendations and promotions to individual customers. Furthermore, cloud services alleviated the need for substantial upfront investments in IT infrastructure, as retailers paid only for the resources they utilized, achieving cost efficiency. The scalability of cloud computing enabled retailers to rapidly adjust their IT resources based on fluctuating demand, effectively managing high volumes of online transactions and seasonal spikes. Moreover, cloud-enabled disaster management ensured business continuity and swift recovery from unforeseen events. These advancements collectively rendered retail operations more dynamic, responsive, and customer-centric, marking a significant shift in how retailers approached technology and business strategies. This also impacted the operationalization of customer loyalty programs and customer relationship management processes.

Data Mining and Extensive Big Data Analysis

In 2014, the advent of data mining, along with extensive big data analysis, revolutionized the retail sector. It empowered retailers to analyze massive volumes of customer data, uncovering hidden patterns and insights. This technological advance enabled more accurate predictions of consumer behavior, leading to highly targeted marketing strategies and personalized shopping experiences. Retailers could segment customers based on purchasing habits, preferences, and demographics, creating tailored promotions and enhancing customer satisfaction. Data mining also optimized inventory management by predicting demand trends, reducing stockouts, and streamlining supply chain operations. This application of data mining significantly enhanced decision-making processes, boosting sales and profitability. The transformative impact of data mining in retailing underscored its importance as a pivotal tool in modern business strategies (Agarwal, 2014).

Emergent Technologies, Smart Retailing, and Digital Transformation in Retail

Emergent Technologies

Retailers are increasingly adopting emergent technologies to enhance strategies and customer engagement. By leveraging advanced data analytics, robotics, and blockchain, they gain insights into consumer behavior, optimize supply chains, and deliver personalized marketing campaigns (Hughes-Castleberry, 2023; Brown, 2024; Retail Insider, 2024).

Pantano & Timmermans (2014) introduce "smart retailing" concept, where integrating new technologies into offline and online activities is essential for success. They identify three key components for integration:

- Technological Integration: Enhancing process efficiency and consumer experience.
- Organizational Structure: Focusing on differentiated organizational structures to leverage these new technologies and operationalize smart retailing.
- Challenges and Opportunities: Addressing the costs and complexity involved, as well as opportunities for innovation and improved service offerings.

Smart Retailing and Smart Stores: A New Set of Technologies Available

Smart retailing technologies revolutionizing retail, both offline and online, include augmented, virtual, and mixed realities, self-checkouts, scan-and-go technologies, automated checkouts, self-scanning, smart shelves, digital signage, pervasive displays, smart shopping carts, shopping assistants, mobile or biometric payment methods, and contactless technologies.

Furthermore, targeted and personalized advertising using facial recognition and other consumer data, alongside mobile loyalty cards and mobile couponing, are transforming retailers' operations, consumer shopping experiences, and perceptions about retailers (Pantano & Dennis, 2019; Pratas et al., 2022; Pratas et al., 2023). These technologies are increasingly numerous and may differ in interfaces and implementation methods (Pratas et al., 2023). A smart retail store empowers customer purchases by combining various smart technologies, including facial recognition, QR codes, smart shelves, virtual shopping carts, product tracking, product recognition settlement, mobile payments, and self-service checkouts throughout the shopping process (Chang & Chen, 2021; Grewal et al., 2020; Shankar et al., 2021).

Smart technology empowers consumers in two key aspects along the purchase process: providing a higher level of convenience and a lower level of social presence (Grewal et al., 2020), and strengthening product offerings, a traditional value shared with conventional retail (Lee & Lee, 2020). Tan et al. (2024) emphasize the role of perceptions, referred to as "cognitive absorption," which significantly influence the perceived usefulness and ease of use of smart retailing technologies, thereby affecting their adoption and recommendation by other users. Pratas et al. (2023) propose a framework to measure the impacts of implementing non-store-based and store-based smart retailing technology pilot projects, with appropriate metrics based on brand leadership, market performance, and word-of-mouth. Chen & Chang (2021) identify four phases of interaction with smart technologies throughout the process: entrance (entering the store and registration), product selection (price and quality evaluations), transaction (self-checkouts and mobile payments), and exit (anti-theft detection and leaving the store).

Robotics and Blockchain

Rivera et al. (2021) emphasize that robotics and blockchain are revolutionizing the retail industry. Regarding customer experience, robots can act as personal shopping assistants, offering real-time recommendations based on customer preferences. AI-powered virtual shopping advisors provide product information, reviews, and advice via smartphones or interactive kiosks. Robots with facial recognition capabilities can also identify loyal customers, offering personalized greetings and promotions. For operational efficiency and inventory management, robots autonomously roam store aisles, scanning shelves to ensure items are adequately stocked. Inventory management drones navigate warehouses swiftly and accurately, conducting inventory checks more efficiently than humans.

Smart shopping carts scan items as customers place them inside, providing real-time information on discounts and promotions. In terms of security and loss prevention, surveillance robots monitor store premises, detecting suspicious activities and potential theft. Robots equipped with RFID technology efficiently track the movement of assets within the store (ProvenRobotics, 2024a; ProvenRobotics, 2024b).

Blockchain, on the other hand, enhances transparency, efficiency, and security across various retail operations. By creating an immutable ledger for transactions, blockchain ensures that every step in the supply chain is recorded and verifiable, reducing counterfeit products and improving product authenticity verification. This transparency allows retailers and consumers to trace the origin and journey of products, fostering trust and accountability. According to Al Kurdi et al (2022), blockchain and smart inventory systems positively impact supply chain performance in the retail industry. The integration of blockchain technology enables real-time tracking of products, reducing errors and fraud, and improving overall efficiency.

Nazir & Fan (2024) highlight that blockchain-enabled Internet of Things (IoT) capabilities can optimize supply chain management, leading to sustainable firm performance. This integration enhances supplier and customer collaboration, minimizes waste, and decreases carbon emissions, contributing to environmental sustainability. Subramanian et al (2020) discusses blockchain's potential in revolutionizing supply chain logistics. By providing a decentralized and transparent system, blockchain reduces intermediaries, lowers operational costs, and ensures data integrity (Al Kurdi et al., 2022).

Blockchain-based loyalty programs and decentralized marketplaces offer innovative ways to engage customers and enhance their shopping experience (Am, 2023; Aaron, 2024). It also supports diverse payment options, including cryptocurrencies, providing customers with more flexibility and security in transactions.

IoT, AI and AIoT in Retail

The IoT has ushered in a transformative era in retail by creating a more interconnected and intelligent shopping environment. Initially, the integration of IoT in retail focused on improving supply chain processes. However, it has since evolved to transform omnichannel approaches and customer interactions. Retailers are now utilizing intelligent sensors, real-time data analysis, and a network of interconnected devices to enhance efficiency and engagement. As IoT technologies advance, the retail sector can harness their full potential, creating dynamic, data-driven ecosystems that enhance both in-store and digital shopping experiences (StarUs Insights, 2025).

IoT empowers retailers to collect real-time data from various sources, including in-store footfall counters, iBeacons, smart carts, temperature sensors, smart shelves, RFID tags, and sensors (Rameshkumar & Shanthi, 2017), to monitor inventory levels, product conditions, analyze customer behavior, and optimize supply chain operations. Sensor-equipped devices, such as camera networks, smartphones, and smartcard chips, cater to consumer demand, while supply-side technologies like RFID tags, Bluetooth, Wi-Fi, and GPS services support this ecosystem (Hossain et al., 2021). This technology reinforces personalized customer experiences by delivering tailored recommendations and offers based on individual preferences and shopping patterns. Furthermore, IoT enhances operational efficiency by automating processes and reducing manual errors. IoT transforms physical stores into intelligent spaces, allowing retailers to monitor inventory, assess store conditions, and elevate customer experiences through personalized interactions (Ng, 2019). The integration of IoT in retail not only improves customer satisfaction but also drives substantial cost savings and amplifies sales (Rameshkumar & Shanti, 2017; Rivera et al., 2021).

Shankara et al. (2015) underscore the significance of embedded systems, cyber-physical systems, and generic sensors in driving this transformation. They examine the legal and commercial ramifications of IoT adoption in retail, focusing on scalability, dynamism, heterogeneity, and interconnectivity. Braun (2015) identifies 2013 as the year when retailers began to collect data massively and innovatively, following Apple's introduction of iBeacon technology, which can track the presence of potential customers with iPhones near an iBeacon. Ajayi et al. (2023) provide a systematic review of the impact of IoT on consumer engagement, pinpointing RFID as the initial IoT technology employed by retailers. Khan et al. (2023) explore the transformative impact of IoT on the retail and e-commerce sectors. Their study elucidates how IoT technologies bolster operational efficiencies, enhance customer experiences, and create new business opportunities. The authors discuss the integration of IoT with existing systems, the challenges of connectivity and data management, and the benefits of real-time data analytics for decision-making.

Lynn et al. (2020) discuss the state-of-the-art in IoT reference architectures, offering insights into the technical and socio-technical perspectives of IoT. In their framework, five core entities are identified and defined: social actors, things, data, networks, and events. IoT revolves around key concepts and enabling technologies, including object identification (e.g., IPv6), information sensing (e.g., RFID, sensors, GPS, etc.), communication technologies for data exchange, and network integration technologies (Shin, 2014). IoT can be leveraged in retail by considering its distinctive characteristics and potentialities. Štofková et al. (2024) estimated the price of various technologies, aiding managers in developing a budget for adopting these technologies in terms of equipment and device costs.

Artificial Intelligence (AI) plays a pivotal role in retail, encompassing several subcomponents such as machine learning, computer vision, deep learning, and image recognition. Machine learning has revolutionized retail by providing valuable insights, streamlining operations, and enhancing customer experiences. By analyzing vast amounts of data, machine learning algorithms can predict consumer behavior, enabling retailers to offer personalized recommendations and dynamic pricing strategies. This not only enhances customer satisfaction but also boosts sales. Additionally, machine learning optimizes inventory management and demand forecasting, reducing stockouts and overstock situations. Retailers can also utilize chatbots and virtual assistants powered by machine learning to provide instant customer support and streamline the shopping process. Overall, the integration of machine learning in retail has led to more efficient operations and a more personalized shopping experience for consumers (Dunlea, 2024; Cummings, 2025).

The integration of computer vision, deep learning, and image recognition has further revolutionized retail by augmenting customer experiences, optimizing operations, and fostering innovation. These technologies enable retailers to analyze visual data in real-time, providing valuable insights into customer behavior and preferences. For instance, computer vision can track footfall and analyze in-store traffic patterns, aiding retailers in optimizing store layouts and enhancing customer flow. Deep learning algorithms can predict trends and personalize recommendations, resulting in more targeted marketing and increased sales. CRM tools empowered by data analytics enable retailers to build comprehensive customer profiles, facilitating targeted marketing campaigns and personalized interactions (Huang & Rust, 2018). Image recognition technology streamlines checkout processes in cashierless stores and enhances inventory management by automatically detecting stock levels. Overall, these advancements have made retail environments more efficient, customer-centric, and adaptive to changing market demands (Boesch, 2024; Assert AI, 2025).

The integration of AI in retail hinges on several pivotal elements: the relevance of data, the challenges in acquiring it, the AI system's performance, and the retailer's capacity to adapt and boost value (Fu et al., 2023). The amalgamation of AI with IoT reshapes the retail landscape. AI facilitates personalized customer experiences, predictive analytics, and virtual assistants, while IoT connects physical objects to the digital realm, enabling smart inventory management and enhanced supply chain visibility.

AIoT, which combines AI with IoT, can help retailers improve their operational efficiency and enhance customer experience and satisfaction. AIoT is at the forefront of transforming retail operations with its cutting-edge applications, offering several critical utilizations that enhance efficiency. Firstly, AIoT excels in optimizing inventory management. By providing real-time tracking and automated restocking, it helps reduce stockouts and overstock situations, ensuring that retailers maintain optimal inventory levels at all times (RameshKumar & Santhi, 2017). Furthermore, AIoT significantly boosts supply chain optimization. With its ability to predict demand, streamline logistics, and minimize operational costs, AIoT ensures a more efficient and cost-effective supply chain. Retailers can thus deliver products faster and more accurately, enhancing overall customer experience. Predictive maintenance is another vital application of AIoT in retail. By forecasting equipment failures and scheduling maintenance proactively, AIoT helps reduce downtime and maintenance costs, keeping operations running smoothly (Oosthuizen et al., 2020). This foresight allows retailers to avoid unexpected disruptions and maintain consistent service quality. Additionally, AIoT offers profound insights into customer behavior through real-time analysis. Retailers can leverage this data to tailor their marketing strategies and improve customer engagement, leading to more personalized and effective interactions (Ahmed, 2024). Understanding customer preferences and behaviors enables retailers to create targeted campaigns that resonate with their audience. Lastly, AIoT-enabled smart shelves are a game-changer for retail environments. These intelligent shelves monitor stock levels, detect theft, and provide valuable data on product performance (Anica-Popa et al., 2021). Retailers can ensure their shelves are always stocked with popular items while minimizing losses and gaining insights into product trends.

AIoT also represents a revolutionary advancement with profound implications for enhancing customer experience in retail. By leveraging AIoT, businesses can transform how they interact with customers through several key applications. One notable utilization is in personalized recommendations. AIoT's capability to analyze vast amounts of customer data allows businesses to offer tailored product suggestions, thereby boosting customer satisfaction and fostering loyalty. Additionally, the deployment of AI-powered conversational agents, such as chatbots and voicebots, can significantly improve customer support by handling inquiries instantly, thus enhancing response times and overall customer satisfaction.

Another critical application of AIoT is predictive analytics. Through the analysis of customer needs and behaviors, AIoT empowers businesses to address potential issues proactively and offer personalized services that meet individual expectations (Peruchini et al., 2024). This predictive capability extends to providing enhanced customer insights. By utilizing advanced AI analytics, companies gain a deeper understanding of customer preferences and behaviors, enabling them to refine their offerings and improve the overall customer experience (Sulastri, 2023). Moreover, AIoT facilitates real-time personalization of customer interactions. This technology ensures that each customer receives a unique and tailored experience by adapting to their preferences in real-time (Chen & Zhang, 2021). Such advancements underscore AIoT's pivotal role in transforming customer service and experience, making interactions more personalized, efficient, and satisfying.

Conceptual Framework and Research Questions

IoT devices collect data from sources like brick-and-mortar stores, retail channels, warehouses, distribution centers, and public spaces. AI algorithms analyze this data, enabling retailers to improve operational efficiency, optimize the value chain, and enhance consumer experiences. Figure 1 illustrates the transformation of data into actionable strategies.

Figure 1. Conceptual framework

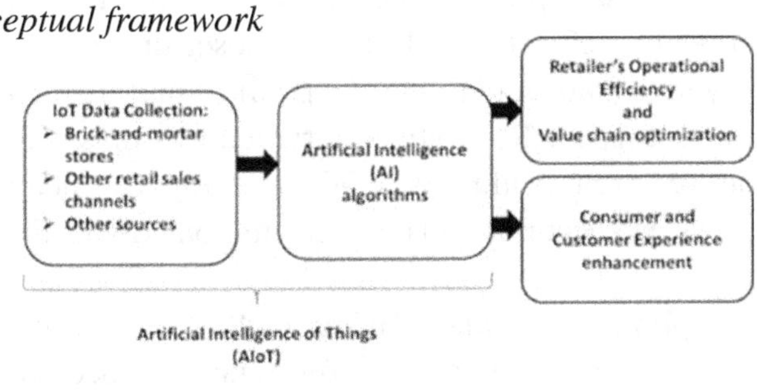

Based on the literature review, the formulated research questions of this work are the following:

- Research question 1: What are the main devices related with IoT that can collect data for retailers?

- Research question 2: How can AI algorithms use this data?
- Research question 3: What are the main utilizations of AIoT for customer experience improvement?
- Research question 4: What are the main utilizations of AIoT for retailers' operations improvement?
- Research question 5: What innovative ideas can be developed for Smart retailing using AIoT-driven solutions?

METHODOLOGY

Research Design

This study employs a qualitative approach, utilizing a bibliometric study with the bibliographical coupling technique to identify primary research cluster topics and perform a content analysis of the articles. Bibliographic coupling is an effective tool for generating research clusters by identifying documents with shared references, indicating thematic or methodological similarities. This method can uncover hidden connections between research works, helping to organize literature into coherent clusters (Ma et al., 2022) and comprehend the current state of knowledge (Pratas & Oliveira, 2023; Pratas et al., 2024).

The analysis collected documents published in the Web of Science (WoS) database, specifically in the categories of Business or Management, focusing on topics such as "Smart Retail," "Smart Retailing," "AIoT," and "Artificial Intelligence of Things." Data collection took place on February 1, 2025, yielding 279 identified and collected documents.WoS database has been chosen due to its selection criteria that ensure that only high-impact journals and publications are included. WoS also integrates seamlessly with specialized bibliometric analysis tools such as VOS Viewer that was used in our research. Additionally WoS employs a structured approach to citation indexing, ensuring accurate and detailed citation linking, allowing a precise impact analysis.

Bibliographic coupling was conducted using VOS Viewer software, with the unit of analysis being "documents," applying the "full counting" method and a minimum citation threshold of five per document. This process highlighted 149 documents that met the criteria, with 65 of these documents interconnected.

The abstracts of all documents were reviewed, and in cases of uncertainty regarding the topics addressed, the entire document was read to gather information on the subjects covered. Additionally, two focus groups, each consisting of eight participants and a moderator, were conducted on December 3, 2024, in Matosinhos, Portugal. These participants, residents, and store customers engaged in focused discussions on the literature review and bibliometric study findings. The participants were chosen as they had direct experience or knowledge about the retail industry, as they were responsible for purchases for their home and family. The sample was based on convenience, but ensuring that all participants lived in the same city and were the main responsible for the purchases to home and family.

In each session, an initial mind map and a subsequent morphological analysis were created to develop innovative ideas for smart retailing management using AIoT. The combined ideas from both focus groups were consolidated by the moderator. Mind mapping encourages free association and visualization of interconnected concepts, aiming to uncover novel perspectives and potential research directions. Morphological analysis systematically explores different dimensions of a problem, generating innovative ideas and identifying critical factors and opportunities.

FINDINGS

Bibliometric Study: bibliographic Coupling Map Main Research Clusters

The goal of bibliographic coupling analysis is to highlight the connections between documents through their shared references. This method is an effective tool for discovering related works and identifying emerging research areas. The first cluster, represented in red, pertains to the topic of "AR and Wearables," exploring the intersection of AR and smart technologies within retail settings and social media contexts. This cluster strongly focuses on consumer acceptance and the practical applications of AR and wearable technologies. Studies on smart retail settings with AR mobile apps investigate how these applications enhance the shopping experience by overlaying digital information onto physical products or environments, including virtual try-ons, interactive product displays, and in-store navigation aids. The acceptance of wearables is another key topic, delving into factors influencing their adoption.

The second cluster, highlighted in dark green, emphasizes the topics of "Emerging Technologies such as IoT in Retail and Big Data". These emerging technologies are transforming retail from back-end logistics to front-end consumer interactions. Technologies such as autonomous shopping systems, logistics 4.0, information systems, self-checkout systems (Thomas-Francois & Somogyi, 2023), and IoT devices and equipment in smart stores (Roe et al., 2022) are examined. This cluster also investigates consumers' reactions to technology in retail settings (Rohden & Espartel, 2024) and the utilization of big data and predictive analytics in retail to predict consumer behavior and optimize retail strategies (Bradlow et al., 2017).

The third cluster, highlighted in dark blue, refers to the topic of "Retail and Hospitality Experiences through Smart Technologies and Intelligent Systems." This cluster examines the integration of smart technologies to enhance shopping value and create intelligent experiences for hospitality customers, focusing on smart retail services, the constituents of a smart customer experience in retail, and the role of WeChat mobile in facilitating these advancements.

The fourth cluster, highlighted in yellow, focuses on "Threats, Privacy, and In-Store Beacons." It underscores the evolving landscape of consumer service systems through co-creation, new smart scenarios, and revisited shopping centers, while addressing privacy threats associated with retail technologies, the use of in-store beacons (Van de Sanden et al., 2019), and the dynamics of B2C smart retailing.

The fifth cluster, highlighted in purple, concentrates on emerging technologies that interact with customers in retail settings. This includes AI (Grewal et al., 2023; Lu et al., 2023), service robots, smart mirrors (Ogunjimi et al., 2021), and cashierless stores (Szabo-Szentgroti et al., 2023), illustrating how technology is fundamentally transforming the retail landscape (Shankar et al., 2021).

The sixth cluster, highlighted in light blue, focuses on the analysis of customer interaction with technologies. This includes exploring the interplay between technology readiness and situational factors, data-driven scanning (Hauser et al., 2021), "Untact" services (Lee & Lee, 2020), consumer-computer interaction (Roy et al., 2020), and shopper-oriented retail technologies (Willems et al., 2017), emphasizing how these elements collectively shape modern retail experiences.

The seventh cluster, highlighted in orange, delves into the realm of luxury retailing and phygital luxury experiences driven by AI. This cluster underscores the progressive domain of luxury retailing, with a specific focus on phygital experiences, innovative smart shopping malls, and omnichannel strategies enhanced by AI technologies in aesthetics.

The eighth cluster, in dusty rose, centers on the framework for classifying retail technologies. This cluster highlights the influence of augmented reality (AR) on purchase intentions, the precision of online sizing solutions such as True Fit, the marketing role of vending channels (Stoyanov, 2021), and the formulation of a classification framework for retail technologies (Wolpert & Roth, 2020). Collectively, these insights propel our comprehension of cutting-edge retail strategies.

In the ninth cluster, marked by pink, the study explores the "Motivation to Shop in Smart Stores and Gamification." It delves into shoppers' motivations within smart stores, the dynamic interplay between physical and online fashion stores, the role of gamification in enhancing smart store experiences, and the impact of technology-enabled personalization in retail environments.

Highlighted in lavender, the tenth cluster examines "Voice Assistants, Mobile AR, and Digital Transformation in Retail." It focuses on the utilization of digital voice assistants like Alexa (Klaus et al., 2022), the advancements in mobile AR (Aw et al., 2024), and the broader digital transformation within the retail value chain (Reinartz et al., 2019).

The eleventh cluster, in light green, focuses on "QR Codes, and the Acceptance and Resistance to Smart Technologies in Retail." This cluster delves into the effects of QR codes, their integration with eco-friendly smartphone apps (Atkinson, 2013), and the acceptance and resistance dynamics surrounding smart technologies in retail (Roy et al, 2018).

Figure 2 presents the bibliographical coupling map, which reveals the opposition of luxury retailing and phygital luxury experiences driven by AI versus IoT devices, big data, and the digital transformation in the retail value chain on the horizontal axis.

This opposition appears to relate to the high-level customer experience versus the operational processes and technology applied to the retail value chain.

On the vertical axis, there is an opposition between the adoption of emerging technologies in retail and their transformative power at the top versus the analysis of consumers' acceptance and resistance to smart retailing technologies below.

Figure 2. Bibliographical coupling map (done with VOS Viewer software)

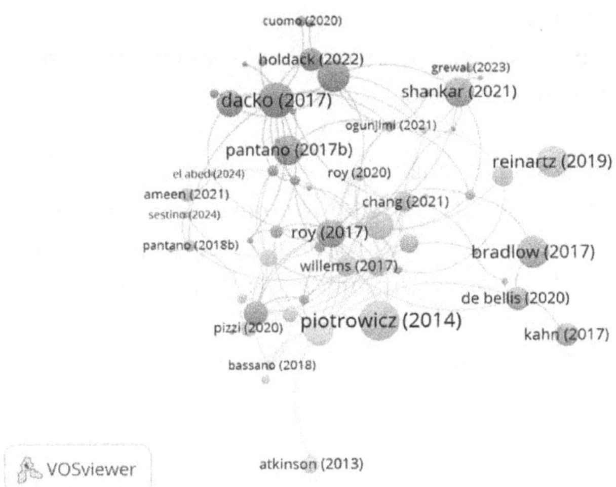

Focus Groups: Mind Maps and Morphological Analysis

A mind map is a visual tool designed to organize information and spark creative ideas by depicting concepts and their connections. Starting with a central idea, it branches outwards to subtopics and related ideas, forming a tree-like structure. This method leverages the brain's preference for visual and associative thinking, facilitating brainstorming and establishing connections (Buzan, 2009; Wheeldon & Ahlberg, 2019). Conversely, morphological analysis is a structured, inventive problem-solving method that generates new ideas by examining all possible combinations of different attributes within each parameter (Zwicky, 1969; Álvarez & Ritchey, 2015).

The main steps for applying morphological analysis are:

a) To define the problem or objetive: clearly outline the creative challenge to tackle.
b) Identify key parameters: the problem has components, attributes or dimensions that need to be identified.
c) List the options for each parameter: the different options for each parameter should be brainstormed.
d) Create a morphological matrix: the key parameters and the options for each parameter should be represented in a grid.
e) Combine the different options: different combinations across the matrix should be experimented. The combinations can be structured by the participants, or randomized to achieve innovative solutions that might not have been considered through traditional brainstorming.
f) Evaluate and refine ideas: the ideas should be assessed in terms of feasibility, originality and impact.
g) Implement and test: the ideas that were chosen should be prototyped, modeled or tested in real-world settings.

The output of morphological analysis is typically represented as a morphological matrix, which explores potential solutions to a complex problem by breaking it down into its components and assessing various options for each component.

The primary goal of this research is to develop innovative ideas for retail management using AIoT-driven solutions, as outlined in Table 1, by systematically exploring combinations of attributes.

Table 1. Morphological analysis matrix output

Key Parameters	Options
Outcomes main type	Customer experience (Customer experience, Customer loyalty, revenue growth); Operational efficiency; Both.
IoT data collection places	Brick-and-mortar stores; Other retail sales channels (transactional websites, Apps, Social media, among other); Others (e.g. distribution centers, supply chain nodes, customer service channels).
Data collection with omnichannel integration	Single sources analysis, multiple sources integration, omnichannel data fusion.
Omnichannel integration outcomes strategy	Single channel, multichannel, cross-channel, omnichannel, customer journey map.
Phase in the customer journey	Awareness, Consideration, Engagement, Purchase, Post-purchase, post-purchase loyalty program.
Retail operation phase	Before the interaction with consumers; During the interaction process with consumers; After the interaction with consumers.
Phase of interaction with smart technologies in the buying process	-In the store entrance phase, in the products selection phase, in the transaction phase, In the exit phases. -Pre-visit online research; Real-time assistance during shopping.
Edge AI	Generative; Predictive; Prescriptive
Operational Efficiency and value chain optimization improvements	-Inventory management (smart shelves, automated restocking, real-time inventory tracking, dynamic pricing) - Supply chain optimization (Product Authenticity and Traceability, Cold Chain Monitoring, Automated Pallets for warehouse optimization) - Supplier Management (Supplier Risk Management, Vendor Scorecards) - Demand Forecasting (AI-driven Forecasting, Seasonal Demand Prediction) - Automation (Automated Checkout Systems; Robotic Assistance; Self-Service Stations) - Layout decisions (layout changes, planogram changes, closing off or opening entrances, or even shuttering stores entirely). - Assortment and space decisions (products listing or delisting, facings number per product) - Security (shoplifting, loss prevention, inventory shrinkage, preventing label switching, mis-scans).

continued on following page

Table 1. Continued

Key Parameters	Options
Consumer and customer experience enhancement Improvements	- Customer interaction and management (Virtual assistants / chatbots, interactive kiosks, Augmented reality shopping; Smart fitting rooms, Smart mirrors, Personalized product recommendations, Smart price tags; Virtual try-on for clothing, eyewear, ...). - AI-driven Personal Shoppers, Real-Time Promotion Adjustments - Automation (Automated Checkout Systems, Robotic Assistance; Self-Service Stations) - Personalization (Personalized Recommendations, Customized Promotions, Tailored In-Store Experiences) - Digital concierge (Avatar, Audio inputs, Visual inputs, Real-time replies) - Dynamic in-store advertising (Store location, localized specials, based or not based on consumer buyer behavior) - Customer monitoring (Shopping Pattern Recognition, Product Interaction Tracking, Customer Feedback Systems) - In-store navagation (Beacon-based navigation, Interactive maps, Emergency response systems) - Automated checkouts (Self checkout kiosks, Smart shopping carts, RFID-enabled checkouts) - Mobile payments (Contactless Transactions, Biometric Payments, Location-based payments)
Data analytics and AI techniques / algorithms	- Predictive Analytics, Customer Behavior Analysis, Sentiment and emotions analysis - Machine Learning, Deep Learning, Natural Language processing; Computer vision, Forecasting, Reiforcement learning, Anomaly detection, Optimization algorithms, Times series analysis and Collaborative filtering, among others.
Integration with other technologies in retail	Barcodes and scanning technologies; Eletronic devices (EPLs, electronic invoices); Internet and E-commerce; RFID; SSTs and self-service checkout systems; Mobile apps; Wireless networks; Mobile cloud computing; Data mining and extensive big data analysis; Blockchain; Conversational AI (Chatbots, Voice Assistants); Digital Twins.
Smart retailing technologies integration	Augmented, virtual, and mixed realities; self-checkouts; scan-and-go technologies; automated checkouts and self-scanning; smart shelves; digital signage and pervasive displays; smart shopping carts and shopping assistants; mobile or biometric payment methods; Contactless technologies; Targeted and personalized advertising using facial recognition and other consumer data; Mobile loyalty cards and mobile couponing.
Sustainability issues and Energy management	Energy-Efficient Systems; Waste Reduction Initiatives; Eco-Friendly Packaging; HVAC Optimization, Smart Lighting, Energy Consumption Monitoring; Renewable Energy Integration; Circular Economy Practices.
Security and Loss Prevention	Biometric Authentication; AI-Driven Surveillance; Secure Payment Gateways; RFID-based Anti theft systems; Employee access control; Smart surveillance systems; AI-Driven Fraud Detection; Contactless Access Control; Intelligent Alarm Systems.

Some suggestions that retailers can effectively use AIoT to enhance customer experience and improve operational efficiency across various aspects of their businesses are:

a) Offer virtual try-on options for clothing and eyewear using smart mirrors and augmented reality: AI-driven product recommendations can be provided through virtual assistants and chatbots, based on data collected from multiple channels, enhancing the customer's shopping experience across both online and in-store. The Outcomes Main Type is "Customer experience" associated with IoT Data Collection Places "Brick-and-mortar stores, transactional websites and apps", Data Collection with Omnichannel Integration "Multiple sources integration", Omnichannel Integration Outcomes Strategy "Cross-channel and omnichannel", Phase in the Customer Journey "Consideration, Engagement and Purchase", Retail Operation "During the interaction process with consumers", the Phase of Interaction with Smart Technologies "In the products selection phase, Pre-visit online research and Real-time assistance during shopping", Edge AI "Generative and Predictive", Consumer and Customer Experience Enhancement Improvements "Virtual try-on for clothing, eyewear, smart mirrors, personalized product recommendations and virtual assistants/chatbots".
b) Leverage data from social media, apps, and in-store sensors, using prescriptive AI to adjust promotions in real-time, to ensure customers receive the most relevant offers based on their behavior and preferences. The Outcomes Main Type is "Customer loyalty and Revenue growth" associated with IoT Data Collection Places: "Social media, apps, brick-and-mortar stores", Data Collection with Omnichannel Integration "Omnichannel data fusion", Omnichannel Integration Outcomes Strategy "Customer journey map", Phase in the Customer Journey "Engagement, Purchase", Retail Operation "During the interaction process with consumers", Phase of Interaction with Smart Technologies "In the store entrance phase, in the products selection phase, in the transaction phase", Edge AI "Prescriptive", and Consumer and Customer Experience Enhancement Improvements "Real-time promotion adjustments, dynamic in-store advertising and personalized recommendations".
c) Implement smart shelves and real-time inventory tracking that can improve stock management, while AI-driven demand forecasting helps retailers anticipate customer needs and optimize stock levels, reducing wastage and improving efficiency. The Outcomes Main Type "Operational efficiency" associates with IoT Data Collection Places "Brick-and-mortar stores and distribution centers", Data Collection with Omnichannel Integration "Single sources analysis", Omnichannel Integration Outcomes Strategy "Single channel", Phase in the Customer Journey "Awareness, Consideration", Retail Operation "Before the interaction with consumers", Edge AI "Predictive", and Operational Efficiency and Value Chain Optimization Improvements "Inventory management (smart shelves, automated restocking, real-time inventory tracking) and demand forecasting".

d) Collect data from various touchpoints and integrate it through omnichannel data fusion, creating a seamless customer journey. Predictive and prescriptive AI can provide personalized recommendations and improve overall customer experience, while feedback systems help refine future interactions. The Outcomes Main Type "Both" associate with IoT Data Collection Places "Brick-and-mortar stores, transactional websites, customer service channels", Data Collection with Omnichannel Integration "Omnichannel data fusion", Omnichannel Integration Outcomes Strategy "Omnichannel, customer journey map", Phase in the Customer Journey "Awareness, Consideration, Engagement, Purchase, Post-purchase, post-purchase loyalty program", Retail Operation "Before, during, and after the interaction with consumers", Phase of Interaction with Smart Technologies: "In the store entrance phase, in the products selection phase, in the transaction phase, Pre-visit online research", Edge AI "Predictive or Prescriptive", and Consumer and Customer Experience Enhancement Improvements: "Personalized recommendations, customer feedback systems and tailored in-store experiences".
e) Implement AI-driven surveillance systems and secure payment gateways that can help retailers reduce incidents of theft and fraud. Predictive AI can analyze patterns to identify potential security threats, ensuring a safer shopping environment. The Outcomes Main Type is "Operational efficiency" associated with IoT Data Collection Places "Brick-and-mortar stores and transactional websites", Data Collection with Omnichannel Integration "Single sources analysis", Omnichannel Integration Outcomes Strategy "Single channel", Phase in the Customer Journey "Awareness and Consideration", Retail Operation "Before the interaction with consumers, during the interaction process with consumers", Phase of Interaction with Smart Technologies "In the store entrance phase or in the products selection phase", Edge AI "Predictive", and Security and Loss Prevention "AI-driven surveillance, secure payment gateways, RFID-based anti-theft systems".

This five ideas presented are only exploratory and examples. The reader can develop a big number of ideas combining the several options and parameters.

Morphological analysis is a powerful method for fostering creativity, especially in problem-solving and innovation management. It systematically explores all possible solutions improving the efficiency of innovation processes.

CONCLUSIONS

Theoretical Contributions

This study makes significant contributions to the existing literature, despite its exploratory nature. The Background section traces the evolution of retail technologies, from barcodes to big data analysis, and discusses emergent technologies, smart retailing, and digital transformation, culminating in the characterization of IoT, AI, and AIoT within the retail sector. The conceptual framework and research questions guide the investigation. A bibliometric study using bibliographical coupling analysis identified eleven research clusters related to AIoT in retail management. Mind maps and morphological analysis, executed through two focus groups, identified different parameters and options. This led to the generation of a matrix combining various options, providing numerous possibilities for retail management using AIoT. The five formulated research questions and their respective answers are prominently highlighted in Table 2.

Table 2. Research questions and main findings summary

Research questions (RQ)	Findings
RQ1) What are the main devices related with IoT that can collect data for retailers?	Key devices identified include RFID sensors, iBeacons, smart shelves, connected cameras, self-checkout systems, smart thermostats, environmental sensors (air quality, noise levels), temperature/humidity sensors, queue management systems, wearable devices, smart carts, inventory drones/robots, smart mirrors, digital price tags, electronic invoicing, and customer feedback devices (touchscreens).
RQ2) How can AI algorithms use this data?	AI algorithms like machine learning, deep learning, natural language processing, computer vision, forecasting, reinforcement learning, anomaly detection, optimization, time series analysis, and collaborative filtering are pivotal. Key data mining types in retail include predictive analytics, customer behavior analysis, and sentiment and emotion analysis. These techniques transform retail operations and customer experiences.
RQ3) What are the main utilizations of AIoT for customer experience improvement?	Key AIoT utilizations for enhancing customer experience include virtual assistants, chatbots, interactive kiosks, AR shopping, smart fitting rooms, smart mirrors, personalized recommendations, QR codes and price tags. Automation involves self-checkout systems, robotic assistance, and tailored in-store experiences. Digital concierges and dynamic in-store advertising are also pivotal. Mobile payments, customer monitoring, in-store navigation, and automated checkouts complete the transformative landscape.

continued on following page

Table 2. Continued

Research questions (RQ)	Findings
RQ4) What are the main utilizations of AIoT for retailers' operations improvement?	Key AIoT applications for improving retail operations include smart inventory management (smart shelves, automated restocking, real-time tracking, dynamic pricing), supply chain optimization (authenticity and traceability, cold chain monitoring, automated pallets), supplier management (risk management, vendor scorecards), demand forecasting (AI-driven predictions), automation (self-checkouts, robotic assistance), layout decisions, assortment management, and enhanced security (shoplifting prevention, inventory accuracy).
RQ5) What innovative ideas can be developed for Smart retailing using AIoT-driven solutions?	The possibilities are almost endless, according to the focus group conducted with the techniques of mind mapping and morphological analysis. Five examples of innovative idea were developed for the application of AIoT in retail management.

Five ideas developed with morphological analysis showcases how readers can spark a multitude of innovative ideas, fostering creativity among managers, consultants, and everyone engaged in the retail management.

Managerial Contributions

The bibliographic coupling analysis reveals the main AIoT topics in retail management. Through morphological analysis and mind mapping in focus groups, the study explores various parameters and strategies for innovation in AIoT retail management. The resulting analysis matrix generates innovative ideas.

Key managerial contributions include AIoT outcomes like customer experience, loyalty, revenue growth, and operational efficiency. The study also connects AIoT to customer journey phases, retail operations, and smart technology interactions, highlighting generative, predictive, and descriptive AI processes.

Identifying main operational efficiencies and value chain improvements is another significant contribution, along with consumer and customer experience enhancements. Data analytics opportunities, technology integrations, and smart retailing technologies are also emphasized. Sustainability, energy management, security, and loss prevention options are included in the matrix output.

Five AIoT utilization ideas for retail emerge, applicable to both large chains and small retailers. Small retailers can now achieve horizontal integration, promoting cooperative efforts. Bourg et al. (2023) introduced a centralized ecosystem enhancing inventory management, geolocated marketing, localized searches, and personalized recommendations. Advanced retail technologies improve communication and data collection, influencing brand leadership perception and market performance (Pratas et al., 2022), supporting consumer purchasing journeys (Chen and Chang, 2023), and boosting retail operations efficiency.

Limitations and Future Research Directions

This research unveils valuable insights into AIoT technology in retail management through bibliographical coupling analysis, mind maps, and morphological analysis. However, several limitations exist.

Firstly, sample representation in focus groups may bias findings, affecting generalizability. Data interpretation can be subjective, reflecting researchers' biases. While morphological analysis provides structure, it may miss critical factors or emerging technologies.

Findings are context-specific and may evolve with new technologies. Implementing conceptual ideas faces practical challenges like technological feasibility, cost, regulatory constraints, and stakeholder acceptance.

For future research, this study lays a solid foundation. Promising directions include investigating AIoT applications in predictive analytics to foresee inventory shortages and supply chain disruptions. Enhancing AIoT device interoperability and exploring blockchain for secure data sharing are crucial.

Ethical implications of AIoT in retail warrant examination, establishing guidelines to address data privacy, surveillance, and biases. Integrating AIoT in sustainable retail management, optimizing energy consumption, and reducing carbon footprints are vital.

Moreover, user-friendly interfaces catering to diverse demographics are essential. Future research should prioritize designing intuitive platforms, ensuring inclusivity and adaptability.

By addressing these areas, AIoT can revolutionize retail management, offering innovative solutions for operational efficiency and enhanced customer experiences.

REFERENCES

Aaron, S. (2024). *Blockchain in retail: Innovative use, cases, benefits and challenges*. Retrieved 3rd February 2025 from https://www.bitdegree.org/crypto/tutorials/blockchain-in-retail

Agarwal, P. (2014). Benefits and Issues Surrounding Data Mining and its Application in the Retail Industry. *International Journal of Scientific and Research Publications, 4 (7),* ISSN 2250-3153.

Ahmed, Z. (2024). Empowering Retailers With IoT: Opportunities, Benefits, And Challenges For Improved Customer Experience And Operational Efficiency. *International Journal of Creative Research Thoughts, 12*(8), 453–461.

Ajayi, S., Loureiro, S. M. C., & Langaro, D. (2023). Internet of things and consumer engagement on retail: State-of-the-art and future directions. *EuroMed Journal of Business, 18*(3), 397–423. DOI: 10.1108/EMJB-10-2021-0164

Al Kurdi, B., Alzoubi, H., Akour, I., & Alshurideh, M. (2022). The effect of blockchain and smart inventory system on supply chain performance: Empirical evidence from retail industry. *Uncertain Supply Chain Management, 10*(4), 1111–1116. DOI: 10.5267/j.uscm.2022.9.001

Álvarez, A., & Ritchey, T. (2015). Applications of general morphological analysis: From engineering design to policy analysis. *Acta Morphologica Generalis, 4*(2).

Anica-Popa, I., Anica-Popa, L., Rădulescu, C., & Vrîncianu, M. (2021). The Integration of Artificial Intelligence in Retail: Benefits, Challenges and a Dedicated Conceptual Article History. *Amfiteatru Economic, 23*(56), 120–136. DOI: 10.24818/EA/2021/56/120

Assert, A. I. (2025). *Transforming Retail: The Game Changing Impact of Computer Vision.* Retrieved 3rd February 2025 from https://www.assertai.com/transforming-retail-the-game-changing-impact-of-computer-vision/

Atkinson, L. (2013). Smart shoppers? Using QR codes and "green" smartphone apps to mobilize sustainable consumption. *International Journal of Consumer Studies, 37*(4), 387–393. DOI: 10.1111/ijcs.12025

Aw, E. C.-X., Tan, G. W.-H., Ooi, K.-B., & Hajli, N. (2024). Tap here to power up! Mobile augmented reality for consumer empowerment. *Internet Research, 34*(3), 960–993. DOI: 10.1108/INTR-07-2021-0477

Bawack, R. E., Wamba, S. F., Carillo, K. D. A., & Akter, S. (2022). Artificial intelligence in E-Commerce: A bibliometric study and literature review. *Electronic Markets*, *32*(1), 297–338. DOI: 10.1007/s12525-022-00537-z PMID: 35600916

Boesch (2024). *The 10 Top Applications of Computer Vision in Retail 2025.* 16th December 2024. Retrieved 3rd Febrauary 2025 from https://viso.ai/applications/computer-vision-in-retail/

Bradlow, E. T., Gangwar, M., Kopalle, P., & Voleti, S. (2017). The Role of Big Data and Predictive Analytics in Retailing. *Journal of Retailing*, *93*(1), 79–95. DOI: 10.1016/j.jretai.2016.12.004

Braun, S. (2015). *The History of Retail: A Timeline*. Retrieved 31th January 2025 from https://www.lightspeedhq.com/blog/the-history-of-retail-a-timeline/

Brown, C. (2024). *Walmart and Quantum Computing: Retail's Future. Augmented QuBit.* Retrieved 3rd February from https://augmentedqubit.com/walmart-and-quantum-computing-impact-to-retail-and-consumers/

Buzan, T. (2009). *The mind map book: Unlock Your Creativity, Boost Your Memory, Change Your Life*. Pearson Education Limited.

Cao, L. (2021). Artificial intelligence in retail: Applications and value creation logics. *International Journal of Retail & Distribution Management*, *49*(7), 958–976. DOI: 10.1108/IJRDM-09-2020-0350

Chang, Y. W., & Chen, J. (2021). What motivates customers to shop in smart shops? The impacts of smart technology and technology readiness. *Journal of Retailing and Consumer Services*, *58*, 102325. DOI: 10.1016/j.jretconser.2020.102325

Chen, J., & Chang, Y. W. (2023). How smart technology empowers consumers in smart retail stores? The perspective of technology readiness and situational factors. *Electronic Markets*, *33*(1), 1. Advance online publication. DOI: 10.1007/s12525-023-00635-6 PMID: 37035262

Chen, L., & Zhang, R. (2021). Real-Time Personalization with AI: Strategies and Outcomes. *International Journal of Market Research*, *43*(4), 295–310. DOI: 10.1177/14707853211001234

Cummings, A. R. (2025). *How Machine Learning Transforms Retail: Benefits & Use Cases (2025).* Retrieved 30th January 2025 from https://www.shopify.com/retail/machine-learning-in-retail

Dunlea, J. (2024). *Machine Learning in Retail: Top Trends & Real Use cases.* 3rd January 2024. Retrieved from https://www.akkio.com/post/machine-learning-in-retail

Fu, H.-P., Chang, T.-H., Lin, S.-W., Teng, Y.-H., & Huang, Y.-Z. (2023). Evaluation and adoption of artificial intelligence in the retail industry. *International Journal of Retail & Distribution Management*, *51*(6), 773–790. DOI: 10.1108/IJRDM-12-2021-0610

Gauri, D. K., Jindal, R. P., Ratchford, B., Fox, E., Bhatnagar, A., Pandey, A., Navallo, J. R., Fogarty, J., Carr, S., & Howerton, E. (2021). Evolution of retail formats: Past, present, and future. *Journal of Retailing*, *97*(1), 42–61. DOI: 10.1016/j.jretai.2020.11.002

Grewal, D., Motyka, S., & Levy, M. (2018). The Evolution and Future of Retailing and Retailing Education. *Journal of Marketing Education*, *40*(1), 85–93. DOI: 10.1177/0273475318755838

Grewal, D., Noble, S. M., Roggeveen, A. L., & Nordfalt, J. (2020). The future of in-store technology. *Journal of the Academy of Marketing Science*, *48*(1), 96–113. DOI: 10.1007/s11747-019-00697-z

Grewal, D., Roggeveen, A. L., & Nordfält, J. (2023). Artificial intelligence applications in retailing. *Journal of Retailing*, *99*(1), 13–27. DOI: 10.1016/j.jretai.2022.11.002

Hauser, J., Urban, G., Liberali, G., & Braun, M. (2021). Dynamic adaptation of scan rates for efficient and congestion-aware internet-wide scanning in IoT security. *JMR, Journal of Marketing Research*, *58*(2), 283–303. DOI: 10.1177/0022243720938837

Heins, C. (2023). Artificial intelligence in retail – a systematic literature review. *Foresight*, *25*(2), 264–286. DOI: 10.1108/FS-10-2021-0210

Hossain, M. S., Chisty, N. M. A., Hargrove, D. L., & Amin, R. (2021). Role of Internet of Things (IoT) in Retail Businсss and Enabling Smart Retailing Experiences. *Asian Business Review*, *11*(2), 75–80. DOI: 10.18034/abr.v11i2.579

Hughes-Castleberry, K. (2023). *Inside Quantum Technology's "Inside Scoop:" Quantum and the Retail Industry.* Retrieved 3rd February from https://www.insidequantumtechnology.com/news-archive/inside-quantum-technologys-inside-scoop-quantum-and-the-retail-industry/

Hunt, W., & Rolf, S. (2022). *Artificial Intelligence and Automation in Retail: Benefits, challenges and implications (a union perspective).* Friedrich Ebert Stiftung. Retrieved from https://library.fes.de/pdf-files/bueros/bruessel/19054.pdf

Insider, R. (2024). *The Retail benefits of Quantum AI.* Retrieved 3rd February 2025 from https://retail-insider.com/articles/2024/01/the-retail-benefits-of-quantum-ai/

Jayakrishnan, S. (2022). Artificial Intelligence (AI) in Retailing - A Systematic Review and Research Agenda. *Contemporary Research in Management: Volume XI - SDM Research Centre for Management Studies.* DOI: 10.2139/ssrn.4134959

Khan, S., Khari, M., & Azrour, M. (2023). IoT in retail and e-commerce. *Electronic Commerce Research.* Advance online publication. DOI: 10.1007/s10660-023-09785-3

Klaus, P., Weijters, G., & Verhoef, P. C. (2022). Voice assistants, mobile AR, and digital transformation in retail. *Journal of Retailing and Consumer Services, 60*, 102–110. DOI: 10.1016/j.jretconser.2022.102110

Lazaris, C., & Vrechopoulos, A. (2014). From Multichannel to "Omnichannel" Retailing: Review of the Literature and Calls for Research. *2nd International Conference on Contemporary Marketing Issues, (ICCMI), 18-20 June 2014At: Athens, Greece.* https://doi.org/DOI: 10.13140/2.1.1802.4967

Lee, S. M., & Lee, D. (2020). "Untact": A new customer service strategy in the digital age. *Service Business, 14*(1), 1–22. DOI: 10.1007/s11628-019-00408-2

Lu, L., Zhang, H., & Song, Y. (2023). AI-driven personalized services in retail: Impacts on customer experience. *Journal of Business Research, 145*, 712–721. DOI: 10.1016/j.jbusres.2022.10.014

Lynn, T., Endo, P. T., Ribeiro, A. M. N. C., Barbosa, G. B. N., & Rosati, P. (2020). The Internet of Things: Definitions, Key Concepts, and Reference Architectures. In Lynn, T., Mooney, J., Lee, B., & Endo, P. (Eds.), *The Cloud-to-Thing Continuum. Palgrave Studies in Digital Business & Enabling Technologies*. Palgrave Macmillan., DOI: 10.1007/978-3-030-41110-7_1

Ma, T-J., Lee, G-G., Liu, J.S., Lan, R., & Weng, J-H. (2022). Bibliographic coupling: a main path analysis from 1963 to 2020. *Information Research,* 27 (1), paper 918. https://doi.org/DOI: 10.47989/irpaper918

Nazir, H., & Fan, J. (2024). Revolutionizing Retail: Examining the Influence of Blockchain-Enabled IoT Capabilities on Sustainable Firm Performance. *Sustainability (Basel), 16*(9), 3534. DOI: 10.3390/su16093534

Ng, K. (2019). IoT in Retail: Enhancing Operational Efficiency and Customer Experience. *Journal of Retail Technology*, 15 (3), 45-58. Retrieved 3rd February from www.gsma.com

Noble, S. M., & Mende, M. (2023). The future of artificial intelligence and robotics in the retail and service sector: Sketching the field of consumer-robot-experiences. *Journal of the Academy of Marketing Science, 51*(4), 747–756. DOI: 10.1007/s11747-023-00948-0 PMID: 37359262

Ogunbiyi, V.O., Bala, G.G. & George, A.C. (2023). Exploring Artificial Intelligence Application and Implication: Evidence From The UK Retail Industry. *IOSR Journal of Business and Management (IOSR-JBM)*, 25 (9), 1-10. https://doi.org/ DOI: 10.9790/487X-2509050110

Ogunjimi, I., Kavak, B., & Seyrek, I. H. (2021). Smart mirrors in retail: Enhancing customer experience with augmented reality. *International Journal of Retail & Distribution Management, 49*(3), 369–383. DOI: 10.1108/IJRDM-12-2020-0465

Oosthuizen, K., Botha, E., Robertson, J., & Montecchi, M. (2020). Artificial Intelligence in Retail: The AI-Enabled Value Chain. [AMJ]. *Australasian Marketing Journal, 29*(3), 264–273. DOI: 10.1016/j.ausmj.2020.07.007

Pantano, E., & Dennis, C. (2019). *Smart Retailing: Technologies and Strategies.* Palgrave Macmillan., DOI: 10.1007/978-3-030-12608-7

Pantano, E., & Timmermans, H. (2014). What is Smart for Retailing? *Procedia Environmental Sciences, 22*, 101–107. DOI: 10.1016/j.proenv.2014.11.010

Peruchini, M., da Silva, G. M., & Teixeira, J. M. (2024). Between artificial intelligence and customer experience: A literature review on the intersection. *Discover Artificial Intelligence, 4*(4), 4. Advance online publication. DOI: 10.1007/s44163-024-00105-8

Pratas, J., Amorim, C., & Reis, J. L. (2022). Smart Retailing Technologies Impact in Brand Leadership and Market Performance: A Conceptual Model. In Reis, J. L., Peter, M. K., Cayolla, R., & Bogdanović, Z. (Eds.), *Marketing and Smart Technologies. Smart Innovation, Systems and Technologies* (Vol. 280). Springer., DOI: 10.1007/978-981-16-9272-7_26

Pratas, J., Amorim, C., & Reis, J. L. (2023). Measuring the Impacts of Smart Retailing Technologies Pilot Implementation – Proposal Framework. *CAPSI 2023 Proceedings. 4.* https://aisel.aisnet.org/capsi2023/4

Pratas, J., Amorim, C., & Reis, J. L. (2024). Subscription Retailing Research Evolution Analysis Using Bibliometric Indicators and Content Analysis. In Reis, J. L., Del Rio Araujo, M., Reis, L. P., & dos Santos, J. P. M. (Eds.), *Marketing and Smart Technologies. ICMarkTech 2022. Smart Innovation, Systems and Technologies* (Vol. 344). Springer., DOI: 10.1007/978-981-99-0333-7_10

Pratas, J., & Brito, P. (2019). *Distribuição - Gestão de pontos de venda e de retalho - Gestão eficiente do negócio.* Actual Editora.

Pratas, J., & Oliveira, Z. (2023). QR Codes Research in Marketing: A Bibliometric and Content Analysis. In Reis, J. L., Peter, M. K., Varela González, J. A., & Bogdanović, Z. (Eds.), *Marketing and Smart Technologies. Smart Innovation, Systems and Technologies* (Vol. 337). Springer., DOI: 10.1007/978-981-19-9099-1_19

ProvenRobotics. (2024 a). *Robots for Retail Stores: Driving Sales & Customer Satisfaction*. 3rd April, Retrieved from https://provenrobotics.ai/robots-for-retail-stores/

ProvenRobotics. (2024 b). *What robots can do for retail: 30 applications*. 27th May, Retrieved from https://provenrobotics.ai/what-robots-can-do-for-retail/

Rameshkumar, P. M., & Shanthi, R. (2017). Internet of Things (IoT's) in Retail Industry - A Study to Trace the Feasible Business Model. *International Journal of Advance Research in Science and Engineering*, *6*(1), 288–292.

Rao, P. H. N., Vihari, N. S., & Jabeen, S. S. (2021). Reimagining the Fashion Retail Industry Through the Implications of COVID-19 in the Gulf Cooperation Council (GCC) Countries. *FIIB Business Review*, *10*(4), 327–338. DOI: 10.1177/23197145211039580

Reinartz, W., Wiegand, N., & Imschloss, M. (2019). The impact of digital transformation on the retailing value chain. *International Journal of Research in Marketing*, *36*(3), 350–366. DOI: 10.1016/j.ijresmar.2018.12.002

Rivera, R., Amorim, M., & Reis, J. (2021). Technological Evolution in Grocery Retail: A systematic literature review. *16th Iberian Conference on Information Systems and Technologies (CISTI),* 23 – 26 June 2021, Chaves, Portugal ISBN: 978-989-54659-1-0 DOI: 10.23919/CISTI52073.2021.9476598

Roe, M., Spanaki, K., Ioannou, A., Zamani, E., & Giannakis, M. (2022). Drivers and challenges of internet of things diffusion in smart stores: A field exploration. *Technological Forecasting and Social Change*, *178*, 121593. DOI: 10.1016/j.techfore.2022.121593

Rohden, S. F., & Espartel, L. B. (2024). Consumer Reactions to Technology in Retail: Choice Uncertainty and Reduced Perceived Control in Decisions Assisted by Recommendation Agents. *Electronic Commerce Research*, *24*(2), 901–923. DOI: 10.1007/s10660-024-09808-7

Roy, S. K., Balaji, M. S., & Quazi, A. (2020). Consumer-computer interaction and in-store smart technology (IST) in the retail industry: The role of motivation, opportunity, and ability. *Journal of Marketing Management*, *36*(5-6), 517–548. DOI: 10.1080/0267257X.2020.1736130

Roy, S. K., Balaji, M. S., Quazi, A., & Quaddus, M. (2018). Predictors of customer acceptance of and resistance to smart technologies in the retail sector. *Journal of Retailing and Consumer Services*, *42*, 147–160. DOI: 10.1016/j.jretconser.2018.02.005

Sagar, S. (2024). The Impact Of Digital Transformation On Retail Management And Consumer Behavior. *IOSR Journal of Business and Management, 26 (1),* 06-14. https://doi.org/DOI: 10.9790/487X-2601010614

Shankar, K., Kalyanam, K., Setia, P., Golmohammadi, A., Tirunillai, S., Douglass, T., Hennessey, J., Bull, J. S., & Waddoups, R. (2021). How technology is changing retail. *Journal of Retailing*, *97*(1), 13–27. DOI: 10.1016/j.jretai.2020.10.006

Shankar, V., & Balasubramanian, S. (2009). Mobile Marketing: A Synthesis and Prognosis. *Journal of Interactive Marketing*, *23*(2), 118–129. DOI: 10.1016/j.intmar.2009.02.002

Shankara, P., Mahanta, P., Arora, E., & Srinivasamurthy, G. (2015). Impact of Internet of Things in the Retail Industry. In Ciuciu, I. (Eds.), Lecture Notes in Computer Science: Vol. 9416. *On the Move to Meaningful Internet Systems: OTM 2015 Workshops. OTM 2015*. Springer., DOI: 10.1007/978-3-319-26138-6_9

Shin, D. (2014). A Socio-technical Framework for Internet-of-Things Design: A Human-Centered Design for the Internet of Things. *Telematics and Informatics*, *31*(4), 519–531. DOI: 10.1016/j.tele.2014.02.003

Singh, S. (2020). AI and IoT in Retail: Its impact on retail value chain & shoppers' behaviour. [IJARET]. *International Journal of Advanced Research in Engineering and Technology*, *11*(7), 766–777. DOI: 10.34218/IJARET.11.7.2020.075

StarUs Insights. (2025). *IoT in Retail: Discover Top 9 Ways it is Reshaping the Industry.* Retrieved 14th February from https://www.startus-insights.com/innovators-guide/iot-in-retail/

Štofková, K. R., Bajza, F., Janošková, P., & Kováčiková, M. (2024). Proposal of innovative smart solutions for retail store in order to support competitiveness and sustainable development. *Frontiers of Computer Science*, *6*, 1328913. DOI: 10.3389/fcomp.2024.1328913

Stoyanov, D. (2021). The role of vending channels in marketing: A systematic review and taxonomy of studies. *The Journal of Consumer Affairs*, *55*(2), 654–679. DOI: 10.1111/joca.12362

Strom, R., Vendel, M., & Bredican, J. (2014). Mobile marketing: A literature review on its value for consumers and retailers. *Journal of Retailing and Consumer Services*, *21*(6), 1001–1012. DOI: 10.1016/j.jretconser.2013.12.003

Subramanian, N., Chaudhuri, A., & Kayıkcı, Y. (2020). Blockchain Applications in Retail Supply Chain. In *Blockchain and Supply Chain Logistics*. Palgrave Pivot., DOI: 10.1007/978-3-030-47531-4_6

Sulastri, L. (2023). The Role of Artificial Intelligence in Enhancing Customer Experience: A Case Study of Global E-commerce Platforms. *The International Journal of Science in Society*, *5*(3), 451–469. DOI: 10.54783/ijsoc.v5i3.1257

Szabo-Szentgroti, G., Gyenge, B., & Papp, B. (2023). The rise of cashierless stores: Implications for the retail industry. *Technological Forecasting and Social Change*, *182*, 121855. DOI: 10.1016/j.techfore.2022.121855

Tan, L., Ren, C., Zhan, Y., Chang, Y. W., Chen, J., & Hsu, M. C. (2024). Exploring consumers' adoption and recommendation in smart retailing: A cognitive absorption perspective. *Current Psychology (New Brunswick, N.J.)*, *43*(26), 22560–22577. DOI: 10.1007/s12144-024-06042-0

Thomas-Francois, K., & Somogyi, S. (2023). Self-Checkout Behaviours at Supermarkets: Does the Technological Acceptance Model (TAM) Predict Smart Grocery Shopping Adoption? *International Review of Retail, Distribution and Consumer Research*, *33*(1), 44–66. DOI: 10.1080/09593969.2022.2051195

Van de Sanden, S., Willems, K., & Brengman, M. (2019). In-store location-based marketing with beacons: From inflated expectations to smart use in retailing. *Journal of Marketing Management*, *35*(15-16), 1514–1541. DOI: 10.1080/0267257X.2019.1689154

Wheeldon, J., & Ahlberg, M. (2019). Mind maps in qualitative research. In Creswell, K. A., & Creswell, S. D. (Eds.), *Handbook of qualitative research methods* (pp. 200–210). Sage Publications.

Willems, K., Smolders, A., Brengman, M., Luyten, K., & Schöning, J. (2017). The path-to-purchase is paved with digital opportunities: An inventory of shopper-oriented retail technologies. *Journal of Retailing and Consumer Services*, *39*, 229–238. DOI: 10.1016/j.jretconser.2017.07.009

Wolpert, R., & Roth, A. (2020). Development of a classification framework for retail technologies. *Journal of Retailing and Consumer Services*, *57*, 102–110. DOI: 10.1016/j.jretconser.2020.102110

Zwicky, F. (1969). *Discovery, invention, research – Through the morphological approach*. Macmillan.

ADDITIONAL READING

Chuprina, R., & Kovalenko, O. (2022). Artificial Intelligence for Retail in 2022: 12 Real-World Use Cases - SPD Group Blog. Full-Cycle Software Development Solutions, September, Retrieved 10th February 2025 from https://spd.group/artificial-intelligence/ai-for-retail

Cranmer, E. E., Papalexi, M., tom Dieck, M. C., & Bamford, D. (2022). Internet of Things: Aspiration, implementation and contribution. *Journal of Business Research*, *139*, 69–80. DOI: 10.1016/j.jbusres.2021.09.025

Kim, S., & Lee, J.-G. (2020). A systematic framework of predicting customer revisit with in-store sensors. *Knowledge and Information Systems*, *62*(3), 1005–1035. DOI: 10.1007/s10115-019-01373-y

Klisenko, O., & Serral Asensio, E. (2022). Towards a maturity model for iot adoption by b2c companies. *Applied Sciences (Basel, Switzerland)*, *12*(3), 982. DOI: 10.3390/app12030982

Shekhawat, S. (2022). Use of AI and IoT to make Retail Smarter. *2022 3rd International Informatics and Software Engineering Conference (IISEC)*, Ankara, Turkey, 1-5, https://doi.org/DOI: 10.1109/IISEC56263.2022.9998202

Shekhawat, S. (2023). Smart retail: How AI and IoT are revolutionising the retail industry. *Journal of AI. Robotics & Workplace Automation*, *2*(2), 145–152. DOI: 10.69554/TCLG1264

Surange, G., & Khatri, P. (2022). Integrated intelligent IOT forensic framework for data acquisition through open-source tools. *International Journal of Information Technology : an Official Journal of Bharati Vidyapeeth's Institute of Computer Applications and Management*, *14*(6), 3011–3018. DOI: 10.1007/s41870-022-01025-5

Xhafa, F. (2023). Towards artificial intelligence internet of things (AIoT) and intelligent edge: The intelligent edge is where action is!: Editorial Preface. *Internet of Things : Engineering Cyber Physical Human Systems*, *22*, 100752. DOI: 10.1016/j.iot.2023.100752

KEY TERMS AND DEFINITIONS

Artificial Intelligence of Things (AIoT): in retail, AIoT integrates Artificial Intelligence (AI) and Internet of Things (IoT) to enhance operations efficiency and customer experiences. This fusion enables smarter processes, personalized shopping, efficient inventory management, and real-time decision-making. Examples of AIoT devices include smart shelves, digital price and RFID tags, automated checkout systems, predictive maintenance sensors, and customer behavior analytics through sensors and cameras.

Creativity techniques: are methods or strategies designed to stimulate creative thinking and generate innovative ideas. They assist individuals and teams in thinking outside the box, breaking free from conventional patterns, and exploring new perspectives. By using these techniques, creative potential is unlocked, and innovative solutions are fostered. These methods can effectively inspire different and new ideas.

Customer experience: in retail, it encompasses the overall perception and feelings a customer has throughout the shopping journey, from first exposure to after-sales service. This includes every touchpoint with the brand. A positive customer experience often involves convenience, personalization, consistency, engagement, and satisfaction. A great customer experience fosters loyalty, encourages repeat business, and enhances the brand's reputation.

Data management in retail: involves collecting, storing, analyzing, and using data from sales (offline and online), inventory, customer behavior, and supply chain activities. Effective data management ensures accurate, timely, and secure data handling. This enables retailers to make informed decisions, optimize operations, personalize customer experiences, and improve overall efficiency. The goal is to transform raw data into valuable insights that drive business success.

Omni-channel: refers to providing a seamless and integrated customer experience across multiple channels, both online and offline. It ensures a consistent and cohesive interaction with a brand, whether customers shop in-store, online, via mobile, or through social media, among other touchpoints. Omni-channel strategies allow customers to switch between channels effortlessly, maintaining the same level of service and personalization throughout their journey.

Retail Innovations: refers to the introduction of new ideas, methods, or technologies to enhance the customer and employee experience or improving business efficiency. Examples include adopting artificial intelligence, personalized shopping, omnichannel strategies, automated checkout systems, and augmented reality for virtual try-ons. These innovations aim is to maintain retailer's competitiveness and leadership image, meet evolving customer expectations, and drive business growth.

Retail Operations: includes all the activities necessary for running a retail business efficiently. This covers day-to-day store functions, inventory control, staffing, customer service, sales management, merchandising, and logistics, among other functions. The aim is to ensure customers have a positive shopping experience, products are readily available, and the business operates smoothly.

Smart Retailing: refers to the use of advanced technologies like Artificial Intelligence (AI), Internet of Things (IoT), data analytics, and automation to improve the retail experience. It aims to boost operational efficiency, offer personalized customer experiences, and streamline processes. This includes personalized shopping, efficient inventory management, automated checkout systems, enhanced customer services, virtual and augmented realities, digital twins, and metaverse retailing. These innovations help retailers stay competitive and meet evolving customer expectations.

Chapter 3
Exploring Personalized Recommendations and AIoT in Retail: Enhancing Consumer Engagement With AR Technology

Usharani Bhimavarapu
https://orcid.org/0000-0002-0246-1420
KDepartment of Computer Science and Engineering, Koneru Lakshmaiah Education Foundation, Vaddeswaram, India

ABSTRACT

Personalized Recommendations and Artificial Intelligence of Things (AIoT) for Retail and Services Management have revolutionized the way businesses interact with consumers, enhancing customer satisfaction and driving sales. This study explores the impact of AI-driven personalized recommendations, powered by AR technology, in the retail sector, specifically focusing on cosmetic products in an online shopping environment. By analyzing data collected through a survey of Shopee users who have used the try-on feature for cosmetic products, the research examines the influence of AI and AR on consumer perceptions, purchase intentions, and satisfaction. The study utilizes Generalized Structured Component Analysis (GSCA) to evaluate the structural relationships between personalized recommendations, AI and AR technology usage, and purchase intentions. The findings reveal that AIoT-based personalized recommendations significantly enhance consumer engagement and purchase decisions.

DOI: 10.4018/979-8-3693-8512-8.ch003

INTRODUCTION

Personalized suggestions are customized suggestions shown to a user based on his/her own behavior, preference, or demographics. In e-commerce and retailing, it is done to provide best shopping by showing something to a user who will likely be interested, thus maximizing interest as well as chances of a purchase. Personalized recommendations draw information from various sources of knowledge like web surfing history, previous buying behavior, search patterns, and social network behavior in an attempt to forecast what is desired or longed for by a user.

Various methods are utilized during model construction for personalized recommendations. Among the methods is collaborative filtering where mass behavior and user-item interaction are utilized, patterns to be analyzed, and suggest something liked or done by users of similar behavior. Another method to content-based filtering is where a recommendation is made based on product features in which a user has interest, i.e., category, price, or brand. Both these approaches can be blended as hybrid models in a manner in which better suggestions can be made. Additionally, machine learning algorithms including matrix factorization, deep neural network models, and reinforcement learning can also be utilized for enhancing suggestions by learning and adapting dynamically according to the user's actions. It requires personalized recommendation models to predict users' preferences, predict future user behavior, and offer the corresponding products in real-time systems and thus influence user satisfaction and boost sales.

Artificial Intelligence of Things (AIoT) is an integration of Artificial Intelligence (AI) and Internet of Things (IoT) where connected devices not only sense data but also process, analyze, and make smart decisions in real-time. In retailing and service management, AIoT improves customer experience, makes business seamless, and drives business innovation since it enables intelligent interaction among customers, products, and systems.

In retailing, AIoT also personalizes customer experience through the assistance of IoT objects such as smart sensors, cameras, and wearables.

Customer behavior can be tracked using monitoring and analysis algorithms driven by AI. For instance, AIoT devices can be programmed to monitor the manner in which customers interact with products and respond accordingly based on contextual markers such as day of week or time of day and past behavior and preference. This results in a more dynamic one-to-one experience that can drive buying behavior.

Aside from this, AIoT enables real-time management of stock, predictive analysis, and lean operation of the supply chain. With AI analytics, the retailers can forecast the demand, control the levels of the stock, and avoid stockouts or overstocking, thus ensuring hassle-free customer experience and optimal resource utilization. AIoT, when it comes to services management, can elevate the effectiveness of processes since it can allow intelligent devices to automate, track performance, and give wisdom-infused feedback when providing a service. Some examples include automating customer support in a shop, tracking machines in real-time for the sake of servicing, and general effectiveness in running business operations.

AIoT enables service providers and retailers to create more personalized, more interactive, and more immersive experiences that lead to greater customer satisfaction, better business decision-making, and ultimately, profitability.

Collaborative Filtering (CF) are the most widely used recommendation models, Collaborative Filtering (CF) operates by looking at a user behavior history (e.g., rating history or purchase history) to suggest something on the basis of similar users. CF performs reasonably but is marred with cold start issues (inequality to suggest products for new users or products) and sparsity (insufficiency of data to suggest a good product) (Adomavicius & Tuzhilin, 2005).

Content-Based Filtering suggests the same items one has engaged with, but based on item properties (price, brand, or genre). Over-specialization (recommended similar items and not appreciating variety) and item attribute dependency, which will not necessarily occur to exist or be functional, are the drawbacks of Content-Based Filtering (Lops et al., 2011).

Matrix Factorization technique breaks the user-item interaction matrix into lower-order matrices in order to discover latent factors. Matrix Factorization techniques like Singular Value Decomposition (SVD) are computationally expensive and plagued with scalability and cold start issues (Koren et al., 2009).

Neural Collaborative Filtering (NCF) are utilized to map the non-linear relationships of user-item interactions. Although NCF models are highly accurate, they are computationally costly and large data, which is not always a case everywhere (He et al., 2017).

Hybrid Techniques Combining Collaborative Filtering and Content-Based Filtering, hybrid techniques try to avoid the limitations of one technique. Model combination complexity, however, makes them hard to apply and optimize (Burke, 2007).

Deep Learning-Based models utilize deep neural networks in learning the user and item embeddings in order to produce more accurate recommendations. While amazingly effective at enhancing recommendation accuracy, deep learning-based models are data-hungry and computationally intensive (Yao et al., 2019).

K-Nearest Neighbors (KNN) makes recommendations by identifying the nearest neighbors for the product or user on similarity dimensions. KNN is computationally costly and doesn't work efficiently with big data (Zhang et al., 2015).

Factorization Machines extend matrix factorization methods used in variable interaction description. They remain very hyperparameter sensitive and susceptible to overfitting very early on unless suitable regularization has been guaranteed for them (Rendle, 2012).

Reinforcement Learning model is trained to find the best recommendation policy by learning to maximize a reward function in a time horizon. Reinforcement learning is extremely powerful for real-time, personal recommendation but is not train-stable and is time-consuming to train (Christiano et al., 2017).

Association Rule Mining model relies on frequent pattern mining to extract associations between items. It is weak in that it requires a large amount of data and does not support user preference-based personal recommendations (Agrawal & Srikant, 1994).

Clustering-Based models group items or users into groups and recommend objects for the interest of a group. Clustering models cannot handle dynamic data and can be ignorant of specific user preferences (Jain et al., 1999).

Decision Trees have the capability to learn decision rules from the data by modeling the user preference. Decision Trees overfit small samples and are not suitable for handling complex, non-linear relationships (Quinlan, 1986).

Latent Dirichlet Allocation (LDA) is content-based topic modeling in systems. LDA is usable in text recommendation but would be useless for non-text data and has extremely high pre-processing (Blei et al., 2003).

Graph-Based Models model user-item interactions as graph representations. Graph-based models are appropriate when modeling intricate relations but are computationally expensive and hard to scale when dealing with large data (Ricci et al., 2015).

Matrix Completion method substitutes missing values of a user-item matrix since it tries to estimate ratings. Powerful but suffering from sparsity and cannot deal with big missing data (Candes & Recht, 2009).

Markov Chains model forecasts what the following activity that the user will be engaged in will be in accordance with their existing engagement. They are constrained by the fact that they can only assume a static state and perhaps may not handle changing user preferences (Sutton & Barto, 2018).

Item-Based Collaborative Filtering is a collaborative filtering algorithm which is concerned with recommending the similar items to the previously interacted items by the user. The drawback of the algorithm is that it could not keep up with the user preferences in the long run (Sarwar et al., 2001).

Personal recommendation tasks can be achieved by Support Vector Machine (SVM) models, especially for user-item interaction classification. SVM models require proper tuning and are not effective in processing large sets (Vapnik, 1995).

Context-Aware Recommender Systems incorporate contextual information such as time, location, or social context in the recommendation. The challenge is how to incorporate contextual information in a reasonable way and how to make the model scalable (Adomavicius & Kwon, 2012).

Probabilistic Graphical models describe dependency among variables as probabilistic graphs. Although they can describe complex dependencies, they are computationally expensive and potentially non-transparent (Jordan, 2004).

Generalized Structured Component Analysis (GSCA) model employed in the paper removes all the limitations of conventional recommendation techniques, like collaborative filtering, content-based filtering, and hybrid approaches. In contrast to such standard models, GSCA combines structural model (latent and observable variables) and measurement model (structural variables' interrelations) within a common framework, thereby making recommendations precise and trustworthy. In this manner, GSCA is able to remove the issues like sparsity, cold start problem, and overfitting concerns typical of traditional models altogether. In addition, the inclusion of user behavior and item attributes in GSCA alleviates the over-specialization issue of standard content-based methods to a certain extent so that the system can suggest extremely similar items. Lastly, the ability of GSCA to capture high-order interdependencies and unobserved variables helps improve generalization because it is able to learn more underlying correlations between users' behaviors and items and therefore produce better recommendation accuracy.

Second, GSCA is also scalable and flexible and hence very efficient with big and dynamic data sets.

By leveraging a generalized model with interaction effects and latent variables, GSCA provides a solution to the shortcomings of the conventional recommender systems such as computationally efficiency, scalability, and real-time response to online users' preferences updates. GSCA hence presents a better and superior model of personalized recommendation than the above methods.

MATERIALS AND METHODOLOGY

Research work involved dissemination of a guided questionnaire via Google Forms. Data were harvested from November 11 to December 1, 2024, on social media platforms like WhatsApp, Instagram, and LinkedIn. The questionnaire utilized a Likert scale to capture the perception of personalized recommendations, AI, and AR technology. GSCA was applied to analyze data to examine relationships among latent variables. GSCA uncovered the effect of AIoT technologies and personal recommendations on purchasing intention.

MATERIALS

Quantitative data were collected through well-crafted and online surveys among professional Shopee users for the use of the try-on feature of beauty products. Participants were requested to give their perception of personal recommendations, use of AI and AR technology, and purchasing intentions. Surveys were also intended to find the impact of the try-on feature on offering personalized products based on personal interests and needs. The users also provided ratings for the ease of used AI and AR technology as well as overall satisfaction for its utilization. Otherwise, the research also investigated the influence of try-on functionality on consumer buying behavior as much as building confidence in the technology and how it influences their consumption patterns. Internet surveys helped gather data in an organized and structured form to enable access among Shopee consumers and derive meaningful and reliable data.

PREPROCESSING

Data preprocessing of data obtained commenced with data cleaning to enable accuracy and uniformity. This included the identification and handling of missing, incomplete, or duplicate records. The incomplete values were handled either through imputation, whereby statistical operations such as mean or median were used, or by excluding missing responses that would skew analysis. Normalization was done on the data by converting categorical responses into numerical form through processes such as one-hot encoding or label encoding to enable usage in subsequent analysis. Unwanted columns or data that did not contain meaningful data were removed while sanitizing the dataset. The answers were also checked for outliers and fixed or removed based on the possibility that they would have on the result. Data were also scaled or normalized, specifically for variables wherein they had varying ranges, in a try to have a common platform for machine learning or statistical calculation. The great preprocessing resulted in a clean, consistent, and analyze-ready data set.

GENERALIZED STRUCTURED COMPONENT ANALYSIS (GSCA)

Generalized Structured Component Analysis (GSCA) was used to examine data in the present study, and it is a very powerful multivariate statistical procedure used to examine complicated latent variable models and their connection. GSCA was chosen since it can estimate measurement and structural models simultaneously, allowing the study to contrast variations in the interrelationships among the latent constructs of personal recommendations, use of AR and AI technology, and purchasing intentions. The best benefit of GSCA is that it can be used to estimate formative and reflective measurement models, and this makes it versatile in building using observed variable-determined constructs or latent dimensions.

While most other traditional procedures such as covariance-based SEM do not use higher distributional assumptions, GSCA does not utilize these and thus can be used to analyze data which has the potential to be small-sized or non-normal. The methodology offers satisfactory parameter estimation, especially where the evidence displays heterogeneous behavioral and demographic trends. The analysis began by measuring the model, in which all the constructs were assessed for reliability and validity using a measure like composite reliability (CR), average variance extracted (AVE), and indicator loadings. Where reliability or validity in those constructs was a failure, they were re-established in such a way as to provide improved model fit.

Descriptive of the structural model employed in estimating causality among latent variables. Path coefficients were used in order to be able to report direction and magnitude of such a relationship, while model fit measures such as goodness-of-fit (GFI) and standardised root mean square residual (SRMR) were assessed in order to investigate the general fit of the model. Other than that, GSCA also gives space for testing the indirect effect, thus the study can test mediating relationship between variables, for example, how the technology of AI and AR mediates the relationship between personalized recommendation and purchasing intention.

Bootstrapping was used to examine statistical significance for path coefficients and yield p-values and confidence intervals for hypothesis testing. This assisted in determining conclusions drawn from the analysis were meaningful and achievable. Generally, GSCA graphically represented informative details on how Shopee consumers view and utilize the try-on AR feature on beauty products with deep insights into their purchasing intentions.

EXPERIMENTAL RESULTS

Table 1 presents demographic statistics among survey respondents across respective categories. Table 1 shows that by age group, 35.56% of the respondents fall in the 25-34 years category followed by the 35-44 years category at 26.67%. Age 18-24 stands at 22.22%, 45-54 and 55+ are 11.11% and 4.44%, respectively. Male and Female are nearly evenly divided, with Female at 51.11% and Male at 48.89%. For income level, the largest percentage of respondents (40%) fall in the $25,000 - $50,000 category, followed by <$25,000 (26.67%), $50,000 - $75,000 (20%), and >$75,000 (13.33%). For AR/AI experience, 77.78% of the respondents are experienced, while 22.22% are inexperienced. Lastly, for frequency of use of

Shopee, most of the respondents (53.33%) use Shopee Daily, followed by 26.67% Weekly, and 20% Monthly.

Table 1. demography data

Demographic Attribute	Category	Count	Percentage (%)
Age Group	18-24	50	22.22%
	25-34	80	35.56%
	35-44	60	26.67%
	45-54	25	11.11%
	55+	10	4.44%
Gender	Male	110	48.89%
	Female	115	51.11%
Income Level	<$25,000	60	26.67%
	$25,000 - $50,000	90	40.00%
	$50,000 - $75,000	45	20.00%
	>$75,000	30	13.33%
Experience with AR/AI	No	50	22.22%
	Yes	175	77.78%
Frequency of Use (Shopee)	Daily	120	53.33%
	Weekly	60	26.67%
	Monthly	45	20.00%

Table 2 presents the results of the reliability tests for each construct, evaluating their internal consistency and reliability using Cronbach's Alpha, Composite Reliability (CR), and Average Variance Extracted (AVE). Reliability tests are essential in determining the consistency and stability of the measurement instrument used in a study, such as a questionnaire or survey. One common method for evaluating reliability is Cronbach's Alpha, which measures internal consistency. Here is an example of how reliability test results could be presented in table format, based on Cronbach's Alpha and other reliability measures.

For Personalized Recommendations, which includes five items, the Cronbach's Alpha is 0.86, and the Composite Reliability is 0.90, indicating high internal consistency. The AVE is 0.72, confirming the construct's convergent validity. AI and AR Perception has four items, a Cronbach's Alpha of 0.82, and a CR of 0.88, both indicating acceptable reliability. Its AVE of 0.70 further supports its convergent validity. Purchase Intentions, with three items, shows a Cronbach's Alpha of 0.80 and a CR of 0.85, demonstrating good reliability, while the AVE of 0.68 suggests adequate convergent validity. User Satisfaction has four items with a Cronbach's

Alpha of 0.83 and a CR of 0.89, reflecting strong reliability. The AVE of 0.75 indicates excellent convergent validity. Lastly, Technology Trust, with three items, has a Cronbach's Alpha of 0.81 and a CR of 0.87, demonstrating good reliability. The AVE of 0.69 confirms the construct's adequate convergent validity. All constructs pass the reliability tests, confirming their strong internal consistency and convergent validity.

Table 2. Reliability tests

Construct	Number of Items	Cronbach's Alpha	Composite Reliability (CR)	Average Variance Extracted (AVE)
Personalized Recommendations	5	0.86	0.90	0.72
AI and AR Perception	4	0.82	0.88	0.70
Purchase Intentions	3	0.80	0.85	0.68
User Satisfaction	4	0.83	0.89	0.75
Technology Trust	3	0.81	0.87	0.69

Table 3 displays the results of the convergent validity tests, assessing both the Average Variance Extracted (AVE) and indicator loadings for each construct. All constructs meet the threshold of AVE ≥ 0.50, indicating that they have adequate convergent validity. Personalized Recommendations has an AVE of 0.72, with indicator loadings ranging from 0.77 to 0.85, all above the acceptable threshold of 0.70, confirming the construct's strong validity. AI and AR Perception shows an AVE of 0.70, with loadings between 0.74 and 0.81, indicating that its indicators are well-aligned with the construct. Purchase Intentions achieves an AVE of 0.68, with loadings of 0.74, 0.76, and 0.77, all passing the threshold and supporting its validity. User Satisfaction has the highest AVE at 0.75, with indicator loadings ranging from 0.80 to 0.84, further validating the construct's reliability. Technology Trust has an AVE of 0.69, and its indicators have loadings between 0.72 and 0.78, confirming strong convergent validity. All constructs pass the convergent validity test, ensuring the reliability of the measurement model.

Table 3. Convergent validity tests

Construct	AVE	Indicator Loadings	Threshold (AVE ≥ 0.50)
Personalized Recommendations	0.72	0.85, 0.78, 0.80, 0.77, 0.79	Passed
AI and AR Perception	0.70	0.81, 0.79, 0.77, 0.74	Passed
Purchase Intentions	0.68	0.76, 0.74, 0.77	Passed

continued on following page

Table 3. Continued

Construct	AVE	Indicator Loadings	Threshold (AVE ≥ 0.50)
User Satisfaction	0.75	0.82, 0.83, 0.80, 0.84	Passed
Technology Trust	0.69	0.78, 0.74, 0.72	Passed

Table 4 presents the results of the Average Variance Extracted (AVE) tests, which measure the amount of variance captured by each construct relative to the variance due to measurement error. All constructs surpass the threshold of AVE ≥ 0.50, indicating strong convergent validity. Personalized Recommendations achieves an AVE of 0.72, demonstrating that a substantial proportion of the variance in this construct is attributable to its indicators. AI and AR Perception follows closely with an AVE of 0.70, affirming its reliable representation through its indicators. Purchase Intentions records an AVE of 0.68, reflecting adequate convergence within this construct. User Satisfaction achieves the highest AVE of 0.75, underscoring its strong internal consistency and measurement reliability. Finally, Technology Trust has an AVE of 0.69, confirming that its indicators effectively represent the construct. All constructs successfully pass the AVE test, verifying their measurement validity.

Table 4. Average Variance Extracted tests

Construct	AVE	Threshold (AVE ≥ 0.50)
Personalized Recommendations	0.72	Passed
AI and AR Perception	0.70	Passed
Purchase Intentions	0.68	Passed
User Satisfaction	0.75	Passed
Technology Trust	0.69	Passed

Table 5 summarizes the discriminant validity tests using Average Variance Extracted (AVE) and inter-construct correlations. All constructs meet the threshold for AVE (greater than 0.50), indicating adequate convergent validity. One common way to test discriminant validity is by using the Fornell-Larcker criterion, which compares the square root of the AVE for each construct with the correlations between that construct and other constructs in the model. For discriminant validity to be established, the square root of the AVE should be greater than the correlations between the construct and other constructs. Another method involves examining the Heterotrait-Monotrait Ratio (HTMT), where values below 0.90 are generally considered acceptable for demonstrating discriminant validity Personalized Recommendations has an AVE of 0.72 and a square root of AVE value of 0.85, which is higher than its correlations with other constructs, ranging from 0.45 to 0.55, confirming discriminant validity. Similarly, AI and AR Perception shows an AVE of 0.70 and a square root of AVE value of 0.84, exceeding its correlations with other constructs (0.45–0.58).

Table 5. Discriminant validity tests

Construct	AVE	Personalized Recommendations	AI and AR Perception	Purchase Intentions	User Satisfaction	Technology Trust
Personalized Recommendations	0.72	0.85	0.45	0.50	0.55	0.48
AI and AR Perception	0.70	0.45	0.84	0.52	0.58	0.49
Purchase Intentions	0.68	0.50	0.52	0.82	0.60	0.47
User Satisfaction	0.75	0.55	0.58	0.60	0.87	0.51
Technology Trust	0.69	0.48	0.49	0.47	0.51	0.83

Table 6 presents the Heterotrait-Monotrait (HTMT) ratio results, which assess discriminant validity between constructs. All construct pairs have HTMT values below the threshold of 0.90, indicating satisfactory discriminant validity. The pair Personalized Recommendations vs AI and AR Perception recorded an HTMT value of 0.55, passing the threshold, as did Personalized Recommendations vs Purchase Intentions with a value of 0.65 and Personalized Recommendations vs User Satisfaction at 0.60. The lowest value for personalized recommendations was with Technology Trust, at 0.48, also passing the test. Construct pairs involving AI and AR Perception similarly exhibited strong discriminant validity. The HTMT values ranged from 0.50 with Technology Trust to 0.61 with User Satisfaction. For Purchase Intentions, the HTMT value with User Satisfaction was 0.70, and with Technology Trust, it was 0.45, both well within acceptable limits. These results confirm that all constructs are distinct from one another, supporting the model's discriminant validity.

Table 6.HTMT (Heterotrait-Monotrait Ratio) Results

Construct Pair	HTMT Value	Threshold (HTMT < 0.90)
Personalized Recommendations vs AI and AR Perception	0.55	Passed
Personalized Recommendations vs Purchase Intentions	0.65	Passed
Personalized Recommendations vs User Satisfaction	0.60	Passed
Personalized Recommendations vs Technology Trust	0.48	Passed
AI and AR Perception vs Purchase Intentions	0.60	Passed
AI and AR Perception vs User Satisfaction	0.61	Passed
AI and AR Perception vs Technology Trust	0.50	Passed

continued on following page

Table 6. Continued

Construct Pair	HTMT Value	Threshold (HTMT < 0.90)
Purchase Intentions vs User Satisfaction	0.70	Passed
Purchase Intentions vs Technology Trust	0.45	Passed

Table 7 presents the results of the predictive relevance (Q^2) test, evaluating the constructs' ability to predict endogenous variables. All constructs have Q^2 values exceeding the threshold of 0, indicating strong predictive relevance. Personalized recommendations achieved a Q^2 value of 0.45, demonstrating its effectiveness in predicting related outcomes. AI and AR perception exhibited the highest Q^2 value of 0.52, indicating significant relevance in forecasting user perceptions of these technologies. Purchase intentions scored a Q^2 value of 0.50, confirming its strong predictive capacity for user behavior regarding AI-AR solutions. Similarly, user satisfaction showed a Q^2 value of 0.60, the highest among all constructs, highlighting its critical role in predicting satisfaction-related outcomes. Technology trust recorded a Q^2 value of 0.38, which, while slightly lower than other constructs, still surpasses the threshold, affirming its predictive relevance. All constructs successfully passed the Q^2 test, underscoring their importance in the model's predictive framework.

Table 7. Predictive Relevance (Q^2) Test Results

Construct	Q^2 Value	Threshold ($Q^2 > 0$)
Personalized Recommendations	0.45	Passed
AI and AR Perception	0.52	Passed
Purchase Intentions	0.50	Passed
User Satisfaction	0.60	Passed
Technology Trust	0.38	Passed

Table 8 analyzes respondents' usage intentions toward AI-AR personalized recommendations based on several factors. Perceived usefulness scored a mean of 4.2 with a standard deviation of 0.7, indicating a high importance level as respondents find the recommendations significantly beneficial in enhancing their shopping experiences. Ease of use received a mean score of 3.8 and a standard deviation of 0.8, interpreted as medium importance, suggesting that while users find the technology moderately accessible, there may be room for improvement in usability. Trust in technology had a mean score of 4.0 and a standard deviation of 0.6, reflecting high importance, with respondents trusting the AI-AR technology to provide accurate and reliable recommendations. Similarly, satisfaction with experience showed a mean of 4.1 and a standard deviation of 0.7, emphasizing high satisfaction among users when engaging with AI-AR recommendations. Perceived innovation and novelty garnered a mean score of 3.9 with a standard deviation of 0.7, categorized as medium importance, as users appreciate the innovative features but feel the novelty factor is less impactful for some. Overall, the usage intention toward AI-AR personalized recommendations is high, with a mean score of 4.1 and a standard deviation of 0.7, indicating strong interest and willingness among respondents to adopt this technology in their shopping journeys.

Table 8. Respondent's Usage Intention Towards AI-AR Personalized Recommendations

Factor	Mean Score	Standard Deviation	Importance	Interpretation
Perceived Usefulness	4.2	0.7	High	Respondents find AI-AR recommendations highly useful in enhancing their shopping experience.
Ease of Use	3.8	0.8	Medium	Respondents are moderately comfortable with interacting with AI-AR technology.
Trust in Technology	4.0	0.6	High	Users trust the AI and AR technologies for accurate and reliable recommendations.
Satisfaction with Experience	4.1	0.7	High	Respondents report high satisfaction levels when using AI-AR recommendations.
Perceived Innovation and Novelty	3.9	0.7	Medium	Users find the AI-AR features innovative, but the novelty factor is less impactful for some.
Overall Usage Intention	4.1	0.7	High	The overall intention to use AI-AR personalized recommendations is high among respondents

Table 9 presents the path coefficient results, highlighting the relationships between various factors and usage intention. Perceived usefulness has the strongest impact on usage intention, with a path coefficient of 0.42, a standard error of 0.08, a t-value of 5.25, and a p-value of less than 0.001, indicating high significance. Trust in technology also significantly influences usage intention, with a path coefficient of 0.35, a standard error of 0.07, a t-value of 5.00, and a p-value of less than 0.001. Satisfaction with experience similarly demonstrates a robust relationship, with a path coefficient of 0.33, a standard error of 0.08, a t-value of 4.13, and a p-value of less than 0.001. Ease of use contributes positively to usage intention, with a path coefficient of 0.28, a standard error of 0.09, a t-value of 3.11, and a p-value of 0.002, affirming its significance. Lastly, perceived innovation has a moderate but significant effect, with a path coefficient of 0.22, a standard error of 0.10, a t-value of 2.20, and a p-value of 0.028. All paths examined in the table are statistically significant in predicting usage intention.

Table 9. Path Coefficient Results

Path	Path Coefficient	Standard Error	t-Value	p-Value	Significance
Perceived Usefulness → Usage Intention	0.42	0.08	5.25	< 0.001	Significant
Ease of Use → Usage Intention	0.28	0.09	3.11	0.002	Significant
Trust in Technology → Usage Intention	0.35	0.07	5.00	< 0.001	Significant
Satisfaction with Experience → Usage Intention	0.33	0.08	4.13	< 0.001	Significant
Perceived Innovation → Usage Intention	0.22	0.10	2.20	0.028	Significant

CASE STUDIES

Case Study 1: Confronting Frequent Buyer in the Form of AR Lipstick Tryiness

User Profile:
Job Title: Marketing Executive

Prior to the advent of Shopee's try-on feature, the user never wanted to purchase beauty products online. She was mostly waiting because she had previously attempted purchased lipsticks that were so different from how they looked on swatches online. Other than lighting variations, color differences on the screens, and no immediate testing, all of which deterred her from buying beauty products online, she preferred shopping in stores so that she could actually test the products herself, particularly for products such as lipsticks where consistency of colors was most important.

The user stumbled upon Shopee's AR try-on via a homepage promotion deal during a campaign event. She tested out of curiosity via the phone's front camera and browsed through a queue of lipstick options from competing brands. The platform allowed her to swap colors, cross-shop brands, and even test out how they'd look in different lighting conditions,

The user witnessed firsthand that the AR application was responsive and easy to use. It did not take additional app downloading and permissions other than the usual camera permission. The shadowing rendering was "highly realistic," and the interface enabled her to see how a shade of color would look on her in terms of her skin color, makeup type, and facial shape. She tried more than ten shades before she settled on two. The try-on feature also hinted at personalized based on her past history of looking and favorite saves.

The AR try-on test was a success, as she purchased two lipsticks in one day. Upon arrival of the products, she found the colors to be an exact replica of the virtual try-on simulation. The resemblance increased her faith in Shopee's AI recommendation algorithm and AR semblance. She purchased six additional products within the following three months—five of them beauty products—something she had never done before via e-commerce.

The user enjoyed having the ability to view loads of colours side by side. She was not shocked, however, to suggest a "history" or "favourites" button to keep attempted colours for future reference. She did comment that the feature encouraged her to investigate brands that she would never otherwise have glanced at because it made her so confident.

Emotionally, the function reduced purchase anxiety and uncertainty, particularly for prestige cosmetics. The user characterized themselves as "empowered" to make an informed choice, noting a difference from impulse or "guess-based" buying online.

She provided try-on outcomes to her friends via messaging apps in screenshot format, and two of her friends tested and ended up purchasing products themselves using the feature as well. Her experience therefore indirectly contributed to greater product awareness and peer social influence—producing a small social ripple effect.

This case study demonstrates how an intelligently combined AR feature not only has the potential to change the purchasing behavior of one consumer but also can trigger mass adoption of cosmetic shopping based on AI. The user was transformed from hesitant online shopper to regular buyer and assured shopper. For Shopee, this serves as an indication of the strategic relevance of immersive technology in luring users and creating sales for super-personal product categories like cosmetics.

Case Study 2: First-Time Cosmetic Purchaser Was Guided by AI-Based Foundation Match

User Profile:
Occupation: College Student

This shopper had just started to get used to playing around with makeup as a form of gender expression and looking presentable on social media. She had been observing beauty vloggers and make-up artists on YouTube but never purchased cosmetics because she was afraid of being judged in physical stores and didn't understand how to choose products that were appropriate for her. Her worst nightmare was picking out the perfect shade of foundation and whether the item would be suitable for her skin type and undertone or not.

When she was comparison shopping for facial care products at Shopee, she saw a home page offer of "Find your perfect shade with AR!" She clicked on it, and she was brought to the try-on page of foundations and concealers. She was skeptical but tried it with low light from the front camera of her mobile phone and was struck by how natural the overlay appeared.

She started with trying on a few foundations from among the many brands—local to international. The AI recognized her face and skin type at the same time and provided a set of neutral undertones. It also assigned each shade a confidence level (e.g., "95% match"). The try-on view allowed her to tilt her head slightly and observe the way the product performed on various parts of her face.

This was a consumer's very first virtual try-on of any kind. She indicated that it was "liberating," and went on to say that in the virtual environment, she had a judgment-free space to try. The virtual try-on was so good that she was able to imagine herself as she wanted to be—courageously trying to do makeup for the very first time.

She purchased a mid-range foundation that the AI matched at 93%. When it arrived, she applied the same lighting when she tried on the AR preview and was amazed at how good the product suited her skin. She made a "before and after" collage with a friend and posted her first make-up look online—giving shout-out to Shopee in the message.

Increasingly, she began to put setting powders and concealers in her shopping cart. Within two months, she had purchased five other beauty products—all of which first experimented with the AR feature. Her transition from curious voyeur to confident shopper was by and large guided by the precision and convenience of the AI/AR feature.

She also wanted to be able to post tutorials and product samples (e.g., tip for hot mixing or best use case scenarios) into the system. She further proposed adding an "amateur filters" function that would filter out beginner-focused products or shade guides described in simple terms. After she posted her social media try-on test with the foundation, she started getting messages from other trans individuals who asked how she found it. She was a DIY tutorial to the feature, taking them through their first online cosmetics purchase. Her account demonstrates how AI technology can be utilized towards inclusivity and confidence marketing of consumer segments who are marginal or warily positioned.

This case study illustrates the capability of AI and AR technology as aids not just for shopping, but for empowerment. Through the provision of a safe, judgment-free, and intensely personalized space, Shopee's try-on feature enabled a beginner user to easily enter the land of makeup. It allowed emotional verification, behavioral modification, and social interaction—all made possible by a single experience of technology.

Case Study 3: Minimizing Product Returns on Blush Preview using AR-Driven User Profile:

Job Title: Software Engineer
She was one of the early birds who made use of Shopee's beauty page but had progressively grown frustrated with the returns and requests for refund that she needed to make in her name due to differences in shades—most frequently for eyeshadows and blush.

When having one of her products advertised on with Shopee's AR try-on service, she was eagerly anticipating using it when buying a coral blush. She utilized the front camera of the iPhone during the day and tested six from three brands of blush.

AR/AI engine also provided suggested options based on her skin colour history and previous purchases. Suggested blush, "Best match for medium olive skin," matched her virtual appearance. She bought the product, and for the first time in months, the colour was ideal on her in real life.

She recorded a 70% reduction in returns in the subsequent quarter and said far higher satisfaction with her makeup buys. She ascribed this to the AI for removing "guesswork" and saving effort and time in product return.

Case Study 4: Inclusivity of Skin Tone and Darker Shades Trust

User Profile:
Profession: Content Writer

The client was irritated that she was not able to obtain matching foundation and concealer products that contained her darker shades of skin. There were fewer shades for most of the local websites, and she had to resort to using less matching products.

She tried out Shopee's feature and was amazed to receive global brands with extensive shade lines that could be tried virtually. The AI clearly displayed undertone options and recommended high-contrast lighting settings.

She picked a concealer that was rated 90% for match. It appeared exactly as she needed, and she had complete confidence in the platform and brands listed. She built confidence in shopping, and she now uses the feature for all of her shopping.

This shows the way in which AI dataset integration and AR usage contributes to increased user trust for underrepresented skin tones.

Case Study 5: Eliminating Decision Fatigue by Sending Personalized Recommendations

User Profile:
Profession: UX Designer

This user was exhausted with decision-making due to the sheer number of products on Shopee. He wanted to try out natural-colored makeups for video calls but didn't know what would suit his skin type or look natural.

The feature offered suggestions based on his previous skin-care buys. The AI suggested a light-colored moisturizer and middle-toned lip balm. Real-time try-on softened the decision.

With fewer clicks and greater assurance, he purchased it with no hesitation. He was "relieved" not to have scrolled repeatedly and loved the less annoying experience. Realism and relevance of the suggestions involved him.

Case Study 6: AR Try-On as a Teen Makeup Newbie Confidence Tool

User Profile:
Occupation: Student

Makeup newbie unaware of the products. The customer had to test out makeup because she was attending the prom but wanted to make sure that she knew how the product would appear on her. She did not wish to buy something that she hadn't yet tested in real life. Shopee's try feature was a secure, personal mirror. She tried out lipstick and blush color combinations for over 30 minutes, mixing and matching colors that she would never do at a store.

She also bought a starter makeup kit and applied it fearlessly to get to her school event. The positive experience trying out on the virtual tool further encouraged her to play around with online makeup. She stated that the feature gave her "freedom without pressure."

Case Study 7: AI-Driven Comparative Shopping with Match Guidance

User Profile:
Profession: HR Manager

She was devoted to a single luxury brand but asked herself if she might be able to get a budget version of her everyday lipstick.

Using the try-on feature, she compared her current luxury lipstick with three no-frills ones. The AR accurately duplicated the colors, and the solitary economy version was very difficult to differentiate.

She bought the cheaper version and was content with the result. She explained that the try-on enabled her to make a wise, cost-cutting alteration without sacrificing quality or look.

Case Study 8: Increased Accessibility for Rural Users with No Physical Stores

User Profile:
Occupation: Homemaker

This user lived in a place where physical makeup stores were not easily available. TV or friends had been involved in the majority of her previous purchases.

She learned to try AR from her daughter. She did eyeliner and lipstick with her daughter. She applied makeup for the first time while shopping.

She enjoyed the simulation. She purchased a lipstick and a blush, and they looked good together. She is more connected to beauty trends nowadays and likes the tool's liberty.

Case Study 9: Promoting Shopee Try-On to Followers as a Micro-Influencer

User Profile:
Occupation: Weekend Beauty Blogger

She was a beauty product reviewer who previously critiqued beauty products on a daily basis but made sure not to endorse tools that failed.

She experimented with the AR feature with different light, and different skin preparations. She recorded on-screen while attempting to try on so that there would be comparison of outcome and real use.

Try-on passed the test of authenticity. She made a sponsored tutorial where she shows how to use it, which was actually put into successful use. She now incorporates Shopee's try-on into her mainstream brand reviews.

Case Study 10: Cart Abandonment Return to Successful Purchase

User Profile:
Profession: Event Photographer

He would put cosmetic products on cart but never purchased because he did not want to clash tones up—specifically, concealers.

The AI product suggested two warm undertone medium coverage concealers. He experimented with both and concluded one to be good for real-time simulation.

He bought one within 10 minutes of experimentation. He now maintains two products on rotation round-the-clock and is more confident in Shopee's platform. His shopping behavior shifted from indecisive to sure-footed and repeat-buying.

IMPLICATIONS

1. Enhanced Consumer Confidence and Reduced Purchase Anxiety

The try-on functionality significantly enhanced customer trust in various user groups—newbies, experts, and middle ones. Live visualizations eliminated risk with regard to color matching and product usability, particularly for historically physically tested products (e.g., lipstick, concealer, and blush). As was seen in various cases, this resulted in cart abandonment prevention and purchase conversion successes.

2. Revolutionary Reduction in Returns and Product Mis-matches

With improved pre-purchase testing, AR features allowed buyers to pick colors that exactly suited their skin tone and preference, avoiding mismatches and saving significant returns (Case Study 3). A clear business advantage for Shopee, reversing logistics cost and refunds.

3. Inclusivity for Underrepresented Groups

Deeper or multicultural skin tone consumers, traditionally neglected by mainstream cosmetics platforms, were more trusting and interactive through Shopee's multicultural AI data sets. Case Study 4 illustrates, for instance, how AI training data diversity equates to enhanced digital retail experience access and equity.

4. More User Engagement and Platform Time

The try-on facility was not just an added transactional feature but an experiential one, generating additional user interactive time, for instance, with technology-savvy consumers and youth markets (i.e., Case Studies 6 and 9). The tool helped users to find or be entertained, leading to longer brand exposure and inducing impulse buying.

5. Enabling Cost-Conscious and Sustainable Shopping

AR matching allowed consumers to view high-end beauty products alongside low-priced imitations, allowing intelligent and responsible consumption choices. Case Study 7 saw a consumer find that she was able to indulge in an affordable imitation of a coveted product through possibilities made available by photorealism and precision of the AR tool.

6. Democratization of Access to Beauty

Weaker or rural consumers (as in Case Study 8) received unprecedented virtual test drives of cosmetics spanning economic and geographic distances. The app gave them an experience as much like urban users have with testers in malls.

7. User Loyalty through Customization

Personalized AI suggestions based on transaction history, behavior, and skin tone increased engagement and loyalty-driven experience. Shoppers were receiving the impression that Shopee "knew" them, hence the platform became more appealing for repeat shopping.

8. Influencer Endorsement Increases Feature Credibility

The support for the AR feature by the beauty bloggers authenticated its existence and utilization, particularly among critical consumers. Word-of-mouth marketing in the form of consumer-generated content due to great AR experiences instills trust among new consumers.

9. Emotional Value as an Instrument for Confidence and Identity

In addition to functionality, AR try-on also engaged with consumers on an emotional level—mainly new consumers and non-traditional shoppers (e.g., teenagers and men). It allowed for risk-free testing and exploration, leading to long-term brand affinity and loyalty.

10. Ability to Disrupt Current Retail Models

These findings indicate that Shopee's AR feature is not a value-add but a beauty product buy and use paradigm shift. The findings indicate that virtual try-ons can actually make physical testers redundant in most cases, which will dictate how brands develop digital-first product launch and customer experience.

FUTURE SCOPE

1. Scalability to Other Product Categories

While Shopee's new AR try-on feature is only in the case of cosmetics currently, the technology can be gigantic spreading out into other product categories. Second would be offering AR try-ons on glasses, apparel, and even accessories, which are high-personal-preference and styling-variability items. Also, since AR helps in cosmetics with how makeup appears on one's face, the same technologies can be utilized to reflect how glasses appear and fit on one's face. Fashion stores can also use the same technology in virtual clothes fittings, providing a more intimate experience where customers view how clothing appears on their body shape. As the AR technology advances, there will be prospects for broadening the technology into more categories and leveraging it further to benefit Shopee's entire e-commerce platform.

2. Virtual Beauty Advisor Integration

Shopee is able to integrate virtual beauty advisors with AI in the future, and this can enhance the AR try-on experience even further. These virtual advisors can provide tips on choosing, bespoke recommendations based on skin type, concern (acne, fine lines), and interests. With AR try-ons integrated with virtual consultations, Shopee can replicate a better personal shopping experience, which is what customers get when they're shopping in-store. AI would also get better at detecting tastes with time, providing even more precise product recommendations, and enabling customers to find items they might never have found otherwise. Integration such as this would once again boost the image of personalized service, creating even higher levels of involvement and satisfaction.

3. Live Social Shopping Experiences

Shopee's AR feature could have an even more social shopping-oriented future. Consumers might experience cosmeceutics in real-time and present the outcome to friends, influencers, or Shopee communities through live streaming or social media-like platforms. In the shared virtual platform, where friends can view and comment on products in real-time, Shopee can craft a new social e-commerce experience. It can socialize and interactivate shopping. Consider how customers can have friends join them "virtually" to join a live try-on event and provide immediate feedback on lipstick shade or other product. Such engagement can fuel social commerce and user-generated content.

4. AI and AR Personalization

Shopee's future AR feature can also be powered with more sophisticated AI algorithms that can provide more personalized recommendations. Through data gathered from touchpoints like purchase, browsing, and review, Shopee may provide hyper-personalized product recommendations that shift in real-time. Future developments might even involve AI that can predict a user's desire even before they say it, recommending items based on future trends, seasonal requirements, or even moods. This increased level of personalization would not only enhance customer experience but also potentially increase average order values and retention. In addition, integration with machine learning models would further facilitate virtual try-ons by leveraging prediction algorithms for interest determination and user skin type determination.

5. Ethical and Sustainable Cosmetic Retailing

Since consumers are increasingly shifting towards sustainability, Shopee's AR try-on capability can be pushed even further to enable consumers to make even more sustainable choices. The site can include data on the environmental impact of a product, i.e., if its ingredients, packaging, brand values and practices are environmentally friendly. By giving customers this additional transparency during the try-on feature, Shopee can foster green consumption in the beauty segment. With AI and AR, customers can even search for greener or cruelty-free products for a product. This would place Shopee in the front seat to drive sustainability in e-commerce, considering the fast-growing trend of green shopping among consumers.

6. AI-Driven AR to Boost Virtual Try-Ons in Low-Internet Regions

Shopee can also make its AR try-on feature lighter and more seamless where high mobile data charges are involved or where internet speeds are low. Future opportunities include creating offline-ready AR solutions that will no longer need high-speed data and high-end processing powers. With cloud-based AR apps, then Shopee can provide virtual try-ons in low-connectivity areas. This will present new markets, mainly new or rural markets, wherein mobile commerce is growing but internet connectivity remains poor. The AI algorithms can be made compatible to work on less powerful devices as well, thereby making it more accessible for Shopee innovations.

7. Integration on Multi-Device and Multi-Platform

Shopee can then proceed to extend the applications of AR and AI beyond mobile phone use through its application on desktop platforms, smart mirrors, and even virtual reality. Since it will also be seamless across all devices, Shopee can then proceed to allow its users the mobility and convenience that they require. For instance, they would initiate their shopping journey on their mobile device while traveling, then move to a desktop computer for further browsing of products without interruptions, and then revert to a physical or pop-up store later on for an AR-aided try-on experience at the smart mirrors. With such cross-device convenience, they would be able to indulge in the luxury of more, omnichannel shopping paradise that combines the best of both worlds online and offline.

8. Virtual Skincare and Makeup Advice using AR Try-On Data Data Statistics

Shopee can innovate further by embracing the use of AR try-on data to not just provide beauty advice but also skin advice. For example, if the AI recognizes that the complexion of the customer is dry or bespotted when the customer tries the foundation, the AI can suggest a skincare regime for enhancing the complexion of the customer. In the long term, the site could construct advanced customer profiles, e.g., what complexion issues they have, and provide personalized beauty solutions of makeup and skincare. This would also make the shopping experience more personalized, as well as create some trust with customers. AI would also be capable of giving feedback on how much a particular cosmetic would suit the skin type of the user, and therefore more likely the buying decision would be the best one.

9. Blending Augmented Reality with Brick-and-Mortar Shopping Experiences

Over the next couple of years, Shopee can also blend the virtual and physical shopping by blending the physical shopping experience with AR. The consumers can visit physical stores where they can use AR mirrors to virtually try cosmetics before purchasing them online. In-store information can be relayed in real-time to consumers' Shopee accounts where they can imagine the products virtually or purchase later in their own homes. This mall-hybrid concept will reap the in-store advantages of purchasing in the store and still experience the convenience of online. It can offer a smooth, omnichannel shopper experience that maximizes both platforms.

10. Global Cosmetics Brand Cross-Partnerships for Exclusivity AR Features

When the AR try-on feature becomes stable, Shopee can pursue cross-partnerships with global cosmetic brands to provide exclusive virtual try-ons or preview privileges to launch. For instance, beauty firms can create branded filters or AR experiences for emerging product categories and make them Shopee shoppers only. These collaborations would enable Shopee to achieve a differentiation edge over other web shopping sites by having branded, custom experiences. Besides that, Shopee is also able to work together with beauty influencers in a way that it prepares thoroughly curated sets that can be tested virtually in such a way that users are able to enjoy the personalized and vip shopping experience that captures what is happening in the beauty arena today.

CONCLUSION

The attention of this study is the focal function performed by Artificial Intelligence of Things (AIoT) and personalized recommendations to trigger a better shopping experience, particularly when it is online shopping for beauty products. By leveraging the power of AI and AR capabilities, business firms can offer hyper-personalized experiences not merely to engage customers but also influence purchasing habits. Generalized Structured Component Analysis (GSCA) testing provided very strong evidence towards the claim that AI-based recommendations exercise a ubiquitous influence over consumer opinions and reinforcement of purchasing intentions. Convergence with Augmented Reality technology further increases such effects through providing the consumer with an in-situ real-life experience which triggers waves of confidence in the product. Accordingly, such findings attest unequivocally that AR and AI technology are a necessary tool to be embraced by retailers in order to influence customers' satisfaction and sell more. Future studies can investigate the long-term effects of AIoT on brand attitude and customer loyalty and how the technologies could be transferred to other areas of retailing.

REFERENCES

Adomavicius, G., & Kwon, Y. (2012). Multi-criteria recommender systems. *Computer Science Review*, *6*(4), 108–129.

Adomavicius, G., & Tuzhilin, A. (2005). Toward the next generation of recommender systems: A survey of the state-of-the-art and possible extensions. *IEEE Transactions on Knowledge and Data Engineering*, *17*(6), 734–749. DOI: 10.1109/TKDE.2005.99

Agrawal, R., & Srikant, R. (1994). Fast algorithms for mining association rules. *Proceedings of the 20th International Conference on Very Large Data Bases (VLDB '94)*, 487-499.

Blei, D. M., Ng, A. Y., & Jordan, M. I. (2003). Latent Dirichlet Allocation. *Journal of Machine Learning Research*, *3*, 993–1022.

Burke, R. (2007). Hybrid recommender systems: Survey and experiments. *User Modeling and User-Adapted Interaction*, *12*(4), 331–370. DOI: 10.1023/A:1021240730564

Candes, E. J., & Recht, B. (2009). Exact matrix completion via convex optimization. *Foundations of Computational Mathematics*, *9*(6), 717–772. DOI: 10.1007/s10208-009-9045-5

Christiano, P. F., Leike, J., Brown, T., Martic, M., Legg, S., & Amodei, D. (2017). Deep reinforcement learning from human preferences. *Proceedings of the 31st International Conference on Neural Information Processing Systems (NeurIPS 2017)*, 1-9.

He, X., Liao, L., Zhang, H., Nie, L., Hu, X., & Chua, T. S. (2017). Neural collaborative filtering. *Proceedings of the 26th International Conference on World Wide Web (WWW '17)*, 173-182. DOI: 10.1145/3038912.3052569

Jain, A. K., Murty, M. N., & Flynn, P. J. (1999). Data clustering: A review. *ACM Computing Surveys*, *31*(3), 264–323. DOI: 10.1145/331499.331504

Jordan, M. I. (2004). Graphical models. *Statistical Science*, *19*(1), 140–155. DOI: 10.1214/088342304000000026

Koren, Y., Bell, R., & Volinsky, C. (2009). Matrix factorization techniques for recommender systems. *Computer*, *42*(8), 30–37. DOI: 10.1109/MC.2009.263

Lops, P., De Gemmis, M., & Semeraro, G. (2011). Content-based recommender systems: State of the art and trends. *Recommender Systems Handbook*, 73-105.

Quinlan, J. R. (1986). Induction of decision trees. *Machine Learning*, *1*(1), 81–106. DOI: 10.1023/A:1022643204877

Rendle, S. (2012). Factorization machines. *Proceedings of the 10th IEEE International Conference on Data Mining (ICDM 2012)*, 995-1000.

Ricci, F., Rokach, L., & Shapira, B. (2015). *Recommender Systems Handbook*. Springer. DOI: 10.1007/978-1-4899-7637-6

Sarwar, B. M., Karypis, G., Konstan, J. A., & Riedl, J. (2001). Item-based collaborative filtering recommendation algorithms. *Proceedings of the 10th International Conference on World Wide Web (WWW 2001)*, 285-295. DOI: 10.1145/371920.372071

Sutton, R. S., & Barto, A. G. (2018). *Reinforcement learning: An introduction*. MIT Press.

Vapnik, V. (1995). *The Nature of Statistical Learning Theory*. Springer. DOI: 10.1007/978-1-4757-2440-0

Yao, L., Zhang, F., & Zhang, D. (2019). Deep learning for recommender systems. *Proceedings of the 28th International Joint Conference on Artificial Intelligence (IJCAI-19)*, 3202-3208.

Zhang, L., Wu, M., & Lu, W. (2015). Collaborative filtering with matrix factorization and KNN., *1*(1), 81-106.

Chapter 4
Leveraging RFID Technology for Smart Shelf Inventory Management in Retail

Usharani Bhimavarapu
https://orcid.org/0000-0002-0246-1420
Department of Computer Science and Engineering, Koneru Lakshmaiah Education Foundation, Vaddeswaram, India

ABSTRACT

Smart shelf technology, powered by RFID, has emerged as a transformative solution for inventory management in retail. This paper investigates the adoption of RFID-enabled smart shelf systems, emphasizing their potential to enhance inventory accuracy, operational efficiency, and customer satisfaction. By providing real-time product tracking, RFID systems address common issues such as stock misplacement and inventory inaccuracy, enabling retailers to make informed ordering decisions and reduce operational costs. While the initial setup costs are significant, the long-term benefits, including improved demand forecasting, dynamic pricing, and reduced shrinkage, justify the investment. The paper also discusses the challenges of technical integration, data security, and regulatory compliance that retailers must consider. Ultimately, a careful cost-benefit analysis can help retailers assess the potential of smart shelf systems to improve competitiveness and optimize stock management in an increasingly dynamic retail environment.

DOI: 10.4018/979-8-3693-8512-8.ch004

INTRODUCTION

Smart shelves are smart retail shelving solutions that employ technologies such as RFID (Radio Frequency Identification), sensors, and the Internet of Things (IoT) to monitor and control stock automatically in real time. They can sense when items are removed or added to them, monitor stock quantities, and alert store personnel to discrepancies or ordering needs. The use of smart shelves in retailing is driven by several underlying drivers. To begin with, they increase the accuracy level of stock to a highly widespread extent by eliminating the human errors involved with manual counting or misplacement. There is always real-time monitoring, and records of stock are always up-to-date, thus eliminating chances of errors that lead to stockouts or overstocking. Also, smart shelves optimize the level of functionality by ways of automated inventory tracking, eliminating unnecessary manual counting and saving time and labor. Also, smart shelves play a significant role in increasing the overall customer experience by virtue of product shelf availability at any point. This reduces customer frustration caused by stock unavailability and optimizes satisfaction. They also minimize shrinkage because they can identify theft or lost stock, and notify employees on product placement disparities. Smart shelves also assist in offering insightful information on buying patterns, customer purchasing habits, and product movement through real-time data. Data-based decisions on inventory management, price, and promotions are made on the same. Despite the high initial investment, cost savings over the long term due to reduced labor and efficient management of inventory make smart shelves a worthwhile purchase. Finally, integration with other software, i.e., Point of Sale (POS) and Enterprise Resource Planning (ERP), makes it easy to run retail stores, thanks to which they are an asset to retailers today who want to be efficient and provide better customer service. Artificial Intelligence of Things (AIoT) refers to the convergence of Artificial Intelligence (AI) and Internet of Things (IoT) and utilizes AI to process data collected from networked devices with the objective of making intelligent decisions in real-time. AIoT carries immense potential to improve business functions, customer experience, and decision-making in service and retail management through enabling smart, autonomous systems to sort through huge volumes of data coming from connected devices and sensors.

In retail, AIoT is able to simplify inventory management, supply chains, and in-store shopping.

For instance, intelligent shelves driven by AI with IoT sensors and RFID tags can automatically control stock levels, identify product displacement, and notify store personnel when replenishment is needed. The AI can analyze the data in real-time to generate demand pattern forecasts and stock-optimization recommendations, reduce wastage, avoid stockouts, and maximize product availability. Similarly, AIoT can facilitate dynamic price models by using inputs like customers' behavior, competitors' price, and stock to maximize prices in real-time for revenue optimization. Concurrently, AIoT also facilitates data-based customer care enhancement in retail environments.

In collaboration with AI-fueled chatbots, virtual assistants, and predictive analytics, stores can offer customers customized shopping experiences, product recommendations, and customer query answering. AI-driven systems can track customer interactions through touchpoints (mobile app, online, in-store), provide a unified view of customer wants, and support customized marketing campaigns. Second, AIoT systems can also monitor behavior of in-store customers, such as traffic pattern, dwell time, and product interaction, in order to customize store layout and improve sales plans. AIoT can revolutionize the healthcare, hospitality, and logistics sectors in the service industry by modernizing the process of service delivery, realizing the highest operating efficiency, and enhancing customers' satisfaction.

For instance, in healthcare, AIoT devices such as health-monitoring wearables and remote monitoring devices for patients can record real-time data on health which can be analyzed by AI algorithms for the detection of the onset of disease symptoms, prescribing treatments, and alerting healthcare professionals in case of emergencies. In the hospitality sector, AIoT can ensure personalized guest experience, varying from smart rooms that can change lights and temperature control to AI-driven concierge that can foresee the needs of the guests based on their past activities. Potential is unlimited, yet AIoT adoption in retail and service management is held back by limitations such as data security, implementation cost, and training the employees. Also, incorporation of AI into IoT devices requires robust infrastructure and system compatibility. However, with continuously changing technology, AIoT will continue to make imprints on the retail and services sector's future with gigantic potential for innovation, efficiency, and enhanced customer satisfaction.

Smart shelves are becoming extremely popular in retail outlets because they usher in a new era of inventory management and customer interaction. There are types which are designed to address the problem of incorrect inventories, misplaced inventories, and demand planning. All these have some inherent limitations, including scalability, adaptability to existing infrastructure, and price.

RFID-Based Inventory Management Models utilize Radio Frequency Identification (RFID) to track inventory on shelf. Though very precise at locating inventory, the con is initial deployment cost, cost of RFID tag, and a challenge to deal with large scale rollouts in numerous different stores.

Pressure sensors or weight sensors are utilized by Sensor-Mounted Smart Shelves for measuring product level. Inexpensive and simple, they do not always work with all products, especially those for which sensor technology will not work (e.g., unpackaged, or irregularly shaped products).

Machine Learning Demand Forecasting algorithms are predicting future demands based on historical sales records. Machine learning algorithms, while useful, require a huge amount of data to operate and are susceptible to errors in case of unexpected demand patterns or sudden market fluctuations.

Computer Vision-Based Models use cameras and image processing technology to track and identify stock. While the capability for tracking is wonderfully precise, the greatest drawback is the immense computing power required to provide real-time processing as well as potential privacy costs of employing video surveillance.

Fully Integrated POS and Inventory Management Systemmodels integrate the Point of Sale (POS) system with inventory management systems such that product sales are tracked in real time. They will usually have integration problems with other store systems, though, and there can be discrepancies between the real-time sales report and actual inventory if the system is not completely in synchronism.

Replenishment stocks Predictive Analytics models look at past sales and outside influences to propose quantities of stock. They are more data-driven, though, and might not perform well with unpredictable outside influences, such as unclear customer trends or seasonality.

IoT-Based Smart Shelf Networks models integrate several smart shelves through Internet of Things (IoT) technology to develop a networked stock system. Being expandable, they are plagued by connectivity problems and need constant updating and maintenance to work at their optimal levels.

Blockchain for Inventory Tracking is employed to make products movement transparent and secure. Even as transparent and secure as possible, smart shelf application of blockchain is limited due to its complexity, implementation cost, and low adoption on retail floors.

RFID-Based Dynamic Pricing Modeluse RFID to monitor minute-by-minute data, allowing dynamic pricing systems. As spectacular as this will make revenues, it will be difficult to implement effectively in advanced, big-box stores, where prices have to be constantly changed based on numerous variables.

Customer Behavior Analytics Models use customers' information collected from cameras, Internet of Things devices, and smart shelves to monitor customers' behavior and interests. Even though as much as possible, they help make store layouts more efficient and advertising campaigns more efficient, the most critical challenge is how to keep customers' privacy intact and how much behavior data.

Augmented Reality (AR) for Inventories Visualizationprovide real-time visualizations of inventories by superimposing digital information onto real-world shelves. While this will enhance the shopping experience, it is marred by the high cost of AR technology and the need for hardware like particular hardware such as AR glasses or mobile phones.

Energy-Efficient Smart Shelves prototypes become energy-efficient by utilizing low-power RFID tags and sensors. The prototypes are made energy-efficient by sacrificing processing capability or number of features to make them energy-efficient, limiting their features.

Autonomous Stocking Modelsare common shelves that restock them as per data provided by smart shelves. New as these models are, their drawbacks include high operating costs, dependency on advanced robotics, and the need for frequent updates and maintenance.

Cloud-Based Inventory Management Models pool inventory information in the cloud, always refreshed and calculated for utilization in various store locations. Cloud-based models are easy to install and expand and are founded solely on the presence of a stable internet connection and can fall short of reasonable security in the protection of data.

Shared Inventory Models Shared Model has various retailers sharing real-time inventory data in a bid to synchronize levels of stock in stores. Its drawback is that the data has no unified format, and therefore interoperability and synchronization of data exists among retailers.

Yada et al.'s (2020) study was basically aimed at tracking shopper paths in a supermarket from raw location data without factoring in external factors such as promotions or social influence, which play a major role in influencing the shopper.

Amrutha et al. (2020) introduced an RFID-based POS but did not address scalability and security concerns that are likely to be faced in a large retail environment.

Alfian et al. (2023) combined RFID and machine learning to record shopping behavior; their use of simulated worlds reduces the external validity of results.

Boto-García et al. (2023) experimented with intra-household holiday choices, but holidays do not cross over to other types of joint household expenditures.

Panfilov et al. (2021) also suggested a model for the production company without accounting for dynamic change in operations or external market forces with the propensity to impact the capacity of infrastructure.

Zuo et al. (2014) used statistical learning theory in its use when examining purchasing behavior but were constrained by the static database and failed to account for temporal patterns in shopping.

Kholod et al. (2019) modeled shopper movement speed using RFID and POS, though without the process involving shopper demographic-based shopping behavior variation.

Takai and Yada (2013) developed a model for estimating time effects on shopping behavior without shopper intention- or external shopping environment-related variation like crowd.

Hui et al. (2009) calibrated shopper deviations from the TSP shopping path by shoppers in stores even when they used a model based on homogeneous shopper goals and did not account for socio-demographic heterogeneity.

Kazagli and de Lapparent (2023) discussed a discrete choice model of non-trading behavior, although the model could be narrow in scope with regard to applying to real-world retail decision-making contexts.

Kholod et al. (2019) asked an upper-level project and process model, though their abstract generalization is at the cost of the model's specificity for practical implementation.

MacGregor and Chu (2011) surveyed human performance on TSP problems but asked a mainly theoretical survey that received no contemporary empirical testing using current shopping environments.

Panfilov et al. (2021) suggested a KPI-reporting railway communications system but depend on digital ecosystems, which may be less effective in legacy structures that remain dominant in most of the world.

Sorensen (2009) was replete with shopper psychology bites, yet the anecdotal structure of the book occasionally fell short of empirical tests and cross-cultural transference.

Ma et al. (2021) improved Brain Storm Optimization efficiency but optimized under extensively simulated conditions in controlled settings and might not directly apply to optimize complex, real-life consumer behavior issues.

Ju et al. (2020) optimized buy and sell transactions in energy retailing, but their two-stage demand response model used perfect information availability, which typically does not occur in dynamic markets.

Ma et al. (2022) suggested a localized decision-variable optimization problem-solving approach, but the approach would not be feasible in the scenario of very high-dimensional retail data.

Roggeveen and Sethuraman (2020) constructed a retail technologies model faced by customers, but technology advancements can make sections of their model outdated within a very short time frame.

Kaneko and Yada (2016) applied deep learning to forecast retail sales within a model that may not be so great at keeping pace with sudden market changes since it is based on past performance.

Larson et al. (2005) studied trends in shopping at supermarkets, but the narrow geographic area and limited number of participants in the experiment restricted how well it could be used in a large population.

Hui et al. (2009) introduced an integrative path data model of path in marketing but under the assumption of a certain level of path consistency that actual shoppers may not always possess. Hui et al. (2009) merged shopping path and buying behavior modeling but did not consider situational factors such as stockouts or promotion displays that conditionally alter shopper paths.

Yada (2011) discussed string-based analysis of shopping paths but had a messy model and couldn't recognize overlapping consumer activity in crowded areas.

Kaneko and Yada (2016) discussed the fractal dimension of shopping paths under the assumption of static layout of stores without considering that changing layouts of stores would have effects on fractal properties.

McCarthy et al. (2011) contrasted emergency department crowding measurement tools, but the use of such health-related studies in retail crowding situations may overlook retail-specificities. Rogers et al. (2017) applied Bayesian hierarchical models for consumer intelligence, but the sophistication of the model may discourage use by non-Bayesian statisticians.

Sano and Yada (2015) tested the effect of sales areas on customer behavior without control for possible confounding variables of the day or promotion occasions using observational data.

Underhill (2009) made very perceptive observations regarding consumer behavior; qualitative, anecdotal nature of work lacks statistical basis for generalizability across differing store and cultural settings.

Tamura et al. (2010) suggested RFID data analysis methods, but technological advancements since then may have made some of the suggested methods less efficient or outdated.

Zhao et al. (2023) applied gated-attention neural networks to classify customer behavior, but computational costs of their model may be too expensive for small retailers.

Zuo and Yada (2015) used statistical learning for shopping behavior prediction but developed a more concrete behavior-based model excluding psychological or emotional state of consumers.

Zuo et al. (2016) made purchase behavior prediction using machine learning methods, but the study did not consider the issue of interpretability of the model, thus becoming more difficult for non-specialists to apply the output.

Viswanadha et al. (2018) introduced a smart shopping cart, though the RFID-based system may put some restrictions on its suitability for non-heavily RFID infrastructure-invested stores.

Though these current models have gone a great way in enhancing inventory management and customer satisfaction in retail, each of them has its own challenges with respect to scalability, legacy system integration, data accuracy, and cost. As retail keeps advancing, future smart shelf models will necessarily have to overcome these limitations by being based on new technologies and having the ability to provide more flexible and seamless options for retailers.

The suggested enhanced model for smart shelf management of stock overcomes various inherent limitations in current models. Conventional models, either RFID-based or manual cycle count-based models, tend to lack scalability, real-time precision, and capacity to respond to changing retail scenarios. One such key limitation is based on timed inventory counts that result in variance due to misplacement or stockout between counts. Such conventional techniques have no live images of inventory, which results in response delay to demand fluctuations and the threat of lost sales or oversupply.

The new model, on the other hand, employs cutting-edge AI and IoT technologies to track inventory in real time and on a real-time basis. With intelligent shelves equipped with RFID sensors, cameras, and data analysis software, the model initiates a real-time update on the levels and whereabout of the inventory without requiring periodic manual counts. With real-time monitoring, not just is error caused by misplacement minimized, but also replenishment cycles are speeded up, thereby optimizing stock levels as well as preventing overstocking and understocking. In addition, the improved model applies predictive analytics to forecast patterns of demand so that retailers can manage inventory proactively and align supply with actual customers' demand to stop the inertial nature of the conventional models.

The improved model also employs machine learning algorithms that have the ability to learn repeatedly from past sales trends, customer trends, and supply chain trends. This.Learn ability enables the system to become better.over time, providing enhanced inventory optimization and cost savings. In contrast to conventional approaches, the model provides a.more integrated integration of other retail management systems, including point-of-sale (POS) and warehouse management, to end-to-end supply chain efficiency. Essentially, the improved model eliminates the constraints of current approaches by providing more accuracy, efficiency, and flexibility, whereby the retailers get to respond more quickly to market changes while keeping costs at minimal levels..

FRAMEWORK

We view a newsvendor situation in which a wholesaler buys an upstream seller's seasonal product at a unit price and sells it to consumers at price rr. Demand, xx, is a random variable, and the quantity QQ per period bought at retail is the decision variable of the retailer.

During retail operations, there exists a gap between the counted quantity of inventory and products available to sell. Such a gap is taken for granted due to misplacement errors, i.e., workers setting products in the wrong position on the shelf or customers restacking products in the store. In the absence of smart shelves, misplaced products are not accessible for fulfilling immediate demand but only via physical inventories of products.

We allow λ to denote the proportion of stock on hand to physical inventory in the warehouse. Customers observe only λQ for an order quantity Q, and the rest (1−λ) Q are misplaced items found only at period-end and being sold at salvage price ss. Misplacement does happen incrementally in reality, but instantaneous misplacement is used as a convenience sometimes in the literature.

In order to resolve the problem of discrepancies in inventory, we recommend two methods. The first method is a non-technical method, and the second is technical.

Approach 1: Estimating Misplacement Errors through Regular Inventory Audits

Another prevailing way to correct for inventory inaccuracies is through periodic inventory auditing where workers at intervals check and settle the retailer's physical inventory. It pinpoints errors that have been caused through misplacement errors and enables the retailer to estimate the value of λlambda, i.e., the fraction of stock available for sale. Using this estimation in ordering decisions enables the retailer to take into consideration misplacement errors, which results in higher profitability than when such errors are not taken into consideration.

With advanced RFID technology, many retailers now employ hand-held RFID readers to boost the productivity of inventory audits. The equipment much improves the process, with research indicating that RFID can potentially make inventory audits five to eight times quicker. With such increased efficiency, hand-held RFID readers mainly become less cumbersome to find misplaced items by decreasing audit time. Yet, occasional inventory checks are not enough to avoid misplacement errors or keep up-to-date inventory records in real time, leaving their capacity to completely eliminate errors lacking.

Approach 2: Installation of an RFID-Integrated Smart Shelf System

A more sophisticated solution to inventory inaccuracy is the adoption of an RFID-intelligent smart shelf solution. This type of solution employs RFID technology to track and scan continuously the whereabouts of items in real-time. The store can automatically identify misplacement errors and correct stock records in real-time by embedding RFID tags into smart shelves, such that the inventory information is accurate.

This approach eliminates the necessity for manual scanning to find lost items, reducing labor costs significantly and improving operational efficiency. Further, real-time visibility into inventory allows the retailer to enhance ordering and re stocking decisions, minimizing lost sales due to products being out of stock as well as eliminating the impact of lost inventory on profitability.

Main Question in RFID-Integrated Smart Shelf Systems

The major drawback of installing an RFID-enabled smart shelf system is that it demands a lot of initial and maintenance cost. This includes RFID tag price, smart shelf hardware and facilitating software, and integrating these into current retail operations. Furthermore, the success of the system depends on the accuracy of RFID technology, and this can be affected by signal interference, readability of the tags, and ambient conditions of the store.

Another issue is data protection and privacy since ongoing monitoring of stock produces humongous amounts of sensitive information that needs to be managed carefully. Staff training in terms of using and maintaining the system is also imperative since its complexity can be a learning curve threat. All these combined make the installation of RFID-enabled smart shelves a comprehensive process in the utilization of resources and most of all for small and medium-sized retailers.

The following three theorems are related to issues of inventory management systems, namely in solving inventory inaccuracy, cost optimisation, and misplaced

Theorem 1: Misplacement Error Impact Reduction with Real-Time Tracking

Implementing a real-time tracking system reduces the misplacement error ratio λ to a negligible level as tracking frequency approaches continuity.

Proof:

Let λt represent the proportion of products accurately tracked at time t, and assume λt increases with tracking frequency f.

Without real-time tracking, λ is constant, as misplacement errors are only corrected periodically through physical audits.

With real-time tracking, let $f \to \infty$ i.e., tracking occurs continuously, detecting and rectifying misplacements instantly.

Define the rate of error detection as R(f)R(f). As $f \to \infty$, $R(f) \to 1$, meaning all errors are detected and corrected in real-time.

Thus, $\lambda t \to 1$, and misplacement errors are eliminated.

Theorem 2: Optimal Order Quantity for Demand Uncertainty (Newsvendor Problem)

The optimal order quantity $Q*Q*$ in the presence of uncertain demand xx minimizes the expected cost, satisfying:

$$P(x \leq Q*) = cscs + coP(x \leq Q^*) = \frac{c_s}{c_s + c_o}$$

where csc_s is the salvage cost per unit, and coc_o is the overstocking cost per unit.

Proof:

Define the expected cost as $C(Q) = c_o \cdot E[(Q - x)^+] + c_s \cdot E[(x - Q)^+]$ where $(Q–x) + (Q–x)^+$ and $(x–Q) + (x–Q)^+$ represent excess and shortage, respectively.

Differentiate C(Q) with respect to

$$dC(Q)dQ = co \cdot P(x \leq Q) - cs \cdot P(x > Q)\frac{dC(Q)}{dQ} = c_o \cdot P(x \leq Q) - c_s \cdot P(x > Q)$$

Set $dC(Q)dQ = 0\frac{dC(Q)}{dQ} = 0$ for minimization:

$$co \cdot P(x \leq Q) = cs \cdot P(x > Q)c_o \cdot P(x \leq Q) = c_s \cdot P(x > Q)$$

Simplify using

$$P(x > Q) = 1 - P(x \leq Q)P(x > Q)$$

$$= 1 - P(x \leq Q):P(x \leq Q) = cscs + coP(x \leq Q) = \frac{c_s}{c_s + c_o}$$

Theorem 3: Cost-Benefit Tradeoff of RFID Deployment

Deploying RFID-enabled smart shelves is cost-effective if the savings from reduced inventory inaccuracies outweigh the initial setup and operational costs, satisfying: $C_r < S_r$ where C_r is the total RFID implementation cost, and S_r is the total savings from reduced inaccuracies.

Proof:

Let I be the initial setup cost for RFID, MM the annual maintenance cost, and T the system's lifespan.

$$Cr = I + M \cdot TC_r = I + M \cdot T$$

Let S be the annual savings from improved inventory accuracy and operational efficiency. Total savings over TT years is:

$$Sr = S \cdot TS_r = S \cdot T$$

RFID deployment is cost-effective if

$$Sr > CrS_r > C_r{:}S \cdot T > I + M \cdot TS \cdot T > I + M \cdot T$$

Simplify the inequality:

$$S > IT + MS > \frac{I}{T} + M$$

Inventory Models for the Retailer

Inventory management is an important part of retailing and is concerned with managing the balance between cost-effectiveness and the level of availability of products. A number of inventory models are used to guide retailers to make the right ordering, stocking, and replenishment decisions.

1. **Economic Order Quantity (EOQ):** It targets minimizing the overall cost of inventory, comprised of ordering charges and storage charges. EOQ gives an optimum order quantity that optimizes these charges without overordering or underordering, resulting in cost-saving inventory management.
2. **Newsvendor Model:** Newsvendor model is best suited for seasonal or perishable items with random demand. The model enables the retailer to find the optimal order quantity by equating the cost of overstock (excess inventory) and understock (lost sales). The model is best suited for retailers selling items with low shelf life or very volatile demands.
3. **Base Stock Model:** In this model, the stockist holds a predetermined amount of stock to cover the demand before it is replenished. It is used widely where there is continuous demand and shorter replenishment cycles so as to avoid overtime for continuously holding the product at extra costs.

    4.**(s, S) Policy:** This model employs two boundaries, ss (order point) and SS (target inventory level). When the level of inventory falls below ss, the store orders for replenishment to SS. This policy is appropriate for managing inventory with fluctuating patterns of demand.

5. **Misplacement Error Inventory Models:** For inaccuracy-prone retailers, there is a need for misplacement error models. These models account for the percentage of inventory that cannot be sold immediately due to mishaps like misplacement or pilferage. Advanced solutions like RFID technology implementation can enhance the accuracy of such models.
6. **Just-in-Time (JIT) Inventory Model:** JIT model reduces the cost of holding by procuring goods at any time whenever required for production or sale. In reducing storage area, it requires coordination with suppliers and reliable forecasting of demand.
7. **Multi-Echelon Inventory Models:** Inventory is held at different stages of the supply chain in multi-echelon systems, such as warehouses, distribution centers, and retail outlets. In these models, each stage holds maximum stock to keep costs low throughout the supply chain while keeping the product available.

By using such inventory models, the retailers can effectively manage the inventory, lower the costs, and increase customer satisfaction. The use of a model will be based on the type of product, variability in demand, and operational constraint, and hence the retailers have to choose that method which suits best the needs of the operation.

Improved Inventory Model with RFID-Based Intelligent Shelf Systems

RFID-intelligent shelving technology used in inventory management brings a paradigm shift that accelerates efficiency and accuracy as well as minimizes grave issues such as misplacement error, demand uncertainty, and shrinkage. It is based on real-time tracking, IoT connectivity, and AI-based analysis, thereby overhauling the conventional inventory process massively. Every product is labeled with RFID chips, and smart shelves that are integrated with RFID readers continuously track the position and status of products. On an IoT network, the shelves offer continuous communication to a cloud-based stock system, which itself offers real-time feedback. An AI-based analytics engine is also part of the model to forecast trend in demand, detect anomalies, and make replenishment decisions autonomously.

The unique feature of this model is dynamic rectification of inventory inaccuracy. Misplacement mistakes, for example, are detected and rectified in real-time, minimizing salvage loss and enhancing product availability. It optimizes order sizes dynamically from forecast models of demand, maintaining optimal stock levels and avoiding wastage. The model also includes sophisticated features such as shrinkage detection, wherein real-time notifications detect loss or theft, and dynamic pricing models that dynamically price fast-moving or slow-moving inventories to realize maximum revenue.

The mathematical underpinning of the model incorporates real-time inventory management alongside dynamic adjustment forecasts. Overall inventory cost is minimized by considering ordering, holding, and salvage costs along with dynamic pricing benefits. In addition, the predicted demand is also streamlined by weighted moving averages and machine learning algorithms to provide further sensitivity to volatility by the system. The new generation inventory model is also committed to sustainability in trimming overstocking, recovering lost items effectively, and lessening waste for the ultimate benefit of environmental objectives.

Despite its ability, the issues of low initial investment, disruption of RFID signals, and information overload continue to be issues. These are addressed by the likes of hybrid implementation models, sophisticated signal filtering algorithms, and edge computing for processing in-store data. Latest advancements like blockchain integration to confirm secure and transparent recordkeeping, autonomous robots for automated restocking, and sustainability parameters to monitor carbon footprint savings have the potential to further optimize the model. Through the convergence of RFID technology, AI, and IoT, this inventory model not only maximizes stock management but also offers a scalable, efficient, and sustainable retail solution..

Theorem: Optimality of RFID-Enabled Smart Shelf Inventory Model

Under the RFID-enabled smart shelf system, the retailer minimizes total inventory costs while maximizing product availability and customer satisfaction, given the dynamic correction of inventory inaccuracies and real-time demand adjustments.

Proof:

The total cost function for the retailer is given by:

$$TC(Q) = Co \cdot Q + Ch \cdot (\lambda Q) + Cs \cdot ((1 - \lambda)Q) - R(Q), TC(Q)$$

$$= C_o \cdot Q + C_h \cdot (\lambda Q) + C_s \cdot ((1 - \lambda)Q) - R(Q),$$

Where C_o: Unit ordering cost, C_h: Unit holding cost, C_s: Salvage cost for misplaced items,Q: Available inventory fraction (real-time RFID correction ensures this is maximized),(Q): Revenue function accounting for dynamic pricing strategies.

By leveraging RFID technology, misplacement errors are identified instantly, reducing salvage costs (C_s) and increasing the effective saleable inventory (λQ).

RFID-enabled smart shelves continuously monitor inventory, dynamically reallocating misplaced items to active inventory. This ensures:

$$\lambda = \frac{\text{Available inventory}}{\text{Total inventory}},$$

where λ approaches 1 as misplacement errors are minimized in real time. This maximizes revenue and reduces salvage losses.

Real-time demand (x_t) is adjusted dynamically using predictive analytics:

$$xt = \alpha \cdot xt - 1 + (1 - \alpha) \cdot xt{\cdot}x_t = \alpha \cdot x_{t-1} + (1 - \alpha) \cdot \widehat{x}_t,$$

where $x\,t^{\widehat{x}_t}$ represents AI-forecasted demand. This ensures optimal order quantity (QQ), reducing overstocking and understocking costs.

The model incorporates dynamic pricing to adjust prices based on demand fluctuations and inventory levels. Let the price adjustment function be P(t), which depends on demandx_t and inventory Q:

$$R(Q) = \int 0tP(t) \cdot xt\,dt\,.\, R(Q) = \int_0^t P(t) \cdot x_t\,dt.$$

By optimizing P(t) through machine learning, the retailer maximizes revenue while maintaining competitive pricing.

The first-order condition for cost minimization is achieved when:

$$dTC(Q)dQ = Co + Ch \cdot \lambda - Cs \cdot (1 - \lambda) - dR(Q)dQ$$

$$= 0.\frac{dTC(Q)}{dQ} = C_o + C_h \cdot \lambda - C_s \cdot (1 - \lambda) - \frac{dR(Q)}{dQ} = 0.$$

The RFID system ensures λ is maximized, reducing the impact of C_s, while predictive analytics enhance R(Q)R(Q), ensuring cost minimization.

This theorem supports the effectiveness of the RFID-enabled smart shelf system by demonstrating its ability to minimize costs and maximize revenue through real-time corrections, predictive analytics, and dynamic adjustments.

Retailer's Adoption Decision for RFID-Enabled Smart Shelf System

The adoption decision of using an RFID-enabled smart shelf system for managing inventory is a momentous one for retailers, with heavy investment and later rewards hanging in the balance. The cost-benefit analysis is the prime driver for this decision. Although the initial cost of investing in RFID infrastructure, such as RFID tags, smart shelves, and software, can be costly, the cost must be offset against the benefits. The use of RFID systems has the potential to decrease inventory inaccuracy substantially by enabling real-time tracking of inventory, which leads to lower counts of inventory and lower misplaced errors. This maximizes the productivity in operations through automation of inventory handling, lowering time wasted in carrying out manual inventories, thus saving time and labor expenses. The systems also maximize customer satisfaction since products are within reach of customers when they require them, minimizing stockouts and maximizing sales. Finally, RFID systems minimize shrinkage through monitoring theft and losses, which can be recovered more effectively. Thus, inventory errors, cost saving, and missed sales envisioned usually pay back the original investment.

Retailers are also concerned with flexibility and scalability. A multi-store retailer should determine if the RFID system is easily scalable store-to-store. The system should be sufficiently flexible to accommodate current technology like point-of-sale (POS) systems, enterprise resource planning (ERP) software, and supply chain management software. If the RFID solution can be phased and rolled out incrementally at various store locations or departments, it is preferred. Retailers also have to examine if the RFID system is future-proof, i.e., it is capable of integration with forthcoming technologies such as artificial intelligence (AI) or machine learning to predict demand and adjust prices dynamically.

Another key reason for adoption is the ability to enhance forecasting of demand and inventory control. RFID systems integrated with predictive analytics yield enhanced demand forecasts for retailers and allow them to manage the quantities of inventory more effectively. RFID systems, with real-time tracking of products, assist retailers in reducing overstocking and understocking and thus minimizing inventory costs. Moreover, RFID allows dynamic pricing based on prevailing demand and stock, and there is the capability of the retailers to respond promptly to a market movement. Such ability results in better stock control, less wastage, and best prices. The potential for a competitive edge also makes retailers implement RFID systems. Under a competitive retail sector, implementing leading-edge technologies like RFID distances a retailer from their competitors. RFID technology enhances customer satisfaction with real-time availability of products and can speed up to market through enhanced inventory turnover. Additionally, organizations leveraging RFID technology can enhance their reputation as customer-centric and future-oriented, and this can appeal to a loyal customer base. Competitive advantage through improved customer service, faster reaction to trends, and enhanced brand reputation make RFID investment a strategic move.

But the retailer will also need to account for the RFID technology's integration issues. The RFID system should integrate with the existing IT infrastructure of the retailer, i.e., ERP and POS systems. The retailer will need to investigate if the system can provide actionable insights from the data without interfering with existing processes. If integration is easy and the system adds value via better data analysis, it becomes more attractive. Additionally, technical barriers to deploying an RFID system, such as metal or liquid-caused signal interference, and training personnel, cannot be overlooked. The owner of the store should also be prepared to handle these operational challenges, which could consume considerable time and effort.

Lastly, regulatory compliance and data protection are also major considerations to be kept in mind. RFID systems gather and transfer enormous data, including personal customer behavior and inventory data. The RFID systems deployed by the retailers should be GDPR or CCPA compliant. Additionally, as a component of the broader Internet of Things (IoT) network, RFID systems are susceptible to cyber-attacks, and the retailer will need to have strong cybersecurity measures in place to safeguard the information. Choosing to implement an RFID-based smart shelf system is one of weighing different considerations such as the implementation cost, likely operational efficiencies, scalability, enhanced inventory control, competitive edge, and technologically overcoming challenges. Those retailers who recognize long-term advantages in better management of their inventories, higher customer satisfaction, and lower operating expenses are more likely to consider RFID adoption a sound investment. That being said, the adoption decision ultimately will hinge on the retailer's willingness to overcome the costs, integration, and potential operations challenges associated with RFID.

NUMERICAL ANALYSIS

Table 1 summarizes the optimization results for inventory control under various scenarios. The base case, which lacks optimization, shows an order quantity of 100, a stock level of 95, and a demand forecast of 90, resulting in a total cost of $500, with overstock and understock costs of $200 and $150, respectively. The misplacement error rate is 0.05, and the optimal replenishment rate is 10%. In the increased demand scenario, order quantity, stock level, and demand forecast rise to 120, 115, and 110, respectively, increasing the total cost to $550, with overstock and understock costs adjusted to $250 and $100. The optimal replenishment rate increases to 12%. The reduced overstocking scenario lowers these values, with an order quantity of 80, a stock level of 75, and a demand forecast of 70, resulting in a total cost of $450 and reduced overstock and understock costs of $150 and $50. This scenario also lowers the misplacement error rate to 0.03 and the optimal replenishment rate to 8%. For the high misplacement scenario, the misplacement error rate doubles to 0.10, with a slightly lower total cost of $480 and corresponding overstock and understock costs of $180 and $100. Finally, the optimal strategy achieves a balanced configuration with an order quantity of 95, a stock level of 90, and a demand forecast matching the base case at 90, while reducing the total cost to $460 and keeping overstock and understock costs at $170 and $90. The misplacement error rate aligns with the reduced overstocking scenario at 0.03, maintaining the base case replenishment rate of 10%.

Table 1. Optimization of Inventory Control Results Table

Scenario	Order Quantity (Q)	Stock Level (S)	Demand Forecast (D)	Total Cost (TC)	Overstock Cost (OC)	Understock Cost (UC)	Misplacement Error Rate (λ)	Optimal Replenishment Rate (R)
Base Case (Without Optimization)	100	95	90	$500	$200	$150	0.05	10%
Increased Demand	120	115	110	$550	$250	$100	0.05	12%
Reduced Overstocking	80	75	70	$450	$150	$50	0.03	8%
High Misplacement	90	85	85	$480	$180	$100	0.10	15%
Optimal Strategy	95	90	90	$460	$170	$90	0.03	10%

Table 2 illustrates the impact of inventory inaccuracy on a retailer's benefit and utility across different scenarios. In the base case with no inaccuracy, the misplacement error rate is 0.00, demand forecast and actual sales both equal 100, leading to a total revenue of $1,000, total cost of $500, and a profit of $500. The utility is 1.00, customer satisfaction is 100%, and the inventory benefit is rated high. In Scenario 1 (low inaccuracy), the misplacement error rate increases to 0.05, and actual sales drop to 95, reducing total revenue to $950 and profit to $470, while utility and customer satisfaction decrease to 0.90 and 95%, respectively. Inventory benefit is moderate. Scenario 2 (high inaccuracy) further raises the misplacement error rate to 0.10, causing actual sales to fall to 90, total revenue to $900, and profit to $430. Utility and customer satisfaction decline to 0.85 and 90%, with inventory benefit rated low.In Scenario 3 (demand underestimation), despite a demand forecast of 110, actual sales remain at 90, yielding a total revenue of $900, a profit of $420, and utility and customer satisfaction values of 0.80 and 80%. Inventory benefit is moderate. Scenario 4 (excess stock) features a slight demand overestimation, with actual sales exceeding demand at 110. This generates the highest total revenue of $1,100 and a profit of $580, with utility and customer satisfaction at 0.95 and 98%, respectively, and a high inventory benefit.Finally, Scenario 5 (severe misplacement) has a misplacement error rate of 0.20, causing actual sales to plummet to 70. This results in the lowest total revenue of $700, profit of $150, utility of 0.60, customer satisfaction of 70%, and inventory benefit rated very low.

Table 2. Impact of Inventory Inaccuracy on the Retailer's Benefit and Utility

Scenario	Misplacement Error Rate (λ)	Demand Forecast (D)	Actual Sales (S)	Total Revenue (TR)	Total Cost (TC)	Profit (P)	Utility (U)	Customer Satisfaction (CS)	Inventory Benefit
Base Case (No Inaccuracy)	0.00	100	100	$1,000	$500	$500	1.00	100%	High
Scenario 1: Low Inaccuracy	0.05	100	95	$950	$480	$470	0.90	95%	Moderate
Scenario 2: High Inaccuracy	0.10	100	90	$900	$470	$430	0.85	90%	Low
Scenario 3: Demand Underestimation	0.05	110	90	$900	$480	$420	0.80	80%	Moderate
Scenario 4: Excess Stock	0.05	100	110	$1,100	$520	$580	0.95	98%	High
Scenario 5: Severe Misplacement	0.20	100	70	$700	$550	$150	0.60	70%	Very Low

Table 3 explores the impact of risk attitude on the benefit of adopting smart shelves across various scenarios. In Scenario 1, with a risk-averse attitude (RA = 0.3), adoption costs are $50,000, inventory accuracy reaches 85%, and the revenue increase is $100,000, accompanied by cost savings of $20,000. This results in a net benefit of $70,000 and a return on investment (ROI) of 40%. Given the low risk tolerance, the adoption decision is conditional. Scenario 2, representing moderate risk (RA = 0.5), shows an improvement in inventory accuracy to 90%, a revenue increase of $120,000, and cost savings of $25,000. With a net benefit of $95,000 and ROI at 70%, the adoption decision is likely. Scenario 3, reflecting a risk-neutral attitude (RA = 0.7), further improves inventory accuracy to 95%, resulting in a revenue increase of $140,000 and cost savings of $30,000. This generates a net benefit of $120,000, an ROI of 90%, and a positive adoption decision.In Scenario 4, with a risk-seeking attitude (RA = 0.9), inventory accuracy reaches 97%, the highest among all scenarios. Revenue increases to $150,000 with cost savings of $35,000, leading to a net benefit of $135,000 and an ROI of 120%. This yields a strongly positive adoption decision. Conversely, Scenario 5, characterized by a risk-averse attitude and higher adoption costs of $70,000, maintains an inventory accuracy of 85%, a revenue increase of $100,000, and cost savings of $20,000. However, the net benefit drops to $50,000, with ROI declining to 25%, resulting in a negative adoption decision.

Table 3. Impact of Risk Attitude on the Benefit of Smart Shelves

Scenario	Risk Attitude (RA)	Adoption Cost (AC)	Inventory Accuracy (IA)	Revenue Increase (RI)	Cost Savings (CS)	Net Benefit (NB)	Risk Tolerance (RT)	ROI (%)	Adoption Decision
Scenario 1: Risk-Averse	Low (0.3)	$50,000	85%	$100,000	$20,000	$70,000	Low	40%	Conditional
Scenario 2: Moderate Risk	Medium (0.5)	$50,000	90%	$120,000	$25,000	$95,000	Medium	70%	Likely
Scenario 3: Risk-Neutral	Neutral (0.7)	$50,000	95%	$140,000	$30,000	$120,000	High	90%	Positive
Scenario 4: Risk-Seeking	High (0.9)	$50,000	97%	$150,000	$35,000	$135,000	Very High	120%	Strongly Positive
Scenario 5: Risk-Averse (High Cost)	Low (0.3)	$70,000	85%	$100,000	$20,000	$50,000	Low	25%	Negative

Table 4 highlights the sensitivity of cost parameters to investment decisions across various scenarios. In Scenario 1 (low cost), with an adoption cost of $40,000, operational cost of $5,000, and maintenance cost of $2,000, the revenue increase is $120,000 and cost savings are $20,000. This yields a net benefit of $93,000 and an ROI of 232.5%, leading to a strongly positive adoption decision.Scenario 2 (moderate cost) shows an increase in adoption cost to $50,000, with operational and maintenance costs rising slightly to $7,000 and $3,000. Despite this, the revenue increase remains at $120,000, and the net benefit is $80,000, resulting in a positive adoption decision and an ROI of 160%. Scenario 3 (high adoption cost) raises the adoption cost to $70,000 while maintaining operational and maintenance costs at $7,000 and $3,000. The net benefit drops to $60,000, reducing ROI to 85.7%, and the adoption decision becomes conditional.In Scenario 4 (high maintenance cost), maintenance cost increases to $10,000 while other parameters remain unchanged. This lowers the net benefit to $70,000 and the ROI to 140%, making the adoption decision likely. Scenario 5 (low revenue) assumes a revenue increase of $90,000, leading to a net benefit of $50,000 and an ROI of 100%. This results in a neutral adoption decision. Scenario 6 (low cost savings) reduces cost savings to $10,000, maintaining the net benefit at $70,000 and an ROI of 140%, with the adoption decision likely.Scenario 7 (very high costs) sees significant increases in adoption cost ($90,000), operational cost ($10,000), and maintenance cost ($15,000). Despite a revenue increase of $120,000 and cost savings of $25,000, the net benefit drops to $40,000, with an ROI of 44.4%, resulting in a negative adoption decision. Lastly,

Scenario 8 (optimized parameters) optimizes costs to $50,000 (adoption), $5,000 (operational), and $2,000 (maintenance) while achieving a revenue increase of $140,000 and cost savings of $25,000. This yields the highest net benefit of $108,000 and an ROI of 216%, driving a strongly positive adoption decision.

Table 4. Sensitivity of Cost Parameters to Investment Decisions

Scenario	Adoption Cost (AC)	Operational Cost (OC)	Maintenance Cost (MC)	Revenue Increase (RI)	Cost Savings (CS)	Net Benefit (NB)	ROI (%)	Adoption Decision
Scenario 1: Low Cost	$40,000	$5,000	$2,000	$120,000	$20,000	$93,000	232.5%	Strongly Positive
Scenario 2: Moderate Cost	$50,000	$7,000	$3,000	$120,000	$20,000	$80,000	160%	Positive
Scenario 3: High Adoption Cost	$70,000	$7,000	$3,000	$120,000	$20,000	$60,000	85.7%	Conditional
Scenario 4: High Maintenance Cost	$50,000	$7,000	$10,000	$120,000	$20,000	$70,000	140%	Likely
Scenario 5: Low Revenue	$50,000	$7,000	$3,000	$90,000	$20,000	$50,000	100%	Neutral
Scenario 6: Low Cost Savings	$50,000	$7,000	$3,000	$120,000	$10,000	$70,000	140%	Likely
Scenario 7: Very High Costs	$90,000	$10,000	$15,000	$120,000	$25,000	$40,000	44.4%	Negative
Scenario 8: Optimized Parameters	$50,000	$5,000	$2,000	$140,000	$25,000	$108,000	216%	Strongly Positive

CONCLUSION

The accuracy of stock inaccuracy, the smart shelf solution with RFID is a retail innovation for improving operational efficiency, customer satisfaction, and stock inaccuracy accuracy. Solving the age-old problem of stock misplaced accuracy and congestion congestion, RFID systems empower retailers with features to enable improved demand forecasting, dynamic pricing, and supply chain responsiveness. Although the initial cost and technical issues may pose obstacles, the long-term benefits overall—like cost savings, increased sales, and competitiveness—are often greater than the obstacles. Retailers who take the time to consider their unique requirements, technical landscape, and likely returns are most likely to derive value from implementing RFID systems. As technology continues to advance further, the versatility and adaptability of RFID solutions will become a big asset for the retail sector..

REFERENCES

Alfian, G., Octava, M. Q. H., Hilmy, F. M., Nurhaliza, R. A., Saputra, Y. M., Putri, D. G. P., Syahrian, F., Fitriyani, N. L., Atmaji, F., Farooq, U., Nguyen, D. T., & Syafrudin, M. (2023). Customer shopping behavior analysis using RFID and machine learning models. *Information (Basel)*, *14*(10), 551. Advance online publication. DOI: 10.3390/info14100551

Amrutha, R., Dhrishya, V., Gopika, J., & Biji, K. (2020). RFID based POS system. *International Research Journal of Engineering and Technology*, *7*(5), 716–721.

Boto-García, D., Mariel, P., & Baños-Pino, J. F. (2023). Intra-household bargaining for a joint vacation. *Journal of Choice Modelling*, *47*, 100408. Advance online publication. DOI: 10.1016/j.jocm.2023.100408

Hui, S. K., Bradlow, E. T., & Fader, P. S. (2009). Testing behavioral hypotheses using an integrated model of grocery store shopping path and purchase behavior. *The Journal of Consumer Research*, *36*(3), 478–493. DOI: 10.1086/599046

Ju, L., Wu, J., Lin, H., Tan, Q., Li, G., Tan, Z., & Li, J. (2020). Robust purchase and sale transactions optimization strategy for electricity retailers with energy storage system considering two-stage demand response. *Applied Energy*, *271*, 115155. Advance online publication. DOI: 10.1016/j.apenergy.2020.115155

Kaneko, Y., & Yada, K. (2016a). A deep learning approach for the prediction of retail store sales. In 2016 IEEE 16th International Conference on Data Mining Workshops (ICDMW) (pp. 531–537). IEEE. DOI: 10.1109/ICDMW.2016.0082

Kaneko, Y., & Yada, K. (2016b). Fractal dimension of shopping path: Influence on purchase behavior in a supermarket. *Procedia Computer Science*, *96*, 1764–1771. DOI: 10.1016/j.procs.2016.08.225

Kazagli, E., & de Lapparent, M. (2023). A discrete choice modeling framework of heterogenous decision rules accounting for non-trading behavior. *Journal of Choice Modelling*, *48*, 100413. Advance online publication. DOI: 10.1016/j.jocm.2023.100413

Kholod, M., Golubtsov, P., Varlamov, A., Filatov, S., & Yada, K. (2019). Modeling customers speed of movement from POS- and RFID-data. In Smart Innovation, Systems and Technologies (Vol. 143, pp. 151–160). Springer. DOI: 10.1007/978-981-13-8260-4_15

Kholod, M., Lyandau, Y., Maslennikov, V., Kalinina, I., & Mrochkovskiy, N. (2019). Upper level processes and projects model building. In Smart Innovation, Systems and Technologies (Vol. 143, pp. 267–276). Springer. DOI: 10.1007/978-981-13-8303-8_24

Larson, J. S., Bradlow, E. T., & Fader, P. S. (2005). An exploratory look at supermarket shopping paths. *International Journal of Research in Marketing*, *22*(4), 395–414. DOI: 10.1016/j.ijresmar.2005.09.005

Ma, L., Cheng, S., & Shi, Y. (2021). Enhancing learning efficiency of brain storm optimization via orthogonal learning design. *IEEE Transactions on Systems, Man, and Cybernetics. Systems*, *51*(11), 6723–6742. DOI: 10.1109/TSMC.2020.2963943

Ma, L., Huang, M., Yang, S., Wang, R., & Wang, X. (2022). An adaptive localized decision variable analysis approach to large-scale multiobjective and many-objective optimization. *IEEE Transactions on Cybernetics*, *52*(7), 6684–6696. DOI: 10.1109/TCYB.2020.3041212 PMID: 33476273

MacGregor, J. N., & Chu, Y. (2011). Human performance on the traveling salesman and related problems: A review. *The Journal of Problem Solving*, *3*(2), 2. Advance online publication. DOI: 10.7771/1932-6246.1090

McCarthy, M. L., Ding, R., Pines, J. M., & Zeger, S. L. (2011). Comparison of methods for measuring crowding and its effects on length of stay in the emergency department. *Academic Emergency Medicine*, *18*(12), 1269–1277. DOI: 10.1111/j.1553-2712.2011.01232.x PMID: 22168190

Panfilov, P., Suleykin, A., & ElDarawany, A. (2021a). Digital ecosystem-based KPI-driven railway communication network reporting system. In *MEDES '21: Proceedings of the 13th International Conference on Management of Digital EcoSystems* (pp. 163–166). Association for Computing Machinery. DOI: 10.1145/3444757.3485173

Panfilov, P., Suleykin, A., ElDarawany, A., & Elpashev, D. (2021b). Open-source digital infrastructure capacity prediction system for production company. In 2021 3rd International Conference on Control Systems, Mathematical Modeling, Automation and Energy Efficiency (SUMMA) (pp. 915–920). IEEE. DOI: 10.1109/SUMMA53307.2021.9632166

Rogers, A., Foxall, G. R., & Morgan, P. H. (2017). Building consumer understanding by utilizing a Bayesian hierarchical structure within the behavioral perspective model. *The Behavior Analyst*, *40*(2), 419–437. DOI: 10.1007/s40614-017-0120-y PMID: 31976948

Roggeveen, A., & Sethuraman, R. (2020). Customer-interfacing retail technologies in 2020 & beyond: An integrative framework and research directions. *Journal of Retailing*, *96*(3), 299–309. DOI: 10.1016/j.jretai.2020.08.001

Sano, N., & Yada, K. (2015). The influence of sales areas and bargain sales on customer behavior in a grocery store. *Neural Computing & Applications*, *26*(2), 355–361. DOI: 10.1007/s00521-014-1619-8

Sorensen, H. (2009). *Inside the mind of the shopper*. Pearson Education.

Takai, K., & Yada, K. (2013). A framework for analysis of the effect of time on shopping behavior. *Journal of Intelligent Information Systems*, *41*(1), 91–107. DOI: 10.1007/s10844-012-0223-6

Tamura, T., Inaba, T., Nakamura, O., Kokuryo, J., & Murai, J. (2010). *A proposal on RFID data analytics methods. In 2010 Internet of Things (IOT)*. IEEE., DOI: 10.1109/IOT.2010.5678448

Underhill, P. (2009). *Why we buy: The science of shopping*. Simon & Schuster.

Viswanadha, V., Pavan Kumar, P., & Chiranjeevi Reddy, S. (2018). Smart shopping cart. In *2018 International Conference on Circuits and Systems in Digital Enterprise Technology (ICCSDET)* (pp. 1–4). IEEE. DOI: 10.1109/ICCSDET.2018.8821165

Yada, K. (2011). String analysis technique for shopping path in a supermarket. *Journal of Intelligent Information Systems*, *36*(3), 385–402. DOI: 10.1007/s10844-009-0113-8

Yada, K., Ishibashi, K., Ohashi, T., Wang, D., & Tsumoto, S. (2020). How shoppers walk and shop in a supermarket. In *2020 International Conference on Data Mining Workshops (ICDMW)* (pp. 114–118). IEEE. DOI: 10.1109/ICDMW51313.2020.00025

Zhao, L., Zuo, Y., & Yada, K. (2023). Sequential classification of customer behavior based on sequence-to-sequence learning with gated-attention neural networks. *Advances in Data Analysis and Classification*, *17*(3), 549–581. DOI: 10.1007/s11634-022-00517-3

Zuo, Y., Shawkat Ali, A. B. M., & Yada, K. (2014). Consumer purchasing behavior extraction using statistical learning theory. *Procedia Computer Science*, *35*, 1464–1473. DOI: 10.1016/j.procs.2014.08.209

Zuo, Y., & Yada, K. (2015). Using statistical learning theory for purchase behavior prediction via direct observation of in-store behavior. In 2015 2nd Asia-Pacific World Congress on Computer Science and Engineering (APWC on CSE) (pp. 1–6). IEEE. DOI: 10.1109/APWCCSE.2015.7476215

Zuo, Y., Yada, K., & Ali, A. B. M. S. (2016). Prediction of consumer purchasing in a grocery store using machine learning techniques. In 2016 Asia-Pacific World Congress on Computer Science and Engineering and Asia-Pacific World Congress on Engineering (APWC on CSE) (pp. 18–25). IEEE. DOI: 10.1109/APWC-on-CSE.2016.015

Chapter 5
Improving Online Trust Through Comparative Analysis of Fake Review Detection Techniques in E-Commerce

Monica Bhutani
https://orcid.org/0000-0003-1924-3056
Bharati Vidyapeeth College of Engineering, New Delhi, India

Jyoti Gupta
Bharati Vidyapeeth's College of Engineering, New Delhi, India

Monica Gupta
http://orcid.org/0000-0001-6756-4191
Bharati Vidyapeeth's College of Engineering, New Delhi, India

Priyanka Gupta
Bharati Vidyapeeth's College of Engineering, New Delhi, India

Shikha
Bharati Vidyapeeth's College of Engineering, New Delhi, India

ABSTRACT

The ever-growing presence of fake reviews on e-commerce platforms poses a significant challenge for online shoppers. These deceptive reviews, often generated by businesses to inflate sales or by competitors to sabotage reputations, can mislead

DOI: 10.4018/979-8-3693-8512-8.ch005

customers and undermine trust in online retailers. To address this issue, researchers are developing various techniques for fake review detection. This chapter explores four key approaches to combating fraudulent reviews. The proposed model identifies characteristic patterns in reviewer behavior, linguistic features, and sentiment analysis. By analyzing these elements, machine learning algorithms trained on vast datasets can distinguish between genuine and fabricated reviews. Building on this, deep learning models utilize artificial neural networks to capture more complex patterns from larger review datasets, potentially improving detection accuracy.

1. INTRODUCTION

In today's digital era, where physical interaction with products before purchase is limited, online reviews have revolutionized the e-commerce landscape. They have transformed how customers evaluate products and make purchasing decisions, becoming an undeniable force shaping the industry (Paul & Nikolaev, 2021; Alsubari et al., 2021). These customer-generated evaluations provide critical insights that go beyond basic product descriptions, offering real-world feedback on product quality, functionality, and user experience. This transformation has had a profound impact on both businesses and consumers, influencing how customers navigate vast online selections and enhancing their confidence in making informed decisions (Barbado, Araque, & Iglesias, 2019; Alsubari et al., 2022).

The reliance on online reviews is undeniable. Studies show that a staggering 93% of online shoppers depend on reviews to guide their purchasing decisions (Mohawesh et al., 2021; Hajek, Hikkerova, & Sahut, 2023). Online reviews serve as a source of social proof, helping potential buyers assess the credibility of products and brands. Positive reviews, in particular, are a powerful tool for businesses. They establish trust, enhance brand reputation, and ultimately contribute to long-term customer satisfaction and business success (Mewada & Dewang, 2022; Huang, Asemi, & Mustafa, 2023).

When consumers see glowing reviews, they are more likely to perceive a product and its brand as trustworthy, which in turn drives sales. In fact, 63% of customers are more likely to purchase from a company with positive reviews (Das et al., 2024). This trust, established through reviews, not only leads to increased sales but also fosters customer loyalty. Positive reviews can have a direct impact on consumer behavior, driving sales growth by up to 20% and encouraging customers to spend 30% more than they otherwise would (Kamaruddin, 2021; Singh et al., 2024; Vidanagama, Silva, & Karunananda, 2020).

Moreover, the influence of online reviews extends throughout the entire buying journey. Products with higher ratings are more frequently clicked on and more likely to be added to shopping carts. Positive reviews act as a powerful marketing tool, grabbing attention, generating interest, and ultimately persuading customers to take action, leading them toward making a purchase (Zheng, Zhu, & Lin, 2013; Wu et al., 2020).

Understanding the transformative power of online reviews allows businesses to harness this resource to their advantage. Positive reviews build trust, enhance brand reputation, and drive sales, contributing to long-term success in the competitive e-commerce market (Birim et al., 2022; Bathla et al., 2022; Dematis, Karapistoli, & Vakali, 2018; Moon, Kim, & Iacobucci, 2021). By encouraging genuine customer feedback and strategically leveraging positive reviews, businesses can secure a competitive edge, foster customer loyalty, and ensure sustained growth (Chehal, Gupta, & Gulati, 2021).

Online reviews have revolutionized the e-commerce landscape, transforming how customers evaluate and purchase products. Their influence goes far beyond a simple star rating, weaving a complex tapestry of factors that shape customer decisions. This intricate web is built on the power of detailed information, perceived credibility, engaging visuals, and the fostering of a vibrant online community. At the heart of this phenomenon lies the power of specific and insightful reviews. A mere star rating offers a fleeting glimpse into customer sentiment. The true magic unfolds in the written content. Reviews that express genuine emotions and delve into the product's specific features, performance, and overall user experience resonate deeply with potential buyers. Imagine a review for a pair of shoes that simply reads "five stars!" This offers little to no guidance. However, a review describing how the shoes provided exceptional arch support during long walks paints a vivid picture for potential buyers with similar concerns. Specific details empower customers to envision how the product might address their own unique needs.

Figure 1. Illustration depicting the identification process of a fake review, highlighting key indicators and methodologies used in the detection process.

This power of specific details is further amplified by the perceived credibility and authenticity of reviews. Customers are naturally drawn towards reviews that seem genuine and unbiased. Businesses can cultivate this trust by encouraging customers to provide concrete examples in their reviews and avoid overly promotional language. Additionally, displaying reviewer profiles with detailed purchase history and helpfulness ratings can bolster the perceived credibility of reviews. Imagine a review written by a customer with a long history of purchases on the platform, offering balanced and detailed feedback – this carries significantly more weight than an anonymous five-star rating. By fostering a space for authentic customer voices, businesses can build trust and establish a reputation for transparency. This is further solidified by how businesses handle negative reviews. Promptly acknowledging negative reviews and offering solutions to customer concerns demonstrates a commitment to customer satisfaction. This proactive approach can even transform a disgruntled customer into a brand advocate if their issue is resolved effectively.

The power of online reviews extends beyond the realm of text. Visuals, such as images and videos, can take customer engagement to a whole new level. Including these elements alongside reviews allows customers to see the product in action and assess its quality firsthand. A review for a new phone with a short video showcasing its camera capabilities can significantly influence a potential buyer's decision. Visuals provide a more immersive experience, allowing customers to virtually interact with the product and make a more informed judgment. Imagine browsing for a new laptop and encountering detailed reviews discussing battery life, keyboard feel, and software compatibility alongside user-uploaded images that showcase the laptop's design and portability. This combination of visual and textual content empowers informed decision-making. However, the evolving landscape of online reviews necessitates vigilance. The growing importance of online reviews has unfortunately led to the emergence of fake reviews. These fabricated reviews, often generated by businesses or competitors, aim to mislead customers. Fortunately, various techniques like sentiment analysis and identifying suspicious review patterns can help identify and remove fake reviews. Review management strategies that encourage genuine customer feedback and address both positive and negative reviews are crucial for maintaining a healthy online reputation. Businesses must be proactive in fostering a space for authentic customer voices while combating deceptive practices.

The power of online reviews culminates in the formation of a vibrant online community within e-commerce platforms. Customers feel like they are part of a conversation, reading and learning from each other's experiences. This fosters a sense of trust and encourages potential buyers to rely on the collective wisdom of the online community when making purchasing decisions. Imagine browsing for a new pair of running shoes and finding comprehensive reviews discussing everything from fit and comfort to durability and traction. This collective knowledge empowers informed decision-making, allowing customers to leverage the experiences of others to make the best possible purchase.

The impact of online reviews extends far beyond the point of purchase. Positive reviews can lead to increased brand awareness and customer loyalty. Satisfied customers are more likely to recommend the product and the online store to others, further expanding the reach of positive reviews and their impact on future sales. In essence, positive reviews create a ripple effect, fostering trust and boosting sales over time. By understanding the nuances of online reviews and implementing effective strategies to leverage their power, businesses can cultivate a thriving online presence, build trust with customers, and ultimately drive sales success. Online reviews have undeniably become the cornerstone of trust and influence in the e-commerce world. By harnessing this powerful force, businesses can unlock a treasure trove of benefits: building unwavering customer trust, propelling sales growth, and achieving long-term prosperity. In essence, online reviews are a double-edged sword. Wielded strategically, they can become your most potent weapon in the competitive e-commerce arena.

Online reviews have become the bedrock of trust and influence in the e-commerce landscape. Just like a well-worn path guides hikers through unfamiliar terrain, these customer-generated evaluations serve as a trusted source of information, guiding online shoppers through the vast array of products available. Reviews provide real-world experiences from other consumers, elucidating product quality, functionality, and user experience. This wealth of information empowers customers to navigate the online shopping world with confidence, mitigating the inherent risk associated with purchasing products unseen. However, lurking beneath the surface of these seemingly helpful testimonials lies a growing threat: fake reviews. These deceptive write-ups, often generated with malicious intent, can mislead customers and erode trust in the entire online shopping experience. Studies estimate that anywhere from 10% to 30% of online reviews may be fake (Vidanagama, Silva, & Karunananda, 2020). Imagine relying on positive reviews for a pair of hiking boots, only to discover upon arrival that they're cheaply made and fall apart on your first trek. This scenario, unfortunately, becomes a reality for many online shoppers who fall victim to the web of fake reviews. These deceptive tactics can take various forms, from businesses inflating their own sales figures with glowing reviews for subpar products to malicious competitors sabotaging a rival's reputation with scathing attacks disguised as customer experiences. The consequences of fake reviews are far-reaching, impacting both consumers and businesses. Misled customers end up with wasted money and a sense of frustration, fostering distrust towards online shopping as a whole. This erosion of trust can have a ripple effect, hindering the growth of e-commerce and creating a climate of scepticism towards online recommendations. Furthermore, fake reviews create an unfair playing field, giving businesses willing to engage in such tactics an undue advantage. Honest businesses that prioritize building trust and rely on genuine customer feedback can be overshadowed by those manipulating the system. Let's delve deeper into the two main sources of fake reviews and their negative impact:

1.1 Sources of Fake Reviews

(Wu et al., 2020):

Online reviews can be a goldmine of information, but beware of manipulation! Businesses may inflate sales through fake positive reviews, either by buying praise from anonymous sources or creating fake accounts to sing their own products' praises. Competitors can also sabotage a business's reputation with fake negative reviews or downvoting positive ones. To be a savvy consumer, develop a critical eye. Unrealistic positivity or negativity across many reviews, generic language, reviews clustered around a product launch, and inactive reviewer profiles are all red flags. Look for reviews on platforms with safeguards against fakery, like purchase verification or suspicious activity detection. Don't ignore negative reviews entirely; constructive criticism can highlight genuine weaknesses. Finally, most platforms allow users to report suspected fake reviews, helping to maintain the integrity of the system. By understanding these tactics and staying vigilant, you can harness the power of online reviews to make informed purchasing decisions.

While online reviews offer a wealth of user experience, navigating their authenticity can be tricky. Businesses might inflate sales through underhanded tactics. One method involves buying glowing reviews, essentially fake praise, from anonymous sources regardless of the product's quality. They might even create fake accounts with fabricated purchase histories to sing their own products' praises. Competitors can also play dirty by posting scathing negative reviews containing false information or exaggerating minor flaws, aiming to dissuade potential customers. They might further manipulate the system by downvoting genuine positive reviews on competitor listings, burying them and making the product appear less appealing. To become a web-savvy consumer, develop a keen eye for red flags. Look for unrealistic positivity or negativity across numerous reviews, generic language lacking specifics, reviews clustered around a product's launch date, and inactive reviewer profiles. Seek out reviews on platforms with safeguards like purchase verification or algorithms that detect suspicious activity patterns. Don't dismiss negative reviews entirely, as they can highlight genuine weaknesses or areas for improvement. Look for constructive criticism that offers valuable insights. Finally, most platforms allow users to report reviews suspected of being fake, helping to maintain the integrity of the online review system. By understanding these tactics and staying vigilant, you can transform online reviews into a powerful tool for informed purchasing decisions.

1.2 Impact of Fake Reviews: A Web of Deception

(Birim et al., 2022; Bathla et al., 2022)

Fake reviews cast a long shadow over the online marketplace, creating a lose-lose situation for both consumers and businesses. Customers, lured by inauthentic praise or discouraged by fabricated negativity, end up making poor purchasing decisions. Imagine trusting glowing reviews for a phone case that ends up shattering easily. This not only leads to financial frustration but also breeds a general distrust towards online shopping, potentially making them hesitant to engage altogether. This erosion of confidence hurts e-commerce growth and fosters a culture of skepticism towards online recommendations. Moreover, fake reviews create an unfair advantage for businesses willing to stoop to such tactics. Ethical companies that prioritize building trust and rely on genuine customer feedback can be overshadowed by those manipulating the system. This fosters an unhealthy competitive environment where honest practices are undermined by a race to the bottom. Essentially, fake reviews become a form of digital deception that weakens the entire online review ecosystem.

Figure 2. Visual representation illustrating the influence and significance of fake reviews on market dynamics, showcasing the potential power they hold in shaping consumer perceptions and market outcomes.

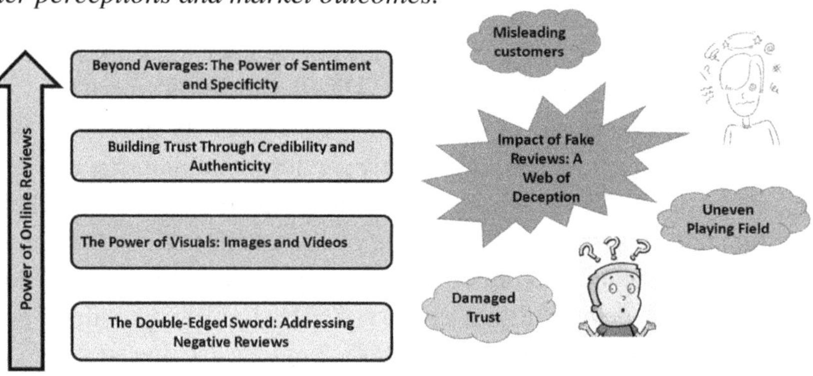

Fake reviews pose a significant threat to the health of e-commerce. To combat this issue, online platforms and businesses need to work together. Platforms can implement stricter review verification methods, utilize technology like Sentiment Analysis to detect suspicious patterns, and encourage transparency by showcasing the reviewer's purchase history. Businesses can prioritize building trust through genuine customer interactions, incentivize honest feedback, and actively address both positive and negative reviews. Only by tackling the problem of fake reviews can we ensure a trustworthy and reliable online shopping experience for everyone.

2 COMBATING FAKE REVIEWS: DETECTION TECHNIQUES

Online reviews have become a crucial element in the digital marketplace, playing a key role in shaping consumer behavior, influencing brand perception, and guiding purchasing decisions. However, the rise of fake reviews threatens to undermine the very foundation of this trust-based system. Fake reviews, which can be either positive or negative, are intentionally crafted to manipulate a product or service's reputation, either boosting it unfairly or sabotaging competitors. The prevalence of such deceptive content has prompted researchers and businesses to seek effective methods to combat fake reviews. In this discussion, we will explore the roles of machine learning (ML) and artificial intelligence (AI) in detecting and eliminating fraudulent reviews, as well as examine the various approaches used to safeguard the integrity of online feedback.

As the volume of e-commerce transactions grows, so too does the challenge of ensuring the authenticity of online reviews. Fake reviews can significantly distort public opinion, leading consumers to make purchasing decisions based on misleading information. These fraudulent reviews can take different forms, such as paid reviews, reviews from bots, or coordinated efforts by groups to manipulate a product's rating. Detecting such content manually is impractical, especially considering the vast amounts of data generated on popular platforms like Amazon, TripAdvisor, and Yelp. The sheer scale of fake reviews requires automated systems capable of filtering out inauthentic content with high accuracy. This is where machine learning and artificial intelligence come into play.

Machine learning has emerged as a powerful tool in the fight against fake reviews. ML algorithms, trained on vast datasets of genuine and fake reviews, are capable of identifying characteristic patterns that distinguish between authentic and fraudulent content. These patterns may include a variety of behavioral, linguistic, and sentiment-based features. One of the most effective ways to detect fake reviews is by analyzing reviewer behavior. For example, fake reviewers may display unusual patterns such as leaving a large number of reviews in a short period, focusing on a narrow range of products, or using similar language across multiple reviews. Machine learning models are trained to detect these anomalies by analyzing user activity, posting frequency, and other metadata that can raise suspicion.

Fake reviews often differ from genuine reviews in terms of linguistic features. By examining factors such as word choice, sentence structure, and tone, machine learning algorithms can identify reviews that deviate from the norm. For instance, fake reviews might contain exaggerated praise or excessively negative language, while genuine reviews are more likely to provide a balanced, nuanced perspective. ML models are trained to recognize such linguistic patterns, allowing them to flag suspicious reviews. Sentiment analysis is another critical tool in fake review detection. This technique involves analyzing the emotional tone of a review to determine whether it aligns with the typical sentiment for that product. Fake reviews often exhibit unusual sentiment patterns, such as extreme positivity or negativity, that are inconsistent with the product's overall rating. By leveraging sentiment analysis, machine learning models can detect reviews that appear artificially polarized.

Building on the foundation of machine learning, deep learning techniques, particularly those involving artificial neural networks, have the potential to further improve the accuracy of fake review detection. Deep learning models, such as Convolutional Neural Networks (CNNs) and Recurrent Neural Networks (RNNs), are capable of learning intricate patterns from large datasets. These models can process vast amounts of review data, identifying subtle patterns that simpler ML models might miss. Deep learning models can be particularly effective in detecting complex patterns in fake reviews, such as inconsistencies in tone, structure, or word choice. These models can also adapt to changing tactics employed by fake reviewers, learning to recognize new types of fraudulent content as they emerge.

Natural Language Processing (NLP) plays a critical role in fake review detection by diving deeper into the language used in reviews. NLP techniques analyze the syntactic and semantic properties of a review, looking for inconsistencies that might indicate inauthentic content. For example, NLP algorithms can detect unusual phrasing, grammar mistakes, or word usage that is uncommon for a native speaker. These linguistic anomalies, when flagged by an NLP system, can help identify reviews that are likely fake.

While machine learning, deep learning, and NLP offer powerful tools for combating fake reviews, combining these approaches can lead to even more effective detection. By leveraging the strengths of each method, researchers can develop comprehensive models capable of analyzing multiple aspects of a review simultaneously. Hybrid models combine different types of analysis to improve accuracy. For example, a model might analyze both reviewer behavior and linguistic features, cross-referencing the results to flag suspicious reviews. By using a combination of techniques, hybrid models can reduce false positives and negatives, leading to more reliable detection. Ensemble learning involves combining multiple machine learning models to improve overall performance. In the context of fake review detection, an ensemble approach might combine a sentiment analysis model, a reviewer behavior analysis model, and an NLP model, each contributing its own insights to the final decision. This multi-faceted approach increases the robustness of the system, making it more difficult for fake reviews to slip through undetected.

Despite the advancements in ML and AI-based fake review detection, there are still significant challenges to overcome. Fake review tactics are constantly evolving, with increasingly sophisticated techniques being used to avoid detection. For example, some fake reviewers may employ more nuanced language or vary their behavior to mimic genuine users. As a result, detection models must continuously adapt to stay ahead of these tactics. Additionally, the effectiveness of ML and AI models depends heavily on the quality and size of the training data. Bias in training data can lead to inaccurate results, while insufficient data may limit the model's ability to generalize across different contexts.

As detection techniques improve, so do the tactics employed by those who create fake reviews. Future research in this area will likely focus on refining existing models, improving scalability, and addressing emerging challenges. Additionally, researchers may explore new techniques, such as graph-based methods for detecting coordinated review manipulation campaigns or blockchain technology for ensuring the transparency and authenticity of online reviews. Combating fake reviews requires a multi-pronged approach that leverages the power of machine learning, deep learning, and natural language processing. By combining these techniques and continuously refining detection models, researchers and businesses can protect the integrity of online reviews, ensuring that consumers can trust the feedback they rely on when making purchasing decisions.

Figure 3. A diagram depicting different approaches for combating fake reviews using Machine-learning algorithms

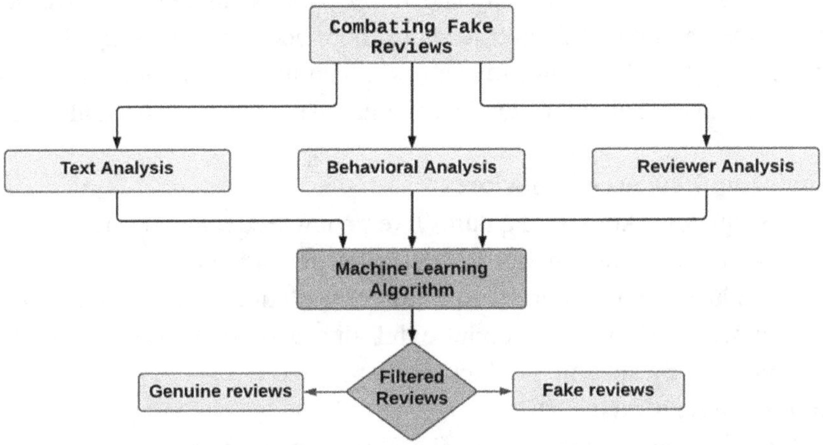

The diagram (Figure 3) depicts the three main categories of detection techniques used to combat fake reviews:

- **Text Analysis:** This section focuses on the content of the review itself. Techniques like Sentiment Analysis compare the written words with the star rating to identify inconsistencies. It also examines unusual vocabulary, repetitive phrases, and generic statements that might indicate automated generation.
- **Behavioral Analysis:** Here, the focus shifts to the reviewer's activity. Factors like review frequency (number of reviews written in a short time), burst patterns (sudden influx of reviews for a product), and activity across different platforms are analyzed to identify suspicious behavior.
- **Reviewer Analysis:** This section investigates the reviewer's profile for red flags. Inconsistencies like a new account with only one review, a suspicious profile picture, or geographically implausible review locations can indicate a fake account.

2.1 Machine Learning Approaches to Combating Fake Reviews

(Dematis, Karapistoli, & Vakali, 2018; Moon, Kim, & Iacobucci, 2021)

Machine learning stands as a powerful weapon in the fight against fake reviews. These algorithms require a massive amount of pre-labeled data, essentially reviews already categorized as real or fake. This data acts as a training ground, teaching the algorithm the "language" of fake reviews by highlighting patterns that differentiate them from genuine ones. The quality and variety of this labeled data are crucial – a diverse and well-annotated dataset leads to more accurate and adaptable models. Here's where machine learning truly shines: it can uncover hidden patterns within reviews and reviewer behavior (details in Figure 4) to sniff out fraudulent activity.

Analyzing Reviewer Behavior:

- Suspicious Activity: Features like review frequency (number of reviews written in a short period), burst patterns (sudden surge of reviews for a product), and activity across different platforms are scrutinized. A reviewer with a new account exhibiting a sudden flurry of positive reviews for a specific product might be a red flag.

Language Analysis:

- Dissecting the Language: The algorithm examines the language used in the review. Features like review length, vocabulary complexity, presence of unusual words or phrases, and repetition are analyzed. Reviews that are extremely short, contain nonsensical phrases, or have very simplistic vocabulary might be indicative of bots or fake accounts.
- Part-of-Speech Distribution: Machine learning can analyze the distribution of different parts of speech (nouns, verbs, adjectives etc.) in a review. Generic or templated reviews often have an unusual distribution, such as a high proportion of adjectives compared to nouns and verbs.

Sentiment Analysis:

- Inconsistency Unmasked: Machine learning models can analyze the sentiment expressed in the review and compare it to the star rating. Inconsistencies, such as a glowing review with a low star rating, or vice versa, can be a sign of manipulation.

Figure 4. Machine Learning Techniques for Analyzing Online Reviews

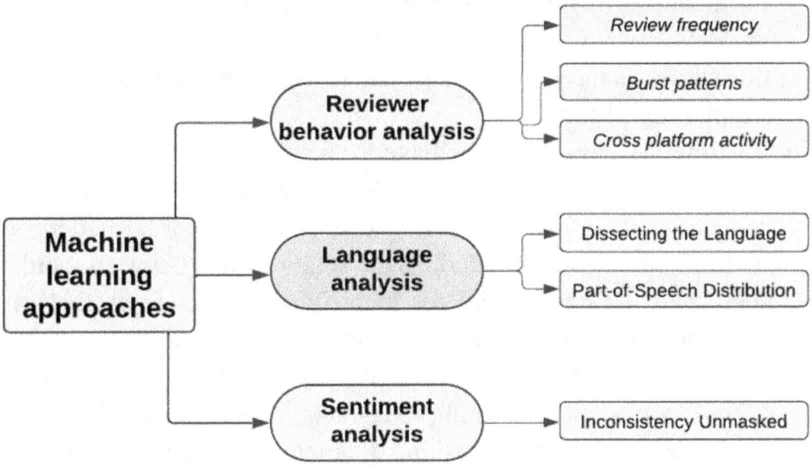

2.2 Deep Learning Techniques for Combating Fake Reviews

(Barbado, Araque, & Iglesias, 2019; Alsubari et al., 2022)

While traditional machine learning algorithms have proven effective in combating fake reviews, deep learning techniques offer a new level of sophistication. By utilizing artificial neural networks with complex architectures, these techniques can learn intricate patterns from massive datasets of reviews, potentially leading to higher accuracy in fake review detection.

Unveiling the Power of Deep Learning:

- Artificial Neural Networks: Deep learning relies on artificial neural networks (ANNs) inspired by the human brain. These networks consist of interconnected layers of processing units (neurons) that learn by adjusting their weights based on the data they are exposed to.
- Complex Pattern Recognition: Compared to traditional algorithms, deep learning models have a much higher capacity for complex pattern recognition. They can analyze not only individual features like word choice but also how these features interact with each other within a review. For instance, a deep learning model might identify a pattern of overly positive adjectives used together alongside a low star rating, potentially indicative of a fake review.

- Large Datasets: Deep learning thrives on vast amounts of data. Fortunately, the realm of online reviews provides a rich source of training data. By leveraging large datasets, deep learning models can capture subtle nuances in language and reviewer behavior that might escape simpler algorithms.

Deep Learning Architectures for Fake Review Detection:

- Recurrent Neural Networks (RNNs): These networks excel at handling sequential data like text. They can capture long-term dependencies within a review, understanding the relationships between words across sentences. This is crucial for identifying fake reviews that might be grammatically correct but lack coherence or logical flow.
- Long Short-Term Memory (LSTM) Networks: A specific type of RNN, LSTMs are adept at learning long-range dependencies. They can effectively deal with the "vanishing gradient" problem, a challenge faced by standard RNNs where earlier information in a sequence can be lost during training. This makes LSTMs particularly suitable for analyzing longer reviews where the overall sentiment or message might depend on information spread across the entire text.

Deep Learning in Action: A Sample Architecture (Chehal, Gupta, & Gulati, 2021; Policarpo et al., 2021; Kauffmann et al., 2020; Kumar et al., 2018)

Figure 5. The Steps of a Deep Learning Model for Review Classification

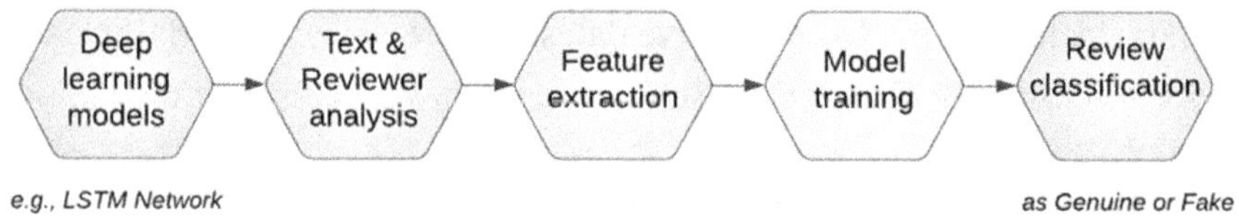

This diagram (Figure 5) depicts a sample deep learning architecture for fake review detection. The text analysis and reviewer analysis sections extract features from the review and reviewer data. A deep learning model, such as an LSTM network, processes these features and learns complex relationships between them. The trained model can then classify new reviews as genuine or fake.

Benefits and Considerations

While machine learning offers a strong foundation for fake review detection, deep learning takes things a step further. Deep learning models have the potential for even higher accuracy, but come at a cost. Training these complex models requires significant computational power, which can be a hurdle for some applications. Additionally, deep learning thrives on massive amounts of training data. To address data limitations, techniques like data augmentation (artificially creating more data) and transfer learning (leveraging knowledge from a different task) can be employed.

In conclusion, deep learning holds immense potential for combating fake reviews by offering a powerful tool for identifying complex patterns and achieving higher accuracy. As research in this area continues to evolve, deep learning techniques will play an increasingly important role in safeguarding the authenticity of online reviews.

2.3 Sentiment Analysis for Combating Fake Reviews

(Hussain et al., 2019; Morid & Shajari, 2012; Sari, Alamsyah, & Wibowo, 2018; Ansari & Gupta, 2021).

Sentiment analysis, a core technique in machine learning approaches to fake review detection, focuses on analyzing the emotional tone of reviews. By identifying unusual sentiment patterns and inconsistencies, it can help expose potentially deceptive reviews. Sentiment analysis is another weapon in the fight against fake reviews. This technique analyzes the emotional tone of a review, categorizing it as positive, negative, or neutral. It does this by examining the words used and their inherent emotional weight. Fake reviews often stick out like sore thumbs under this scrutiny. For instance, a glowing review filled with positive adjectives for a low-quality product might be flagged as suspicious. Sentiment analysis can also identify inconsistencies between the expressed emotion and the product itself. A scathing review of a children's toy raises more red flags than a similar review for a complex appliance.

2.3.1 Sentiment Analysis Techniques

(Hajek, Hikkerova, & Sahut, 2023)

To understand a review's emotional tone, sentiment analysis employs two main techniques. The lexicon-based approach relies on pre-built dictionaries. These dictionaries assign sentiment scores (positive, negative, or neutral) to individual words. The sentiment of a whole review is then calculated by adding up the scores of the words it contains. This offers a quick and easy analysis. However, it can struggle with sarcasm or slang. To overcome such limitations, machine learning comes into play. Here, models are trained on a massive dataset of reviews with already-determined sentiment. This allows the model to learn complex relationships between words and their emotional weight, resulting in a more nuanced analysis that can better capture the true sentiment behind a review.

Sentiment Analysis in Action: A Sample Workflow

Figure 6. A flowchart outlining the stages involved in Sentiment Analysis

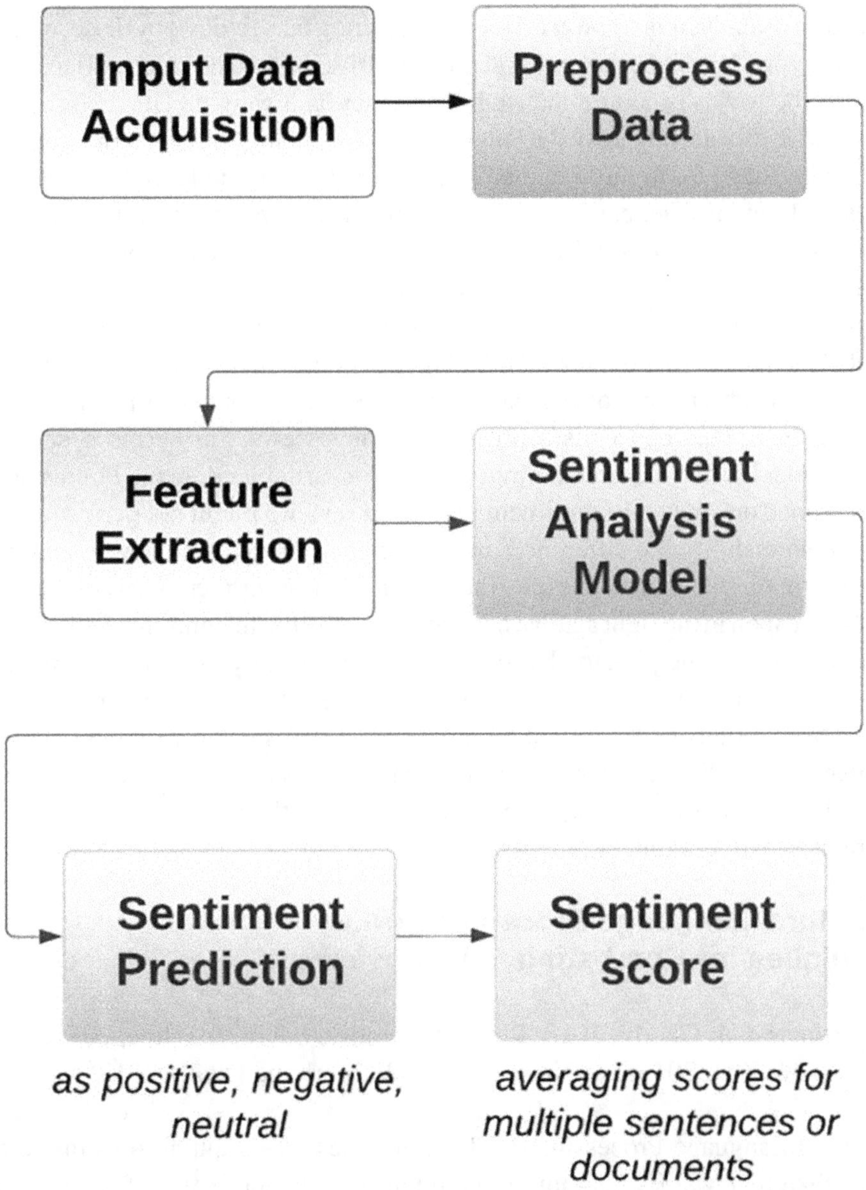

This diagram (Figure 6) depicts a basic Sentiment Analysis workflow. The Sentiment Analysis module takes the review text as input and analyzes it using either a lexicon-based approach or a machine learning model. The output is a sentiment score indicating the overall emotional tone of the review.

Sentiment analysis is a powerful tool for detecting fake reviews by dissecting their emotional core. It assigns sentiment scores (positive, negative, or neutral) to reviews based on the words used and their inherent emotional weight. This helps identify reviews with excessively positive language for low-quality products or excessively negative language for highly-rated products – a red flag for potential manipulation. Additionally, inconsistencies between the sentiment analysis score and the reviewer's star rating can be unearthed. Imagine a review expressing frustration but awarding a perfect 5-star rating – this dissonance might indicate a manipulated review.

However, sentiment analysis has its limitations. Sarcasm and irony, where the intended meaning is the opposite of the literal words, can be tricky. A review laced with sarcasm that's meant to be negative might be misinterpreted as positive by sentiment analysis, leading to misidentified genuine reviews. Furthermore, sentiment analysis models often require training specific to a particular domain. For instance, a model trained on analyzing sentiment in product reviews might not perform well on movie reviews due to the differences in how language is used and how emotions are expressed in those contexts. Despite these limitations, sentiment analysis remains a valuable weapon in the fight against fake reviews, offering insights into the emotional tone of reviews and helping to identify inconsistencies that can signal manipulation.

In conclusion, Sentiment Analysis plays a crucial role in detecting fake reviews. By identifying unusual sentiment patterns and inconsistencies, it helps safeguard the integrity of online reviews and promote a more trustworthy online environment. As Sentiment Analysis techniques continue to evolve, their accuracy in uncovering fake reviews will continue to improve.

2.4 Natural Language Processing (NLP) Techniques for Combating Fake Reviews

(Elmurngi & Gherbi, 2018; Reyes-Menendez, Saura, & Filipe, 2019; Zhang, Bian, & Zhu, 2013; Salminen et al., 2022; Carbonell et al., 2019)

Natural Language Processing (NLP) techniques are essential tools in the fight against fake reviews. By examining the linguistic characteristics of reviews, NLP can analyze word choice, grammar, and sentence structure to identify inconsistencies or unusual phrasing that might be indicative of fake reviews.

To truly understand the language of reviews and sniff out fakes, Natural Language Processing (NLP) dives deeper. NLP techniques extract features from review text that can be fingerprints of deception. One such feature is vocabulary complexity – fake reviews often rely on a simpler vocabulary compared to genuine reviews with a richer word choice. Readability scores also come into play – fake reviews may have lower scores due to less complex sentence structures. NLP can also analyze the grammatical makeup of reviews through Part-of-Speech (POS) tagging. Here, an unusual distribution of parts of speech, like an abundance of adjectives compared to nouns and verbs, can raise a red flag for potentially fake reviews. Finally, Named Entity Recognition (NER) identifies and classifies specific entities within the review text. Fake reviews might contain unusual or irrelevant named entities that don't fit the context of the product or service being reviewed. By analyzing these features in combination, NLP helps us pierce the veil of language used in fake reviews and expose potential deception.

NLP in Action: A Sample Workflow

Figure 7. Feature extraction using Natural Language Processing (NLP)

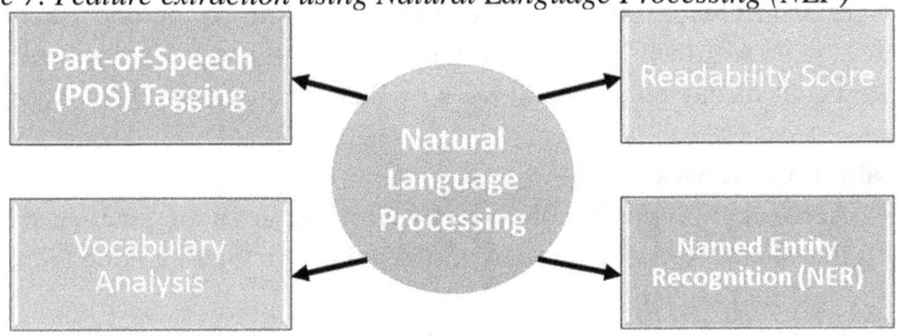

This diagram (Figure 7) depicts a basic NLP workflow for fake review detection. The NLP module analyzes the review text and extracts various linguistic features. These features then become input for further analysis or machine learning models designed to identify fake reviews. NLP peels back another layer in the fight against fake reviews by analyzing the language itself to find patterns indicative of deception. Imagine a review filled with generic statements and cliches, lacking specifics about the product – this might be a red flag. Similarly, repetitive use of specific phrases or a sudden shift in writing style within a single review (like vocabulary or sentence structure) could point to a bot-generated review or a template used for churning out fakes. NLP can even pick up on grammatical errors, though it's important to consider that genuine reviews might also contain them. The key lies in the frequency – an unusually high number of errors could signal a non-native speaker or a hastily written fake review. However, NLP has limitations. Online reviews are full of informal language, slang, and emojis, so NLP models need to be trained on data that reflects this informality to avoid misinterpreting genuine reviews. Additionally, language use can vary greatly between different domains, like tech reviews versus restaurant reviews. To achieve optimal performance, NLP models might require specific training for the domain they're analyzing.

NLP techniques provide a powerful lens for examining the linguistic characteristics of reviews. By identifying inconsistencies, unusual phrasing, and generic language patterns, NLP plays a vital role in detecting fake reviews and ensuring the authenticity of online reviews.

3 EVALUATING AND COMPARING TECHNIQUES FOR COMBATING FAKE REVIEWS

(Thirunarayan et al., 2014; Zhang et al., 2022; Mohawesh et al., 2021; Ahmed et al., 2021; Alamdari et al., 2020; Lau et al., 2012)

The fight against fake reviews necessitates a multi-pronged approach, leveraging various techniques with their individual strengths and weaknesses. Here's a breakdown of the techniques discussed earlier, along with their evaluation and comparison:

Evaluation Metrics:

- **Accuracy:** Proportion of correctly classified reviews (genuine vs. fake)
- **Precision:** Ratio of correctly identified fake reviews among all reviews classified as fake
- **Recall:** Proportion of true fake reviews identified out of all actual fake reviews
- **F1-Score:** Harmonic mean of precision and recall, balancing both metrics

3.1 Comparing Strengths and Weaknesses of Techniques for Combating Fake Reviews

(Beatty et al., 2011; Tan et al., 2016; Wang et al., 2012; Wang et al., 2022)

The fight against fake reviews necessitates a multi-pronged approach, leveraging various techniques with their individual strengths and weaknesses. The analysis results, after comparing Sentiment Analysis, Natural Language Processing (NLP), and Deep Learning (DL) techniques, are tabulated in Table 1.

Table 1. A Comparison of Strengths and Weaknesses of Techniques for Combating Fake Reviews

Technique	*Strengths*	*Weaknesses*
Sentiment Analysis (Beatty et al., 2011; Tan et al., 2016)	- Simple to implement	- Struggles with sarcasm and irony
	- Effective for identifying unusual sentiment patterns	- Domain specificity
Natural Language Processing (Wang et al., 2012)	- Identifies inconsistencies in language use	- Informal language can be misinterpreted
	- Captures grammatical errors	- Domain specificity can affect performance
Deep Learning (Wang et al., 2022)	- High accuracy potential	- High computational cost
	- Learns complex patterns from large datasets	- Data scarcity can hinder model performance

(Beatty et al., 2011; Tan et al., 2016; Wang et al., 2012; Wang et al., 2022).

Figure 8. Effectiveness of fake review detection techniques

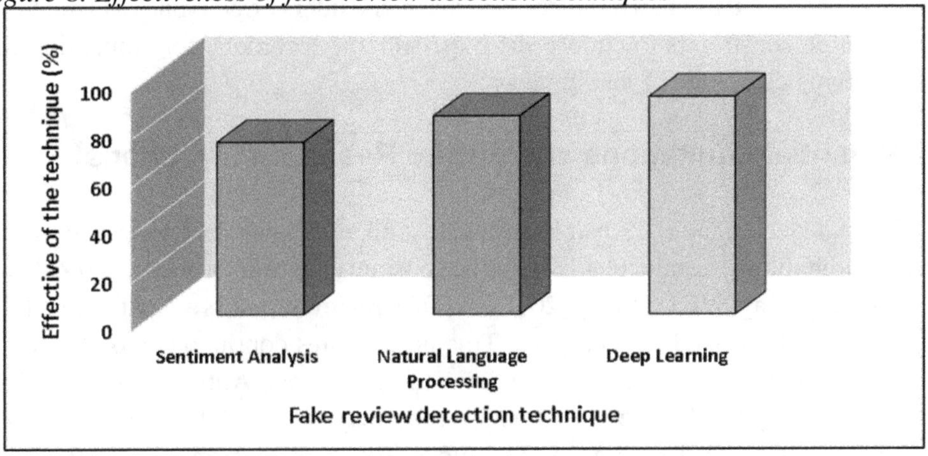

In Figure 8, Deep Learning technique proves to be highly effective, followed by NLP technique, indicating their stronger ability to identify fake reviews compared to Sentiment Analysis technique. However, it's important to remember that these results depend on the data and methods used, and other factors like efficiency and resource requirements should also be considered when choosing the most suitable technique. The chart leans heavily towards Deep Learning (DL) as the most effective technique. Its towering bar signifies a clear advantage in accurately identifying fake reviews compared to Sentiment Analysis and NLP. This dominance likely stems from DL's ability to analyze complex patterns in text data, uncovering subtle cues that human-crafted rules or Sentiment Analysis might miss.

Natural Language Processing (NLP) comes in a respectable second place. Its bar height suggests a solid capability in detecting fake reviews. NLP techniques excel at understanding the structure and meaning of language, allowing them to identify unusual phrasing, grammatical anomalies, or inconsistencies often present in fabricated content. While still valuable, Sentiment Analysis appears less effective based on the shorter bar. This technique focuses on gauging emotional tone, which can be a helpful indicator, but fake reviews creators can manipulate sentiment to deceive readers. Sentiment Analysis might struggle to differentiate between genuine outrage at a real event and outrage fabricated for a fake story. It's crucial to remember that this visualization is a snapshot based on specific data and evaluation methods. The effectiveness of each technique can vary depending on the type of fake reviews being targeted. For instance, NLP might shine with heavily manipulated grammar in political hoaxes, while Deep Learning might excel at identifying cleverly disguised clickbait articles. Highlighting Deep Learning's potential for robust fake reviews detection. However, NLP remains a strong contender, and Sentiment Analysis retains value in specific contexts. Ultimately, the best approach considers effectiveness, efficiency, and resource constraints to choose the most suitable technique for combating the ever-evolving challenge of fake reviews.

3.2 Potential Limitations and Future Research Directions:

No single technique is a silver bullet against fake reviews. Each has its strengths but also limitations. A major challenge is the constant evolution of deception (Zahara, Rini, & Sembiring, 2021; Huang, 2018). As fake review creators adapt their tactics, detection methods need to keep pace. This necessitates continuous monitoring of these evolving tactics and ongoing updates to the models. Another hurdle is data scarcity. Training machine learning models requires a substantial amount of labeled data, which can be hard to come by. Techniques like data augmentation (artificially creating more data) and transfer learning (leveraging knowledge from a different task) can help bridge this gap. Finally, the specter of bias looms large. Machine learning models can inherit biases present in the data they're trained on. To mitigate this, careful data curation and a focus on fairness are essential (Daskalakis et al., 2022; Badotra & Sundas, 2021; Zhang et al., 2023; Bawack et al., 2022).

3.3 Future Research Directions

- **Explainable AI:** Developing models that can explain their reasoning behind classifying a review as fake, fostering trust and transparency.

- **Real-time Detection:** Implementing systems that can detect fake reviews in real-time, preventing their spread and impact.
- **Multimodal Analysis:** Incorporating additional data sources like reviewer profile pictures and review location verification for a more comprehensive analysis.
- **Hybrid Approaches:** Combining various techniques (e.g., Sentiment Analysis + NLP) can leverage their collective

3.3.1 Limitations and Future Research Directions of Fake reviews Detection Techniques

While the bar chart (shown previously) highlights the effectiveness of various techniques for fake reviews detection, each approach has limitations that ongoing research aims to overcome. Here's a detailed analysis of these limitations and promising future research directions for Sentiment Analysis, Natural Language Processing (NLP), and Deep Learning.

3.3.1.1 Sentiment Analysis

Limitation: Oversimplification of Emotions

Sentiment analysis often categorizes emotions into positive, negative, or neutral. Fake reviews creators can exploit this by strategically using positive or negative language to mask their true intent. For instance, an article promoting a fake medical product might use overly positive language about its "miraculous" effects, even though it has no scientific backing.

Figure 9. Limitations of Sentiment Analysis technique in identifying the labels correctly.

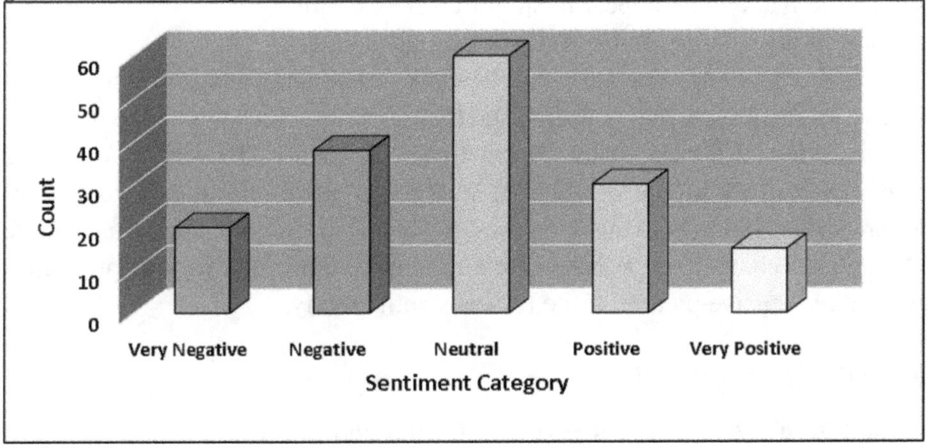

The data displayed in Figure 9 highlights the constraints associated with Sentiment Analysis. The graph depicts various identified labels, spanning from highly negative to highly positive, with the predominant labels being categorized as Neutral.

Future Direction: Multi-Dimensional Sentiment Analysis

The fight against fake reviews constantly evolves, with researchers exploring ways to capture the subtler nuances of human emotion within reviews. One promising area is sarcasm detection, which aims to identify and interpret sarcastic language – a red flag for potentially manipulative content. Additionally, emotional intensity analysis delves deeper, gauging the strength of emotions expressed in the text. A strongly negative sentiment might be more suspicious than a mildly negative one. Finally, contextual sentiment analysis takes things a step further by analyzing words' sentiment within the surrounding text's broader context (Kumar et al., 2022; Benlahbib, Boumhidi, & Nfaoui, 2022; Krishnaiah, 2023). This would help differentiate between genuine expressions of opinion and those strategically used to mislead readers. By incorporating these techniques, researchers are pushing the boundaries of sentiment analysis, making it a more powerful weapon in the fight against deceptive online reviews.

3.3.1.2 Natural Language Processing (NLP)

Limitation: Limited Understanding of Context

NLP excels at identifying patterns in language structure, but it often struggles to grasp the overall context of the content. Fake reviews creators might use grammatically correct language but manipulate the context to mislead readers (Chawla & Kumar, 2022). For example, a fabricated news story might quote someone out of context to make them appear to support a false claim.

Research is focusing on integrating techniques like:

NLP's reach extends beyond the review text itself. Knowledge graphs, massive databases of interconnected concepts and relationships, can be linked to the review text. This allows NLP to understand the factual background of the review and identify inconsistencies. Additionally, NLP can leverage external information sources like news archives or fact-checking databases. By incorporating these external sources, NLP can gain context and verify the claims made within the review, providing a more comprehensive picture of the review's authenticity.

3.3.1.3 Deep Learning (DL)

Limitation: Data Dependence and Explainability

Deep Learning models heavily rely on the quality and quantity of training data. Biases present in the training data can be reflected in the model's outputs (Daskalakis et al., 2022). Additionally, Deep Learning models often lack transparency, making understanding their reasoning behind classifications challenging. For instance, a Deep Learning model trained on biased datasets might be more likely to misclassify news content critical of certain groups.

Figure 10. Limitations of the Deep Learning Technique

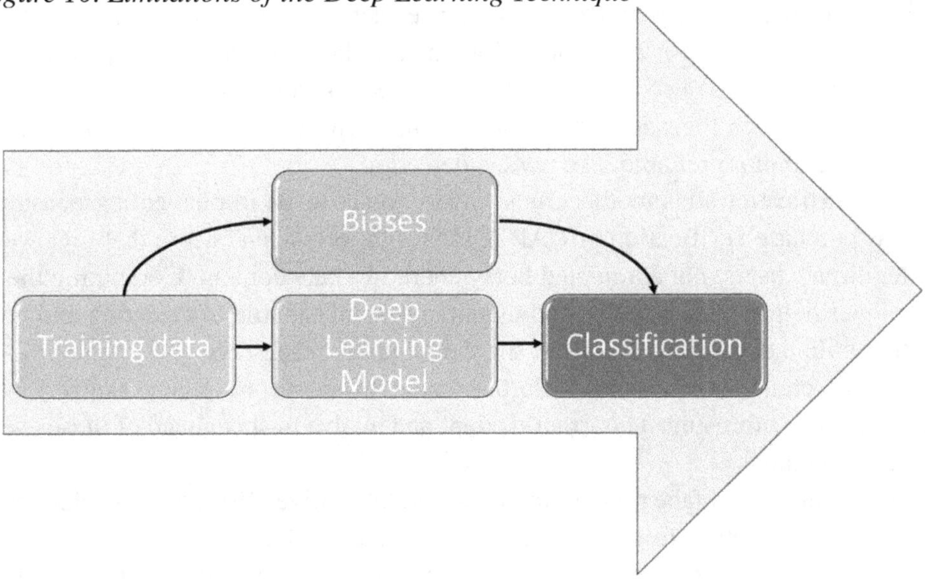

Figure 10 illustrates the limitations of Deep Learning techniques and indicates how biases in the training data can influence the model's output.

3.3.1.4 Explainable AI (XAI)

Explainable AI (XAI) strives to make complex AI models, especially Deep Learning, more transparent. These models often act like black boxes, delivering accurate results but leaving us clueless about their reasoning. XAI techniques like feature importance analysis and attention mechanisms aim to illuminate the decision-making process, fostering trust, enabling bias detection, and guiding model improvements for reliable AI applications.

4 CONCLUSION: THE ENDURING FIGHT FOR ONLINE TRUST

Fake reviews pose a significant threat to online trust and safety. Consumers rely heavily on reviews to make informed decisions, and the presence of misleading or deceptive content can lead to financial losses, wasted time, and even safety concerns. In our analysis, we have unveiled several key tools in the fight against fake reviews, with machine learning, particularly deep learning, playing a crucial role. These models, trained on vast datasets, can identify patterns indicative of deception, such as unusual language use, suspicious user activity, or inconsistencies within the review itself. However, as detection models become increasingly complex, explainable AI (XAI) becomes essential. XAI techniques help us understand how these models reach their decisions, enabling us to mitigate biases that might arise and leading to more reliable fake review detection.

User verification adds another crucial layer of defense. By implementing measures such as purchase verification or CAPTCHAs, platforms can ensure that reviewers are legitimate users, not automated bots generating fake content. Combining these techniques helps create a robust and dynamic system capable of detecting and preventing online deception. However, the battle against fake reviews is ongoing. As detection techniques advance, so do the tactics of those producing fake reviews. Detection algorithms must constantly adapt and evolve to stay ahead of these ever-changing methods.

This fight against fake reviews requires a collaborative effort. Review platforms need to work together to implement more effective safeguards, consumers must remain vigilant and report suspicious activity, and regulatory bodies should play a role in enforcing standards that contribute to a comprehensive solution. The most critical defense, however, lies in empowering consumers. By equipping users with the critical thinking skills to evaluate reviews and identify potential red flags, we can foster a more informed online community that is less susceptible to manipulation by fake reviews.

A multi-pronged approach, combining cutting-edge technology, responsible platform practices, and user empowerment, is essential in creating a more trustworthy and secure online environment. This collective effort will ultimately lead to a healthier e-commerce ecosystem and a safer online experience for everyone. By employing a combination of advanced techniques and fostering a culture of responsibility, we can build an online marketplace where consumers can make informed decisions based on genuine opinions and experiences, and businesses can thrive in a fair and transparent review system.

Looking ahead, future studies should focus on further refining machine learning models, exploring hybrid approaches that integrate multiple detection techniques, and investigating new strategies for user verification. As fake review tactics continue to evolve, research into more sophisticated AI-driven solutions will be crucial in staying ahead of these challenges. Additionally, collaboration between platforms, researchers, and regulatory bodies will be essential in establishing industry-wide standards and best practices for detecting and preventing fake reviews. Ultimately, the ongoing commitment to innovation, collaboration, and user awareness will be the key to ensuring a more trustworthy and reliable online environment for all.

5. FUTURE SCOPE

The pervasive impact of fake reviews on consumer trust and business credibility underscores the critical need for advanced and adaptive detection mechanisms. As the digital landscape evolves, so too do the methods employed by those intent on manipulating online platforms through deceptive reviews. To this end, the future scope of research and development in fake review detection is both expansive and essential, encompassing several promising areas aimed at enhancing the accuracy, efficiency, and adaptability of current technologies.

1. **Integration of Multi-Modal Data Sources:** Future studies could explore the integration of multi-modal data sources to improve fake review detection systems. Currently, most models primarily analyze text. However, integrating other data types, such as metadata, user profile information, and interaction patterns, could provide a more holistic view of reviewer behavior. This approach would allow for the identification of subtle patterns and anomalies that might not be evident through text analysis alone. For instance, combining text analysis with temporal patterns of reviews and the social network structure among reviewers can help detect coordinated fake review campaigns.
2. **Real-Time Detection Systems:** As online platforms continually update their offerings and interact with users in real time, there is a significant need for real-time detection of fake reviews. Developing algorithms that can operate in real time, providing instant assessments of review authenticity, would be a major step forward. This capability would prevent fake reviews from influencing consumer decisions before they are flagged and reviewed by human moderators. Real-time processing involves challenges related to scalability and computational efficiency, which future research will need to address.
3. **Application of Federated Learning: Federated** learning presents a novel opportunity in the realm of fake review detection by enabling multiple organizations to collaborate on model training without sharing sensitive data. This method ensures privacy and data security, encouraging more companies to participate in collective efforts to improve detection algorithms. Research could focus on

developing federated systems that learn from diverse data sources across different platforms and geographies, enhancing the model's ability to generalize across various types of fake reviews.

4. **Advancements in Explainable AI (XAI):** As detection techniques become more sophisticated, the need for transparency and explainability increases. Future work should focus on enhancing the explainability of AI models used in fake review detection. This research would involve developing new frameworks and algorithms that provide clear explanations of the decisions made by AI, making these systems more understandable and trustworthy to humans. Improved explainability will not only increase trust in AI systems but also make it easier for reviewers to understand and improve the detection process.
5. **Deeper Behavioral Analysis:** Incorporating deeper behavioral analysis into detection systems can provide more nuanced insights into the authenticity of reviews. Future research could explore psychological profiling, where AI models identify psychological cues that indicate deception. This approach could also include the analysis of emotional intelligence components, such as empathy or sincerity, which are difficult for deceptive reviewers to mimic convincingly.
6. **Regulatory and Ethical Frameworks:** As technology advances, so must the regulatory and ethical frameworks that govern its use. Future studies should also consider the ethical implications of fake review detection, particularly in terms of privacy, consent, and the potential for bias. Research should aim to establish clear guidelines and standards for ethical AI use in this context, ensuring that detection technologies respect user privacy and are free from biases that could harm certain groups.
7. **Cross-Platform Collaboration:** Enhanced collaboration between different online platforms could significantly improve the effectiveness of fake review detection systems. By sharing insights, data, and successful detection techniques, platforms can create a more unified front against fake review activities. Future research could explore the development of standardized APIs and protocols for data sharing and joint detection efforts, respecting privacy and data security concerns.

REFERENCES

Ahmed, A., Saleem, K., Khalid, O., & Rashid, U. (2021). On deep neural network for trust aware cross domain recommendations in E-commerce. *Expert Systems with Applications, 174*, 114757. DOI: 10.1016/j.eswa.2021.114757

Alamdari, P. M., Navimipour, N. J., Hosseinzadeh, M., Safaei, A. A., & Darwesh, A. (2020). A systematic study on the recommender systems in the E-commerce. *IEEE Access : Practical Innovations, Open Solutions, 8*, 115694–115716. DOI: 10.1109/ACCESS.2020.3002803

Alsubari, S. N., Deshmukh, S. N., Al-Adhaileh, M. H., Alsaade, F. W., & Aldhyani, T. H. (2021). Development of integrated neural network model for identification of fake reviews in E-commerce using multidomain datasets. *Applied Bionics and Biomechanics, 2021*, 2021. DOI: 10.1155/2021/5522574 PMID: 33953796

Alsubari, S. N., Deshmukh, S. N., Alqarni, A. A., Alsharif, N., Aldhyani, T. H., Alsaade, F. W., & Khalaf, O. I. (2022). Data analytics for the identification of fake reviews using supervised learning. *Computers, Materials & Continua, 70*(2), 3189–3204. DOI: 10.32604/cmc.2022.019625

Ansari, S., & Gupta, S. (2021). Customer perception of the deceptiveness of online product reviews: A speech act theory perspective. *International Journal of Information Management, 57*, 102286. DOI: 10.1016/j.ijinfomgt.2020.102286

Badotra, S., & Sundas, A. (2021). A systematic review on security of E-commerce systems. *International Journal of Applied Science and Engineering, 18*(2), 1–19.

Barbado, R., Araque, O., & Iglesias, C. A. (2019). A framework for fake review detection in online consumer electronics retailers. *Information Processing & Management, 56*(4), 1234–1244. DOI: 10.1016/j.ipm.2019.03.002

Bathla, G., Singh, P., Singh, R. K., Cambria, E., & Tiwari, R. (2022). Intelligent fake reviews detection based on aspect extraction and analysis using deep learning. *Neural Computing & Applications, 34*(22), 20213–20229. DOI: 10.1007/s00521-022-07531-8

Bawack, R. E., Wamba, S. F., Carillo, K. D. A., & Akter, S. (2022). Artificial intelligence in E-Commerce: A bibliometric study and literature review. *Electronic Markets, 32*(1), 297–338. DOI: 10.1007/s12525-022-00537-z PMID: 35600916

Beatty, P., Reay, I., Dick, S., & Miller, J. (2011). Consumer trust in e-commerce web sites: A meta-study. *ACM Computing Surveys, 43*(3), 1–46. DOI: 10.1145/1922649.1922651

Benlahbib, A., Boumhidi, A., & Nfaoui, E. H. (2022). Mining online reviews to support customers' decision-making process in e-commerce platforms: A narrative literature review. *Journal of Organizational Computing and Electronic Commerce, 32*(1), 69–97. DOI: 10.1080/10919392.2022.2053454

Birim, Ş. Ö., Kazancoglu, I., Mangla, S. K., Kahraman, A., Kumar, S., & Kazancoglu, Y. (2022). Detecting fake reviews through topic modelling. *Journal of Business Research, 149*, 884–900. DOI: 10.1016/j.jbusres.2022.05.081

Carbonell, G., Barbu, C. M., Vorgerd, L., & Brand, M. (2019). The impact of emotionality and trust cues on the perceived trustworthiness of online reviews. *Cogent Business & Management, 6*(1), 1586062. DOI: 10.1080/23311975.2019.1586062

Chawla, N., & Kumar, B. (2022). E-commerce and consumer protection in India: The emerging trend. *Journal of Business Ethics, 180*(2), 581–604. DOI: 10.1007/s10551-021-04884-3 PMID: 34257470

Chehal, D., Gupta, P., & Gulati, P. (2021). Implementation and comparison of topic modeling techniques based on user reviews in e-commerce recommendations. *Journal of Ambient Intelligence and Humanized Computing, 12*(5), 5055–5070. DOI: 10.1007/s12652-020-01956-6

Das, R., Ahmed, W., Sharma, K., Hardey, M., Dwivedi, Y. K., Zhang, Z., Apostolidis, C., & Filieri, R. (2024). Towards the development of an explainable e-commerce fake review index: An attribute analytics approach. *European Journal of Operational Research, 317*(2), 382–400. DOI: 10.1016/j.ejor.2024.03.008

Daskalakis, E., Remoundou, K., Peppes, N., Alexakis, T., Demestichas, K., Adamopoulou, E., & Sykas, E. (2022). Applications of fusion techniques in e-commerce environments: A literature review. *Sensors (Basel), 22*(11), 3998. DOI: 10.3390/s22113998 PMID: 35684619

Dematis, I., Karapistoli, E., & Vakali, A. (2018). Fake review detection via exploitation of spam indicators and reviewer behavior characteristics. In SOFSEM 2018: Theory and Practice of Computer Science: 44th International Conference on Current Trends in Theory and Practice of Computer Science, Krems, Austria, January 29-February 2, 2018 [Springer International Publishing.]. *Proceedings, 44*, 581–595.

Elmurngi, E. I., & Gherbi, A. (2018). Unfair reviews detection on amazon reviews using Sentiment Analysis with supervised learning techniques. *Journal of Computational Science, 14*(5), 714–726. DOI: 10.3844/jcssp.2018.714.726

Hajek, P., Hikkerova, L., & Sahut, J. M. (2023). Fake review detection in e-Commerce platforms using aspect-based Sentiment Analysis. *Journal of Business Research, 167*, 114143. DOI: 10.1016/j.jbusres.2023.114143

Huang, A. (2018). A risk detection system of e-commerce: Researches based on soft information extracted by affective computing web texts. *Electronic Commerce Research, 18*(1), 143–157. DOI: 10.1007/s10660-017-9262-y

Huang, H., Asemi, A., & Mustafa, M. B. (2023). Sentiment analysis in e-commerce platforms: A review of current techniques and future directions. *IEEE Access : Practical Innovations, Open Solutions, 11*, 90367–90382. DOI: 10.1109/ACCESS.2023.3307308

Hussain, N., Turab Mirza, H., Rasool, G., Hussain, I., & Kaleem, M. (2019). Spam review detection techniques: A systematic literature review. *Applied Sciences (Basel, Switzerland), 9*(5), 987. DOI: 10.3390/app9050987

Kamaruddin, N. (2021). Comparative Study on Sentiment Analysis Approach for Online Shopping Review. [TURCOMAT]. *Turkish Journal of Computer and Mathematics Education, 12*(3), 1358–1370.

Kauffmann, E., Peral, J., Gil, D., Ferrández, A., Sellers, R., & Mora, H. (2020). A framework for big data analytics in commercial social networks: A case study on Sentiment Analysis and fake review detection for marketing decision-making. *Industrial Marketing Management, 90*, 523–537. DOI: 10.1016/j.indmarman.2019.08.003

Krishnaiah, K. R. (2023). Predicting Fake Online Reviews: A Comprehensive Study of Supervised and Semi-Supervised Learning Models. [TURCOMAT]. *Turkish Journal of Computer and Mathematics Education, 14*(03), 392–399.

Kumar, A., Gopal, R. D., Shankar, R., & Tan, K. H. (2022). Fraudulent review detection model focusing on emotional expressions and explicit aspects: Investigating the potential of feature engineering. *Decision Support Systems, 155*, 113728. DOI: 10.1016/j.dss.2021.113728

Kumar, A., Gopal, R. D., Shankar, R., & Tan, K. H. (2022). Fraudulent review detection model focusing on emotional expressions and explicit aspects: Investigating the potential of feature engineering. *Decision Support Systems, 155*, 113728. DOI: 10.1016/j.dss.2021.113728

Kumar, N., Venugopal, D., Qiu, L., & Kumar, S. (2018). Detecting review manipulation on online platforms with hierarchical supervised learning. *Journal of Management Information Systems, 35*(1), 350–380. DOI: 10.1080/07421222.2018.1440758

Lau, R. Y., Liao, S. Y., Kwok, R. C. W., Xu, K., Xia, Y., & Li, Y. (2012). Text mining and probabilistic language modeling for online review spam detection. [TMIS]. *ACM Transactions on Management Information Systems*, *2*(4), 1–30. DOI: 10.1145/2070710.2070716

Mewada, A., & Dewang, R. K. (2022). Research on False Review Detection Methods: A state-of-the-art review. *Journal of King Saud University. Computer and Information Sciences*, *34*(9), 7530–7546. DOI: 10.1016/j.jksuci.2021.07.021

Mohawesh, R., Tran, S., Ollington, R., & Xu, S. (2021). Analysis of concept drift in fake reviews detection. *Expert Systems with Applications*, *169*, 114318. DOI: 10.1016/j.eswa.2020.114318

Mohawesh, R., Xu, S., Tran, S. N., Ollington, R., Springer, M., Jararweh, Y., & Maqsood, S. (2021). Fake reviews detection: A survey. *IEEE Access : Practical Innovations, Open Solutions*, *9*, 65771–65802. DOI: 10.1109/ACCESS.2021.3075573

Moon, S., Kim, M. Y., & Iacobucci, D. (2021). Content analysis of fake consumer reviews by survey-based text categorization. *International Journal of Research in Marketing*, *38*(2), 343–364. DOI: 10.1016/j.ijresmar.2020.08.001

Morid, M. A., & Shajari, M. (2012). An enhanced e-commerce trust model for community based centralized systems. *Electronic Commerce Research*, *12*(4), 409–427. DOI: 10.1007/s10660-012-9099-3

Paul, H., & Nikolaev, A. (2021). Fake review detection on online E-commerce platforms: A systematic literature review. *Data Mining and Knowledge Discovery*, *35*(5), 1830–1881. DOI: 10.1007/s10618-021-00772-6

Policarpo, L. M., da Silveira, D. E., da Rosa Righi, R., Stoffel, R. A., da Costa, C. A., Barbosa, J. L. V., & Arcot, T. (2021). Machine learning through the lens of e-commerce initiatives: An up-to-date systematic literature review. *Computer Science Review*, *41*, 100414. DOI: 10.1016/j.cosrev.2021.100414

Reyes-Menendez, A., Saura, J. R., & Filipe, F. (2019). The importance of behavioral data to identify online fake reviews for tourism businesses: A systematic review. *PeerJ. Computer Science*, *5*, e219. DOI: 10.7717/peerj-cs.219 PMID: 33816872

Salminen, J., Kandpal, C., Kamel, A. M., Jung, S. G., & Jansen, B. J. (2022). Creating and detecting fake reviews of online products. *Journal of Retailing and Consumer Services*, *64*, 102771. DOI: 10.1016/j.jretconser.2021.102771

Sari, P. K., Alamsyah, A., & Wibowo, S. (2018, March). Measuring e-Commerce service quality from online customer review using Sentiment Analysis. []. IOP Publishing.]. *Journal of Physics: Conference Series, 971*, 012053. DOI: 10.1088/1742-6596/971/1/012053

[] Singh, Y., Teotia, R., Kadian, K., Garhwal, S., & Dwivedi, V. (2024). Fake Review Detection and Removal: A Comparative Analysis using ML and DL Models. Grenze International Journal of Engineering & Technology (GIJET), 10(1).

Tan, F. T. C., Guo, Z., Cahalane, M., & Cheng, D. (2016). Developing business analytic capabilities for combating e-commerce identity fraud: A study of Trustev's digital verification solution. *Information & Management, 53*(7), 878–891. DOI: 10.1016/j.im.2016.07.002

Thirunarayan, K., Anantharam, P., Henson, C., & Sheth, A. (2014). Comparative trust management with applications: Bayesian approaches emphasis. *Future Generation Computer Systems, 31*, 182–199. DOI: 10.1016/j.future.2013.05.006

Vidanagama, D. U., Silva, T. P., & Karunananda, A. S. (2020). Deceptive consumer review detection: A survey. *Artificial Intelligence Review, 53*(2), 1323–1352. DOI: 10.1007/s10462-019-09697-5

Wang, G., Xie, S., Liu, B., & Yu, P. S. (2012). Identify online store review spammers via social review graph. [TIST]. *ACM Transactions on Intelligent Systems and Technology, 3*(4), 1–21. DOI: 10.1145/2337542.2337546

Wang, Q., Zhang, W., Li, J., Mai, F., & Ma, Z. (2022). Effect of online review sentiment on product sales: The moderating role of review credibility perception. *Computers in Human Behavior, 133*, 107272. DOI: 10.1016/j.chb.2022.107272

Wu, Y., Ngai, E. W., Wu, P., & Wu, C. (2020). Fake online reviews: Literature review, synthesis, and directions for future research. *Decision Support Systems, 132*, 113280. DOI: 10.1016/j.dss.2020.113280

Zahara, A. N., Rini, E. S., & Sembiring, B. K. F. (2021). The Influence of Seller Reputation and Online Customer Reviews towards Purchase Decisions through Consumer Trust from C2C E-Commerce Platform Users in Medan, North Sumatera, Indonesia. *International Journal of Research and Review, 8*(2), 422–438.

Zhang, G., Li, Z., Huang, J., Wu, J., Zhou, C., Yang, J., & Gao, J. (2022). efraudcom: An e-commerce fraud detection system via competitive graph neural networks. [TOIS]. *ACM Transactions on Information Systems, 40*(3), 1–29. DOI: 10.1145/3474379

Zhang, X., Guo, F., Chen, T., Pan, L., Beliakov, G., & Wu, J. (2023). A Brief Survey of Machine Learning and Deep Learning Techniques for E-Commerce Research. *Journal of Theoretical and Applied Electronic Commerce Research*, *18*(4), 2188–2216. DOI: 10.3390/jtaer18040110

Zhang, Y., Bian, J., & Zhu, W. (2013). Trust fraud: A crucial challenge for China's e-commerce market. *Electronic Commerce Research and Applications*, *12*(5), 299–308. DOI: 10.1016/j.elerap.2012.11.005

Zheng, X., Zhu, S., & Lin, Z. (2013). Capturing the essence of word-of-mouth for social commerce: Assessing the quality of online e-commerce reviews by a semi-supervised approach. *Decision Support Systems*, *56*, 211–222. DOI: 10.1016/j.dss.2013.06.002

Chapter 6
Direct to Consumer Brands (D2C): Business Model Innovation Using Artificial Intelligence

Rahul Gupta
https://orcid.org/0000-0003-2823-9526
Jain University, India

Rupesh Kumar M.
https://orcid.org/0000-0002-6229-6885
Alliance University, India

Bharathi S. Gopal
IBS School, India

ABSTRACT

The convergence of evolving consumer profiles, digital access, and ease of online product discovery in the mid-2010s created a virtuous cycle. This gave rise to first-generation entrepreneurs who launched D2C brands with minimal capital, relying on consumer insights and identifying gaps in a competitive market. D2C websites acted as consumer labs, offering insights into consumer behavior. As these brands faced distribution bottlenecks, they began diversifying their channels. Savings from streamlined inventory and distribution were reinvested into customer acquisition via aggressive search engine and social media campaigns. D2C brands adopted various technologies—such as voice search, AI-driven conversations, augmented reality, recommender systems, image recognition, and blockchain—to enhance

DOI: 10.4018/979-8-3693-8512-8.ch006

customer experiences. These technologies not only simplified website navigation but also boosted engagement and conversions. The future of D2C brands lies in vertical integration and the digital transformation of offline businesses.

1. INTRODUCTION

For decades, consumer brands in the Indian market were dominated by family businesses and multinational corporations in consumer-packaged goods (also known as fast-moving consumer goods or FMCG as an acronym), fashion, beauty and personal care and electronics categories. The entry barriers to starting a business such as capital requirements to set up a factory, establish brand differentiation through mass media advertising and setting up a nationwide distribution network were a few of the deterrents, even after abolishing industrial licensing and economic reforms of 1991.

1.1 Evolution of D2C Brands

Then the proliferation of the internet helped in mass-adoption of tools required in starting and scaling a business. Over the next two decades, direct to consumer (D2C) brands emerged in the USA. Bonobos (2007), Dollar Shave Club (Shaving Razors in 2010), Casper (mattresses), Warby Parker (eyeglasses), and the Honest Company (baby and beauty products) were a few of them. This marked an inflection point for the sector. Direct to consumer brands (D2C) started to emerge in India around the same time with many of the startups imitating the business model of their US counterparts, Lens kart and Wakefit being a couple of them.

Building a brand in India was not just expensive but also took several years as the retail landscape was heavily dotted with mom-and-pop stores. The distribution costs and the costs to reach a customer were high. The mom-and-pop stores had store formats of about 200 sq. ft space with a countertop and had shelves behind with a wide range of products. The advent of supermarket formats in the late 1990s allowed customers to touch, feel, glance and find the brand and then the online retail caught up with customers in the late 2000s. There was also the emergence of millennial consumers **(See Figures 1 and 2)** in the second decade (2010-2020) who were willing to shop online, spend more and live on credit. As a result, there were more efficient and less capital-intensive ways of reaching customers such as optimization of marketing and inventory investments.

Figure 1. Population by Age Cohort

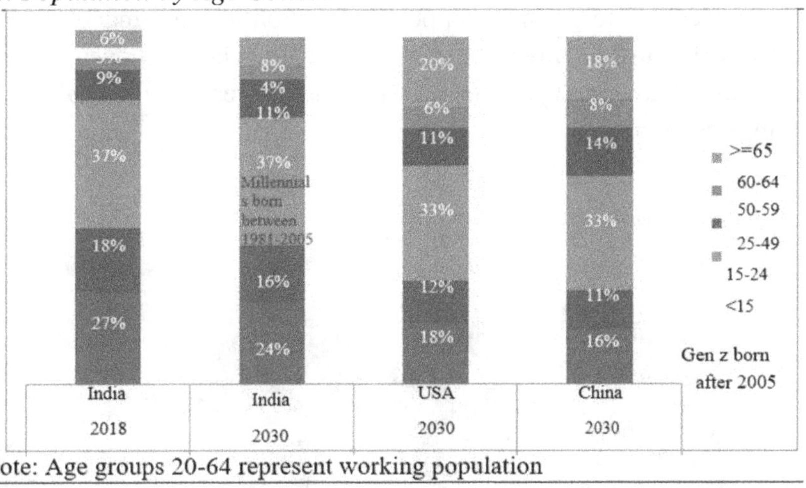

Note: Age groups 20-64 represent working population
Source: https://www.euromonitor.com/population

Figure 2. Online Shoppers by Age Group

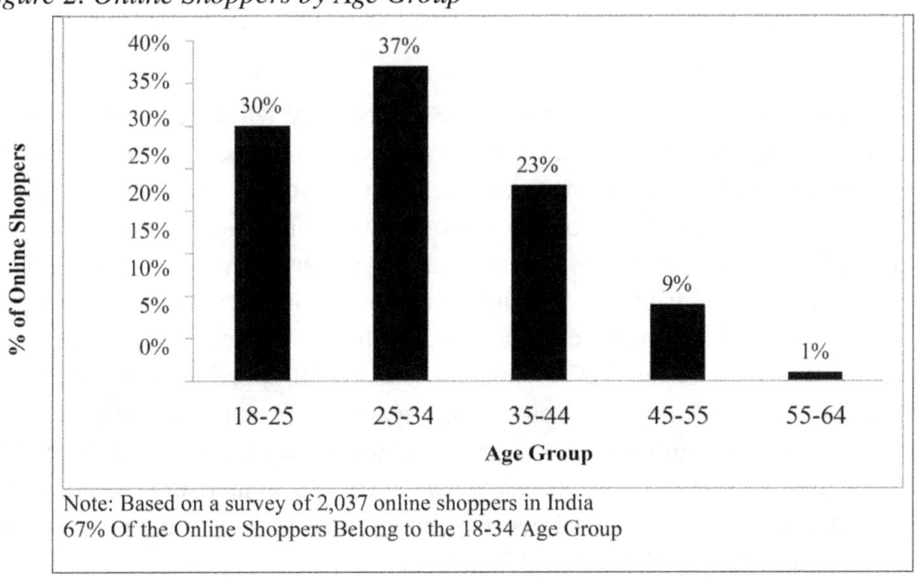

Source: https://inc42.com/reports/decoding-indias-100-bn-d2c-opportunity-market-landscape- and-trends-report-2021/

The large, established brands were seeing the opportunity further down in the customer pyramid, which was an underserved, tougher but a larger market. But the customer pyramid itself is changing with a bulge in the middle **(See Figure 3)**. D2C startups decided to go in the opposite direction of mass market brands such as those from Hindustan Unilever Ltd. (HUL), India's largest consumer packaged goods company that were trying to crack the code of reaching out to customers at the bottom of the pyramid.

Figure 3. Income Segments

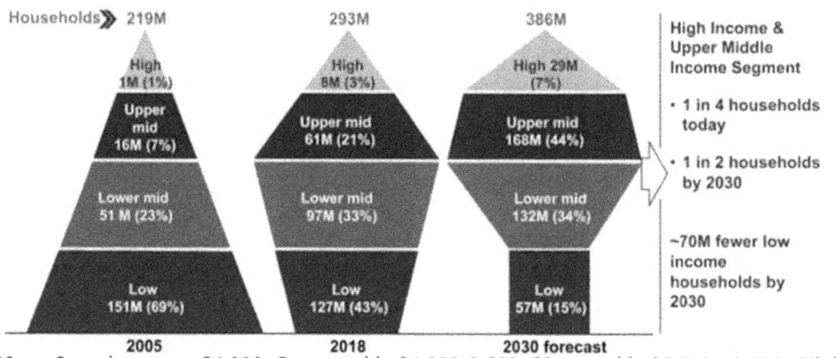

Note: Low income: <$4,000, Lower-mid: $4,000-8,500, Upper-mid: $8,500-40,000, High income: >$40,000 basis income per household in real terms; Projections with annual GDP growth assumed at 7.5%

Source: https://www.weforum.org/docs/WEF_Future_of_Consumption_Fast-Growth_Consumers_markets_India_report_2019.pdf

The middle of the second decade of the 21st century witnessed a convergence of the trends such as changing consumer profile, consumer access modalities and ease of product and brand discovery online. The traditional way of marketing and advertising was being upended by the rise of digital marketing. Social media marketing platforms allowed brands to reach consumers far and wide by getting word out of their product offerings through influencer marketing, organic social and paid social. This created a virtuous cycle and led to the emergence of first-generation entrepreneurs. They started D2C companies with bootstrapped capital armed with consumer insights and identification of white spaces in a competitive market. They disrupted the way consumer brands were being built in India and even globally. The first generation of D2C companies were characterized by rented and shared supply chains, internet-only presence, direct distribution, use of social media to acquire customers and a unique visual brand identity.

Many D2C brands emerged in market niches such as Tata Coffee's Sonnets and Tata Tea 1868, a luxury tea range. Sonnets was a premium roast and ground coffee range priced upwards of 10,000/kg compared to a standard pack of 500- 1000/kg. Similarly, the number of new brand launches in women's lingerie category went up from 24 a month in offline channels to 150 a month in online channel. Customers increasingly favored the ease, convenience, customizability and the choice of ordering directly from D2C brands. The D2C companies were able to scale up faster and achieve revenues of 1 billion in 3 years, which would have otherwise taken 5-7 years using offline channel **(See Figure 4)**.

Figure 4. Number of Years Taken by D2C Brands to Cross 1Billion Revenue in India

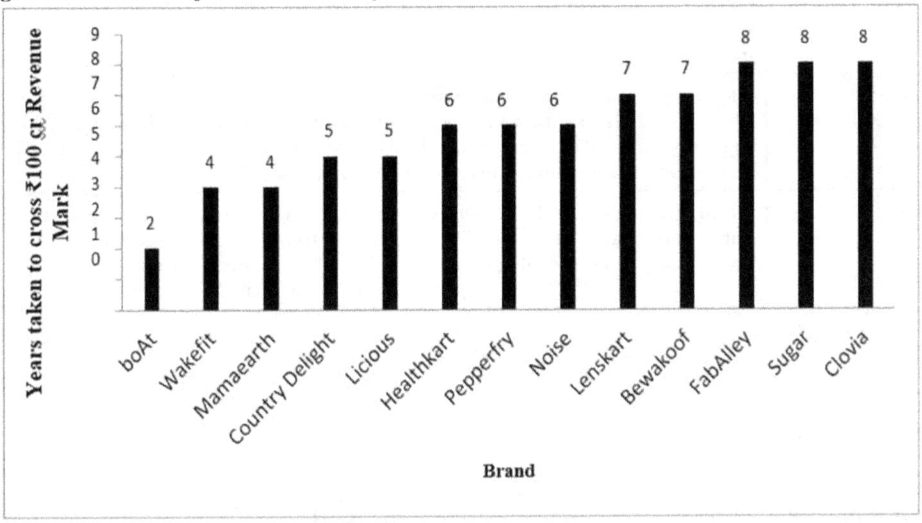

Source: https://inc42.com/reports/decoding-indias-100-bn-d2c-opportunity-market-landscape-and-trends-report-2021/

1.2 Salient Characteristics of D2C Industry

Grocery, fashion, Beauty and Personal Care and Electronics are the biggest categories in the India D2C market

Table 1. Key Trends and Success Factors of D2C Market

	Key Trends	Key Success Factors
Electronics	Increasing demand for premium products Rising popularity of wearables, fitness and audio devices Shift towards Indian manufacturers	Achieving Product market fit User driven innovation Amplifying brand narrative Engagement led communication
Beauty and Personal Care	Leveraging digital channels and Technology Offering Personalization and subscription-based solutions Increasing demand for sustainable products	Innovation and Product Development Sustainability
Fashion	Integrating technology for better experience Shift towards sustainable fashion Celebrity and influencer owned labels Personalization and customization of offerings	Revenue optimization due to higher AOV's Demand driven product assortment by leveraging data analytics Enhanced Customer Experience
Grocery	Unadulterated and fresh offers Subscription and customization model Transparency in Product offering	Quality and Differentiation Optimizing E-commerce platforms to enhance conversion rates Supply Chain Management

Source: 1lattice.com

1.3 Market Size

A report by Goldman Sachs mentioned that the workforce from the urban middle class (having an annual income of over $11,000) was 27 million. This was just 2% of India's population. But for an emerging brand, it becomes a big enough target group. Another study by KEN showed that the number of active internet users in India (consumers who did at least one e-commerce transaction in a year in 2023, excluding entertainment apps and digital wallets) were approximately 140 million (80 million first time users, 40 million occasional and 20 million frequent users) which is a mere 10 percent of India's population.

Marketers tracking the industry have taken a leaf out of China's e-commerce growth story and are of the opinion that e-commerce in India will grow in proportion to the growth in per capita GDP which was $2000 in 2018. A Bain & Co. and Flipkart report projects online shoppers to reach 350 million in India by 2025 growing at a CAGR of 28.5% **(See Figure 5)**. The D2C segment in India will be a $61 billion opportunity by 2027, according to a report by 1lattice.

Figure 5. Growth in online shopper in India till 2025

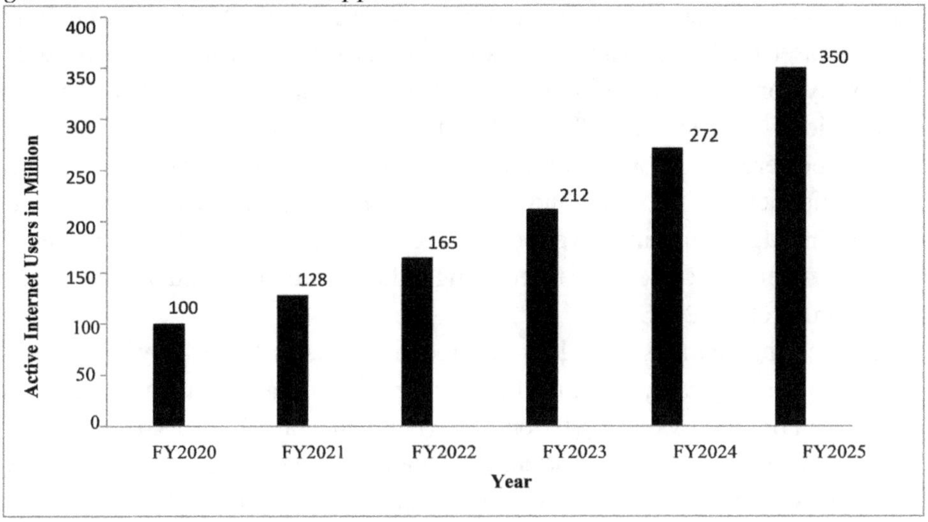

Source: https://www.bain.com/insights/how-india-shops-online/

2. LITERATURE REVIEW

The Direct-to-Consumer Model has redefined the traditional retail businesses by eliminating the mediators and developing a direct relationship with the consumers because disintermediation reduces costs, enabling better margins and pricing control (Chatterjee, 2020). The digital platforms, such as e-commerce, mobile apps, and social media, replace traditional distribution and retail models (Lemon & Verhoef, 2016). If we look at the example of Dollar Shave Club, they focused on viral marketing and subscription models (Wirtz et al., 2016).

This model is particularly relevant in the context of digital transformation and evolving consumer preferences for personalized, accessible, and value-driven products (Gielens & Steenkamp, 2019). The high competition on digital platforms leads to expensive customer acquisition strategies (Chen et al., 2020). According to a report by Deloitte (2021), millennials and Gen Z consumers prefer brands with direct interaction, faster delivery, and value transparency.

AI-driven social ad platforms like Meta use reinforcement to optimize ad delivery for D2C brands (Chatterjee, 2020). Subscription-based and bundled pricing models are also optimized using AI-driven analytics (Chen & Bell, 2020). A company named Stich Fit uses AI based Style Algorithm for personalized cloth curation (Chen et al., 2020). Unlike traditional retail, D2C enables brands to establish a direct digital interface with consumers, while AI augments their ability to personalize, automate, and optimize customer experiences and operations. Furthermore, AI, big data analytics, and cloud-based CRM tools support personalized experiences (Shankar et al., 2021).

Nowadays, brands utilize AI to transform the customer data into real-time product customization (Nguyen et al., 2021). Brands like Lenskart use chatbots and voice assistance powered by NLP which reduces the operational cost and increases the customer interaction efficiency and AI help them in effective eyewear selection. Deep learning algorithms improve forecast accuracy by analyzing historical and external data. AI-enhanced demand forecasting reduces stock-outs and overproduction (Fosso Wamba et al., 2018).

The emerging markets may lack the technical maturity to fully leverage AI tools (Fosso Wamba et al., 2021). The overuse of automation may reduce human connection in brand-customer relationships (Nguyen et al., 2021). The AI promise in Direct to Consumer is vast, but ethical handrails are essential. AI models may inherit biases from training data, leading to ethical issues in customer treatment (Zeng et al., 2022).

3. OBJECTIVES OF THE STUDY

1. To understand the evolution and growth of D2C market.
2. To comprehend the market with market research and use of marketing channels.
3. To know the consumer behaviour and customer acquisition through above the line and below the line activities.
4. To appreciate the supply chain and the use of technology to enhance customer experience.
5. To recognize the importance of engagement through community building.
6. To understand the role of venture capitalist in crafting the D2C market.
7. To know the outlook for the future of D2C Brands in the competitive market.

4. MARKET RESEARCH

Market Research was the domain of large Consumer Packaged Goods (CPG) and consumer companies facing companies to measure product and brand performance to generate shopper insights. About a decade back (2010), it took 3 months to launch a campaign or brand, involving a lengthy process of questionnaire design, recruitment of respondents, analysis and finally converting the insight into action. D2C startups cannot wait for 2-3 months running large surveys and have to onboard online much faster. The campaign lifecycles have crunched to an extent that content can be produced overnight. This ensures that go to market, feedback and measurement is fast.

The direct website acts as a consumer lab and helps companies better understand consumer behavior. Instead of obtaining information through consumer surveys which are sometimes notorious for false positives or negatives as the findings are based on small sample size, D2C brands undertake review mining of the visitors and transactions on their website by analyzing the search queries to understand shifts in consumer behavior, complaints and feedback.

For instance, the founders of SkinKraft and Vedix, Chaitanya Nallan, Sangram Simha, and Veerendra Shivhara, considered launching the venture after understanding consumer insights from their websites stylecraze.com and momjunction.com. These two sites attracted 40-50 million visitors a month. Data mining of consumer logs and reviews revealed that each woman's skin and hair was different and that a single product does not work for everyone. Prospects who visited the company website were asked to participate in an online survey to seek information on location, climate, lifestyle, color and fragrances. The algorithms crunched the customer data to devise the right products with specific ingredients. SkinKraft deployed data science to carve a unique identity in the cluttered space of both online and offline brands by leveraging personalized recommendations for winning customer loyalty.

Another interesting D2C model was boAt, founded by Aman Gupta in 2016. The founder gained access to user pain points after analyzing the reviews on Amazon as customers complained of broken cord for apple chargers. The first product the company launched was an indestructible Apple charger and cable as the Apple cable used to break near the electrical socket end. This was priced on par with the Apple cable. boAt launched its second product, earphones with loud bass as the differentiator as it dawned on the product team that the Indian culture exposes individuals to musical instruments such as tabla and dhol, both high bass musical instruments. The brand signed on celebrities like Hardik Pandya, Kiara Advani and Diljit Dosanjh to attract youth, and collaborated with brands, events, movies and influencers restating its youth centric and lifestyle brand image e.g., Marvel. Bira 91`Masaba, Lakme Fashion Week. The company has since positioned itself as an ear-wear brand selling lifestyle electronics accessories.

D2C brands can collect four types of data- videos, chats, photographs and surveys to generate insights in a matter of days. D2C Companies can carry out A/B testing on a scale. They can test messages, packaging, product ingredients, and campaigns on their website before going omni channel to distribute their products through marketplaces and modern trade. D2C companies can obtain qualitative feedback which is important to understand the gap the brand is trying to address, customers' online behavior, their pain points, reasons for customer delight and the possibility of offering reviews and ratings.

D2C brands can measure Net Promoter Score (NPS) at checkout and monitor after a usage period of 15 days if the customers are detractors or promoters. D2C brands can also check for campaign effectiveness on YouTube and Facebook. Brand lift studies can be conducted by simulating sales before running an advertising campaign on YouTube with an experiment group and a control group. Social listening helps in understanding the consumer sentiment towards the brand.

5. CONSUMER BEHAVIOR

One of the trends and themes which many D2C companies' rode was the consumer shift away from synthetic to organic, natural products, pioneered by the poster boy of the industry, Baba Ramdev of Patanjali Ayurveda. Many others latched on to the bandwagon inspired by brands earlier launched in the US market. For instance, in 2019, clean beauty was the biggest celebrity trend resulting in a demand for products that were vegan and cruelty- free. These brands were further promoted with celebrities like Kourtney Kardashian and Gwyneth Paltrow regaling fans by extolling the virtues of clean beauty. Many home-grown clean beauty brands like Mama Earth and WOW were providing sustainable alternatives to chemical-laden skin care products from big multinationals. However, the US brands were different from their Indian counterparts in using a simple design built to offer a great customer experience and use of marketing methods to build an audience swiftly by creating unique and viral sales campaigns.

A young couple in India, Varun and Gazal Alagh could not find a suitable baby care product for their newborn which was safe and free of chemicals. This led them to start a company named Mamaearth by launching natural, plant-based baby care products catering to millennial parents. According to the founders, the ingredients for the products are sourced from around the world. These ingredients were ISO, GMP and non-GMO compliant. The company followed an asset light model by outsourcing R&D to freelance scientists in Australia and Switzerland for initial product development, the production to contract manufacturers in both India and China and warehousing and last mile deliveries to customers through third party logistics providers. Since then, Mamaearth has diversified into a wide range of skin care, hair care, body care and color cosmetics. To stay relevant among millennial parents, Mamaearth signed actress Shilpa Shetty to talk directly to customers from a mother's point of view. The company clocked revenues of 17 billion in 2023 and has gone on to launch brands such as Derma, Aqualogic, Ayuga, etc. The success of Mamaearth spawned a series of imitators like Priyanka Raina's Maate, Mother Sparsh, Bumchum and the baby Atelier.

Suhasini and Anindita Sampath who were sisters and educated in the US teamed up to launch Yoga Bar in 2014, a health food brand for the Indian market that suffered from an entrenched belief that health does not sell. The founder-sisters realized the lack of healthy snacking options and launched a natural energy bar which is a great source of protein and essential nutrients like quinoa, millets, flax, peanuts, oats, almonds and chia seeds. The duo was very mindful of what goes on inside the product and ensured that their products do not contain any sugar, corn starch, additives or preservatives and are gluten free. They successfully extended their products into breakfast by launching muesli, oats and peanut butter.

Bala Sarda founded Vahdam teas in 2015 with a mission to make better tea available in every corner of the world. He was a 4th generation entrepreneur to enter the eight-decade old family business. He discovered that prime flavor and freshness found in tea was lost with passage of time as it passed through auction houses and several middlemen. He took this revolutionary idea and tied it all up in a modern approach of wellness to launch Vahdam teas, which brings fresh tea to the cup of consumers, by sourcing and packaging directly from the plantations. Every Vahdam tea pack is sent to the customer with a note from the CEO explaining the origins of the company and the tea heritage. The herbal teas of Vahdam are 100% organic, caffeine free and non-toxic. The whole leaf teas are non-bitter, more nutritious and better for the health of consumers. And if consumers don't like the tea, Vahdam offers a 7-days Money Back Guarantee, no questions asked. Vahdam teas is today shipped to more than 100 countries.

Founded by Vivek Gupta in 2015, Licious is a direct-to-home clean meat and seafood delivery company in a highly unorganized, fragmented industry valued at $40 billion. In India, 99 percent of the meat and seafood sold was in the wet markets and the product was characterized by high perishability. The brand promised its meat to be free of chemicals and antibiotics, non-fibrous and tender. This promise was fulfilled by the company's farm-to-fork model. It owned the entire back-end supply chain fueled by strict cold chain control (temperature-controlled environment between 0 and 4 degrees). This helped to maintain the quality and freshness of each product across all stages, from procurement, processing, storage and delivery to the customer.

HRX, owned by actor Hrithik Roshan, started off as an affordable active wear and positioned itself as a collection inspired by Hrithik Roshan's style and his lifelong dedication to achieving fitness. The brand has forged strategic partnerships with online fashion platform MYNTRA and health platform cult fit, which has helped it achieve rapid customer acquisition. The brand created engaging content, including workout videos, fitness tips and motivational messages to build brand loyalty. HRX collaborated with four IPL teams by becoming the official fan merchandise partner. The brand has evolved from a fitness brand to a lifestyle brand by expanding presence in cross category product lines and ventured into healthy food habits by launching HRX by Eat fit in CY22.

The advantages of buying from D2C channels include price benefits, quality assurance, authenticity assurance, improved customer service, wide selection, exclusive benefits, convenience, loyalty benefits, expert advice, availability, customization options and specialized services.

The disadvantages of buying from D2C channels include higher prices, limited variety, lack of product diversity, long shipping times, no disadvantages, limited availability, limited discounts, high shipping costs, limited comparison, quality uncertainty, customer service issues, delivery problems, time consuming, separate purchasing inconvenience, no price matching and lack of direct purchase knowhow.

6. CUSTOMER ACQUISITION

The D2C startups growth was aided by availability of venture capital, few players and an advertising arbitrage by leveraging cost-effective social media platforms. The direct-to-consumer companies invested in establishing a web presence and a team of digital marketers to acquire customers in contrast to the brick-and-mortar retailers who relied on above-the-line (ATL) activities such as mass media advertising and below-the-line (BTL) activities such as sales promotion to acquire customers. The savings in inventory and distribution costs were ploughed back into customer acquisitions by running aggressive campaigns on search engines and social media platforms. As a result, a value migration could be seen from offline channel intermediaries who used to act as a front to acquire customers to new age social media companies.

The social media strategy of a DTC brand entails having an appealing online brand identity and voice through organic social content, influencer partnerships on social media platforms such as Instagram and YouTube to get the initial loyal customer base, on platform advertising and commerce feature to streamline the customer journey from product discovery to purchase. Brand deals with influencers, once deemed pivotal for D2C success has started waning in favor of social influence. There is a perceptible shift towards paid and sponsored marketing as it is viewed as unbiased and unincentivized, relatable user generated content and daily product reviews. Some D2C companies used referral programs to acquire new customers but the channel and reward structure started to mimic that of multi-level marketing companies.

This new model with cheaper advertising costs meant that brands could be priced competitively or enjoy higher margins. The DTC space became crowded, driving up the costs of gaining consumer attention. Frequent lockdown due to Covid-19 pandemic resulted in shut stores, supply chain disruption and inventory sitting idle encouraging offline brands to rethink their business models. The online traffic surged, both from online and offline brands. This increased the pricing of paid promotions in social media platforms, search marketing and other digital platforms, obliterating the price advantage.

D2C brands maintain databases of consumers and build profiles at the backend based on multiple data points to serve the most relevant product. Direct access to customers gave much higher lifetime value, brand recall and communication leading to loyalty. Loyalty programs and rewards cultivate a sense of recognition and belonging among customers, strengthening their bond with the brand. The benefits of building a customer community are numerous such as positive word of mouth and authentic reviews, besides repeat purchases. D2C brands need to ensure that the average order value is \$10-12 to cover the cost of customer acquisition from digital channels. The brands had to turn in a profit in the first transaction itself if it was a less frequently bought product as cookies expired within a year and retargeting could not be done. Subscription based and frequently bought products turned into a higher lifetime value for D2C brands.

7. BRANDING

Branding goes back to history as early as 2700 BC when ancient Egyptians burnt a symbol on livestock as a way of differentiating from other cattle, providing a seal of ownership and delivering the promise of consistency and quality. The millennial customers have added purpose as a third dimension to branding – Why does the brand exist? Why should customers remember the brand? Millennials also connect personalization as a fourth dimension of branding - How does the brand treat me differently? Is the brand tailoring the message around me? What about the user experience? These are the four core pillars that will define a brand's functional, emotional and experience perspectives.

The brand building journey needs to evolve through three stages for a D2C brand. In the first stage, the brand will introduce itself to as many customers as possible by creating awareness through digital media and trumpeting a few points around differentiation and USP. The company should continue market messaging with high frequency till the measurement yields the brand as standing out on one or two measures. In the second stage the brand starts talking about the role of brand in the consumer's life (benefits), building relationships, leveraging LTV to cross sell and emotional storytelling. A D2C presence gives brand flexibility to talk to the customer about lifestyle regime or habit compared to marketplaces which are more transactional in nature. In the third phase the brand tries to stand on certain values and beliefs, who they are and shares its perspective with the world.

Mamaearth, a D2C personal care brand promoted the goodness in the product with no toxic ingredients and plant-based actives in the first phase. In the second phase, the brand talked about being plastic positive by planting a tree, PETA certified and started conversations around the relevance of the brand in making the world a better place to live in. In the third phase the brand started shaping perspectives around the topic - What do you believe beauty care stands for & what is wrong with the world? The brand in its final leg of evolution has turned Omni channel by using influencers and a Bollywood celebrity and investor to endorse traditional media. It ramped up stores from 3,000 to 10,000; sponsored a popular television reality show - Big Boss, used YouTube influencers to increase brand awareness and connected with mothers through a parenting blog and word-of-mouth.

Category building requires very different kinds of budget and mixes of channels (websites, marketplace, offline) vis-vis market share goals. Every message the company sends out helps build the brand and a texture around the brand. D2C brands can synchronize their website to reviews and customer testimonials on marketplaces which can reinforce the influence led to credibility on their own website. The choice of media is decided by reach and the frequency the brand wants for reach. The brand can compare the impact of its digital campaigns across platforms as use of specific media can enhance transactions and drive performance. The brand needs to analyze which paid, earned and owned touchpoints work together to optimize media and marketing spending by changing the message and content without deviating from the core strategy.

8. SUPPLY CHAIN

While traditional retailers flourish by selling fewer fast moving stock keeping units (SKUs) in greater volume, e-commerce platforms have prospered by making a disproportionate amount of revenue from the far greater variety of products to sell **(See Figure 6)**. Thus, the factor driving the adoption of D2C brands was the availability and fulfillment of slow-moving SKUs which were part of the long tail of a product line and were not available in stock in physical stores, e.g., a customer buying a bottle of Rice Water Shampoo with an oil for damaged, dry and frizzy hair containing rice water, rice keratin and lavender in a 650 ml pack. The inventory gets centralized in a single warehouse, bringing down the safety stock requirements and resulting in substantial savings in inventory holding costs. Inventory planning is more efficient as forecasting is based on end consumer sales and not primary and secondary sales of offline marketing channel partners, with little visibility on tertiary sales. D2C brands usually start with small number of SKUs and experiment with pack sizes and flavors. Each SKU is tracked like a graduation metric as it passes through different channels for repeat customers.

Figure 6. Traditional Retailers vs. Platform Retailers

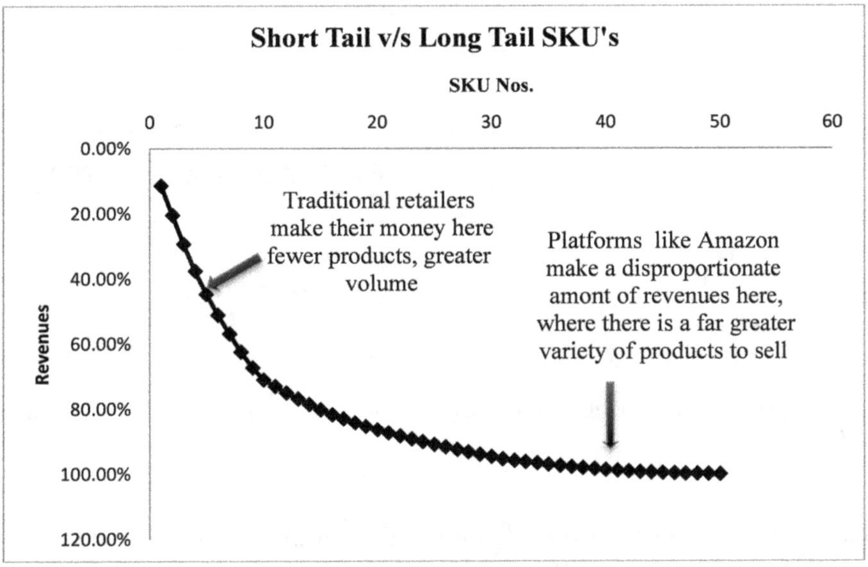

Source: https://www.cbinsights.com/research/direct-to-consumer-retail-strategies/

Figure 7. D2C Landscape in India

Source: https://inc42.com/reports/decoding-indias-100-bn-d2c-opportunity-market-landscape-and-trends-report-2021/

D2C companies start with single digit orders in the first week and scale up to 100,000 orders in the first 12-18 months of start date using an owned central warehouse and shipping partners. This approach pushes up the shipping time to 5-7 days for 65-70 percent of the orders in a large market like India. But shipping time is driving customer experience for DTC companies which require distributed storage. To help DTC companies, achieve this goal, specialized companies in logistics have sprung up which have set up pan India fulfillment centers for 24–48-hour delivery. Further, setting up a technology platform connects all the channels to last mile delivery companies as well as hyperlocal partners.

For omni channel brands, the technology platform also forecasts the inventory to be maintained in each fulfillment center closest to the demand center and the shipping time for the pin code of the customer while browsing the product catalogue on the DTC website. The new age warehousing and logistics aggregators like Delhivery and shiprocket are also experimenting with dark stores (not stocking products) in dense city centers to shore up delivery times. They also differ from third-party logistic providers as there is no minimum commitment on volumes and offer multiple services in managing the post shipping workflow.

Some of the KPIs which D2C companies use to monitor their supply chain include topline conversions, cancellations, repeat purchase, return percentage or return to origin (RTO) and speed of delivery. The RTO queries land in a call center via chat, SMS or phone call and is traced to the courier partner. D2C brands are also incentivizing customers to shift from cash on delivery (COD) to prepaid options with the advent of Unified Payment Interface (UPI) backed digital payment systems as the RTO is lower for prepaid customers.

The logistics sector has also transformed itself during the period and adapted itself to cater to the requirements of online marketplaces and D2C brands for single unit deliveries instead of cases, pallets and less than truck load (LTL) or full truck load (FTL) to more than 20,000 pin codes, thus overcoming the barriers of accessibility. This has been made possible due to the early adoption and integration of technologies like automation, robotics, and machine vision. Experimentation with drone delivery has the potential to change the unit economics of the industry.

Artificial Intelligence (AI) software can optimize inventory management ensuring optimal stock levels, minimize excess inventory and reduce holding costs and avoid customer dissatisfaction due to shortages. D2C companies can integrate AI software with their existing ERP and MRP systems to support closed loop action and real time feedback. The AI software will forecast the demand for a SKU in the right quantity at the right time (day, week, month, quarter, year) and in the right place (specific warehouse), lead time predictions with configurable alerts for projected late orders and supplier deliveries. The AI system can quickly adapt to changing market conditions, engineering combinations, business objectives and supply chain constraints.

9. MARKETING CHANNELS

D2C brands must diversify into multiple channels to cross the chasm as direct website only will constrict growth after gaining a beachhead in the market. Once the DTC brands have perfected the product market fit, understood customer preferences, price points and the brand narrative they can get their products listed on vertical marketplaces like Nykaa for cosmetics, Firstcry for baby products, Myntra and Ajio for fashion which attract a lot of early adopters, and finally on horizontal marketplaces like Amazon and Flipkart which facilitate brand discovery. Finally, D2C brands can complete the Omni channel journey by getting inside brick-and-mortar retail chains. D2C brands can also make their products available through company-owned stores like Zivame and Lenskart.

Some brands which are bootstrapped start with horizontal marketplaces as the cost of customer acquisition is lower and plough back the cash flows into D2C website. The risk of starting off on horizontal marketplaces is delisting in case the product-market fit turns out to be wrong. When the average selling price (ASP) is low, D2C brands can route the transaction through sellers who are aggregators for marketplaces to make the economics more favorable. Average order value (AOV) on DTC ends up being 1.5-1.6 times on marketplaces. In January 2021, Amazon launched Amazon Global Selling Propel (AGSP). It was an accelerator programme for helping new D2C brands to launch in the international market. Slurrp farm and Wellbeing nutrition are among the D2C brands selected under AGSP in 2021 from India.

Social Selling

D2C brands which want to expand to tier-II and tier-III cities can tap the social commerce platforms. The social selling model appeals to small stores, traders and individuals (housewives, students and retirees) who want to supplement their family income without the hassle of incurring expense in setting up an e-commerce business and carrying inventory. The listed resellers are responsible for customer acquisition by finding customers amongst their social groups by sharing the product details via WhatsApp or Instagram and picking which items to include in their online store. This arrangement benefits all stakeholders in the value chain. The suppliers can save on marketing and logistics costs; the reseller gets his revenue through the mark-up on each product and finally, the social commerce company receives its commission from the supplier. Social ecommerce companies provide an online platform with tools that allow resellers to manage purchases, process payments and logistics providers for drop shipping from a network of wholesalers or suppliers. Social e-commerce Company's product range is in the unbranded and long tail categories such as beauty, fashion, home appliances and furnishings and target tier-2 and 3 cities. Meesho, Glowroad and Zepo are a few social commerce start-ups in India.

Micro Markets

Omni Channel D2C brands can take advantage of the presence of target customers in dense micro markets such as university townships, industrial townships and busy tourist circuits. The companies can enhance customer engagement by organizing events around their offline stores and nudge them online for more routine purchases.

Quick Commerce Apps

Niche D2C brands in the CPG, Beauty and personal care and health and fitness are listed on Quick commerce apps like Blinkit, Instamart and Zepto due to the traffic they were driving, leading to the discovery of new brands. Quick commerce apps promise delivery within 10 minutes of the order being placed. Factors such as what people are searching for, a brand's scale and image, comparison with competitors and depth of the category on the platform are key criteria when listing on these apps. D2C brands may have to pay a hefty 30-45% commission to quick commerce companies besides paying 20% of the sales revenue for advertising on the platform and product discounts of 20-22%.

10. OMNI-CHANNEL APPROACH

Large consumer brands have formed internal teams to drive competitive differentiation by offering Omni channel buying options to consumers and becoming more responsive. Brick and mortar companies realize that the brands built over decades can be better monetized and scaled by incorporating D2C model in the Omni channel transition journey. The companies find themselves at an inflection point as it coincides with an enabling digital ecosystem falling in place. The companies embracing the web can witness a 10x ROI on their digital investments.

Haldiram's, a manufacturer of savories and sweets and the largest packaged foods company in India, currently sells 240-250 SKUs in the domestic market through offline channel whereas the biggest supermarkets are willing to display or stock not more than 10% of its range of SKUs. Although the company used to take online orders for a shipping fee, the frequent lockdowns due to COVID-19 pandemic disrupted supplies to physical retailers and saw the company making free deliveries for order value above 500. Online ordering on websites may result in discovery of consumer behavior never understood before in terms of product and SKU preferences. Moreover, since Haldiram's already has a supply chain in place, the company can turbocharge its growth by faster fulfillment of online orders through multi-city distributor warehouses. This will bring down the shipping time from 5-7 days from their distribution center in Nagpur to well under a day in key markets.

Alternatively digital native brands like Mamaearth and boAt are expanding into offline channels through tie-up with retail chains and appointing distributors and wholesalers to enable them to reach small stores. The extent and choice of channels will depend on the strength of the customer community; the level of control needed in storytelling and the target to achieve a particular scale. Marketplace (64%) continues to dominate the overall sales channel mix followed by brand.com (21%) and offline (15%).

Table 2. Comparison of Market Place vs. Brand.com vs. Offline

Particulars	Offline	Marketplace	Brand.com
Definition	Traditional brick and mortar stores, consumer physically visit for purchases)	Digital platforms that connect buyers and sellers, facilitating transaction between them	Digital-first brands, selling products directly to consumers, bypassing intermediaries
Customer Experience	In-person shopping experience, with the ability to touch and feel products	Vast array of options but less direct interaction with individual brands	Direct interaction allowing for a personalized and controlled customer experience
Control over branding	Limited control as products are displayed within the store's context	Brands share space with competitors, potentially impacting individual brand visibility	Full control over brand image and opportunity to drive customer loyalty
Supply Chain & Logistics	Inventory management is crucial, and distribution is typically centralized	Dependence on the marketplace's logistics, however benefit of economies of scale	Higher supply chain control, but full-scale benefits take time
Market Reach	Localized presence required coupled with distributor and stockiest relationship	Global reach with access to a diversified customer base	Benefit of targeting specific demographics, but with smaller reach initially
Incurred Expenses	High overhead cost as rent, staff and physical infrastructure incur significant expenses	Minimal overhead cost, however significant commissions paid out to marketplaces	While no commissions and lesser overhead costs. Significant performance marketing and branding expenses required
Outlook	Offline retail expected to remain an important touchpoint for brands	Marketplace penetration expected to increase due to a plethora of choices and customers convenience	Brand.com brands expected to emerge on the back of innovative marketing strategies

Source: 1lattice.com

11. INVESTORS AND VENTURE CAPITALISTS

Venture Capitalists brought Series A, B and C funding to D2C startups once the proof of concept was established, and companies were clocking revenue run rate of approximately $1 million a year. The VCs brought their domain expertise of investing in similar consumer startups and provided a strategic direction to the firms with the aim of growing revenues 10- 15 times during a period of five years before exiting the company through a secondary sale of shares to private equity or listing on the capital markets. D2C startups utilize the capital to build competencies using data science, expand product portfolio and build and strengthen the brand.

The investors in venture funds are the family offices of Indian billionaires such as Mariwala family, Munjal family, Sanjiv Goenka group and Premji invest besides large multinationals in the consumer goods space like Unilever, Colgate Palmolive, Reckitt Benckiser, L'Oreal and ITC. Many celebrities from the movie industry (Bollywood) and Sports World have also made personal investment in D2C companies. Instead of being content with charging hefty fees for endorsement of big brands, the celebrities want to be the face of the brand e.g., Shilpa Shetty in Mamaearth, a personal care products company and Deepika Padukone in Epigemia, a probiotic foods startup.

12. TECHNOLOGY

The emergence of specialist E-Commerce technology providers like Shopify, WordPress, Woocommerce, Wix and Magento have made technology which powers a D2C website a plug and play affair. Although consumer companies deploy information technology to bring in efficiency and handle back-end processes and operations, some of the emerging AI technologies are helping shape consumer experience of the brands.

***Voice Search*:** Customers in future will increasingly be using voice commands to search for the website or app as it is both convenient and faster. Voice search will also have to be offered in multiple Indian languages as most of the voice searches will be in vernacular. For instance, "Parda" was one of the top three searches for curtains in India.

***Conversational AI*:** Conversational AI is to understand questions and answer them with a human like level of experience. Conversational AI differs from earlier generations of AI or chatbots in its ability to understand context. Context means the ability to understand all kinds of past data such as user engagement, online behaviour, advertisement impressions and purchases made.

The drop-off rate (no conversion) for a D2C website is 95 percent and conversational AI has given D2C brands the power to automate conversations by giving a human-like experience and engagement and in the process increasing conversion rates to 15-20 percent. Moreover, the customers might be intimidated by the amount of information available on the website. Conversational AI helps solve these problems by taking care of the customer throughout the buying journey by bringing that customer on a chat platform like WhatsApp from website seamlessly, engaging them, helping them with product discovery to find the right products for themselves and purchase inside chat itself.

There are categories in the offline world which require more involved purchasing through beauty advisors or store assistants to help the customer navigate the category at the store and help them to consummate the transaction. Conversational AI is the digital equivalent of a beauty consultant in the online D2C world. Since customers are not experts in determining the right solution, conversational AI helps customers seek the relevant solutions. For instance, while there are several face packs, only an expert can analyze based on age, skin type and other skin problems, the right kind of face pack for the customer. The role of an expert is fulfilled by a conversational AI.

***Augmented Reality*:** Furniture brands can use an augmented reality app which will provide customers with a realistically rendered 3D image of furniture scaled to dimensions of a room. The app will scan the expanse of the room through the smartphone camera and users will browse through the product catalogue online to make a product choice. Once chosen the user will point the device to a desired space in the room, drag and drop the selected furniture image in the space. The app will also save the user's favorite products and share their choice on social media which is similar to crowdsourcing the best idea.

***Recommender Systems*:** These are algorithms that recommend relevant items to users based on some criteria. Recommender systems are a source of competitive advantage and generate a significant amount of revenue for e-commerce companies as they help them up sell and cross sell. Recommender systems help companies make predictions about future preferences of users based on past interactions recorded between users and items. Recommendation systems become more accurate over a period as more users interact with items i.e. more transactions are executed.

***Image Recognition*:** It is a system or software employed to identify objects, places, people and actions in images. Customers in categories such as apparel, jewelry and furniture have a specific product design in mind but cannot articulate it in the form of a text. The customer can discover the product through browsing the customer catalogue which can be a painstakingly time-consuming process and may test the patience of customers. (A Bain Capital-Flipkart report mentions that an Indian e-commerce customer browses through 20 webpages before making a purchase and 50-60 webpages for categories such as apparel). Alternatively, the customer can drop the image of the product in the search bar of a DTC website which will show the images of products most closely resembling the object in the search bar.

***Blockchain*:** It is a distributed ledger technology that offers the advantages of transparency and tracking in the supply chain. Customers want to know the source and origin of the product, is not manufactured using conflict minerals or were manufactured in factories with fair wages and did not use child labor e.g. the distributed ledger for a D2C brand like Licious collects data about the source of the meat, the story of the farm where the animal was reared, its owner and location. All this information is made available to a customer on a website in the form of a QR code.

Google Analytics: This service offered by Google helps in tracking traffic to a website. The data is reported on a dashboard. It tracks website information such as pages per session, session duration, bounce rate etc. of browsers using the website along with information on the source of traffic. Google Analytics can also be integrated with Google Ads with which users can create reviewing online campaigns by tracking the landing page quality and conversions (goals). Goals might include sales, lead generation or viewing a specific page.

***Multi touchpoint Attribution*:** Statistical Attribution modelling helps understand the effects of a multimedia campaign on conversions and assign chunks of conversion back to campaign interaction i.e., how much credit each touchpoint interaction gets for conversion. D2C brands need to build an attribution model for conversion tracking and bidding to optimize conversion journeys. The benefits of attribution include reaching customers early in the purchase cycle, matching the offer with how people search and improving the bidding for paid campaigns on digital media including display, search and social.

13. ENGAGEMENT THROUGH COMMUNITY

Communities are a living, breathing surrogate family filled with like-minded individuals who want to improve their lives and the lives of others. The communities are on an inexpensive way to keep members interested in the brand on a continuous basis and evangelize about it without the company making efforts to preach on its own. This further emphasizes the need to make and deliver a brand promise and create opportunities to be attentive to customer conversations.

Mamaearth, the baby and personal care products company, runs a parenting blog which helps would be parents or parents of new born navigate the challenges that come with parenting as many of them reside in big towns and cities and do not have the company of their parents and in-laws. The blog covers a wide range of topics from foods to eat during pregnancy, losing baby weight, getting rid of stretchmarks and the ritual of baby shower to name a few.

Gynoveda which sells ayurvedic pills for treatment of PCOS and irregular menstrual cycles is well suited for community building. The community "Circle of sisterhood" on Facebook is a space for women to discuss intimate issues such as PCOS facts and myths, Can PCOS be cured? What is permanent PCOS treatment? How to cure PCOS naturally? and many more.

boAt sells affordable, durable and fashionable audio products and accessories to millennials. The brand has built an online community of 80,000 members who share their musical experiences of singing out their individual styles. The members also have access to new Bollywood movie releases, music festivals and thus provide a platform to interact with musicians. This helps the brand to influence purchase decisions, integrate the brand into customers' lives and become part of their identity.

D2C brands should focus on creating unique offerings and organic brand building practices for sustainable growth in the long run. Different tools and enablers exist to help D2C brands optimize operations, enhance personalization capabilities and drive business growth through the brand's value chain.

Table 3. Comparison between Budding vs. Growing vs. Established Brands

	Budding Brands	Growing Brands	Established Brands
Marketing Initiatives	Website traction and content marketing Develop customers organically in a cost-effective manner	Paid advertisements and partnerships Focus on increasing the customer outreach for more brand trial	Personalized marketing and loyalty programs Create brand loyalists and drive repeat purchase
Operating Activities	Process and Inventory Optimization Focus on core offerings and effectively manage inventory	Process and Warehousing streamline Use inventory management tools and software for better control and planning	Logistics optimization and presence expansion Optimize logistics and create omnichannel presence, geographical expansion
Technology Usage	Website optimization and Tracking Utilize DIY platforms like Shopify and Wix track website traffic and conversion	Automation and Data Analytics automate platforms to gather data on different metrics, analyze to create personalized offerings	Integration and Forecasting Integrate all business functions, optimize resource allocation deploy demand forecast models
Team Building	Founders and core team Small lean team focusing on essential roles, developing interchangeable skills	Department structure and specialized roles Create separate departments with defines roles and responsibilities	Cross functional team and leadership development Create collaborative roles with focus on knowledge sharing, investment in training and development
Funding Medium	Business incubators, microloans, accrued cashflow Focus on raising funds effectively without diluting the equity	Angel investments, venture capital, accrued cashflow Capital expansion for business growth	Private equity investment, debt raising sustainable growth Large capital source, focus on growing sustainably maximizing profits

Source: 1lattice.com

14. OUTLOOK FOR FUTURE MARKET

Direct to consumer companies must grow by engineering changes in consumer behavior, gain market share from offline channels and convert customers from unbranded to branded products and services. In the ever-changing ecosystem, D2C brands must invest in integration as the battle for competitive advantage intensifies.

Brands in traditional channels are upbeat with the new chance of reaching customers directly. At the same time, as witnessed in many industries, consolidation could result in massive changes with market power in the hands of a few and mighty.

Process Automation:

Digital transformation enables digitization of the entire business process and workflows including customer experience. Automating key decision support systems will enable the brand to make the right decision based on different parameters. This will also help prioritize channel and marketing campaigns based on product preference.

Rampant adoption of Artificial Intelligence (AI):

Generative AI enables brands to create compelling and personalized content utilizing vast datasets catering to specific audience preferences e.g., brands can use generative AI to create multiple Tik Tok videos daily to engage with their customers. Predictive AI can help decode consumer behavior by analyzing historical data and patterns to anticipate consumer needs and forecast trends e.g., identifying the reasons for customer churn.

Subscription based Model:

D2C platform provides an opportunity for companies to customize and control the experience of their customers. The subscription model is a great way for D2C companies to get customers invest in the company by providing periodic replenishments at a predetermined price so as to produce consistent revenues for the business, and in the process helping them to scale and grow. Thus, the subscription model caveats frustration around having to make one off purchase. By subscribing, Bombay shaving company makes it convenient for their customers to buy razors, razor blades and shaving cream without having to worry about running out of products regularly used by them. Country Delight, a D2C company in the business of daily essentials such as milk, bread and eggs, a highly perishable item relies on subscription services for better forecasting of demand and predictability of revenues.

Social Commerce Integration:

D2C brands need to undertake seamless integration of social media platforms with their online brand stores for product discovery and purchase in anticipation of gaining vast potential of online shoppers. Sugar cosmetics hosts live commerce events on social media allowing direct purchase.

Vertical Integration:

Borrowed or shared supply chains may work for D2C brands in the early stages but may not be supportive over the long term. As incumbent brands compete with scrappy startups for the same impressions across digital media, they deceive the initial advantages of D2C brands. The brands must gain more control over their manufacturing operations by vertical integration to bring down costs, assure quality and preserve margins. Anusha Chandrashekhar and Alok Paul started the D2C women western wear apparel brand Berrylush in Noida in 2018. They started off by reaching out to fabricators and discovered that the final product was different from the sample shown to them. They also had issues related to the timelines promised by the fabricators resulting in delays in the launch of season collection. With a bank loan, they set up a factory with 120 machines and designers to manufacture the apparel on their own. This helped alleviate the issues faced with fabricators. The company's initial sales were through their own website but vertically online marketplaces like Myntra and Ajio now account for 70 percent of its sales.

Diversifying into Adjacencies:

Many D2C brands start off with a single category before eventually branching into adjacent categories e.g., Wakefit started as a mattress brand but has since diversified into furniture and home furnishings. D2C companies can also launch new brands if it is capital efficient to do so.

D2C brands partnership and acquisition:

The narrative among large companies in consumer business has changed in the last decade from acquiring companies to partnering with startups in the D2C space and engaging with the ecosystem to create value. Although these investors had complimentary and sometimes competing business lines, they allowed D2C startups to build and nurture their own brands e.g., Colgate Palmolive and Reckitt Benckiser have invested in Bombay Shaving Company which sells subscription of male grooming products, Emami in the Man Company which is a premium men's grooming brand enriched with natural essential oils, Unilever in Plum which is a cruelty free and vegan cosmetics brand and Marico which has picked up a stake in Nykaa, a vertical marketplace for cosmetics.

The digital native startups worked in tandem with Amazon, Unilever, P&G, Nestle, L'Oreal as partners to create new business understanding of product, R&D, supply chain, sourcing, expansion in offline channels but marketing and branding was separated. These investors want to witness how the business models of D2C startups evolve before deciding to either scale up their existing brands' online presence or acquire the fledgling D2C companies e.g., Marico acquired Beardo, a men's grooming brand and Just herbs, a premium ayurvedic cosmetics brand. Unilever acquired Dollar Shave Club, a men's shaving products startup allowing the company to gain D2C expertise and customer base without having to build out brand strategy from scratch. Dollar Shave Club proved to be a promising model as Gillette share of the US razor market fell from 70% to 50%. Such relationships will always pose a dilemma of build versus buy for the goliaths of the industry. The legacy heritage brands are acquiring D2C brands to undergo crucial digital transformation and serve as a strategy initiative to stay relevant and connect with consumers.

Established players launching their own DTC brands:

Large Indian and MNC CPG companies have created separate business unit to focus on digital only brands that operate independently in terms of processes and systems, will not cannibalize their existing brands and may act as flanker to successful D2C brands. By forging direct links with consumers, these brands acquire valuable insights, customize offerings and swiftly adopt to changing trends. In 2020 Pepsico, a packaged snacks and beverage company, demonstrated leadership by launching Pantryshop.com and snacks.com. The closure of brick-and-mortar salons during the Covid-19 pandemic led L'Oreal to launch an e-commerce platform for Keratase, their salon grade hair care brand, mitigating the effects of lockdown.

Consolidation of D2C brands under a single umbrella:

Online marketplaces, Amazon and Flipkart, have helped small private brands to gain considerable momentum in growth. However, it is a challenge to scale beyond a particular revenue threshold as they lack resources. More investments are needed in optimization tools, technology, marketing, category management, operations and supply chain. E-Commerce experts view it as an opportunity to provide these investments, services and tools to accelerate growth. US-based Thrasio, also the world's largest acquirer of third-party private label businesses on Amazon, was the first to adopt such a model. Within a span of three years, it bought, consolidated and scaled up about 100 brands on the platform.

GlobalBees in India had raised $150 million for a Thrasio-style investment platform in a mix of debt and equity. This was led by Firstcry and a few of its investors in April 2021. Mensa Brands, another Thrasio-style investment platform in India is a venture of former Myntra CEO and Medlife co-founder, Ananth Narayanan. It rose around $50 million in a mix of debt and equity during May 2021. Mensa invests in brands that are profitable, have a revenue run rate of $1-$10 million and at a 5-7X the EBITDA (Earnings Before Interest Tax, Depreciation and Amortization) of the company. Mensa had bought the majority stakes (50-60%) in 10 D2C startups within six months of its launch and is looking at a target of 50 ventures across fashion, home, garden, personal care and beauty in its portfolio by 2024.

15. CONCLUSION

While many D2C brands make humble beginnings, sustenance is questioned in the absence of scale ambitions. And scale cannot be only driven through distribution. As seen earlier, while omni-channel seems to be the obvious route, it also creates a dilemma of scaling up the community against the established one-to-one customer relationships. So D2C brands need to monitor the dilution of relationships while on the path to scale. It is worthwhile focusing on profit margins as promotion and customer acquisition costs can result in losses while chasing scale opportunities. Backward and forward integration can provide substantial benefits and thus improve profit margins. D2C brands must also be ready to predict and brace for the next big technology disruption. This helps in being ahead of the game and minimizing the impact as well. To sum up, D2C brands must aim to achieve leadership status in their respective categories as the quote by the reputed American author, John Maxwell goes, *a leader is one who knows the way, goes the way and shows the way*. In the D2C conundrum, it will always be the leaders who will grow the market and make it beneficial for all stakeholders.

REFERENCES

Chatterjee, R. (2020). Digital Marketing Transformation of D2C Brands. *International Journal of Business and Management, 15*(4), 110–121.

Chen, J., & Bell, D. R. (2020). Predictive Analytics for Direct-to-Consumer Retail. *Journal of Marketing Analytics, 8*(3), 134–145.

Fosso Wamba, S., Gunasekaran, A., Papadopoulos, T., & Ngai, E. (2018). Big data analytics in logistics and supply chain management. *International Journal of Logistics Management, 29*(2), 478–484. DOI: 10.1108/IJLM-02-2018-0026

Gielens, K., & Steenkamp, J. B. E. (2019). Branding in the Era of Digital. *Journal of Marketing*.

Lemon, K. N., & Verhoef, P. C. (2016). Understanding Customer Experience Throughout the Customer Journey. *Journal of Marketing, 80*(6), 69–96. DOI: 10.1509/jm.15.0420

Nguyen, B., Simkin, L., & Canhoto, A. (2021). The Dark Side of AI in Customer Experience. *Journal of Services Marketing*.

Shankar, V.. (2021). How Artificial Intelligence is Reshaping Retailing. *Journal of Retailing*.

Zeng, J., Lu, Y., & Huang, Y. (2022). Algorithmic Bias in Marketing AI. *Journal of Business Research, 145*, 678–689.

ADDITIONAL READINGS

Matthew W Ragas, Bolivar J Bueno. The Power of Cult Branding: How 9 magnetic brands turned customers into loyal followers. Crown Business

https://www.deloitte.com/global/en/issues/work/genz-millennial-survey.html

https://firesideventures.com/

https://www.vahdamteas.in/

http://www.businessworld.in/article/Where-Health-Creates-Wealth-Anindita-Sampath-Co-founder-CEO-Yoga-Bars-/13-11-2019-178917/

https://www.bain.com/insights/how-india-shops-online/

https://www.cbinsights.com/research/direct-to-consumer-retail-strategies/

https://hbr.org/2020/03/reinventing-the-direct-to-consumer-business-model

https://yourstory.com/2021/05/turning-point-entrepreneur-couple-mamaearth - chemical-free-baby-care-d2c-brand/amp

https://yourstory.com/smbstory/berrylush-womens-apparel-brand-western-wear - myntra-ajio/amp

https://timesofindia.indiatimes.com/world/rest-of-world/skin-in-the-game-beauty - tech-firms-drive-market-makeover/articleshow/72216921.cms

https://timesofindia.indiatimes.com/business/india-business/investors-double-down - on-direct-to-consumer-brands/articleshow/78817340.cms

https://www.architectmagazine.com/technology/ikea-launches-augmented-reality - application

https://economictimes.indiatimes.com/markets/stocks/news/price-to-imagination-for -pe-raamdeo-lists-out-pitfalls-of-dealing-with-digital- stocks/articleshow/84475032. cms?from=mdr

https://economictimes.indiatimes.com/tech/funding/globalbees-a-thrasio-style - investment-platform-raises-150-million/articleshow/84550608.cms?from=mdr

https://economictimes.indiatimes.com/tech/funding/ananth-narayanans-mensa-brands- raises-50-million-from-accel-others/articleshow/83110325.cms?from=mdr

https://www.1lattice.com/verticals/consumer-retail/retail

https://inc42.com/reports/decoding-indias-100-bn-d2c-opportunity-market-landscape-and-trends-report-2021/

https://www.cbinsights.com/research/direct-to-consumer-retail-strategies/

https://www.weforum.org/docs/WEF_Future_of_Consumption_Fast-Growth_Consumers_markets_India_report_2019.pdf

https://www.euromonitor.com/population

Chapter 7
Revolutionizing Customer Support:
Business Impact Analysis of Automated Models

Usharani Bhimavarapu
https://orcid.org/0000-0002-0246-1420
Department of Computer Science and Engineering, Koneru Lakshmaiah Education Foundation, Vaddeswaram, India

ABSTRACT

Automated customer support systems have become essential in enhancing the efficiency and responsiveness of service industries. This paper presents a proposed automated customer support tool designed to overcome the limitations of traditional support models by leveraging advanced data processing techniques. The system utilizes Data Extraction, Data Transformation, and Data Import using Business Intelligence (BI) tools to create a dynamic, adaptive framework for real-time, personalized customer assistance. By extracting relevant data from various sources, transforming it into usable formats, and integrating it into BI tools for enhanced visualization and analysis, the tool enables a proactive, data-driven approach to customer support. The system also incorporates AI-powered analytics to predict customer issues and adapt to ongoing interactions, ensuring that responses remain relevant and timely. Moreover, the tool ensures seamless integration with human agents for escalation, providing a hybrid solution that combines automation with human expertise.

DOI: 10.4018/979-8-3693-8512-8.ch007

INTRODUCTION

Automated Customer Support refers to the application of artificial intelligence (AI), machine learning, and other advanced technologies to serve the customer automatically without direct human intervention. The technique involves the employment of chatbots, virtual assistants, and automated ticketing systems to reply to customer inquiries, resolve issues, and reply at any time. Automated systems are able to undertake a range of customer service activities, including answering repeated queries, taking orders, resolving problems, and making individualized recommendations.

The most significant benefit of automated customer support is that it can eliminate the problems of companies in terms of scaling rapidly and efficiently, giving immediate responses to customers round the clock and delivering a superior customer experience. It also lowers the cost of operation because it does not allow human representatives to handle unwanted calls, hence leaving them enough time to resolve complex ones. Customer support systems have been improved by the use of AI, with increased accuracy, natural language handling, and customized chat.

This computerized revolution has been a major driving force in the evolving customer support environment. As businesses seek to cope with escalating customer demands for instant, effective, and personalized support, computerized customer service systems offer the avenues for sustaining such interactions ongoing. This introduction will attempt to characterize the features, advantages, and limitations of computerized customer support, describing its revolutionary impact on modern business practice.

Automated Customer Service has been an increasing need in recent years against the premise of technological innovation, changing customer expectations, and increasing business complexity. Customers today, in today's fast, digitally driven times, want 24/7, real-time support anywhere in the world. 24/7 support is achievable through automation technologies like chatbots and virtual assistants without asking human agents to work round-the-clock. Also, since more companies are being formed, customer inquiries become higher in numbers, and maintaining high response levels with human agents is impossible. Automation customer support software can answer multiple questions at once, significantly curtailing waiting time and enhancing customer overall satisfaction. Cost-effectiveness is one of the largest advantages of automation. By taking away the routine job of attending to redundant questions or addressing simple requests, companies can minimize their need for huge customer service teams, hence lesser operational costs. This frees human agents from performing less complicated tasks and enables them to attend to more complex ones, hence becoming more efficient and effective. Besides, computerized systems provide real-time same-treatment to customers, and this eliminates delay in support functions as well as human-error. Computerized systems also have the capability to provide recommendations from customer data, enhancing customer experience further.

Computerized systems used for customer support also provide scalability and flexibility. They can scale up to handle increasing demands of an expanding organization without requiring additional resources. Whether they are managing peak loads for specific periods of time or managing gigantic volumes of questions, automation allows firms to provide high-quality levels of service. Finally, automated systems give valuable data-driven feedback on customer behavior, preference, and routine grievances, which help firms make their product, services, and overall customer care policy better.

Automated customer support is no longer an indulgence but a requirement of today's competitive business environment. It assists organizations to provide efficient, scalable, and affordable solutions and improve customer experience as well. With the evolving technology and growing customer expectations, the need for automated customer support can only intensify.

Artificial Intelligence of Things (AIoT) is a robust union between two revolutionary technologies: Artificial Intelligence (AI) and Internet of Things (IoT). AIoT uses data collected through IoT devices and applies AI rules to scan, read, and respond to the data in real-time. This union produces smarter, self-regulated solutions that are able to deliver personalized, data-driven insights, and solutions to business segments, i.e., Retail and Services Management.

In the store floor, AIoT has the potential to enhance customer satisfaction and shop floor efficiency. Intelligent sensors in the products and shelves monitor inventory in real time, so that inventory balance is ensured and risk of stockout or overstocking condition is avoided. AI-driven algorithms learn this data and use it to predict demand, streamline supply chains, and remotely restock. Furthermore, AIoT also facilitates customers' individual shopping experience by sensing and analyzing customers' behavior data via smart devices, which offers customers' consumption habits, tendencies, and preferences for retailers' customers. According to the data, the retailers can offer customers' personalized promotions, recommendations, and dynamic pricing, which can enhance customers' satisfaction and sales.

When it comes to managing services, AIoT is also crucial in enhancing operating efficiency and service quality. For instance, in a hotel setting, intelligent sensors and IoT devices can track guest preferences, temperature, and service requirements in real-time. AI-based systems can automate the adjustment of lighting, temperature, and other environmental conditions to enhance guest comfort or predict when a customer might require assistance and optimize the service experience as a whole. AIoT can also maximize the use of resources, be it energy consumption in the rooms of a hotel or equipment services within service organizations, for efficient and cost-saving operation.

AIoT also allows customers to engage with messages via mobile phone applications, chatbots, and voice assistants for round-the-clock attention and bespoke interaction. In retail to consumers, consumers are permitted to interact with virtual AI-powered personal assistants either for suggestion or even status of available stock availability, and service companies can simplify day-to-day work and make it faster through AI. AIoT enables companies to gain precious feedback, either from intelligent devices or computerized questionnaires, to individualize their product and services as well as respond better to customers' needs.

AIoT, as a whole, opens retail and service management companies to working more smartly, delivering better quality customer experiences, and optimizing resources. With real-time intelligence, predictive analytics, and automation, AIoT is enabling businesses to deal with the changing needs of customers in today's connected consumers and driving profitability as well as operating efficiency. As the technology of AI and IoT keeps on evolving, the overall potential of both for retail and service management companies will evolve further with more possibilities of expansion and innovation.

Automated Customer Support comes in a few models with each one being good for some but not for all. Chatbots (Rule-Based) is one of the most widely used solutions, as it carries pre-stored responses to certain questions asked. They are appropriate for basic and repetitive questions but fail to deliver when it comes to advanced or complex customer specifications. Rule-based chatbots lack competency in contextual knowledge, jargon, or off-topics as well as need human intervention to be highly responsive to the changing needs of customers.

Artificial intelligence-powered Virtual Assistants such as Google Assistant and Amazon Alexa read and respond to customer inquiries through natural language processing. Whilst providing more conversational interfaces, they are still limited by their programming, exposed to misreading common, especially accent, slang, or highly particular customer service queries. Privacy concerns are also generated by the data harvesting associated with these assistants.

Interactive Voice Response (IVR) Systems are automated voice-read systems that navigate customers step-by-step. Although they simplify straightforward procedures such as account details or balance inquiries, they frustrate customers where voice instructions cannot be understood by the system or provides monotonous, pre-programmed responses. Customers are also frustrated because of deep menu trees, and thus become unhappy.

Automated Ticketing Systems create and assign priority to the customer issue support tickets and automatically send them to their corresponding team. But they are not smart enough to fix intricate issues and require manual intervention. If the ticket is sent or given wrong priority, then it can lead to the delay in solving the customer issue, which in mission-critical environments is extremely frustrating.

Self-Service Knowledge Bases are websites where customers can self-solve their issues by reading solutions to frequent questions and step-by-step troubleshooting processes. Although they permit the customer to fix their issue on their own, knowledge bases will fail if customers require assistance beyond the model created or need customized help.

All of these models are vital to customer care automation but do have intrinsic limitations, especially when it comes to handling complex, personalized, or sensitive questions. For overcoming them, the combined use of automated systems with human intervention and ongoing training through AI can be critical to responsiveness and efficiency of customer care centers.

The self-service customer support mechanism established here is founded on weaknesses of conventional models of customer servicing with advanced methods to data processing, integration, and analysis. They are Data Extraction, Data Transformation, and Data Import using BI Tools as the foundation for establishing a constantly adaptable and smart system.

Data Extraction presents everything that is required, including customer history, interactions, and preferences, to be supplemented on for further processing. This enables the system to execute dynamically by holding each customer's history, interactions, and reviews in real-time, giving a more solid base for personalized replies. Pre-processing beforehand ensures the extracted data is clean, structured, and error-free, another accuracy boost in the tool.

After retrieving data, Data Transformation can be utilized for decision-making and analysis. The software has already been processed through multiple steps of data transformation to clean and normalize the data. These include categorical variables being encoded, missing data being handled, and response types such as responses from a Likert-scale being encoded into useful numeric data. Other forms of insight such as levels of customer satisfaction or sentiment scores are also calculated in the process of producing a more comprehensive dataset. This further aids in data structuring for integration with Business Intelligence tools easily, enabling the system to report and analyze information correspondingly. Transformation makes the data useful and aggregated for maximum potential for real-time customer care.

Data Import from BI Tools is a key process through which the tool imports data such as Power BI, Tableau, or Qlik Sense for further analysis. Loading the prepared and cleaned data in these tools, the system can generate dynamic dashboards and build reports that highlight key learnings, i.e., customer attitude, quality of service, and behavior trends. It incorporates openness to the customer, bringing in the information and presenting it in real time and also to respond to any issue causing a problem with it being resolved instantly. This also enables the system to learn patterns and gain intelligence to further enhance proactive customer service and raise operational efficiency as well as levels of satisfaction.

The study by Balagué et al. (2016) is flawed even as it brings a convincing equivalence between non-authentic and authentic hotel reviews in the sense that it is taking into account just two websites, namely TripAdvisor and Booking.com, and the chances of these merely giving a fraction of the total number of review systems created by users across all areas or domains. In addition, user involvement and review verification processes could have been altered since the years 2016 and therefore their relevance these days may have been reduced.

Borrego and Comalat Navarra (2021) provide insightful figures based on Google Maps users' comments about public libraries, but the limitation of this research is that it is platform-dependent, and that might be subject to bias by Google users and its creators. Users' comments might not continue to represent users' satisfaction or subtlety of value from public library services.

The MarketsandMarkets (2024) business report projects that the business intelligence market will evolve considerably but is constrained by the limitations of foresight and business agendas. The projection is not peer-reviewed empirical research and does not account for the economic depressions or unforeseen interference that would alter the trajectories of markets (MarketsandMarkets, 2024).

Czerepicki (2019) is use-case-specific but fairly technology-aware research on column databases for measuring data processing in electric vehicles. Its results can be irrelevant for another use case or against a different database schema with different workloads or in real-time conditions.

Edmondson's (2018) original publication on psychological safety is strong theoretically within the working innovation context. It is indirectly, not directly, transferred to the green technology and logistics domain. It is qualitative in nature versus an empirical evidence base and therefore not transferable to technical domains directly.

Eurostat's NACE Rev. 2 (2008) is an economic activity basis for classification but can fail to have the capability to capture future new activities such as green logistics or hybrid digital services activities. The 2008 classification does not have the emerging context of sustainability firms (Eurostat, 2008).

Although Google Forms (2024) is extremely popular for gathering survey data, it falls short in response bias for the need for access online and security issues with data on sensitive subjects. Analytics tools for the platform are similarly not as extensive as other software specifically designed for surveys.

Howson (2013) outlines strategic business intelligence methods, but the book is old in relation to much of the more current advancements in AI and real-time analytics. The delay may minimize the application of some of the recommendations in today's cloud-enabled and high-speed BI environments.

Jachimowski et al. (2017) present a warehouse simulation database example but provide a solution to an existence that may not be as freely transferable to other supply chain situations or technology settings. The study does not also provide a full comparison with other competing simulation platforms.

Jacyna et al. (2015) provide strategic advice on specialized transport systems but are technically limited by inadequate data and are theory-oriented. Operational impacts on green logistics technology or real-time decision support tools are not widely studied.

Kim's (2007) study on virtual call centers jumps to conclusions regarding quality monitoring but is technology outdated when used on contemporary AI-based customer service platforms. The results may not be representative of today's AI-based chatbots and changing customer expectations (Kim, 2007).

Kubina et al. (2015) suggested BI effectiveness enhancement in business corporations, but case study limitation within industries limits its results to be narrow. Typical results of this research might not offer solutions to e-commerce or logistics organizations with sustainability-specific needs.

Lokman and Aberdeen (2019) have authored a piece on chatbot technology, which is good in terms of system architecture awareness but poor as far as domain application considerations, e.g., for CEP or green logistics environments. In addition, the speed at which technology has progressed since the review makes some comments obsolete.

Loshin's (2003) first venture in business intelligence implementation offers basic guidelines but much of the technology ground it covers is old. Leaving artificial intelligence integration, cloud computing, and mobile BI out of the domain reduces its applicability to current use (Loshin, 2003).

Martin-Fuentes et al. (2020) mention the effect of review and rating quantity but do not differentiate between unverified and verified reviews that may have the potential to affect perceived credibility. It also fails to mention the effect of platform algorithms to display reviews.

McBride (2014) analyzes BI in magazine distribution but does not utilize substantial empirical evidence and relies on descriptive narratives instead. The pre-digital context and field specificity of the research reduce its applicability to the diversified e-commerce landscape of the modern day.

Nujic and Ambrusec (2021) have a business influencer marketing perspective but consumer opinion or ROI data is given lesser consideration. Its firm sentiment emphasis restricts a broader discussion of influencer effects in digital logistics situations.

The Climber 2022 report positions Qlik as a leader in BI but is limited on the fact that it is promotional and there is no peer review by others. It lacks comparative performance by comparison and may not even offer user experience by markets (Climber, 2022).

Selamat and Windasari (2021) refer to a two-viewpoint SME chatbot strategy, but their study was carried out on small enterprises, and it cannot be generalized for large-scale, sophisticated logistic operations. The findings are not highly generalizable to industry-scale chatbot systems.

Stone and Heen (2014) offer writing on feedback as a psychological asset but less directly usable in operations of logistic or customer interface systems with artificial intelligence. Their model would not carry over so easily into operational modes for internet services.

Swani and Milne (2017) measure Facebook brand engagement but direct their studies towards viral content rather than customer loyalty or long-term conversion. Expansion of their studies into strategic logistics or long-term environmental marketing campaigns is thus minimal.

Zapier's tool (2021) for comparison, being a proper introduction to form builders, is too elaborate and detailed, not being the object of methodological study. Moreover, it does not consider data security, scalability, or integration with business systems which are essential in research environments (Zapier, 2021).

Watson and Wixom (2007) provide the context in BI during the mid-2000s. Although of historical interest, the study is old-fashioned and does not address issues in data privacy, real-time analysis, or AI-based decision making (Watson and Wixom, 2007).

Yongho Hyun et al. (2014) contrast satisfaction by place and system in tourism but mention nothing about new technology such as mobile commerce or green logistics platforms. The conditions under which the sample are being taken may be unrepresentative of trends for customers in our multi-platform world today.

Aside from utilizing AI-assisted analytics, the product is much more advanced than reporting. The system is based on AI models to forecast customer problems beforehand to enable proactive steps. For instance, if a customer is repeatedly asking for help for the same problems, the system would identify the trend and send solutions even before the customer asks for them. This proactive ability guarantees that the system will be able to react with prompt and sufficient help without having to depend on the reactive methods, a characteristic not found in traditional models.

Secondarily, real-time flexibility is another critical aspect of the system presented here. Since the customer information is being updated in real-time, so is the system, tailoring responses based on new interactions and feedback. This device is not like static pre-computed responses from standard models but rather adjusts its behavior based on its history, offering a more personalized customer experience.

Finally, the human intervention is also incorporated within the system. As a safeguard feature, if the automated support system is unable to resolve a problem, the tool can escalate the problem to a human agent. With automation and human support integration, the customers are assured that they would never have pending problems, benefiting from the speed and efficiency of automation and the expertise of human agents.

In total, through the intervention of Data Extraction, Data Transformation, and Data Import through BI tools, the envisioned automated customer service system here is better equipped to manage a variety of questions from customers and reply in timely, personalized messages. It is superior to the traditional ones as it is flexible, predictive, and symbiotically leveraging both AI and human resources to empower the customers to extract the best out of it..

MATERIALS AND METHODOLOGY

This research explores the effect of green logistics process innovation on customers' decision to choose bidders and the requirement of CEP companies to implement green logistics. The research was carried out during early 2023 and 2024 and utilized explanatory and descriptive approaches and was targeting Indian consumers of online shopping. The scope of the study was divided into broken and deterministic to a particular category of internet shoppers.

The data were gathered using a user-diagnostic questionnaire with the assistance of Computer-Assisted Web Interview (CAWI) technique. 48-item closed-ended professional questionnaire out of which 18 used measurement by Likert scale attitude was placed on the research portal ebadania.pl. The portal was available on August 31, 2024.

The respondents of the survey were above 14 years old and had placed one or more orders online from e-commerce websites in the past three months before the survey. The research was primarily on the last-mile operation of logistics business to know the effects of technological innovation promoting sustainable development on the demand of supply bidders among customers. The research did not include every online consumer who had consumed a product in December 2023 and January 2024, however.

PREPROCESSING

Preprocessing of the survey data collected is needed in order to preserve the quality and relevance of data and aid in appropriate analysis. Data cleaning by missing value handling by imputation, such as mean or mode imputation for quantitative data and categorical data or omission of missing response in case they are not significant and insignificant, comes first. Duplicates are eliminated and deleted to eliminate redundancy, and inconsistent responses are handled to maintain consistency, particularly for Likert-scale responses. These data are then transformed where categorical answers are transformed into numerical values, like labeling Likert scale statements (e.g., Strongly Agree = 5, Agree = 4). Dates are transformed into default format to be able to conduct temporal analysis.

Feature engineering is subsequently conducted in order to obtain new information, i.e., deriving satisfaction ratings from Likert scales or aggregating purchase frequency across respondents. Quantitative variables such as age are scaled or normalized for inter-variable comparison, particularly for machine learning. Redundant feature removal or dimension reduction using techniques such as PCA, if necessary, is conducted using data reduction methods. Outliers are identified and removed using statistical tests such as Z-score or Interquartile Range (IQR) testing in order to remove anomalies.

Statistical tests are carried out for consistency to ensure that it meets rational criteria, i.e., people under 16 years of age are excluded since they are out of the research scope. Cross-checking accounts for the fact that identical questions are answered in a similar manner. All server crashes and mistakenly completed forms are corrected, and Likert-scale data are recalmed in terms of interpreter difference. In the event that predictive modeling is needed, data are divided into test and training sets, ideally 80:20.

Once pre-processed, data are now clean, organized, and free from discrepancies and are ready to be applied within exploratory data analysis or modeling to establish customer preference results as well as the contribution of sustainable innovation to last-mile logistics business.

BI TOOLS

Data Extraction is the activity of pulling out useful data from information repositories like databases, APIs, spreadsheets, or web pages. Like survey data extraction, it commences with the retrieval of the unprocessed data set within the warehouse facility or system in which the answers were captured, i.e., database or CSV file. In the course of the process, all delivery methods, demographic data, Likert-scale response sets, and records are retrieved except none. When records are available from many different sources, they are brought together into a single point using queries or APIs. Data integrity is maintained during the process by ensuring that the retrieved records are intact as in the original source and not lost or duplicated.

Data Transformation is the process of getting the data accessed into a state ready for analysis by reorganizing data into its normal and usable form. It includes data cleaning and normalization, e.g., categorical data conversion to numbers, correct date field formatting, and numerical feature normalization to ensure they are all in the same format. For example, Likert-scale items are converted into numeric values, but demographic customer information like age can be binned for convenience. Transformation also includes management of missing data, i.e., deletion or imputation of missing records, and treatment of outliers for the sake of preserving the original shape of the dataset. Secondly, measurable fields such as satisfaction scores or purchase frequency can be defined here with the aim of optimizing the value of the dataset. The goal is to clean the data and prepare it to be imported into Business Intelligence tools.

Data Import with BI Tools is importing processed data into Business Intelligence tools like Tableau, Power BI, or Qlik Sense to analyze and visualize. This is achieved by initiating the selection of optimal import mode, i.e., joining to a database, importing supported file formats (e.g., Excel, CSV), or joining by way of use of APIs. After importing data, data hierarchies and associations are created to facilitate analysis. Data relationships could include demographic customer characteristics being associated with buying habits in order to analyze trends. BI solutions would generally be paired with functionality for guaranteeing imported data through preview and cross-checks with the source to confirm correctness. Upon import, advanced features like calculated fields, aggregations, and custom dashboards seek to extract insights and display data in graphical form. Decision-making is facilitated by using BI tools through interactive analysis and real-time reporting of the most important trends and patterns within the set of data.

SMART LOGISTICS

Smart Logistics means the implementation of technology and data-driven strategy for the optimization of supply chain operations based on efficiency, sustainability, and customer satisfaction. Based on data gathered through selecting e-commerce consumers and adopting last-mile delivery technologies, smart logistics plans can be planned and implemented efficiently.

The information gives customer choice, green operating attitude, and delivery mode. These can be used to build intelligent logistics solutions, like optimized last-mile delivery routes with dynamic qualities. Customers' locations, desired delivery times, and the neighborhood environment can be used by logistics businesses with predictive logic to build the least-fuel-consuming and lowest-emission delivery routes.

In addition, data can lead to the adoption of green logistics best practices. Feedback from customers regarding green delivery innovation such as electric transport or drone delivery can inform investment in cleaner transport. Qualitative analysis of customer feedback through surveys, for instance, can determine carbon-neutral delivery demand and push logistics stakeholders to get greener.

Smart logistics can also involve IoT-based tracking systems, where customers can receive real-time updates regarding their delivery. The system can utilize customer preference and satisfaction information in the survey to develop features that are more transparent and offer a better customer experience, such as delay in delivery alert or allowing alternative pickup.

In addition to this, customer segmentation based on data can be used for offering customized logistics services. Regular customers, for instance, can be serviced with subscription plans or priority plans, and low-frequency ones can be provided with low-cost options. Questions in Likert scale can be answered in a way that responses will be used for such segment identification and customization of logistics operations as well.

Lastly, in integrating this data set into Business Intelligence (BI) solutions, the logistics service providers can build dynamic dashboards upon which to track key performance indexes (KPIs) such as hours of delivery, customer satisfaction rates, and environmental footprint. This allows for very informed decisions so that logistial activity remains attuned to customer demand and to sustainability performance.

SMARTCLIENT

A Smart Client is a rich application that combines the richness of desktop applications and web-based system connectivity and scalability.

A smart client delivers an intuitive experience to the customers by combining sophisticated features like offline support, smart caching, and dynamic updates. For an e-commerce logistics dataset, an intelligent client can be extremely beneficial in improving customers' experience by delivering interactive and personalized functionality. For instance, a smart client program may provide customers with a minute-by-minute order tracking console, enable them to select delivery options, and communicate with providers. Data analysis indicates the app can forecast user needs, i.e., eco-friendly ways of transport, and provide them in advance to satisfy their demands. The smart client would enable users "to see major features even offline, to see history of delivery and preferences offline. All that has been altered offline can be synchronized automatically when the device comes online again, providing continuity. Dynamic updates provide the application with ongoing access to the most current features and information without having to reinstall it, and smart caching improves performance by storing major data in high demand locally.".

In addition to this, the smart client may also deliver real-time order status, delay, or sustainability data alerts based on customer preference. Additionally, it may offer interactive analytics like delivery performance metrics or carbon footprint visibility to allow customers to make informed decisions. With a strong front-end platform, i.e., .NET or Java, and supported by a back end on the cloud, smart client enables data management and business logic integration to be made simpler. In e-commerce logistics business, it fills the gap between service providers and customers by offering efficient, data-driven, and customer-centric services. Synching customer expectations and encouraging environmentally friendly behavior, the smart client triggers customer experience and induces green logistics and innovation.

EXPERIMENTAL RESULTS

Table 1 presents a comparative overview of the Efficiency Metrics of the proposed automated customer service model and ten typical customer service automation systems. The parameters are measure parameters such as response time, resolution rate, automation rate, error rate, and customer satisfaction (CSAT), highlighting the accessibility of the proposed model.

The Proposed Model is best when it experiences the shortest response time of 2.5 seconds, which is quicker compared to the response time of the rest of the models ranging between 2.8 and 3.5 seconds.

It has a resolution rate of 90%, which is better compared to the majority of the other models including Rule-based Chatbots and Zendesk Answer Bot's 80%.

92% automation percentage of the model proposed here is significantly higher than other models like Amazon Lex at 85% and Google Dialogflow at 75% because of the large percentage of tasks being automated. On the error rate, the system here achieves a worst-case error percentage of 2%, as opposed to other systems like Rule-based Chatbots and Freshdesk, which have an error percentage of 6% and above. This indicates the system's reliability and accuracy. Furthermore, customer satisfaction (CSAT) of the system under consideration is 88%, higher than that in other systems, e.g., Intercom and Zoho Desk, with respective CSAT scores of 78% and 77%..

Table 1. Efficiency Measures of the proposed model with existing customer support automation models

Model	Response Time (Seconds)	Resolution Rate (%)	Automation Rate (%)	Error Rate (%)	Customer Satisfaction (CSAT)
Proposed Model	2.5	90%	92%	2%	88%
Rule-based Chatbots	3.1	80%	70%	6%	75%
IBM Watson Assistant	2.9	85%	80%	5%	80%
Google Dialogflow	3.0	83%	75%	4%	78%
Zendesk Answer Bot	3.5	80%	72%	6%	76%
Amazon Lex	2.8	88%	85%	3%	85%
LivePerson	3.2	85%	78%	4%	80%
Intercom	3.3	82%	77%	4%	78%
Drift	3.0	81%	80%	5%	79%
Freshdesk	3.1	80%	75%	6%	78%
Zoho Desk	3.4	79%	74%	7%	77%

Table 2 compares the Accuracy and Reliability Measures of the proposed customer support automation model with ten existing systems, highlighting metrics such as accuracy, reliability (uptime), precision, recall, and F1-score. The proposed model consistently delivers superior performance across all thesemeasures.The proposed model achieves the highest accuracy of 92%, outperforming all other systems, such as Rule-based Chatbots and Zoho Desk, which recorded 78% and 77%, respectively. It also excels in reliability (uptime), with an impressive 99.9%, surpassing most other models like Zendesk Answer Bot (99%) and Drift (99.4%). This ensures that the proposed model is highly dependable for continuous operations.In terms of precision, the proposed model scores 91%, which is higher than competitors like IBM Watson Assistant (83%) and Freshdesk (76%), indicating its capability to provide accurate responses with minimal errors. Its recall score of 94% is also outstanding, reflecting its ability to effectively identify and resolve a broad range of customer queries, surpassing systems like LivePerson (85%) and Drift (83%).The F1-score, a harmonic mean of precision and recall, is 92.5 for the proposed model, making it the top performer in balancing accuracy and completeness. Other models, such as Amazon Lex (86%) and Google Dialogflow (88.5%), fall behind in this critical measure.

Table 2. Accuracy and Reliability Measures for the Proposed Model with existing customer support automation models

Model	Accuracy (%)	Reliability (Uptime %)	Precision (%)	Recall (%)	F1-Score
Proposed Model	92%	99.9%	91%	94%	92.5
Rule-based Chatbots	78%	98%	75%	80%	77%
IBM Watson Assistant	85%	99.5%	83%	86%	84.5
Google Dialogflow	88%	99.6%	87%	89%	88.5
Zendesk Answer Bot	80%	99%	78%	82%	80%
Amazon Lex	89%	99.7%	85%	87%	86%
LivePerson	84%	99.8%	82%	85%	83.5
Intercom	82%	99.5%	80%	84%	82%
Drift	83%	99.4%	81%	83%	82%
Freshdesk	79%	99.5%	76%	79%	77.5
Zoho Desk	77%	99.4%	74%	78%	76%

Table 3 evaluates Customer Experience Measures for the proposed customer support automation model compared with ten existing models, focusing on Customer Satisfaction (CSAT), First Contact Resolution (FCR), Average Handling Time (AHT), Customer Effort Score (CES), and Net Promoter Score (NPS). The proposed model demonstrates superior performance across nearly all metrics, enhancing overall user experience.The proposed model achieves an impressive CSAT score of 88%, significantly surpassing systems such as Rule-based Chatbots (75%) and Zoho Desk (70%). Similarly, its FCR rate of 92% highlights its ability to resolve customer issues efficiently on the first interaction, outperforming competitors like IBM Watson Assistant (80%) and Freshdesk (70%).In terms of operational efficiency, the proposed model's AHT is just 3.5 minutes, reflecting its fast query resolution capabilities. This is far quicker than alternatives like Zendesk Answer Bot (6.5 minutes) and Rule-based Chatbots (6.0 minutes), demonstrating significant time savings for customers.The CES, which measures how much effort customers need to exert during interactions, is exceptionally low at 1.2 for the proposed model. This reflects a seamless and user-friendly experience compared to higher scores like 3.9 for Zoho Desk and 3.8 for Freshdesk, which indicate more effort is required in those systems. Finally, the proposed model achieves a strong NPS of 75%, indicating high customer loyalty and satisfaction. It outperforms systems like Google Dialogflow (58%) and LivePerson (63%), while closely rivaling Amazon Lex, which has an NPS of 70%.

Table 3. Customer Experience Measures for the Proposed Model with existing customer support automation models

Model	Customer Satisfaction (CSAT) (%)	First Contact Resolution (FCR) (%)	Average Handling Time (AHT) (Minutes)	Customer Effort Score (CES)	Net Promoter Score (NPS)
Proposed Model	88%	92%	3.5	1.2	75%
Rule-based Chatbots	75%	70%	6.0	3.5	55%
IBM Watson Assistant	80%	80%	5.5	3.0	60%
Google Dialogflow	78%	78%	5.0	2.8	58%
Zendesk Answer Bot	76%	72%	6.5	3.6	57%
Amazon Lex	85%	82%	4.2	2.5	70%
LivePerson	80%	79%	5.2	3.1	63%
Intercom	78%	74%	5.5	3.3	60%
Drift	77%	75%	5.3	3.4	59%
Freshdesk	72%	70%	6.2	3.8	56%
Zoho Desk	70%	68%	6.5	3.9	54%

Table 4 provides a comparative analysis of Business Impact Measures for the proposed model and ten existing customer support automation models, focusing on metrics like Cost Savings, Operational Efficiency, Return on Investment (ROI), Revenue Growth, and Customer Retention. The proposed model demonstrates a significant edge in driving business value and operational success.The proposed model achieves remarkable cost savings of 35%, far exceeding systems like Rule-based Chatbots (10%) and Zoho Desk (10%). Its operational efficiency is also the highest at 40%, outperforming competitors such as IBM Watson Assistant (25%) and Drift (20%), showcasing its ability to optimize resources effectively.In terms of financial outcomes, the proposed model boasts an impressive ROI of 120%, setting a benchmark for profitability. This is nearly double the ROI of Google Dialogflow (60%) and significantly higher than the 35% achieved by Rule-based Chatbots. The revenue growth metric further highlights its impact, with the proposed model driving a 15% increase, compared to 5% for systems like Freshdesk and Rule-based Chatbots.The proposed model also excels in customer-centric metrics, achieving a customer retention rate of 88%, the highest among all models. It outshines competitors like Amazon Lex (65%) and LivePerson (63%), ensuring continued customer engagement and loyalty over time.

Table 4. Business Impact Measures for the Proposed Model with existing customer support automation models

Model	Cost Savings (%)	Operational Efficiency (%)	Return on Investment (ROI) (%)	Revenue Growth (%)	Customer Retention (%)
Proposed Model	35%	40%	120%	15%	88%
Rule-based Chatbots	10%	15%	35%	5%	55%
IBM Watson Assistant	18%	25%	50%	8%	60%
Google Dialogflow	20%	30%	60%	10%	62%
Zendesk Answer Bot	15%	20%	45%	6%	57%
Amazon Lex	22%	28%	65%	12%	65%
LivePerson	18%	22%	55%	9%	63%
Intercom	16%	18%	45%	7%	60%
Drift	14%	20%	42%	6%	58%
Freshdesk	12%	17%	40%	5%	55%
Zoho Desk	10%	15%	38%	4%	54%

IMPLICATIONS OF THE STUDY

Shift in Consumer Preference towards Green Logistics: Massive shift in consumer preference towards green logistics practices is certified by the study. The evidence certified through the results indicates that customers are becoming more environmentally conscious regarding the responsibility of e-commerce operations, particularly at the stage of last-mile delivery. Thus, e-commerce business firms must revisit their logistics choices in an effort to catch up with sustainability demands. Green logistics preference would imply that the business operations would have to be aligned with not only their environmental sustainability objective but also meeting the evolving demands of green consumers. The companies that fail to integrate green schemes would lose their customers to competition from companies that provide sustainable logistic services.

Economic Advantage to CEP Companies for Green Logistics Implementation: The environmental advantages are more than green logistics implementation brings to CEP companies. The study reveals that green consumers are willing to pay a premium for services they perceive as sustainable. This presents a competitive advantage to CEP companies through the inclusion of aspects which enable green logistics, i.e., electric vehicles, routing optimization, and environmentally friendly packaging. By aligning operations with customers' values of sustainability, companies can build brand loyalty, earn good reputation, and differentiate in the competitive e-business environment.

Implementation Problems of Green Logistics: Besides the apparent advantages of green logistics, the study uncovers problems and hurdles to companies in adopting green logistics practices. The main issue is that adopting green technology, e.g., electric vehicles of transport and warehouses with energy from renewable energy-harvested sources, demands higher cost. Opposition from a few of the stakeholders, e.g., supply chain allies and logistics companies, will also be present with lower incentives or funds to go greener. Technology barriers in certain regions are also reported to discourage mass adoption of green logistics, particularly in rural or underdeveloped regions. This will require collective effort on the part of both the public and private sectors regarding the issue of incentives to firms to embrace greenness and investment in infrastructure.

Transparency and Communication Role in Building Trust: The research postulates the extent of the role of transparency and communication in trust building. To benefit from the shift towards green logistics, not only must businesses incorporate green business practices but also make such practices known in an open fashion to customers. Customers are going to trust and patronize businesses that provide such open revelations of attempts at sustainability, such as curbing carbon footprints, minimizing waste, and optimizing the use of resources, based on studies. CEP companies and online shopping websites need to establish trust by disclosing their commitment towards sustainability in tangible proof through transparent reporting as well as marketing. Policy Implications and Government Policy: The study also identifies how government policy as well as legislation could be catalysts for the take-up of green logistics.

With policies encouraging the take-up of sustainable concepts, governments could easily mobilize the logistics industry. It can mean providing tax credits or subsidies to companies that are investing in green technology and stricter environmental rules for logistics operations. More companies looking for green logistics, the regulatory bodies must remake policies such that electronic business also falls under environmental policy. This can be a cleaner system of e-commerce without providing each business an uneven playing field to do business.

DISCUSSION

Consumer Awareness and Technological Consciousness: The research shows rising awareness of Indian consumers towards the green practices of logistics, specifically at the last-mile delivery stage.

This is being initiated by rising media focus towards climate change and the green footprint left by e-commerce. The research is demonstrating that individuals are becoming more and more technologically aware with a large percentage proactively looking for information regarding the sustainability actions of online retailers. But even given such an awareness, to pay more for cleaner delivery is not best at best, with the study putting that price sensitivity is still high. So much so that as consumers are able to tell the truth that they want sustainable logistics, price and convenience continue to be top purchase drivers. Adoption of green technology by e-commerce companies and CEP operators: Apart from the above, adoption is still in its initial stage among the e-commerce companies and CEP operators.

The practice is commonest among the companies to have thought about how they need green logistics but not ready to invest a lot because green technologies are expensive in the very initial phase. For instance, electric vehicles (EVs), since they are environmentally friendly, cost more to acquire and maintain than traditional vehicles. Similarly, the establishment of green logistics centers such as power charging centers and energy-saving storage houses is a capital-intensive venture. However, as people become increasingly concerned with sustainability, the e-commerce and CEP industry sectors can discover that profitability will cost itself in the long term. Effect of Green Logistics on Supply Chain Dynamics: The research has an interesting point in the scenario of the effect of green logistics on supply chain dynamics.

When businesses adopt green operations, the dynamics in the supply chain will surely shift. E-commerce businesses may be compelled to deal with new suppliers who are experts in green technology, thereby transforming the face of logistics. This would lead to new sustainability-focused business models in the supply chain, from procurement through to end delivery. Second, with increased innovation in green logistics technologies, supply chain efficiency would increase, hence reducing long-term operational expenses. Consumer Values for Green Logistics and Competitive Advantage: Customer values, the research says, are shifting towards companies that offer green logistics services.

Those e-commerce companies that are unable to position themselves along these lines risk losing their customers to those companies that move faster to adopt customers' values. The study supported customers' willingness to pay additional for environmentally friendly services, i.e., last-mile delivery. This shift in consumers' preference creates space for business firms to compete with one another to offer greener logistics services that are not only greener but also more embracing of the values of green consumers. The Role of Collaboration in Green Logistics: The research highlights the importance of collaboration of the stakeholders in the logistics industry to ease the adoption of green logistics.

As part of realization of effective green logistics practices, online business traders need to collaborate with the government, leaders in technology innovation, and logistics service providers. Electric trucks and warehouses powered by renewable energy need to be developed by collaboration among the above players. Secondly, the encouragement of green logistics by the government and the creation of a facilitation environment by the government for innovation also support the improvement in the extensive use of green practices in the sector.

FUTURE SCOPE

More Deployment of AI and Data Analytics to Optimize Green Logistics: Optimizing logistics in the future will qualify employing superior technology, such as artificial intelligence (AI) and data analysis, to optimize logistics.

AI can be used to predict more fuel-efficient and lower carbon emission delivery routes, while data analytics can be used to identify regions of inefficiency within supply chain operations. With such technologies, e-commerce and CEP businesses can render their logistics more environmentally friendly while realizing more cost savings. One of the areas for research in the future is employing AI tools to enhance green logistics practice and analyze their impact on business performance and customer satisfaction. Synthesizing Green Logistics and Circular Economy Models: The research area for the future for this study would be examining how green logistics is combined with circular economy models that are aimed at reducing waste and promoting reusing and recycling of the products.

E-commerce companies may have take-back schemes on products and packaging that reduce the environmental impact of waste and returns. Green logistics activities of product return through reverse logistics, recycling, and remanufacturing might be the hallmark of green e-commerce. Opportunities of intersection of green logistics with circular economy strategies and how, and its significance in brand identity and customer loyalty are to be explored by future research. Adoption of Green Logistics in Emerging Economies: While the research work is being carried out in India, there is huge scope for studying the adoption of green logistics in other emerging economies as well.

Where the industries of e-commerce are growing very rapidly, such as Southeast Asia and Africa, green logistics can be one among the main determinants to decide the sustainability of logistics activities. Future research will be able to examine the implementation of green logistics practices for addressing the specific needs and issues of such markets, such as infrastructural limitations, budgetary limitations, and local environmental concerns. Information on how such practices can be implemented in emerging markets can be highly useful to companies having international e-commerce business. Government Policy and Regulation to Encourage Green Logistics: Future research can explore how government policy and regulation can encourage the adoption of green logistics.

Governments can also play a very strong role through providing incentives to firms for adopting green initiatives, such as tax credits, grants, and subsidies for green infrastructure. Additionally, stricter environmental policy regarding logistics activity could prompt firms to adopt more sustainable conduct. Future studies can also consider how policy from the government can affect take-up of green logistics and the most appropriate mechanisms to promote sustainability in the logistics sector.

Consumer Education towards Green Logistics: Greater awareness among consumers about environmental issues becomes the key driving factor in compelling the adoption of green logistics.

Future studies can explore how the educational initiatives among consumers will drive greater demand for green logistics services. By educating customers with proper information about the environmental impact of their purchases, e-commerce companies can help customers make better choices. Educational campaigns enlightening consumers about the benefits of green logistics and how the latter can minimize carbon prints can create demand for eco-friendly procedures in e-commerce. Researching here is a review of the impact of green logistics on the consumer's decision in e-commerce. With sustainability now the forefront issue of consumers, adopting green logistics processes presents opportunities and challenges for e-commerce as well as CEP players. There are enough opportunities for green logistics innovation in the future and further research can be done as to how to upgrade and expand such processes in a manner that would make the industry sustainable.

CONCLUSION

Comparison of the performance of the Proposed Model with that of existing computerized customer service systems reveals that the Proposed Model has better business results. It reveals greater cost savings (35%), enhanced operating efficiency (40%), and a high ROI of 120%. The Proposed Model also reveals high top-line growth and customer satisfaction and performs better on these most important business metrics. The research shows the significance of embracing high-tech automation technology into customer service, which, in addition to enhancing customer satisfaction, also facilitated business expansion. Business firms who would like to use their customer service operations and improve their bottom line are urged in this study to prioritize automated solutions when it comes to measures and performance targets spelled out in this study.

REFERENCES

Balagué, C., Martin-Fuentes, E., & Gómez, M. J. (2016). Fiabilidad de las críticas hoteleras autenticadas y no autenticadas: El caso de TripAdvisor y Booking.com. *Cuadernos de Turismo*, *38*(38), 67–86. DOI: 10.6018/turismo.38.271351

Borrego, Á., & Comalat Navarra, M. (2021). What users say about public libraries: An analysis of Google Maps reviews. *Online Information Review*, *45*(1), 84–98. DOI: 10.1108/OIR-09-2019-0291

Climber. (2022). Qlik a leader in the 2022 Gartner Magic Quadrant. https://www.climber.eu/qlik-a-leader-in-the-2022-gartner-magic-quadrant/

Czerepicki, A. (2019). Study on effectiveness of using column-oriented databases in the processing of measurement characteristics of an electric vehicle. *Archives of Transport*, *51*(3), 77–84. DOI: 10.5604/01.3001.0013.6164

Edmondson, A. C. (2018). *The fearless organization: Creating psychological safety in the workplace for learning, innovation, and growth.* John Wiley & Sons.

Eurostat. (2008). NACE Rev. 2: Statistical classification of economic activities in the European Community. Office for Official Publications of the European Communities.

Howson, C. (2013). Successful business intelligence (2nd ed.): Unlock the value of BI & big data. McGraw-Hill Professional.

Jachimowski, R., Gołębiowski, P., Izdebski, M., Pyza, D., & Szczepański, E. (2017). Designing and efficiency of database for simulation of processes in systems: Case study for the simulation of warehouse processes. *Archives of Transport*, *41*(1), 31–42. DOI: 10.5604/01.3001.0009.7380

Jacyna, M., Semenov, I., & Trojanowski, P. (2015). The research directions of increase effectiveness of the functioning of the RSA with regard to specialized transport. *Archives of Transport*, *35*(3), 27–39. DOI: 10.5604/08669546.1185181

Kim, W. (2007). Online call quality monitoring for automating agent-based call centers. In *Proceedings of Interspeech 2007* (pp. 130–133). ISCA. DOI: 10.21437/Interspeech.2007-56

Kubina, M., Koman, G., & Kubinova, I. (2015). Possibility of improving efficiency within business intelligence systems in companies. *Procedia Economics and Finance*, *26*, 300–305. DOI: 10.1016/S2212-5671(15)00856-4

Lokman, A. S., & Aberdeen, M. A. (2019). Modern chatbot systems: A technical review. In K. Arai, R. Bhatia, & S. Kapoor (Eds.), Proceedings of the Future Technologies Conference (FTC) 2018 (pp. 1012–1023). Springer International Publishing. DOI: 10.1007/978-3-030-02683-7_75

Loshin, D. (2003). *Business intelligence: The savvy manager's guide, getting onboard with emerging IT*. Morgan Kaufmann. DOI: 10.1016/B978-155860916-7/50003-8

MarketsandMarkets. (2024, October 2). Business intelligence market worth $33.3 billion by 2025. https://www.marketsandmarkets.com/PressReleases/social-business-intelligence-bi.asp

Martin-Fuentes, E., Mateu, C., & Fernandez, C. (2020). The more the merrier? Number of reviews versus score on TripAdvisor and Booking.com. *International Journal of Hospitality & Tourism Administration*, *21*(4), 1–14. DOI: 10.1080/15256480.2018.1429337

McBride, N. (2014). Business intelligence in magazine distribution. *International Journal of Information Management*, *34*(1), 58–62. DOI: 10.1016/j.ijinfomgt.2013.09.006

Nujic, L., & Ambrusec, M. (2021). Influencer marketing in the tourism sector: A company's perspective. In *Proceedings of the Interdisciplinary Management Research*. Opatija, Croatia.

Selamat, M. A., & Windasari, N. A. (2021). Chatbot for SMEs: Integrating customer and business owner perspectives. *Technology in Society*, *66*, 101685. DOI: 10.1016/j.techsoc.2021.101685

Stone, D., & Heen, S. (2014). *Thanks for the feedback: The science and art of receiving feedback well*. Penguin.

Swani, K., & Milne, G. (2017). Evaluating Facebook brand content popularity for service versus goods offerings. *Journal of Business Research*, *79*, 123–133. DOI: 10.1016/j.jbusres.2017.06.003

Watson, H. J., & Wixom, B. H. (2007). The current state of business intelligence. *Computer*, *40*(9), 96–99. DOI: 10.1109/MC.2007.331

Yongho Hyun, M., Kim, H.-C., & O'Keefe, R. M. (2014). Inter-satisfaction between website and automated call distribution (ACD) systems. *Journal of Travel & Tourism Marketing*, *31*(8), 1039–1056. DOI: 10.1080/10548408.2014.892467

Zapier. (2021). The 9 best free form builders and survey tools in 2021. https://zapier.com/blog/best-free-survey-tool-form-app/

Chapter 8
Human-AI Fusion:
Elevating Customer Experience Across Selected Service Industries

Razia Nagina
https://orcid.org/0000-0002-0305-8393
Lovely Professional University, India

ABSTRACT

The integration of Artificial Intelligence (AI) technologies, such as chatbots and virtual assistants, has profoundly transformed customer experiences across various industries. This chapter explores the enhancement of customer experiences through AI in retail, finance, and healthcare sectors. It investigates the key factors necessary for the successful implementation of human-AI collaboration and examines real-world applications to draw valuable lessons. Furthermore, it outlines best practices for integrating AI to anticipate customer needs and improve decision-making processes. By analyzing these aspects, the chapter aims to provide a comprehensive understanding of how AI can be effectively employed to revolutionize customer experience and drive business growth.

1. INTRODUCTION

The rapid advancement of Artificial Intelligence (AI) has significantly transformed multiple sectors, redefining how businesses interact with customers and enhancing the overall value delivery process (Enholm et al., 2022). In particular, tools such as chatbots and virtual assistants have revolutionized Customer Experience (CX) by introducing intelligent, responsive solutions that increase customer satisfaction, improve operational efficiency, and offer organizations a competitive edge. As businesses across industries continue to explore digital transformation opportunities, the

DOI: 10.4018/979-8-3693-8512-8.ch008

integration of AI into customer-facing functions has emerged as a strategic priority and an essential component of modern CX frameworks (Ali, 2024).

The increasing adoption of AI in customer experience is largely driven by the growing demand for faster, more consistent, and more efficient service delivery. Traditional service models, which rely heavily on human agents, often struggle to manage the rising volume of customer queries and meet the evolving expectation of 24/7 service availability. In this context, AI technologies have gained prominence due to their ability to process large volumes of data and provide real-time, automated responses (Hoyer et al., 2020). Early applications primarily consisted of rule-based chatbots that were limited to handling repetitive and predefined queries. Despite their simplicity, these early systems laid the foundational groundwork for more advanced AI-powered solutions that are now capable of understanding context, learning from interactions, and responding to complex customer needs (Adamopoulou & Moussiades, 2020).

With the progression of AI technologies, their applications in customer experience have broadened significantly. Machine learning and natural language processing (NLP) led to the development of advanced chatbots and virtual assistants that could understand context, learn from interactions, and provide personalized responses (Maria et al., 2022). This evolution marked a significant shift from reactive customer service to proactive customer engagement. Businesses began to use AI not just to respond to inquiries but to anticipate customer needs, offer tailored recommendations, and create more meaningful interactions (Haleem et al., 2022). For instance, in retail, AI-powered chatbots analyze browsing history and purchase patterns to suggest products; in finance, virtual assistants provide personalized financial advice; in healthcare, AI tools assist patients with medical queries, appointments, and preliminary diagnoses.

AI's impact on customer experience goes beyond efficiency and personalization. These advancements have empowered businesses to gather and analyze large volumes of customer data, providing deeper insights into consumer behavior and preferences. This data-driven strategy enables companies to make well-informed decisions, optimize their operations, and continually enhance their services (Ameen et al., 2021). For example, analyzing customer interactions with AI systems helps businesses identify common pain points, refine processes, and enhance the overall experience. Additionally, AI's ability to process data in real-time allows businesses to swiftly respond to evolving customer needs and market dynamics, thus preserving their agility and competitive edge (Foltean & van Bruggen, 2022).

However, integrating AI into customer experience presents challenges. The quality of data is crucial for training AI systems; inaccurate or poor-quality data can result in flawed predictions and less effective customer interactions (Liang et al., 2022). Ensuring data accuracy, privacy, and security is crucial for successful AI implementation. Additionally, integrating AI with existing systems requires technical expertise and a clear understanding of how AI can complement and enhance human roles within customer service (Jarrahi et al., 2023). Ethical considerations also arise as AI systems become more autonomous, particularly in areas like finance and healthcare, where decisions can significantly impact customers' lives. Businesses must establish robust governance frameworks to oversee AI applications, ensuring they adhere to ethical standards (Whittlestone et al., 2019).

Despite these challenges, the advantages of integrating AI into customer experience are substantial. AI technologies present businesses with the chance to offer more personalized, efficient, and scalable customer service, ultimately fostering higher satisfaction and loyalty. By automating routine tasks, AI allows human agents to concentrate on more intricate and value-adding interactions, thereby enhancing overall service quality. As AI continues to develop, its influence on customer experience is expected to grow, providing businesses with new avenues for innovation and market differentiation (Kumar et al., 2024).

Given the rapid integration of AI into customer service across industries, it is crucial to study how these technologies influence customer experiences and service delivery. Grasping the impact of AI on customer interactions is crucial for businesses that aim to remain competitive and meet the evolving expectations of their customers. This chapter addresses this need by focusing on specific research objectives that explore AI's role in customer experience.

To meet the above objectives, this chapter adopts a systematic literature review methodology. The process involved collecting and analyzing relevant scholarly and industry sources published over the last decade. Using a structured search across academic databases such as Scopus, Web of Science, and Google Scholar, the review included peer-reviewed journal articles, books, and conference proceedings relevant to AI in customer experience across retail, finance, and healthcare sectors. The review followed a structured approach to literature analysis, emphasizing thematic categorization, synthesis of findings, and identification of research gaps. Through this focused exploration, the chapter aims to offer both theoretical insights and practical recommendations that contribute meaningfully to ongoing academic and professional conversations about AI's transformative potential in customer experience.

2. RESEARCH QUESTIONS

- How are AI technologies, such as chatbots and virtual assistants, enhancing customer experience across various industries?
- What are the key factors for successful implementation of human-AI collaboration in retail, finance, and healthcare?

- What lessons can be learned from real-world applications of AI in customer experience?
- What are the best practices for integrating AI to anticipate customer needs and enhance decision-making processes?

2.1 How are AI Technologies, Such as Chatbots and Virtual Assistants, Enhancing Customer Experience Across Various Industries?

In an era characterized by rapid technological advancements, businesses are continually seeking innovative ways to enhance the Customer Experience (CX). The importance of delivering exceptional CX cannot be overstated, as it directly impacts customer satisfaction, loyalty, and overall business success (Srivastava et al., 2021). One of the most significant developments in this realm is the integration of Artificial Intelligence (AI) technologies, particularly chatbots and virtual assistants. These AI-driven tools are revolutionizing how companies interact with their customers, providing real-time, personalized, and efficient interactions that meet the ever-growing expectations of modern consumers (Aslam, 2023).

AI technologies have evolved from being experimental tools to becoming integral elements of customer service strategies. These technologies empower businesses to deliver round-the-clock support, offer personalized recommendations, and swiftly resolve customer inquiries, thereby greatly enhancing customer satisfaction. The transformative impact of AI on customer experience is well-documented in the literature. For instance, El Bakkouri et al. (2022) underscore the vital role of chatbots in customer service, highlighting their capacity to provide immediate assistance and manage a high volume of inquiries at once. Likewise, Hoyer et al. (2020) explore how emerging technologies, including AI, are revolutionizing customer interactions by making them more seamless and tailored to individual needs.

2.1.1 The Shift from Experimental to Essential

AI technologies have transitioned from being mere experimental tools to becoming essential components of customer service strategies. Initially, AI was explored in pilot projects and limited implementations to gauge its potential benefits and address any technical challenges. However, as these technologies have matured, their capabilities have expanded, and their value has become increasingly evident. Today, AI-driven tools like chatbots and virtual assistants are integral to the customer service operations of many businesses across various industries. This evolution is driven by several key factors (Chaturvedi & Verma, 2023):

Technological Advancements: Ongoing advancements in AI algorithms, machine learning models, and natural language processing (NLP) have greatly improved the capability of chatbots and virtual assistants to accurately comprehend and contextually address customer inquiries.

Increased Customer Expectations: Modern consumers demand quick, efficient, and personalized interactions. They expect businesses to be available 24/7, provide instant support, and offer solutions tailored to their specific needs and preferences. AI technologies are well-equipped to meet these high expectations by leveraging data-driven insights and automation.

Business Efficiency and Cost Savings: AI-powered customer service tools can handle a large volume of queries simultaneously, reducing the burden on human agents and allowing businesses to operate more efficiently. This not only improves response times but also leads to significant cost savings, making AI an attractive investment for companies.

2.1.2 The Role of AI in Enhancing Customer Experience

A growing body of literature underscores the transformative potential of AI in elevating the customer experience (CX). Researchers and industry experts have extensively studied and documented the benefits and applications of AI in customer service. Several key aspects illustrate how AI technologies are revolutionizing CX:

Real-Time Support: AI chatbots and virtual assistants provide instant responses to customer inquiries, eliminating the wait times typically associated with traditional customer service channels. In today's fast-paced world, where customers demand instant assistance, real-time support has become essential.

Reference: El Bakkouri et al. (2022) emphasize the important role that chatbots play in customer service, particularly their capacity to deliver instant support and manage numerous inquiries at once. Their research demonstrates that chatbots can greatly enhance response times and boost customer satisfaction by providing round-the-clock availability and prompt solutions to common problems.

Personalized Interactions: AI technologies utilize advanced data analytics and machine learning to gain insights into customer preferences and behavior. This allows businesses to provide highly personalized recommendations and solutions, thereby improving the overall customer experience.

Reference: Hoyer et al. (2020) explore how emerging technologies, such as AI, are revolutionizing the customer experience by enhancing the smoothness and personalization of interactions. Their study demonstrates that AI-driven tools can analyze customer data to provide tailored recommendations, leading to higher engagement and satisfaction.

Efficiency in Handling Inquiries: AI chatbots are capable of handling a large number of customer inquiries at the same time, efficiently addressing routine questions. This capability allows human agents to concentrate on more complex problems, thereby enhancing the overall efficiency and effectiveness of customer service operations.

For instance, in the banking industry, chatbots like Erica from Bank of America manage tasks such as checking account balances, processing payments, and offering financial advice. This approach not only accelerates service delivery but also improves the user experience by making it more interactive and convenient (Polireddi, 2024).

Cost Reduction: Integrating AI technologies into customer service can result in substantial cost savings. Automating routine tasks and managing inquiries through AI allows businesses to lessen their reliance on large customer service teams, cut down on operational costs, and reallocate resources to more strategic areas.

Case Study: HDFC Bank's chatbot, EVA (Electronic Virtual Assistant), handled over 2.7 million customer queries within its first six months, demonstrating substantial efficiency gains and cost savings. This example showcases the potential of AI to optimize resources and improve service delivery in the banking sector (Mathew, 2023).

Data-Driven Insights: AI chatbots and virtual assistants gather important data from customer interactions, which businesses can analyze to better understand customer needs and preferences. This data-driven approach facilitates continuous improvement in customer experience strategies and helps businesses stay competitive.

Study Reference: According to research by Hoyer et al. (2020), data-driven insights derived from AI interactions are essential for businesses to remain competitive and effectively respond to customer needs. These insights help refine marketing strategies and product offerings, ensuring they remain aligned with customer desires.

2.1.3 AI and Human Collaboration in Enhancing CX

The integration of AI technologies in customer service is a transformative approach that focuses on enhancing human agents' capabilities rather than replacing them. By leveraging AI to handle routine and repetitive tasks, such as answering common customer queries or processing simple transactions, human agents are freed to concentrate on more complex issues that require emotional intelligence, creativity, and problem-solving skills. This collaborative approach leads to a synergistic effect, where the strengths of both AI and human agents are combined to deliver a more personalized and efficient customer experience (CX). Numerous studies and books highlight that this human-AI partnership is crucial for optimizing customer interactions, reducing response times, and providing tailored solutions, ultimately leading to higher customer satisfaction and loyalty.

2.1.3.1 Real Stories of Human-Machine Collaboration

Davenport and Miller (2022), in their book "Working with AI: Real Stories of Human-Machine Collaboration," provide numerous examples of how AI and human workers can collaborate effectively to enhance business operations, including customer service. They highlight several key points:

- Routine Task Handling: AI can handle repetitive and time-consuming tasks, such as responding to frequently asked questions or managing simple transactions. This enables human agents to concentrate on more complex interactions that require empathy and creative problem-solving skills.
- Enhanced Decision Making: The collaboration between AI and humans leads to better decision-making processes. AI can rapidly analyze large datasets and uncover patterns that may elude human detection. Meanwhile, humans are able to interpret these patterns and apply them within relevant contexts.

2.1.3.2 Enhancing Prediction Accuracy in Retail

Revilla et al. (2023), in their study "Human–Artificial Intelligence Collaboration in Prediction: A Field Experiment in the Retail Industry," explore how AI and human collaboration can enhance prediction accuracy in the retail sector. Their findings indicate:

- Improved Inventory Management: By combining AI's data analysis capabilities with human intuition and experience, retailers can predict demand more accurately. This leads to better inventory management, reducing both stockouts and overstock situations.
- Customer Satisfaction: Enhanced prediction accuracy means that products are more likely to be available when customers need them, leading to higher satisfaction levels. The study showed that collaboration between AI and humans resulted in more precise stocking strategies, directly impacting customer satisfaction positively.

2.1.3.3 Hybrid Intelligence in Marketing Analytics

Petrescu and Krishen (2023), in their article "Hybrid Intelligence: Human–AI Collaboration in Marketing Analytics," discuss how combining AI's data processing power with human creativity and strategic thinking leads to more effective marketing strategies. Key insights from their research include:

- Personalized Marketing Campaigns: AI can examine customer data to discern trends and preferences, allowing marketers to design highly personalized campaigns. When combined with human creativity, these campaigns are more engaging and effective.
- Strategic Insights: While AI excels at processing large datasets and identifying patterns, human marketers can use these insights to develop strategies that resonate with target audiences. This hybrid approach ensures that marketing efforts are both data-driven and creatively compelling.

2.1.3.4 Financial Planning and AI Collaboration

Kunnathuvalappil Hariharan (2018), in "Artificial Intelligence and Human Collaboration in Financial Planning," explores the role of AI in enhancing financial planning services. The study highlights several important findings:

- Personalized Investment Recommendations: AI can process extensive financial data to deliver personalized investment recommendations that align with each client's specific needs. This includes risk assessments, financial forecasts, and portfolio management.
- Enhanced Advisor Capabilities: By collaborating with human financial advisors, AI can augment their capabilities, allowing advisors to offer more precise and personalized advice. This collaboration ensures that clients receive comprehensive financial planning services that are both data-driven and human-centric.

2.1.3.5 Research Findings on Human-AI Collaboration

Enhanced Efficiency and Customer Satisfaction

Research across various industries demonstrates that human-AI collaboration significantly enhances both efficiency and customer satisfaction. For example:

- Retail: Revilla et al. (2023) showed that human-AI collaboration in retail prediction led to improved inventory management and customer satisfaction. Retailers who utilized this collaborative approach were able to reduce stock-outs and overstock situations, ensuring that customers found the products they needed when they needed them.
- Marketing: Petrescu and Krishen (2023) found that hybrid intelligence in marketing analytics resulted in more effective and personalized marketing campaigns. By combining AI's data processing capabilities with human cre-

ativity, businesses were able to develop strategies that better resonated with their audiences, leading to higher engagement and conversion rates.

- Financial Services: Kunnathuvalappil Hariharan (2018) highlighted that AI-human collaboration in financial planning led to more accurate and personalized financial advice. Clients benefited from data-driven insights provided by AI, while human advisors offered context and personalized guidance, resulting in better financial outcomes for clients.

2.1.4 The Interconnectedness of AI, CX, and Business Success

The integration of AI technologies into customer service strategies is not just about improving CX in isolation; it is deeply interconnected with overall business success. Enhanced CX leads to higher customer satisfaction, which in turn drives customer loyalty and retention. Content customers are more inclined to make repeat purchases, recommend the brand to others, and become advocates for the business (Bilgeri, 2020).

Moreover, the efficiencies and cost savings achieved through AI implementation contribute to better financial performance. Businesses can allocate resources more strategically, invest in innovation, and scale their operations more effectively. This holistic approach to leveraging AI for CX enhancement creates a virtuous cycle of improvement, where better customer experiences lead to stronger business performance, which then enables further investments in AI and customer service enhancements (Enholm et al., 2022).

The integration of AI technologies, particularly chatbots and virtual assistants, is transforming the landscape of customer experience. These AI-driven tools provide real-time, personalized, and efficient interactions that meet the ever-growing expectations of modern consumers (Bilgeri, 2020). The advantages of AI in enhancing customer experience (CX) are well-documented in the literature. These benefits include offering round-the-clock support, delivering personalized recommendations, increasing efficiency, lowering costs, and producing valuable data-driven insights (Zhang, 2024). As businesses increasingly adopt AI, the impact of these technologies in creating outstanding customer experiences and driving business success will become even more significant.

2.1.5 Enhancing Customer Experience with AI Technologies

1. Round-the-clock Availability and Instant Responses

A key advantage of AI chatbots and virtual assistants is their capacity to offer round-the-clock support. This 24/7 availability guarantees that customers can access assistance at any time, which is especially valuable in industries where timely support is crucial.

Example: E-commerce: Leading e-commerce platforms such as Amazon and Alibaba utilize AI chatbots to manage a wide range of customer inquiries, from order tracking to product recommendations. According to Daqar and Smoudy (2019), these chatbots significantly reduce wait times and enhance the shopping experience by providing instant responses to customer queries. This continuous availability not only boosts customer satisfaction but also aids businesses in retaining their customers by providing prompt and efficient service.

2. Personalization and Predictive Analytics

AI technologies excel in analyzing large datasets to provide personalized customer experiences. By analyzing individual tastes, preferences and habits, AI chatbots can deliver personalized recommendations and solutions that improve the overall customer experience.

Case Study: Netflix: Netflix exemplifies how AI can be utilized to personalize the customer experience. The platform uses sophisticated AI algorithms to analyze users' viewing habits and preferences, allowing it to recommend content that aligns with each viewer's tastes. This level of personalization, as highlighted by Kushwaha, Kumar, and Kar (2021), not only keeps users engaged but also increases subscription retention rates by enhancing the viewing experience to be more enjoyable and relevant to individual preferences.

3. Efficient Issue Resolution

AI chatbots are adept at handling common customer issues quickly and efficiently. By resolving simple queries, they free up human agents to focus on more complex problems, ensuring that all customer issues are addressed promptly and effectively.

Example: Banking: Financial institutions such as Bank of America have implemented AI chatbots like Erica to assist customers with routine tasks. Erica helps users check account balances, make payments, and receive financial guidance. This quick resolution of simple queries enhances the user experience by making banking more interactive and convenient, as noted by Reddy (2022) in his exploration of AI-powered marketing automation in enhancing customer experience.

4. Cost Reduction and Resource Optimization

The implementation of AI chatbots leads to significant cost savings for businesses by reducing the need for large customer service teams. This enables companies to use their resources more efficiently and invest in other aspects of customer service enhancement.

Case Study: HDFC Bank: HDFC Bank's chatbot, EVA (Electronic Virtual Assistant), handled over 2.7 million customer queries within its first six months, demonstrating substantial efficiency gains and cost savings. This example, discussed by Mathew (2023) and Khan et al. (2021), showcase the potential of AI to optimize resources and improve service delivery in the banking sector.

5. Improved Customer Engagement

AI chatbots engage customers through interactive and conversational interfaces. By providing quick responses and maintaining consistent communication, they significantly enhance customer engagement and satisfaction.

Example: Hospitality Industry: Hotels such as Hilton have integrated AI-powered chatbots to manage bookings, offer local recommendations, and address guest inquiries. These chatbots provide a seamless and interactive way for guests to access services and information, greatly enhancing their overall experience (Vashishth et al., 2024). Ahmad et al. (2024) highlights how AI chatbots in the hospitality industry not only improve customer engagement but also streamline operations, making the guest experience more enjoyable and efficient.

6. Enhanced Data Collection and Insights

AI chatbots collect valuable data on customer interactions, which businesses can analyze to gain insights into customer needs and preferences. This data-driven approach facilitates continuous improvement in customer experience strategies.

Case Study: Sephora: Sephora's chatbot on platforms like Facebook Messenger not only assists customers with product recommendations but also gathers data on customer preferences and feedback. This information helps Sephora refine its marketing strategies and product offerings, ensuring they remain aligned with customer desires (Eyada & Ahmed, 2022). According to research by Hoyer et al. (2020), such data-driven insights are crucial for businesses to stay competitive and responsive to customer needs.

7. Multilingual Support

AI chatbots can provide support in multiple languages, allowing businesses to serve a global customer base and improve accessibility.

Example: Travel Industry: Airlines such as KLM utilize chatbots to assist customers in various languages, helping with tasks such as booking flights, providing travel updates, and answering travel-related queries (BR, 2022). This multilingual capability ensures that language barriers do not hinder the customer experience, as highlighted by El Bakkouri, Raki, and Belgnaoui (2022) in their discussion on the role of chatbots in customer service.

8. Proactive Customer Service

AI technologies can anticipate customer needs and offer proactive assistance, further enhancing the customer experience.

Case Study: Starbucks: The Starbucks Barista chatbot allows customers to place orders via voice or text before arriving at the store. This proactive service saves time for customers and streamlines the ordering process, contributing to a more efficient and enjoyable customer experience (Sharma & Aggarwal, 2024; Hasan et al., 2021). Reddy (2022) emphasizes how proactive AI solutions can significantly enhance customer satisfaction by addressing needs before they arise.

2.2 What Are the Key Factors for Successful Implementation of Human-AI Collaboration in Retail, Finance, and Healthcare?

Successful implementation of human-AI collaboration in retail, finance, and healthcare requires careful consideration of several key factors. These factors ensure that the integration of AI technologies enhances human capabilities, improves efficiency, and delivers superior customer or patient experiences. Here are the critical factors for each sector:

2.2.1 Retail

a) Data Integration and Management:

Effective AI systems require high-quality data. Retailers must ensure that their data is accurate, up-to-date, and well-integrated across various platforms (e.g., POS systems, CRM, and supply chain management systems) (Fragkiskaki, 2023).

Investing in robust data management solutions helps in gathering and processing data efficiently.

Example: Walmart, a global retail giant, employs AI for inventory management and supply chain optimization. Their AI systems analyze historical sales data, current inventory levels, and external variables such as weather forecasts to accurately predict demand. This integration helps Walmart maintain optimal stock levels and reduce inventory costs (Frank & Henry, 2024).

b) User-Friendly Interfaces:

AI tools must have intuitive interfaces that employees can easily interact with. This minimizes the learning curve and ensures smooth adoption.

User interfaces should provide clear insights and actionable recommendations based on AI analyses.

Example: Amazon's AI-powered recommendation engine is a prime example of a user-friendly interface. It examines customer browsing and purchase history to recommend relevant products, thereby enhancing the user experience and boosting sales conversion rates (Pyarelal & Das, 2018).

c) Training and Change Management:

Employees must be trained to work with AI systems, understanding both the technology's capabilities and its limitations.

Change management strategies are essential for overcoming resistance and ensuring a seamless transition to AI-enhanced workflows.

Example: Tesco, a leading UK retailer, implemented AI chatbots to handle customer inquiries and complaints. They conducted extensive training programs for their customer service teams to work effectively alongside AI, ensuring smooth integration and improved customer satisfaction (Bird, 2021).

d) Personalization Capabilities:

AI should be used to offer personalized shopping experiences, from personalized marketing campaigns to customized product recommendations.

This requires leveraging customer data to understand preferences and predict future buying behaviors.

Example: Starbucks uses AI to personalize customer experiences through its mobile app. The app recommends personalized drink suggestions based on past purchases and user preferences, enhancing customer loyalty and satisfaction (Naim et al., 2024).

e) Scalability and Flexibility:

AI solutions should be scalable to accommodate growing data volumes and adaptable to evolving retail trends.

Flexibility in AI systems ensures they can integrate with new technologies and platforms as needed.

Example: Alibaba, a global e-commerce giant based in China, uses AI to scale its operations during peak shopping seasons like Singles' Day. AI algorithms analyze user behavior in real time to handle millions of transactions simultaneously, ensuring a seamless shopping experience for customers (Berning, 2021).

Finance

f) Regulatory Compliance and Security:

AI implementations must adhere to financial regulations and standards to maintain data privacy and security.

Regular audits and security assessments help in maintaining compliance and protecting sensitive financial data.

Example: HSBC, a multinational bank, employs AI for fraud detection and risk management. AI algorithms analyze transaction patterns and detect anomalies that may indicate fraudulent activities, ensuring compliance with financial regulations and protecting customer accounts (Mohanty & Mishra, 2023).

g) Integration with Existing Systems:

AI tools need to seamlessly integrate with existing financial systems such as trading platforms, customer relationship management (CRM) systems, and financial databases.

Integration ensures a unified approach to data processing and decision-making.

Example: ICICI Bank in India utilizes AI-powered chatbots for customer service. These chatbots are integrated with the bank's core banking system, allowing customers to perform transactions, check balances, and obtain account information through conversational interfaces (Patil & Kulkarni, 2019).

h) Transparency and Explainability:

AI algorithms should be transparent and explainable to build trust among financial advisors and clients.

Understanding how AI reaches its conclusions is crucial for compliance and for clients to feel confident in AI-driven recommendations.

Example: JPMorgan Chase uses AI in asset management to provide investment recommendations. The AI systems provide transparent explanations of their recommendations, helping financial advisors and clients understand the rationale behind investment decisions (Byrum, 2022).

i) Real-Time Data Processing:

Financial markets operate in real time, so AI systems must process and analyze data quickly to provide timely insights and recommendations.

High-frequency trading and real-time fraud detection are examples where real-time processing is critical.

Example: Goldman Sachs uses AI algorithms for high-frequency trading. These algorithms process market data in real time and execute trades at high speeds to seize market opportunities, highlighting the critical role of real-time data processing in finance (Fathia, 2024).

j) Enhancing Human Expertise:

AI should augment, not replace, human expertise in finance. AI can handle complex data analysis, while human advisors focus on strategy and client relationships.

Collaborative tools should enable financial professionals to make more informed decisions based on AI-driven insights.

Example: Vanguard, an investment management company, integrates AI in financial planning tools for advisors. AI analyzes client financial data to provide personalized investment strategies, empowering advisors to offer tailored advice that meets individual client goals (Mohammed et al., 2021).

2.2.2 Healthcare

a) Clinical Integration:

AI systems must integrate seamlessly with existing clinical workflows and electronic health records (EHR) systems.

This integration ensures that AI recommendations are easily accessible and actionable by healthcare providers.

Example: Apollo Hospitals in India utilizes AI for medical imaging analysis. AI algorithms examine medical images, such as MRI scans and X-rays, to identify anomalies and support radiologists in making precise diagnoses, thereby enhancing patient care outcomes (Agarwal et al., 2020).

b) Data Privacy and Security:

Healthcare data is highly sensitive, so AI implementations must adhere to strict privacy and security standards, such as HIPAA in the United States.

Ensuring data encryption, secure access controls, and regular security audits are essential.

Example: Mayo Clinic in the United States employs AI for patient data analytics while ensuring strict adherence to HIPAA regulations. AI systems anonymize patient data and analyze trends to enhance treatment protocols without compromising patient privacy (Adler-Milstein et al., 2022).

c) Interdisciplinary Collaboration:

Effective AI implementation in healthcare demands collaboration among data scientists, IT professionals, and healthcare practitioners.

Interdisciplinary teams ensure that AI tools are clinically relevant and practically useful.

Example: NHS (National Health Service) in the UK collaborates with AI startups to develop AI-powered healthcare applications. These applications range from virtual health assistants to predictive analytics for patient management, illustrating effective interdisciplinary collaboration in healthcare (Kakkad et al., 2023).

d) Patient-Centric Design:

AI systems should focus on improving patient outcomes and experiences. This includes personalized treatment plans and predictive analytics to prevent illnesses.

Patient-centric design also involves ensuring that patients understand and trust AI-driven recommendations.

Example: Ping An Good Doctor in China uses AI-powered chatbots for remote patient consultations. Patients can interact with AI chatbots to describe symptoms, receive preliminary diagnoses, and schedule appointments with healthcare providers, enhancing access to healthcare services (Harrison, 2021).

e) Continuous Learning and Improvement:

AI systems in healthcare should continually learn from new data and clinical outcomes to enhance their accuracy and effectiveness.

Implementing feedback loops where healthcare providers can input their observations and outcomes can help in refining AI models.

Example: Philips Healthcare utilizes AI for predictive analytics in intensive care units (ICUs). AI algorithms analyze patient data in real time to predict deteriorations in health, enabling early interventions and improving patient outcomes through continuous learning and refinement (McAdams et al., 2022).

f) Regulatory Compliance:

Healthcare AI systems must comply with medical regulations and standards, such as FDA approval for AI diagnostic tools.

Ensuring that AI applications meet regulatory standards helps in building trust and ensuring safety.

Cross-Industry Considerations

g) Ethical AI Use:

Across all sectors, ethical considerations must guide AI use. This includes ensuring fairness, avoiding biases, and maintaining transparency.

Ethical frameworks and guidelines should be established to govern AI deployment.

h) Stakeholder Engagement:

Involving all relevant stakeholders (employees, customers, clients, patients, and regulators) in the planning and implementation stages is crucial.

Ongoing communication and feedback mechanisms are essential to ensure that AI solutions align with the needs and expectations of all stakeholders.

i) Performance Monitoring and Evaluation:

Continuous monitoring and evaluation of AI systems help in assessing their impact and effectiveness.

Key performance indicators (KPIs) should be defined to measure the success of AI implementations and guide future improvements.

By focusing on these key factors, businesses in retail, finance, and healthcare can successfully implement AI-human collaboration, leading to enhanced customer experiences, improved operational efficiency, and better overall outcomes.

2.3 Lessons Learned From Real-World Applications of AI in Customer Experience

a) Data Privacy and Transparency:

Lesson: Data privacy involves safeguarding personal information from unauthorized access, use, or disclosure. In the context of AI-driven interactions, businesses collect vast amounts of customer data to personalize services, improve operational efficiencies, and enhance overall customer experience. However, this data often includes sensitive information such as contact details, purchase history, preferences, and even behavioral patterns. Data privacy and transparency in AI-driven interactions are pivotal for building and maintaining trust with customers. In today's digital age, where personal data is increasingly valuable and vulnerable, businesses must prioritize robust measures to safeguard customer information while being transparent about how AI technologies utilize this data.

Example: Apple has consistently prioritized user privacy, embedding robust data protection measures into its AI-driven services like Siri. Apple ensures that user data used for AI personalization remains on the device whenever possible, reducing the need to transmit personal information over the internet. This approach has helped Apple maintain high levels of customer trust and satisfaction (Loideain & Adams, 2020).

b) Robust Measures for Data Protection:

Compliance with Regulations: Adherence to data protection regulations such as GDPR in Europe or CCPA in California is non-negotiable. These regulations mandate that businesses must secure explicit consent from customers before gathering their personal data and must ensure secure storage and processing practices.

Secure Data Handling: Adopting robust cybersecurity measures is crucial for safeguarding customer data against cyber threats, unauthorized access, and data breaches. This includes encryption of sensitive data both at rest and in transit, regular security audits, and access controls.

Data Minimization: Collecting only the necessary data required for specific purposes reduces the risk associated with data breaches. It's essential to periodically review and purge unnecessary data to minimize exposure.

c) Transparency in AI Utilization:

Transparency involves clearly informing customers about how their data is collected, used, and shared, especially in AI-driven interactions. This transparency builds trust by providing customers with clarity on how businesses leverage AI technologies to enhance their experiences.

Communicating AI Usage:

Clear Privacy Policies: Businesses should articulate their data handling practices clearly in privacy policies accessible to customers. These policies should detail what data is collected, how it is used (e.g., for personalization or analytics), and who has access to it.

User Consent: Obtaining explicit consent from customers before utilizing their data for AI-driven personalization or other purposes is essential. This consent should be informed, meaning customers understand the implications of providing their data.

Explainable AI: Businesses should strive to make AI algorithms explainable, particularly in decision-making processes that impact customers. Customers should have visibility into how AI systems reach conclusions or recommendations to maintain trust and ensure fairness.

d) Building Trust and Customer Confidence:

Customer Control: Empowering customers with control over their data enhances trust. Providing options for customers to manage their preferences, including opting out of data collection or AI-driven personalization, demonstrates respect for their privacy.

Educational Initiatives: Educating customers about data privacy practices and the benefits of AI-enhanced services can alleviate concerns and foster a positive perception of AI technologies.

e) Personalization with User Consent:

Lesson: Effective personalization enhances CX when implemented with clear user consent and control over data.

Personalization with user consent is a cornerstone of effective Customer Experience (CX) in the digital age. Personalization refers to tailoring services, communications, and experiences to individual customer preferences and behaviors. When implemented correctly, it can significantly enhance customer satisfaction, loyalty, and engagement. However, achieving this without compromising user privacy and consent is crucial. Here's an in-depth look at this lesson, emphasizing the importance of user consent and control over data in personalization strategies.

Importance of Personalization in CX:

Personalization involves using data to create customized experiences for customers, which can include personalized product recommendations, tailored marketing messages, and customized user interfaces. Personalization is highly effective because it makes customers feel understood and valued, leading to increased satisfaction and loyalty.

f) Role of User Consent:

User consent is the permission given by customers for businesses to collect, store, and use their personal data for personalization. Clear, informed consent is crucial for several reasons:

Trust Building: When customers understand how their data will be used and give permission for its use, they are more likely to trust the business. Trust is a foundational element of any customer relationship.

Regulatory Compliance: Many jurisdictions have stringent data protection regulations that mandate explicit user consent for data collection and use. For example, the General Data Protection Regulation (GDPR) in Europe and the California Consumer Privacy Act (CCPA) in California enforce these requirements. In India, the Personal Data Protection Bill (PDPB) outlines similar obligations, requiring businesses to obtain clear consent from users and ensure responsible data handling practices. Compliance with these regulations is mandatory to avoid legal repercussions.

Ethical Responsibility: Respecting user privacy and consent is an ethical obligation. It ensures that businesses do not exploit customer data and use it in a manner that aligns with customer expectations and preferences.

g) Effective Implementation Strategies:

To implement effective personalization with user consent, businesses must adopt clear, transparent, and user-friendly practices:

- Clear Communication:

Privacy Policies: Clearly articulate privacy policies, explaining what data is collected, how it will be used, and the benefits of data-driven personalization.

Consent Forms: Use straightforward and non-technical language in consent forms to ensure customers fully understand what they are agreeing to.

- Opt-in Mechanisms:

Voluntary Participation: Ensure that customers have the choice to opt-in to data collection and personalization features rather than being automatically enrolled.

Granular Consent: Enable customers to provide granular consent, allowing them to specify which types of data they are comfortable sharing and how that data will be used.

- User Control:

Data Management: Provide customers with easy-to-use tools to manage their data preferences, including options to view, edit, or delete their data.

Preference Centers: Implement preference centers where customers can update their personalization settings and consent choices.

- Transparency and Feedback:

Usage Notifications: Inform customers about how their data is being used and the impact of their consent decisions. Regular updates on data usage build transparency.

Feedback Mechanisms: Establish channels for customers to share their input on personalization efforts, which can help refine and enhance the approach.

- Real-World Examples:

Spotify:

Personalized Playlists: Spotify uses listening data to create personalized playlists like "Discover Weekly" and "Release Radar." The company clearly explains how user data enhances these features and allows users to manage their data preferences through account settings (Skutle, 2022).

Netflix:

Content Recommendations: Netflix analyzes viewing history to recommend shows and movies. Users are informed about how their viewing data is used, and they can customize their preferences or reset their recommendation settings (Frey, 2021).

Amazon:

Product Recommendations: Amazon leverages browsing and purchase history to recommend products to users. The platform provides detailed information about data usage in its privacy notice and offers options for users to manage their data preferences (Schafer et al., 2001).

Starbucks:

Personalized Offers: Through its mobile app, Starbucks personalizes offers and recommendations based on purchase history. The app includes clear privacy settings where users can control data sharing and personalization preferences (Kang & Namkung, 2019).

h) Integration Across Channels for Seamless Experience:

Lesson: AI's ability to integrate data and insights across multiple channels enables a seamless customer journey.

Example: McKinsey's research showcases how businesses leverage AI to unify CX across channels. For example, a retail chain integrates AI-powered chatbots across its website, mobile app, and social media platforms. These chatbots provide consistent responses to customer inquiries, ensuring a cohesive brand experience regardless of the channel used. Customers benefit from immediate assistance and personalized recommendations, fostering loyalty (Naslednikov, 2024).

i) Enhanced Customer Service Efficiency:

Lesson: AI improves operational efficiency by handling routine inquiries, allowing human agents to focus on complex customer needs.

Example: Zendesk illustrates how AI chatbots streamline customer service operations. For instance, a telecommunications company implements AI chatbots on its support portal. These bots handle common customer queries such as billing inquiries or service troubleshooting. By handling routine tasks automatically, AI allows human agents to focus on more complex issues, leading to reduced wait times and improved overall service efficiency (Nirala et al., 2022).

j) Predictive Analytics for Proactive Service:

Lesson: AI's predictive capabilities enable proactive customer service and personalized recommendations.

Example: Yellow Systems explores AI's impact on predicting customer behavior. For instance, a subscription-based service uses AI-driven analytics to anticipate customer preferences and renewal patterns. Using historical data and current trends, the AI system detects high-risk customers who are likely to churn and suggests targeted retention strategies. This proactive method helps prevent customer attrition and boosts satisfaction by providing personalized solutions before issues escalate (Mitchell, 2020).

k) Continuous Learning and Adaptation:

Lesson: AI systems that persistently analyze customer interactions and feedback can adapt and improve their performance over time.

Example: Harvard Business Review (HBR) discusses AI's role in adaptive CX strategies. For example, a hospitality chain uses AI-powered sentiment analysis tools to monitor social media conversations about its brand. By analyzing real-time sentiment data, the AI system identifies emerging trends or customer concerns. This feedback loop enables the chain to adjust marketing campaigns, refine service offerings, or address customer grievances promptly, thereby enhancing CX and brand reputation (De Keyser & Van Vaerenbergh, 2024).

l) Human-AI Collaboration for Complex Problem Solving:

Lesson: Effective collaboration between AI and human agents enhances problem-solving capabilities and customer satisfaction.

Example: Thomas H. Davenport's book "The AI Advantage: How to Put the Artificial Intelligence Revolution to Work" provides cases where AI supports human agents in complex scenarios, enhancing decision-making and improving customer satisfaction. For example, a financial services entity uses AI-powered analytics to assess customer investment portfolios. AI algorithms analyze market trends and client preferences, providing data-driven insights to human advisors. Armed with these insights, advisors can offer personalized investment strategies that align with clients' financial goals and risk profiles. This collaborative approach not only improves decision-making accuracy but also strengthens client relationships through informed, empathetic interactions (Davenport, 2018).

2.4 What Are the Best Practices for Integrating AI To Anticipate Customer Needs and Enhance Decision-Making Processes?

Integrating AI to anticipate customer needs and enhance decision-making processes involves several best practices to ensure effectiveness, ethical considerations, and customer satisfaction. Here are some key best practices:

1. Data Collection and Management

Data Quality: Ensure high-quality, clean, and relevant data is collected. Data should be precise, comprehensive, and up-to-date.

Data Privacy and Security: Implement robust data privacy and security measures to protect customer data and comply with regulations like GDPR and CCPA.

Data Integration: Integrate data from various sources (e.g., CRM systems, social media, transaction records) to create a comprehensive customer profile.

Example: Amazon gathers extensive data from its customers, such as purchase history, search queries, and browsing behavior. This data is carefully managed and analyzed to maintain high quality and relevance (Wei & Xia, 2022).

Case: Netflix uses its extensive data collection on viewing habits to recommend shows and movies. The platform's recommendation engine is responsible for more than 80% of the content watched on the platform (Van Es, 2023).

2. Customer-Centric Approach

Understand Customer Journeys: Map out customer journeys to identify key touchpoints and pain points where AI can add value.

Personalization: Use AI to provide personalized experiences, recommendations, and offers tailored to customer behavior and preferences.

Feedback Loops: Continuously gather customer feedback to refine AI models and ensure they remain aligned with customer needs.

Example: Spotify's Discover Weekly playlist exemplifies a customer-centric AI application. By analyzing listening habits, Spotify generates personalized playlists for each user (Wheeler, 2023).

Case: Stitch Fix, an online personal styling service, leverages AI to tailor clothing recommendations to individual preferences. Their AI algorithms analyze customer preferences, feedback, and purchase history to suggest outfits that customers are likely to buy (Chan et al., 2022).

3. Advanced Analytics and Modeling

Predictive Analytics: Implement predictive analytics to anticipate customer needs and behaviors. Use historical data to forecast future trends.

Real-Time Analysis: Employ real-time data processing to make instant decisions and provide timely responses to customers.

Behavioral Analytics: Analyze customer behavior to understand patterns and predict future actions.

Example: Uber uses predictive analytics to anticipate demand in various locations and times, ensuring an optimal number of drivers are available, which reduces wait times and improves customer satisfaction (He et al., 2022).

Case: The Royal Bank of Scotland (RBS) uses AI to predict customer needs and offer personalized banking solutions. By analyzing transaction data, RBS can predict when a customer might need a loan or a new financial product (Kasturi, 2023).

4. Ethical AI Practices

Bias Mitigation: Conduct regular audits of AI models to identify and address bias, and implement corrective actions to ensure fairness and equity.

Transparency: Maintain transparency with customers about how their data is used and how AI-driven decisions are made.

Ethical Guidelines: Develop and adhere to ethical guidelines for AI use, ensuring respect for customer rights and societal norms.

Example: IBM's Watson ensures transparency in AI by providing explanations for its recommendations, helping businesses understand how decisions are made (Olateju et al., 2024).

Case: Microsoft has established guidelines to promote ethical AI use, emphasizing fairness, reliability, safety, privacy, security, inclusiveness, transparency, and accountability. This commitment is reflected in their AI for Good initiatives (Shneiderman, 2020).

5. Technology Integration

Scalable Infrastructure: Invest in scalable and flexible infrastructure to support AI initiatives.

Interoperability: Ensure AI systems can seamlessly integrate with existing business systems and workflows.

Automation: Leverage AI to automate routine tasks and processes, freeing up human resources for more strategic activities.

Example: Salesforce's Einstein AI integrates seamlessly with its CRM, providing sales teams with predictive insights and next-best-action recommendations based on customer data (Picareta et al., 2021).

Case: GE uses Predix, an industrial IoT platform, to integrate AI with its machinery. This allows for predictive maintenance, which reduces downtime and operational costs by predicting when equipment will fail and scheduling timely maintenance (Demir, 2023).

6. Skill Development and Culture

Upskilling Employees: Train employees on AI tools and technologies to enhance their decision-making capabilities.

Collaborative Culture: Foster a culture of collaboration between data scientists, IT professionals, and business teams to ensure successful AI implementation.

Change Management: Manage change effectively by communicating the benefits of AI and addressing any resistance within the organization.

Example: Google fosters a culture of continuous learning and experimentation. Employees are encouraged to develop AI skills and apply them to improve products and services (Zulfan et al., 2020).

Case: Deloitte has invested heavily in upskilling its workforce to ensure they can leverage AI effectively. This includes training programs and workshops focused on data science and AI technologies (Arif, 2021).

7. Continuous Improvement

Performance Monitoring: Continuously monitor AI performance and impact on customer satisfaction and business outcomes.

Iterative Development: Adopt an iterative approach to AI development, regularly updating models based on new data and feedback.

Benchmarking: Benchmark AI performance against industry standards and competitors to identify areas for improvement.

Example: Facebook continually updates its AI algorithms to improve user experience. This includes refining its newsfeed algorithm to show more relevant content based on user interactions (Schwartz & Mahnke, 2021).

Case: Tesla continuously improves its Autopilot system by collecting and analyzing data from its fleet of vehicles. This iterative approach allows Tesla to enhance the system's capabilities over time, making it safer and more reliable (Lyyra et al., 2023).

8. Customer Engagement and Communication

Proactive Engagement: Use AI to proactively engage with customers, anticipating their needs before they reach out.

Seamless Experiences: Ensure AI-driven interactions are seamless and complement human customer service efforts.

Value Addition: Focus on how AI can add value to the customer experience, whether through enhanced support, personalized recommendations, or streamlined processes.

Example: Sephora uses AI in its Virtual Artist app to engage customers by allowing them to try on makeup virtually. This enhances the shopping experience and drives sales (Raj et al., 2024).

Case: H&M uses AI to enhance customer engagement by offering personalized outfit suggestions through its chatbot on the H&M app. This not only helps customers find products they like but also increases the likelihood of purchase (Alduraywish et al., 2021).

3. CONCLUSION

The integration of AI technologies in customer service is revolutionizing the way businesses interact with their customers by offering personalized, efficient, and engaging experiences across various industries. By leveraging the strengths of both AI and human capabilities, businesses can create real-time, tailored customer experiences that drive higher satisfaction and operational efficiency. The synergistic effect of human-AI collaboration enhances decision-making, fosters proactive service delivery, and ultimately strengthens customer loyalty and business growth. Studies and real-world examples from diverse sectors, including e-commerce, banking, entertainment, hospitality, and travel, demonstrate the transformative potential of this collaboration, highlighting AI's role in providing valuable insights for continuous improvement while respecting user consent and privacy. As AI continues to evolve, its importance in customer experience strategies will only grow, ensuring that businesses remain competitive, responsive, and aligned with the evolving needs and expectations of their customers. By adhering to best practices such as data privacy, transparency, and seamless integration across channels, businesses can effectively harness AI to anticipate customer needs, improve decision-making processes, and achieve sustainable success in an increasingly digital marketplace.

The key contributions of this chapter include a comprehensive synthesis of the current literature on artificial intelligence (AI) in customer experience (CX), with insights drawn from a range of industries. It identifies best practices for integrating AI tools to anticipate customer needs and support more informed, data-driven decision-making. The chapter offers a detailed examination of the evolving human-AI collaboration model, emphasizing how such integration enhances service delivery and augments overall quality. Additionally, it provides real-world examples that bridge theoretical concepts with practical, sector-specific applications, making the discussion both academically grounded and practically relevant.

Suggestions for Future Practice and Research: Organizations should embrace AI not as a replacement for human talent but as a complementary force that enhances customer relationships. Investing in explainable AI, employee training, and ethical data governance frameworks will be crucial for maximizing AI's benefits while maintaining public trust. Furthermore, future studies could examine AI adoption in under-researched sectors or explore the long-term impacts of AI-driven personalization on customer loyalty and brand perception.

Limitations of the Study: While the chapter provides a robust review of academic and practical insights, it is limited by its focus on literature published primarily in English. Additionally, the absence of empirical data collection or interviews means the findings are based on secondary sources and may not capture every contextual nuance of AI deployment across diverse cultural or organizational settings.

REFERENCES

Adamopoulou, E., & Moussiades, L. (2020). An overview of chatbot technology. In *IFIP international conference on artificial intelligence applications and innovations* (pp. 373–383). Springer.

Adler-Milstein, J., Aggarwal, N., Ahmed, M., Castner, J., Evans, B. J., Gonzalez, A. A., James, C. A., Lin, S., Mandl, K. D., Matheny, M. E., Sendak, M. P., Shachar, C., & Williams, A. (2022). Meeting the moment: Addressing barriers and facilitating clinical adoption of artificial intelligence in medical diagnosis. *NAM Perspectives*, *22*(9), 2022. DOI: 10.31478/202209c PMID: 36713769

Agarwal, Y., Jain, M., Sinha, S., & Dhir, S. (2020). Delivering high-tech, AI-based health care at Apollo Hospitals. *Global Business and Organizational Excellence*, *39*(2), 20–30. DOI: 10.1002/joe.21981

Ahmad, M., Naeem, M. K. H., Mobo, F. D., Tahir, M. W., & Akram, M. (2024). Navigating the Journey: How Chatbots Are Transforming Tourism and Hospitality. In *Design and Development of Emerging Chatbot Technology* (pp. 236-255). IGI Global.

Alduraywish, M., Unhelkar, B., Singh, S., & Prasad, M. (2021, October). Application of Artificial Intelligence in Recommendation Systems and Chatbots for Online Stores in Fast Fashion Industry. In *International Conference on Intelligent Vision and Computing* (pp. 558-567). Cham: Springer International Publishing.

Ali, A. (2024). *Revolutionizing Customer Support: The Impact of AI-Powered Chatbots and Virtual Assistants* (No. 12037). EasyChair.

Ameen, N., Tarhini, A., Reppel, A., & Anand, A. (2021). Customer experiences in the age of artificial intelligence. *Computers in Human Behavior*, *114*, 106548. DOI: 10.1016/j.chb.2020.106548 PMID: 32905175

Arif, F. V. (2021). The Future of Work: How Ai and Blockchain Technologies will impact HR and the Job Market.

Aslam, F. (2023). The impact of artificial intelligence on chatbot technology: A study on the current advancements and leading innovations. *European Journal of Technology*, *7*(3), 62–72. DOI: 10.47672/ejt.1561

Berning, S. C. (2021). Alibaba's International Digital Marketing Practices and Strategies. In *Advanced Digital Marketing Strategies in a Data-Driven Era* (pp. 80–98). IGI Global. DOI: 10.4018/978-1-7998-8003-5.ch005

Bilgeri, N. (2020). *Artificial intelligence improving CRM, sales and customer experience: An analysis of an international B2B company* (Doctoral dissertation, FH Vorarlberg (Fachhochschule Vorarlberg)).

Bird, J. J. (2021). Improving customer service chatbots with attention-based transfer learning. *arXiv preprint arXiv:2111.14621.*

BR. S. R. (2022). Information and Communication Technology Application in the Asian Tourism Industry. In *Handbook of Technology Application in Tourism in Asia* (pp. 19-48). Singapore: Springer Nature Singapore.

Byrum, J. (2022). AI in financial portfolio management: Practical considerations and use cases. *Innovative Technology at the Interface of Finance and Operations, I*, 249–270. DOI: 10.1007/978-3-030-75729-8_9

Chan, L., Hogaboam, L., & Cao, R. (2022). Artificial Intelligence in Fashion. In *Applied Artificial Intelligence in Business: Concepts and Cases* (pp. 325–334). Springer International Publishing. DOI: 10.1007/978-3-031-05740-3_21

Chaturvedi, R., & Verma, S. (2023). Opportunities and challenges of AI-driven customer service. *Artificial Intelligence in customer service: The next frontier for personalized engagement*, 33-71.

Daqar, M. A. A., & Smoudy, A. K. (2019). The role of artificial intelligence on enhancing customer experience. *International Review of Management and Marketing, 9*(4), 22–31. DOI: 10.32479/irmm.8166

Davenport, T. H. (2018). *The AI advantage: How to put the artificial intelligence revolution to work.* mit Press.

Davenport, T. H., & Miller, S. M. (2022). *Working with AI: real stories of human-machine collaboration.* MIT Press. DOI: 10.7551/mitpress/14453.001.0001

De Keyser, A., & Van Vaerenbergh, Y. (2024). Beyond the snafu: Research directions in customer experience-led business transformation. *AMS Review, 14*(1-2), 1–14. DOI: 10.1007/s13162-024-00279-5

Demir, I. B. (2023). Artificial Intelligence for predictive maintenance.

El Bakkouri, B., Raki, S., & Belgnaoui, T. (2022). The role of chatbots in enhancing customer experience: Literature review. *Procedia Computer Science, 203*, 432–437. DOI: 10.1016/j.procs.2022.07.057

Enholm, I. M., Papagiannidis, E., Mikalef, P., & Krogstie, J. (2022). Artificial intelligence and business value: A literature review. *Information Systems Frontiers, 24*(5), 1709–1734. DOI: 10.1007/s10796-021-10186-w

Eyada, B., & Ahmed, N. (2022). Effectiveness of CHATBOT Advertising on Consumer Buying Decision: An Analytical Study. *Journal of Design Sciences and Applied Arts*, *3*(2), 74–87. DOI: 10.21608/jdsaa.2022.121166.1158

Fathia, A. (2024). Combining AI-Driven Knowledge Frameworks with ML for Real-Time Financial Decision Support and Automation.

Foltean, F. S., & van Bruggen, G. H. (2022). Digital Technologies, marketing agility, and Marketing Management Support Systems: How to remain competitive in changing markets. In *Organizational Innovation in the Digital Age* (pp. 1–38). Springer International Publishing. DOI: 10.1007/978-3-030-98183-9_1

Fragkiskaki, K. (2023). Big data and analytics in enhancing procurement and supply chain efficiency: a literature and empirical study.

Frank, E., & Henry, E. (2024). *AI-Driven Demand Forecasting for Optimized Inventory Management* (No. 13214). EasyChair.

Frey, M. (2021). *Netflix recommends: algorithms, film choice, and the history of taste*. Univ of California Press.

Haleem, A., Javaid, M., Qadri, M. A., Singh, R. P., & Suman, R. (2022). Artificial intelligence (AI) applications for marketing: A literature-based study. *International Journal of Intelligent Networks*, *3*, 119–132. DOI: 10.1016/j.ijin.2022.08.005

Harrison, V. J. (2021). *Leveraging Pharma, Digital Innovation, and Partnerships to Increase Healthcare Access in China: A COVID-19 Case Study* (Doctoral dissertation, Harvard University).

Hasan, R., Thaichon, P., & Weaven, S. (2021). Are we already living with Skynet? Anthropomorphic artificial intelligence to enhance customer experience. In *Developing digital marketing* (pp. 103–134). Emerald Publishing Limited. DOI: 10.1108/978-1-80071-348-220211007

He, L., Liu, S., & Shen, Z. J. M. (2022). Smart urban transport and logistics: A business analytics perspective. *Production and Operations Management*, *31*(10), 3771–3787. DOI: 10.1111/poms.13775

Hoyer, W. D., Kroschke, M., Schmitt, B., Kraume, K., & Shankar, V. (2020). Transforming the customer experience through new technologies. *Journal of Interactive Marketing*, *51*(1), 57–71. DOI: 10.1016/j.intmar.2020.04.001

Jarrahi, M. H., Askay, D., Eshraghi, A., & Smith, P. (2023). Artificial intelligence and knowledge management: A partnership between human and AI. *Business Horizons*, *66*(1), 87–99. DOI: 10.1016/j.bushor.2022.03.002

Kakkad, J., Macon-Cooney, B., Northend, J., Phillips, J., Rajkumar, N., Stanley, L., & Westgarth, T. (2023). *A New National Purpose: Innovation Can Power the Future of Britain*. Tony Blair Institute for Global Change.

Kang, J. W., & Namkung, Y. (2019). The role of personalization on continuance intention in food service mobile apps: A privacy calculus perspective. *International Journal of Contemporary Hospitality Management*, *31*(2), 734–752. DOI: 10.1108/IJCHM-12-2017-0783

Kasturi, S. (2023). Evolving consumer expectations and the future of digital banking. *Journal of Digital Banking*, *8*(1), 37–48. DOI: 10.69554/LURA3454

Khan, M. S. U., Hasan, M. F., Islam, M. S., & Hassan, S. T. (2021). Artificial intelligenc e in the banking sector of Bangladesh: Applicability and the challenges. *Roundtabl e discussion series-2021. Keynote Paper of Roundtable Discussion of BIBM, 6*(2).

Kumar, S., Talukder, M. B., & Tyagi, P. K. (2024). The Impact of Artificial Intelligence on Improving Efficiency in Service and Implementing Best Practices in Service Marketing. In *AI Innovations in Service and Tourism Marketing* (pp. 57–79). IGI Global. DOI: 10.4018/979-8-3693-7909-7.ch004

Kunnathuvalappil Hariharan, N. (2018). Artificial Intelligence and human collaboration in financial planning.

Kushwaha, A. K., Kumar, P., & Kar, A. K. (2021). What impacts customer experience for B2B enterprises on using AI-enabled chatbots? Insights from Big data analytics. *Industrial Marketing Management*, *98*, 207–221. DOI: 10.1016/j.indmarman.2021.08.011

Liang, W., Tadesse, G. A., Ho, D., Fei-Fei, L., Zaharia, M., Zhang, C., & Zou, J. (2022). Advances, challenges and opportunities in creating data for trustworthy AI. *Nature Machine Intelligence*, *4*(8), 669–677. DOI: 10.1038/s42256-022-00516-1

Loideain, N. N., & Adams, R. (2020). From Alexa to Siri and the GDPR: The gendering of virtual personal assistants and the role of data protection impact assessments. *Computer Law & Security Review*, *36*, 105366. DOI: 10.1016/j.clsr.2019.105366

Lyyra, A., Koskinen, K., Sørensen, C., & Marion, T. (2023). Tethered Architectures in Cyber-Physical System Development: The Case of Tesla's Autopilot System. *Available at SSRN* 4515061. DOI: 10.2139/ssrn.4515061

Maria, K., Drigas, A., & Skianis, C. (2022). Chatbots as cognitive, educational, advisory & coaching systems. *Technium Soc. Sci. J.*, *30*, 109.

Mathew, S. M. (2023). Banking 4.0-AI Driven Chatbots-Sun Setting of the Traditional Banking. *Innovatus: An Ivanian Journal of Economics and Business Studies*, 8-16.

McAdams, R. M., Kaur, R., Sun, Y., Bindra, H., Cho, S. J., & Singh, H. (2022). Predicting clinical outcomes using artificial intelligence and machine learning in neonatal intensive care units: A systematic review. *Journal of Perinatology*, *42*(12), 1561–1575. DOI: 10.1038/s41372-022-01392-8 PMID: 35562414

Mitchell, W. D. (2020). *Proactive Predictive Analytics Within the Customer Lifecycle to Prevent Customer Churn*. Northcentral University.

Mohammed, S., Bealer, R., & Cohen, J. (2021). Embracing advanced AI/ML to help investors achieve success: Vanguard Reinforcement Learning for Financial Goal Planning. *arXiv preprint arXiv:2110.12003*.

Mohanty, B., & Mishra, S. (2023). Role of Artificial Intelligence in Financial Fraud Detection. *Academy of Marketing Studies Journal*, *27*(S4).

Naim, I., Rajuddin, W. O. N., & Ansyori, A. (2024). Customer Relationship Management In The Digital Era To Enhance Customer Experience Through Technology. *Transforma Jurnal Manajemen*, *2*(2), 77–85. DOI: 10.56457/tjm.v2i2.131

Naslednikov, M. (2024). The Impact of Artificial Intelligence on Customer Relationship Management (CRM). *Strategies (La Jolla, Calif.)*.

Nirala, K. K., Singh, N. K., & Purani, V. S. (2022). A survey on providing customer and public administration based services using AI: Chatbot. *Multimedia Tools and Applications*, *81*(16), 22215–22246. DOI: 10.1007/s11042-021-11458-y PMID: 35002470

Olateju, O., Okon, S. U., Olaniyi, O. O., Samuel-Okon, A. D., & Asonze, C. U. (2024). Exploring the concept of explainable AI and developing information governance standards for enhancing trust and transparency in handling customer data. *Available at SSRN*. DOI: 10.2139/ssrn.4879025

Patil, K., & Kulkarni, M. S. (2019). Artificial intelligence in financial services: Customer chatbot advisor adoption. *International Journal of Innovative Technology and Exploring Engineering*, *9*(1), 4296–4303. DOI: 10.35940/ijitee.A4928.119119

Petrescu, M., & Krishen, A. S. (2023). Hybrid intelligence: human–AI collaboration in marketing analytics. *Journal of Marketing Analytics*, *11*(3), 263–274. DOI: 10.1057/s41270-023-00245-3

Picareta, G., Weissheim, E., & Klöhn, M. (2021). Intelligent applications in the modern sales organization. In *The Machine Age of Customer Insight* (pp. 19–35). Emerald Publishing Limited. DOI: 10.1108/978-1-83909-694-520211003

Polireddi, N. S. A. (2024). Artificial intelligence in banking and financial services. *Research Advances in Intelligent Computing*, *2*, 139–152. DOI: 10.1201/9781003433941-9

Pyarelal, S., & Das, A. K. (2018). Automating the design of user interfaces using artificial intelligence. *DS 91: Proceedings of NordDesign 2018,* Linköping, Sweden, 14th-17th August 2018.

Raj, R., Kumar, K., Prakash, A., Kumar, A., Kumari, S., & Kumar, G. (2024, May). Enhancing E-Commerce Engagement: Exploring AR and VR-Based Marketing Strategies. In *2024 International Conference on Computational Intelligence and Computing Applications (ICCICA)* (Vol. 1, pp. 448-453). IEEE. DOI: 10.1109/ICCICA60014.2024.10585182

Reddy, S. R. B. (2022). Enhancing Customer Experience through AI-Powered Marketing Automation: Strategies and Best Practices for Industry 4.0. *Journal of Artificial Intelligence Research*, *2*(1), 36–46.

Revilla, E., Saenz, M. J., Seifert, M., & Ma, Y. (2023). Human–Artificial Intelligence Collaboration in Prediction: A Field Experiment in the Retail Industry. *Journal of Management Information Systems*, *40*(4), 1071–1098. DOI: 10.1080/07421222.2023.2267317

Schafer, J. B., Konstan, J. A., & Riedl, J. (2001). E-commerce recommendation applications. *Data Mining and Knowledge Discovery*, *5*(1-2), 115–153. DOI: 10.1023/A:1009804230409

Schwartz, S. A., & Mahnke, M. S. (2021). Facebook use as a communicative relation: Exploring the relation between Facebook users and the algorithmic news feed. *Information Communication and Society*, *24*(7), 1041–1056. DOI: 10.1080/1369118X.2020.1718179

Sharma, I., & Aggarwal, A. (2024). Revolutionizing Creative Tourism: Integrating AI in Marketing for Immersive Travel Experiences. *Innovative Technologies for Increasing Service Productivity*, 179-197.

Shneiderman, B. (2020). Bridging the gap between ethics and practice: Guidelines for reliable, safe, and trustworthy human-centered AI systems. [TiiS]. *ACM Transactions on Interactive Intelligent Systems*, *10*(4), 1–31. DOI: 10.1145/3419764

Skutle, M. (2022). *Discovering music in the streaming era: How online recommendation engines and application design influence users' habits and discoveries in online music streaming services* (Master's thesis, The University of Bergen).

Srivastava, V., Kishore, S., & Dhingra, D. (2021). Technology and the future of customer experience. In *Crafting customer experience strategy* (pp. 91–116). Emerald Publishing Limited. DOI: 10.1108/978-1-83909-710-220211006

Van Es, K. (2023). Netflix & big data: The strategic ambivalence of an entertainment company. *Television & New Media*, *24*(6), 656–672. DOI: 10.1177/15274764221125745

Vashishth, T. K., Sharma, V., Sharma, K. K., Kumar, B., Kumar, A., & Panwar, R. (2024). Artificial Intelligence (AI)–Powered Chatbots: Providing Instant Support and Personalized Recommendations to Guests 24/7. In *Technology and Luxury Hospitality* (pp. 211-236). Routledge.

Wei, L., & Xia, Z. (2022). Big Data-Driven Personalization in E-Commerce: Algorithms, Privacy Concerns, and Consumer Behavior Implications. *International Journal of Applied Machine Learning and Computational Intelligence*, *12*(4).

Wheeler, J. (2023). *The Digital-First Customer Experience: Seven Design Strategies from the World's Leading Brands*. Kogan Page Publishers.

Whittlestone, J., Nyrup, R., Alexandrova, A., Dihal, K., & Cave, S. (2019). *Ethical and societal implications of algorithms, data, and artificial intelligence: a roadmap for research*. Nuffield Foundation.

Zhang, S. (2024). The role of Artificial Intelligence in enhancing online sales and the customer experience.

Zulfan, G., Kee, D. M. H., Khor, T. W., Lee, S. Y., Ali, H. J., Hanan, A., & Akansha, V. (2020). The Influence of Organizational Culture on Employee Retention: A Case of Google. *Journal of the community development in Asia, 3*(1), 25-32.

Chapter 9
Innovative Ideas for Smart City Management Using AIoTt-Driven Solutions

Joaquim Monteiro Pratas
https://orcid.org/0000-0002-7432-9242
Instituto Superior de Contabilidade e Administração, Instituto Politécnico do Porto, Portugal

Ana Isabel Melo
Águeda School of Technology and Management, University of Aveiro, Portugal

ABSTRACT

This study delves into AIoT solutions to spark innovative ideas for smart city management. It starts with a literature review on smart city characteristics, objectives, indicators, IoT devices, sensors, and AI data utilization possibilities. The methodology includes a bibliometric study and qualitative analysis through focus groups using mind maps and morphological analysis. The bibliometric study identified ten research clusters. Additionally, two focus groups generated innovative ideas, highlighting key IoT devices, data collection agents, AI algorithms, and methods for data access and use in smart cities. The innovative ideas generation process suggested main parameters and options of morphological analysis, with an example provided to illustrate an innovative idea. This tool can inspire numerous innovative ideas for AIoT-driven smart city management by the readers. The study also discusses theoretical and managerial contributions, limitations, and future research directions.

DOI: 10.4018/979-8-3693-8512-8.ch009

INTRODUCTION

In recent years, the prominence of smart cities has risen, as urban areas globally address challenges posed by population growth, climate change, and globalization. A smart city leverages technology and data collection to enhance quality of life, and improve sustainability and efficiency in city operations (Soares et al., 2020; Kumar & Singh, 2024).

Using information and communication technologies (ICT), smart cities optimize urban planning, transportation, energy efficiency, and essential services (Myeong et al., 2022). Emerging technologies facilitate real-time problem detection and resolution, enabling swift public and private stakeholder responses through automated systems or human intervention. Statista reports a significant surge in investments in smart city technologies, with investments doubling from 2018 to 2023, highlighting the commitment to innovation for sustainable urban growth (Thormundsson, 2022). At the heart of these investments is the convergence of the Internet-of-Things (IoT) and Artificial Intelligence (AI). The proliferation of IoT devices embedded in urban infrastructure, vehicles, machinery, drones, robots, and smartphones creates a data-rich urban nervous system (Mohamed, 2023). Millions of sensors strategically positioned across streets, bus stops, billboards, and public buildings, continuously collect data. This information wealth enables precise management and control of critical variables, such as traffic flow, energy consumption and infrastructure maintenance (Bedi et al., 2022). These systems, associated with AI, resemble digital neural networks, intricately weaving together sensor data, predictive algorithms, and real-time analytics to enhance urban infrastructure and services (Xu et al., 2024). AI techniques, such as Artificial Neural Network (ANN), Support Vector Machine (SVM), Genetic Algorithm (GA), and Linear Regression (LR) are applied alongside IoT and Big Data technologies in smart cities (Bibri et al., 2023). The resulting Artificial Intelligence of Things (AIoT) systems, merging AI and IoT, serve as the backbone for managing vast amounts of urban data. Forkan et al. (2023) present a systematic framework for implementing AIoT systems, comprising distinct layers: the Mobile IoT layer for data capture; the Data Ingestion layer for processing; the Analytics layer for advanced AI models; and the Decision Support layer for informed choices.

In urban development, the monitoring, evaluation, and communication of smart city performance are paramount. These integrated digital ecosystems hold the promise of sustainable urban growth. Despite the growing integration of AIoT in urban environments, comprehensive studies analyzing its impact and effectiveness within Smart Cities remain notably lacking (Wolniak & Stecula, 2024; Matei & Cocosatu, 2024).

This research aims to identify the main devices used for data collection in smart city management, the agents involved in collecting this data, the primary AI applications utilizing IoT-collected data, and current data access by smart city stakeholders. Concurrently, we aim to develop innovative AIoT-driven solutions for smart city management through creativity and idea-generation techniques. Our methodology involves an extensive literature review, a bibliometric study using bibliographic coupling, followed by focus group sessions to perform idea-generation techniques, such as mind maps and morphological analysis to develop innovative AIoT-driven solutions for smart city management.

The structure of this text includes the Introductory section, followed by the Background section, highlighting the general characterization of smart cities, their objectives, indicators, main IoT devices (types of sensors used), data utilization possibilities by AI algorithms, and methods to acess and use IoT data in smart cities. Additionally, the conceptual model and research questions are presented. The Methodology section details the research design, including the bibliographic coupling methodology and the process of developing two focus groups to generate innovative ideas using mind maps and morphological analysis. In the Findings section, we describe the bibliographic coupling results, highlighting the main research clusters and presenting the key ideas developed by focus group participants, along with the processes, to enable the reader to develop new ideas.

Finally, the Conclusions section underscores the theoretical and managerial contributions of this work and its limitations, suggesting directions for future research.

BACKGROUND

Smart cities Characterization, Objectives and Main Indicators

A smart city integrates physical, digital, and human systems to foster a sustainable, prosperous, and inclusive urban environment. This involves deploying electronic data collection sensors in infrastructures, buildings, vehicles, and IoT devices to gather real-time city operations information. The data is integrated into information and communication technology (ICT) platforms, enabling city managers to optimize efficiency and resilience across key areas (Moura & Abreu Silva, 2021). These areas are generally identified in the literature (Soares et al., 2020; Jakubcinova & Poruban, 2023; Myeong et al., 2022) as:

- Infrastructure Management: Development and maintenance of roads, bridges, and public buildings.

- Energy Management: Efficiently using and distributing energy resources, including renewables.
- Transportation Management: Optimizing traffic flow, public transit systems, and reducing congestion.
- Environmental Monitoring: Tracking air and water quality and managing waste to ensure a healthy environment.
- Public Safety: Enhancing security through surveillance, emergency response systems, and disaster management.
- Healthcare Services: Providing accessible and efficient healthcare to residents and visitors.
- Economic Development: Promoting local businesses, job creation, and economic growth.
- Citizen Engagement: Encouraging public participation in decision-making and improving communication channels.

A smart city aims to satisfy various stakeholders, including citizens, residents, tourists, private sector organizations, local government, academic and research institutions, Non-Governmental Organizations (NGOs), utility providers, transportation agencies, financial institutions, and international organizations, like the United Nations (UN) and World Bank, which promote smart city development. Often, stakeholders such as residents, tourists, workers, and investors (Kotler et al., 1993; Aragonez and Alves, 2013) are unaware of initiatives or fail to recognize their contributions (Dameri, 2017). Nonetheless, public value remains central to the smart city vision.

Smart cities rely on indicators and metrics to assess effectiveness. Determining a smart city's success is complex. Initiatives are launched to benefit stakeholders, but assessing their impact involves diverse models and indicators (Giffinger et al., 2007; Komninos, 2008; Fondazione Ambrosetti, 2012). The ISO 37122 standard defines terms and evaluation methodologies for a comprehensive set of Smart City indicators. These indicators align with the UN's Sustainable Development Goals, covering Health and Well-being, Quality of Education, Gender Equality, Clean Water and Sanitation, Decent Work and Economic Growth, Reduction of Inequalities, Sustainable Cities and Communities, Climate Action, and Peace, Justice, and Strong Institutions (ISO, 2019). The ISO 37122 standard outlines 19 key areas: Economy, Education, Energy, Environment and Climate Change, Finance, Governance, Health, Housing, Population and Social Conditions, Recreation, Security, Solid Waste Management, Sports and Culture, Telecommunications, Transportation, Urban Agriculture/Local Food Security, Urban Planning, Wastewater Management, and Water Resources. These indicators are vital tools for assessing smart city progress, promoting sustainable development, and ensuring a balance between economic, social, and environmental dimensions.

Effective smart city management relies on robust indicators, geospatial dashboards, indicator-driven approach, and real-time data. Geospatial Dashboards are crucial tools for decision-makers, integrating maps, spatial data analytics, and geographic visualization to provide real-time insights into smart city performance. Researchers and practitioners address challenges related to large geospatial datasets and uncover spatiotemporal patterns within urban spaces (Jing et al., 2019). An indicator-driven approach is essential, as smart city indicators assess a city's progress toward greater intelligence. The temporal dimension (tracking development over years, quarters or months) is vital for evaluating progress. These indicators act as yardsticks, gauging whether overarching policy objectives are met or within reach (Babinov, 2016). Leveraging real-time data is also fundamental, as smart cities utilize it to inform decision-making. Comprehensive data sources enable agencies to understand dynamic demand patterns and respond swiftly.with cost-effective solutions (Woetzel et al., 2018). In practice, such real-time monitoring, without IoT devices hinges on unstructured feedback from citizens and other stakeholders, as well as on-site verification by municipal workers. Unfortunately, this approach tends to be resource-intensive, time-consuming, and financially burdensome. Consequently, frequent delays in addressing community needs can adversely impact the well-being of residents and other city's stakeholders (Forkan et al, 2023). Thus, a new approach using the IoT technology seems crucial.

Main IoT Devices and Data Utilization Possibilities by AI Algorithms

Smart cities employ various IoT devices to enhance their operations (Particle, 2021; Yen, 2022). For instance, Smart Parking Lots use sensors and real-time data to guide drivers to available spaces, eliminating the need to circle the block. In Smart Waste Management, IoT-enabled garbage bins monitor fill levels, optimizing collection routes. Smart Traffic Control Systems use sensors to detect traffic flow and congestion, enabling data analytics to synchronize traffic lights, easing commutes and boosting safety. Smart Street Lighting adapts brightness based on real-time conditions, saving energy and ensuring well-lit pathways for pedestrians. Smart Utility Meters, discreetly measuring water, gas, and electricity consumption, provide accurate data that empowers city planners to allocate resources effectively, promoting sustainability.

All these IoT devices tend to be related with sensors. In the context of smart cities, sensors are devices that collect and transmit data about various environmental and infrastructural parameters.

The primary agents that can collect IoT data for smart city management are (Bhardwaj et al, 2024; Omrany et al, 2024; Zaman et al, 2024):

- Government Agencies: Local and municipal governments are the main players in smart city initiatives. They implement and manage IoT devices for public services, like traffic management, environmental monitoring, waste management, and public safety.
- Private Companies: Businesses, especially those in technology and telecommunications, often collaborate with governments to deploy IoT solutions. They provide the infrastructure, devices, and platforms needed for data collection and analysis.
- Utility Providers: Companies that supply water, electricity, and gas use IoT devices to monitor usage and manage distribution networks. This helps in optimizing resource consumption and improving service delivery.
- Transportation Authorities: Agencies responsible for public transportation systems use IoT devices to manage and monitor traffic flow, public transit schedules, and vehicle maintenance.
- Healthcare Institutions: Hospitals and healthcare providers use IoT devices to monitor patient health, manage medical equipment, and track the spread of diseases in urban areas.
- Research Institutions and Universities: Academic institutions often participate in smart city projects to study and improve urban living conditions. They use IoT data for research and development purposes.
- Citizens: Individuals contribute to data collection through personal IoT devices, such as smartphones and wearable technology. Crowdsourced data from citizens can enhance the accuracy and coverage of smart city systems.

The IoT sensors can have different types, and be characterized as follows (Syed et al, 2021; Morais et al, 2019).

Presence Sensors

Presence sensors detect the presence of humans or objects. Popular examples include Passive InfraRed (PIR) sensors, which detect human motion, and reed switches for security on windows and doors. Inductive loop sensors, employing electromagnetic induction, are used in transport systems to detect presence. Ultrasonic sensors determine the distance of objects, while capacitive sensors are used to ascertain position.

AI algorithms leverage data from presence sensors in IoT devices for various applications (Park & Yen, 2018; Adi et al., 2020; Merenda et al., 2020):

- Security and Surveillance: AI analyzes data from presence sensors to detect unusual activity or unauthorized access in real-time, enhancing security in homes, offices, and public spaces.
- Energy Management: Presence sensors provide occupancy data, which AI uses to optimize energy consumption by adjusting lighting and HVAC systems based on room occupancy, reducing energy waste.
- Healthcare Monitoring: In healthcare settings, presence sensors track the movement of patients and staff. AI analyzes this data to monitor patient activity, detect falls, and ensure timely assistance.
- Smart Home Automation: Presence sensors inform AI algorithms about room occupancy. This data is used to automate tasks such as adjusting lighting, temperature, and entertainment systems based on user preferences and presence.
- Retail Analytics: In retail environments, presence sensors track customer traffic and behavior. AI analyzes this data to optimize store layouts, manage inventory, and enhance customer experience, including opening checkout systems.

Position Sensors

These sensors identify an object's position on a global scale (like GPS) or local scale (such as small beacons). Examples include GPS, magnetometers, direction sensors, and ultrasonic sensors. AI algorithms can leverage data from position sensors in IoT devices for various applications (Almomani & Al-Turjman, 2024; Shahbazian et al., 2023), namely:

- Indoor Localization: AI analyzes data from position sensors to locate objects or individuals in environments where GPS is weak or unavailable, useful in smart buildings, healthcare facilities and retail stores.
- Asset Tracking: In industrial settings, AI uses position sensor data to track assets like equipment and inventory, optimizing utilization, reducing losses, and improving efficiency.
- Smart Environment Management: AI analyzes data from position sensors to monitor and control environmental conditions (temperature, humidity, lighting) based on people's presence and movement.
- Healthcare Monitoring: Position sensors track patients and medical staff. AI analyzes this data to ensure safety, monitor activity, and provide personalized care.

- Smart Agriculture: Position sensors monitor agricultural equipment and livestock locations. AI uses this data to optimize farming practices, improve resource management, and enhance productivity.

Machine Vision Sensors

Machine vision sensors capture images for computer processing to generate valuable information. Examples include camcorders, IR camcorders, lane perception sensors, and thermal cameras. AI algorithms can leverage data from these sensors in various applications (Adi et al., 2020; Merenda et al., 2020; Rao et al., 2025):

- Object Recognition: AI analyzes images from machine vision sensors to identify and classify objects, useful in retail for automatic product recognition and tracking.
- Quality Control: In manufacturing, machine vision sensors capture images of products on assembly lines. AI analyzes these images to detect defects, ensuring only high-quality products are shipped.
- Autonomous Navigation: In robotics and autonomous vehicles, machine vision sensors provide environmental data. AI processes this data to navigate safely and avoid obstacles.
- Facial Recognition: In security and surveillance, machine vision sensors capture images of individuals. AI analyzes these images to recognize faces and identify persons of interest.
- Medical Imaging: In healthcare, machine vision sensors capture medical scans. AI analyzes these images to assist in diagnosing diseases and planning treatments.

Motion Sensors

Motion sensors detect movement using inertial sensors like accelerometers and gyroscopes. They are crucial in smart health applications such as activity tracking and in smart homes and industry for vibration sensing. Examples include accelerometers, gyroscopes, laser scanners, proximity sensors, and tilt sensors.

AI algorithms utilize data from motion sensors in various applications (Merenda et al., 2020; Chen et al., 2018; Panduman et al., 2024):

- Activity Recognition: AI analyzes motion sensor data to identify activities like walking, running, or sitting. This is valuable in healthcare for monitoring patients' activities and in smart homes for automating tasks based on user behavior.

- Fall Detection: In elderly care, AI uses motion sensor data to detect falls and alert caregivers or emergency services, ensuring timely assistance.
- Smart Home Automation: Motion sensors detect room occupancy. AI controls lighting, heating, and appliances based on this data, optimizing energy use and comfort.
- Industrial Automation: In manufacturing, motion sensors track machinery and worker movement. AI analyzes this data to optimize production processes, improve safety, and reduce downtime.
- Sports, Fitness, and Health: Motion sensors monitor athletes' movements during training. AI analyzes this data to provide performance feedback, prevent injuries, and personalize training programs.

Identification Sensors

Identification sensors include RFID tags and Near Field Communication (NFC) devices, commonly used in payments, data exchange, smart transportation, and smart city services. AI algorithms can leverage data from these sensors in various applications (Merenda et al., 2020; Sehito et al., 2024; Rao et al., 2025):

- Security: Biometric scanners capture unique identifiers like fingerprints or facial features. AI algorithms analyze this data to enhance security by verifying identities and detecting unauthorized access.
- Access Control: In smart buildings and facilities, identification sensors grant or restrict access based on recognized individuals. AI dynamically manages access permissions, ensuring only authorized personnel enter specific areas.
- Personalized Services: Identification sensors recognize individuals and tailor services to their preferences. In retail, AI uses this data to provide personalized recommendations and enhance customer experiences.
- Healthcare: Identification sensors monitor patient identities and track medical histories. AI analyzes this data to ensure accurate patient identification and deliver personalized healthcare services.

Interaction Sensors

Interaction sensors are human-activated devices, such as buttons or levers, that trigger events. AI algorithms can harness data from these sensors in various IoT applications (Sehito et al., 2024; Rao et al., 2025; Kush, 2025):

- Enhancing User Experiences: Interaction sensors detect user inputs like touch, gestures, and voice commands. AI analyzes this data to deliver personalized, context-sensitive responses, improving user interactions.
- Improving Accessibility: For individuals with disabilities, interaction sensors capture specific movements or sounds. AI adapts interfaces and devices to be more accessible and user-friendly.
- Smart Environments: In smart homes and offices, interaction sensors monitor user activities and preferences. AI automates tasks, such as adjusting lighting and temperature, based on user behavior.
- Healthcare: Interaction sensors track patient movements and interactions with medical devices. AI analyzes this data to monitor progress, detect anomalies, and provide real-time feedback to healthcare providers.

Hydraulic Sensors

Hydraulic sensors measure liquids, such as levels, flow, and leak detection in tanks. Examples include float and flow sensors. AI algorithms can utilize data from these sensors in various applications (Chang & Chang, 2022; Kim & Heo, 2022; Sefu & Tudor, 2022):

- Condition Monitoring: AI analyzes hydraulic sensor data to monitor system health in real-time, detecting early signs of wear, ensuring timely maintenance, and reducing downtime.
- Anomaly Detection: Hydraulic sensors identify unusual patterns or performance deviations. AI algorithms analyze this data to predict potential failures and enable proactive interventions.
- Predictive Maintenance: AI uses hydraulic sensor data to forecast maintenance needs, optimizing schedules and extending system lifespan.
- Energy Efficiency: AI optimizes hydraulic system operations using sensor data, reducing energy consumption and enhancing efficiency.

Acoustic Sensors

Acoustic sensors activated via soundwaves, capture data from ambient sound changes. AI algorithms leverage this data for various applications (Shankar & Zennaro, 2023; Yu et al., 2024; Zennaro & Manzoni, 2021):

- Sound Recognition: AI analyzes acoustic data to classify sounds like speech, music, or environmental noises, useful in voice assistants, security systems, and wildlife monitoring.

- Environmental Monitoring: Acoustic sensors detect sounds related to environmental changes, such as animal vocalizations or storms. AI analyzes this data to monitor biodiversity and detect disturbances.
- Healthcare: In healthcare, acoustic sensors capture sounds like breathing or heartbeats. AI analyzes this data to monitor patient health and detect anomalies.
- Industrial Applications: Acoustic sensors detect sounds indicating machinery malfunctions or operational issues. AI analyzes this data to predict equipment failures and optimize maintenance schedules.

Force/Load Sensors

Force/load sensors detect external forces, capturing deformation or intensity. Examples include load, speed, and wind velocity sensors. AI algorithms leverage data from these sensors in various applications (Park & Yen, 2018; Merenda et al., 2020; Arockia et al., 2024):

- Structural Health Monitoring: AI analyzes sensor data to detect structural damage or stress in buildings, bridges, and infrastructure, enabling early failure detection and timely maintenance.
- Robotics: In robotics, force/load sensors provide feedback on forces experienced by robotic arms and grippers. AI improves the precision and efficiency of robotic movements.
- Industrial Automation: Sensors monitor forces on machinery and equipment. AI optimizes production processes, reduces wear and tear, and enhances safety.
- Human-Machine Interaction: Sensors detect forces exerted by users in human-machine interactions. AI adapts the machine's response, improving user experience and safety.

Electric Sensors

Electric sensors measure electrical power and are widely used in smart grids and homes to monitor power consumption. They include current transformers and voltage sensors. Examples encompass AC analyzers, energy consumption monitors, current and voltage sensors, capacitance meters, and conductivity sensors.

AI algorithms leverage data from electric sensors in various applications (IAEME, 2024):

- Predictive Maintenance: AI analyzes sensor data to predict equipment failures before they occur, enabling proactive maintenance and reducing downtime.
- Energy Management: Sensors monitor real-time energy consumption. AI optimizes energy usage, reduces waste, and promotes efficiency.
- Fault Detection: AI detects anomalies and faults in electrical systems early, preventing potential failures.
- Load Forecasting: AI analyzes historical sensor data to forecast future energy demand, aiding utilities in managing supply and demand effectively.

Chemical Sensors

Chemical sensors measure chemical properties, including gas sensors detecting carbon monoxide (CO), carbon dioxide (CO2), and other gases for air quality monitoring, as well as sensors for detecting smoke, pH, and water quality. Examples include chemical detectors, pH sensors, CO2 sensors, ORP sensors, smoke sensors, and water quality sensors.

AI algorithms utilize data from chemical sensors for various applications (Noh & Oh, 2025; Rao et al., 2025; Park & Yen, 2018):

- Environmental Monitoring: AI analyzes data from chemical sensors to detect pollutants and monitor air quality, identifying pollution sources and implementing mitigation measures.
- Industrial Safety: Chemical sensors detect hazardous gases and chemicals in industrial settings. AI provides early warnings and ensures worker safety by analyzing this data.
- Healthcare: Chemical sensors monitor biomarkers in bodily fluids. AI analyzes this data to diagnose diseases, monitor treatment effectiveness, and personalize medical interventions.
- Food Safety: Chemical sensors detect contaminants and spoilage in food products. AI ensures food safety and quality by analyzing this data.

Bio Sensors

Biosensors are essential in smart city services, homes, and transport, measuring health parameters of living organisms. In smart cities, biosensors monitor patients for healthcare purposes, including ElectroEncephaloGram (EEG), ElectroMyoGram (EMG), ElectroCardioGram (ECG), skin resistance, heartbeat, breath sensors, pulse oximetry, and blood pressure. Examples include ECG, heartbeat, blood pressure, breath sensors, discomfort index, EEG, and swallow sensors.

AI algorithms leverage data from biosensors for various applications (Singh et al., 2022; Shirgir et al., 2024; Wang et al., 2023):

- Healthcare Monitoring: AI analyzes biosensor data to monitor vital signs, such as heart rate, blood pressure, and glucose levels, enabling continuous health monitoring and early detection of potential issues.
- Disease Diagnosis: Biosensors detect specific disease biomarkers. AI analyzes this data for accurate diagnoses and personalized treatment recommendations.
- Personalized Medicine: AI uses biosensor data to tailor medical treatments based on individual physiological characteristics and health conditions.
- Remote Patient Monitoring: Biosensors collect data on patients' health status remotely. AI provides real-time feedback to healthcare providers, enabling timely interventions.

Ambient Sensors

Ambient sensors measure environmental conditions such as temperature, humidity, light intensity, and pressure. Examples include temperature, humidity, light sensors, pressure, soil humidity, soil microorganism sensors, soil temperature, and solar irradiation index.

AI algorithms can leverage data from ambient sensors in various applications (Park & Yen, 2018; Panduman et al., 2024; Popescu et al., 2024):

- Environmental Monitoring: AI analyzes data from ambient sensors to monitor air quality, temperature, and humidity, helping detect pollution and predict environmental changes.
- Smart Home Automation: Ambient sensors detect occupancy and environmental changes. AI uses this data to automate home systems, such as adjusting lighting, heating, and cooling based on preferences.
- Health and Wellness Tracking: Ambient sensors monitor air quality and noise levels in homes and workplaces. AI analyzes this data to provide health insights, aiding individuals in making informed decisions about their environment.
- Energy Management: AI optimizes energy usage in buildings by analyzing data from ambient sensors. Adjusting HVAC systems based on occupancy and environmental conditions leads to significant energy savings.

Other Sensors

Other sensors are employed in smart agriculture, city services, health, homes, industry, infrastructure, and transport. Smart city applications utilize diverse sensing modalities, including audio, visual, and signal measurement devices, such as Bluetooth and Wi-Fi signal strength. These sensors capture raw signal information, which is further processed to derive the target variable being measured.

Methods to Access and Use IoT Data in Smart Cities

Accessing and utilizing data collected through IoT devices, coupled with AI analysis in smart cities, involves a meticulous and multifaceted process that encompasses several critical phases. Initially, data acquisition is paramount, typically achieved through sensors strategically embedded within urban infrastructures, vehicles, and personal devices (Ullah et al., 2023). These sensors facilitate the seamless transmission of data to centralized systems via robust communication networks, thereby ensuring real-time data flow.

Subsequently, the transmitted data must be systematically stored, often within cloud-based platforms or localized data centers, to maintain accessibility and security (Wolniak & Stecula, 2024). The next pivotal step involves data processing, wherein raw data is transformed into a structured and usable format, enabling comprehensive analysis. Advanced AI and machine learning algorithms are then deployed to analyze the data, leveraging techniques such as predictive analytics, pattern recognition, and optimization processes to extract valuable insights.

Upon deriving these insights, informed decision-making becomes feasible, empowering stakeholders to implement strategic actions through automated systems or manual interventions (Ullah et al., 2023). Sometimes automated decisions occur without the need to storage data, if the sensors are smart sensors or edge sensors. These devices are capable of processing data locally and performing actions based on that data, reducing the need for constant communication with central servers (Stetter, 2012).

To ensure the efficacy of these actions, a feedback loop is essential, whereby the outcomes of the implemented decisions are continuously monitored. This iterative loop allows the data to be reintegrated into the system, fostering an environment of continuous improvement and refinement in future decision-making processes (Wolniak & Stecula, 2024).

The smart city data analysis comprises the phases of data aquisition (through sensors, smartphones, WiFi, devices and IoT), Data pre-processing (data cleaning, selection, normalization and interpolation), Data analytics (classification, clarification, regression, anomaly detection), and Service Provision (in terms of Transportation, Healthcare, Environment and Public Safety) (Ullah et al, 2023).

The network protocols used in the data transmission can be of different types, such as radio frequency identification (RFID), near field communication (NFC), bluetooth, Z-wave or Zensys wave, Light fidelity (Li-Fi), wireless fidelity (Wi-Fi), Zigbee, Wireless Smart Utility Network (Wi-SUN), cellular (3G, 4G and 5G communications), Long Range Wide Area Network (LoRaWAN), 6LoWPAN, SigFox and Narrow Band IoT (NB-Iot). The home area networks are designed for distances below one kilometer. It comprises the network protocols of NFC, RFID, Li-Fi, Bluetooth, Z-Wave, Zigbee, Wi-Fi and 6LoWPAN. The Field/Neighborhood Area networks are designed for distances between more than one kilometer and below ten kilometers. It comprises the Wi-SUN network protocol. The Wide area networks are designed for distances higher than 10 kilometers. It comprises the NB-IoT, LoRaWAN, SigFox and Cellular network protocols (Syed et al, 2021).

Conceptual Model and Research Questions

Smart cities operate through distinct phases of data collection, storage, processing, and decision-making. From a thorough literature review, a conceptual model was crafted to delve into this fascinating venture. Data acquisition is conducted via sensors and Internet-of-Things (IoT) technology. When sensors are smart or edge sensors embedded with AI, processing happens within the sensor itself, leading to automated decision-making processes. For instance, consider a smoke detector that not only provides immediate voice alerts and guidance to occupants, but also directly calls the firefighters.

Conversely, when sensors gather data and store it on cloud-based platforms or data centers, AI steps in to process this information, make decisions, and automate responses. This entire cycle culminates in a feedback loop, enhancing the efficiency and responsiveness of smart city systems. This conceptual framework is represented in figure 1.

Figure 1. Conceptual framework

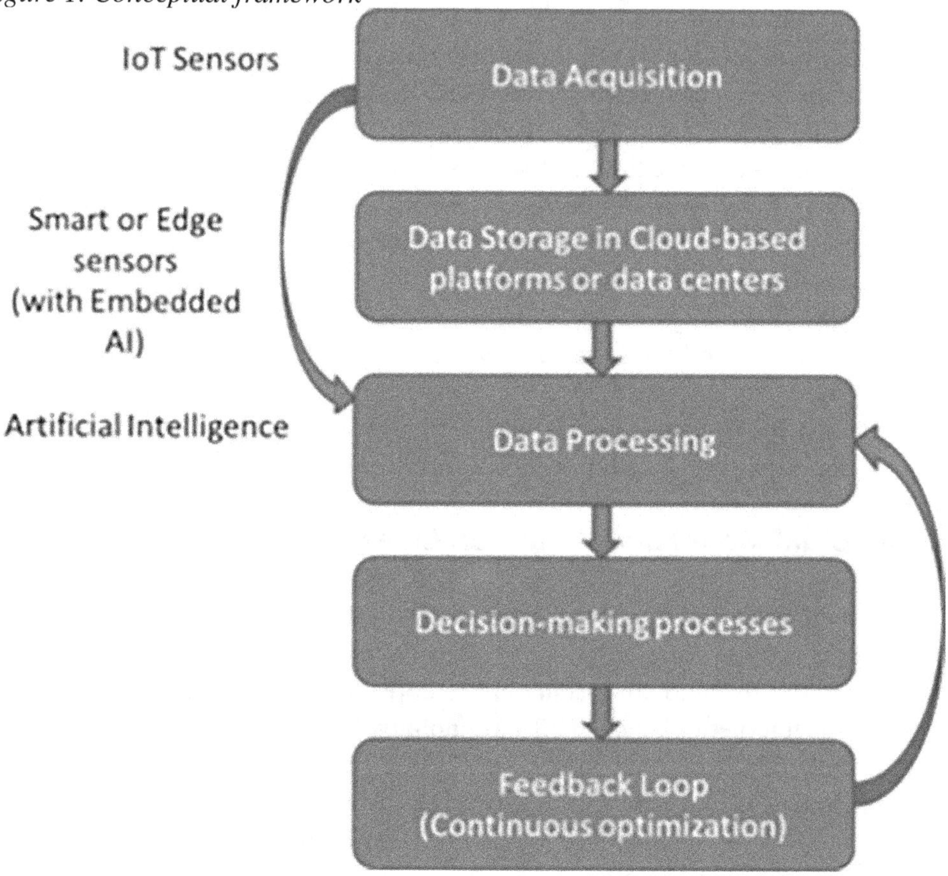

Based on the literature review, the formulated research questions of this work are the following:

1. What are the main devices related to the IoT that can collect data for smart city management?
2. Who are the primary agents that can collect this data?
3. How can AI algorithms utilize this data?
4. What methods allow smart city stakeholders to access and use this data?
5. What innovative ideas can be developed for Smart City management using AIoT-driven solutions?

METHODOLOGY

Research Design

This study follows a mixed approach. First, the methodology employed was a bibliometric study, which is very important to academic research to understand the state of the art of the knowledge (Pratas & Oliveira, 2023), with a bibliographic coupling analysis. The research strategy included the collection of data from the Web of Science Core Collection (WoSCC), searching for topics with the keywords related with Artificial Intelligence of Things (AIoT) and Smart cities, such as "AIoT", or "artificial intelligence internet of things", or "Artificial intelligence*of Things", or "artificial intelligence internet of things aiot", or "artificial intelligence of things", or "artificial intelligence of things aiot", or "artificial intelligence over the internet of things aiot", or "artificial intelligence-of-things", or "artificial internet of things", and "Smart cities", or "smart city", in the Web of Science categories of Business and Management. The WoSCC was chosen because is the database with stricter journal selection, meaning it includes highly reputable journals. It also includes Impact Factor metrics and extensive citation connections, making it ideal for assessing research influence.

The data was retrieved on the 1st of February 2025, and the data analysis was performed using VOS Viewer software. The articles were filtered by the year of publication - between 2021 and 2025 - in order to have the most recent publications, and post-COVID period. Additionally, a content analysis was done on the documents highlighted in the bibliographic coupling analysis. The Abstract was read in all the documents, and in some cases all the document was read, if there was a doubt about the topics issues by the document in the Abstract session.

Then, two focus groups with eight participants and a moderator in each session were conducted, using a convenience sample of residents, workers and students of Matosinhos, Portugal, on the 3rd of February 2025. The participants were chosen as they had direct experience or knowledge about living, studying or working at this city. The sample was based on convenience, but ensuring that all participants lived in the same city.

These participants engaged in focused discussions related to the literature review and bibliometric study findings. In each of these sessions, one initial mind map was done based on participants' inputs, and one morphological analysis (resuming the mind map and added with new ideas) was done to develop innovative ideas for smart cities management using AIoT based on the initial mind map that was developed. The morphological analysis done highlighted the key parameters used, as well as the options for each key parameter.

Finally, the two focus groups ideas were joined by the moderator. Mind mapping encourages free association and visualization of interconnected concepts. By creating mind maps, we aim to uncover novel perspectives and potential research directions. Morphological Analysis systematically explores different dimensions of a problem. By dissecting the components of smart city management, we can generate innovative ideas and identify critical factors and opportunities.

FINDINGS

Bibliographic Coupling Map: Main Topics Studied

The purpose of bibliographic coupling analysis is to illuminate the relationships between documents based on shared references, serving as a powerful tool for identifying related works and emerging research trends. Our analysis utilized the unit of analysis "documents" and the counting method "Full counting," with a minimum threshold of five citations per document. From a total of 426 documents, 179 met this criterion, leading to the identification of ten distinct research clusters.

The first cluster, represented in red, pertains to innovative "Smart City Technologies and Services", encompassing diverse topics, such as AI systems, smart mobility, green management, public health, and technology adoption. This cluster underscores the theme of innovation within smart city contexts.

The second cluster, highlighted in green, relates to "Advanced Technological Innovations and Management". It spans a broad array of topics, including dynamic capabilities, risk management, big data, blockchain, AI in smart cities, education, open innovation, and applications in smart homes, aircraft systems, and wearables.

The third cluster, depicted in blue, focuses on "Governance and Innovation in Smart Cities". This cluster emphasizes governance, innovation, performance, and citizen participation in the development and implementation of smart city initiatives.

The fourth cluster, shown in yellow, addresses "Smart Urban Mobility and Logistics". It covers diverse topics related to transportation services, urban logistics, smart mobility, and the integration of advanced technologies to enhance urban transportation systems.

The fifth cluster, in purple, revolves around "Sustainable Urban Innovation and Development". It includes themes of green development, smart city construction, employment, public health, and technological advancements within the context of emerging economies, highlighting sustainability, innovation, and urban improvement.

The sixth cluster, highlighted in lavender, is associated with "Electric Mobility and Smart Cities Sustainable Governance". This cluster captures the integration of electric mobility, sustainability, governance, and advanced urban mobility solutions within smart cities.

The seventh cluster, depicted in orange, pertains to "Smart Tourism and Sustainable Destinations". It emphasizes smart hospitality, tourism destinations, local energy systems, digital twins, and the governance and progress of smart destinations, considering travel mobility patterns and tourist experiences.

The eighth cluster, illustrated in dusty rose, focuses on "Sustainable Urban Entrepreneurship and Smart Governance". This cluster encompasses entrepreneurial ecosystems, start-up ecosystems, municipal solid waste management, and smart governance applications tailored for digital immigrants and digital natives, emphasizing sustainability, entrepreneurship, and urban governance.

The ninth cluster, depicted in dark pink, concerns "Sustainability and Innovation in Smart Cities". It covers big data analytics for sustainability, blockchain technology, local policy, public-private partnerships, innovative companies, smart city mobility, water supply chain management, and specific applications in smart cities like Jakarta.

The tenth cluster, shown in pink, relates to "Innovative Design and Optimization in Urban Bioinformatics". It includes themes of bioinformatics optimization, design thinking, text mining, and citizen involvement in city design, emphasizing collaboration and innovation.

Figure 2 presents the bibliographical coupling map, which reveals an intriguing opposition on the horizontal axis: generic presentations of smart city technologies and initiatives on the left versus specific topics of smart urban mobility and logistics on the right. Vertically, there is an opposition between static variables such as innovative design and sustainable urban innovation and development at the top versus the involvement of people, namely tourists, at the bottom.

Figure 2. Bibliographical coupling map (done with VOS Viewer software)

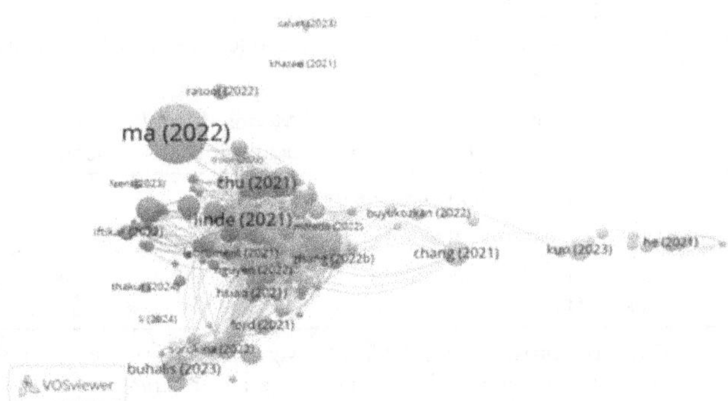

Focus Groups, Mind Maps and Morphological Analysis

A mind map is a visual tool used to organize information and generate creative ideas by visually mapping out concepts and their relationships. It starts with a central idea or theme, and branches out to subtopics and related ideas, creating a tree-like structure. This technique leverages the brain's natural inclination for visual and associative thinking, making it easier to brainstorm and connect ideas (Buzan, 2009; Wheeldon & Ahlberg, 2019).

Morphological analysis on the other hand, is a structured, creative problem-solving technique used to generate new ideas by exploring all possible combinations of different attributes in each parameter (Zwicky, 1969; Álvarez & Ritchey, 2015).

The output of a morphological analysis in idea generation techniques is typically a morphological matrix or chart. This matrix is a structured tool that helps to explore all possible solutions to a complex problem by breaking it down into its core components and examining the various options for each component (not all the parameters need to be used). The initial problem is to develop innovative ideas for smart city management using AIoT-driven solutions. The parameters found by the participants in the focus groups are identified in table 1, as well as the options for each parameter.

By systematically exploring all possible combinations of attributes, morphological analysis helps generate a wide range of ideas, some of which may lead to innovative and practical solutions.

Table 1. Morphological analysis matrix output

Key Parameters	Options
Data collection spaces	Indoor; Outdoor; Both.
Data collection modes	Static (fixed places); Mobile; Satellite.
Devices used to collect data	IoT devices and sensors; wearables; mobile apps; social media; aircraft systems; satellite imagery.
IoT sensor types	Presence; Position; Machine vision; Motion; Identification; Interaction; Hydraulic; Accoustic; Force / Load; Electric; Chemical; Bio; Ambient; Other.
IoT sensor characteristics	Smart or edge sensors; non-smart sensors.
Data input types	Images; sounds; videos; texts; graphs; geospatial data; network data; other types of sensor data.
Agents that collect the data	Citizens; tourists; residents; local government; private sector organizations; non-government organizations; utility providers; transport agencies; financial institutions; Other.

continued on following page

Table 1. Continued

Key Parameters	Options
Network protocols	RFID; NFC; Bluetooth; Z-wave; Li-Fi; Wi-Fi; Zigbee; Wi-SUN; cellular; LoRaWAN; 6LoWPAN; SigFox; NB-IoT.
Smart city component (SCC): Infrastructure management	Smart buildings (analyzing structural damage or stress in buildings and bridges, voice assistants, environmental noises); Construction; Waste management (bins, electronic traps for insects and pests); Street lighting; Accessibility (for individual with disabilities movements analysis); Security systems; Wildlife monitoring interaction with infrastructures; Access controls; Security and surveillance (with camera vision sensors, biometric scanners and other types of sensors analysis); Indoor location and asset tracking (of objects, individuals, equipmments and inventory).
SCC: Energy management	Electric mobility (electric vehicle chargers, other maintenance and consumption analysis); Energy management in buildings (analyze occupancy and adjust lighting and HVAC systems); Forecast future energy demand; Fault detection and performance deviations analysis; Predictive maintenance of equipments and systems; Hydraulic system operations; Other.
SCC: Transportation and mobility	Smart traffic management systems; Smart parking; Road maintenance issues (including pothole detection and correction); Smart roads (powering street lights and mobile electric vehicles); Smart and eletric mobility (apps and smart parking lots, public transports, traffic lights); Security systems; Voice assistants; Autonomous cars and taxis; Autonomous navigation (in robotics and autonomous vehicles, with safety and avoiding obstacles); Sustainability issues (air pollution and energy consumption); Accessibility (for individuals with disabilities); Wildlife monitoring interacting with transport infrastructure, Other.
SCC: Environmental monitoring	Water supply chain; Sewers' analysis; Air quality; Noise levels; Temperature; Humidity; Pollution and pollutants detection; Environmental changes detections; Animal vocalizations and wildlife detection; Storms; Analysis of people's presence and movement; Other.
SCC: Public safety	Food safety and quality; Wildlife monitoring; Facial recognition of individuals; Indoor location and asset tracking (of objects, individuals, equipments and inventory); Security and surveillance (with alarms promptly alerting authorities); Other.
SCC: Healthcare services	Wearables; Public health monitoring; Remote patient monitoring and anomalies detection; Personalized medicine; Disease diagnosis; Monitoring of vital signs (heart rate, blood pressure, glucose levels, biomarkers in bodily fluids, breathing or heartbeats); Fall detection in elderly care; Monitor movements of individuals outdoor and in smart homes; Medical imaging; Indoor location of objects, equipments and individuals in healthcare facilities; Other.
SCC: Economic development and smart retailing	Smart tourism and smart destinations (voice assistants, wildlife monitoring; tourist experiences; personalization of offers); Hospitality (voice assistants, security systems, user experience, personalization of offers, facial recognition, indoor location, object recognition and asset tracking); Start-up systems; Smart retailing (voice assistants, security systems, user experience, personalization of offers – recommendations, experiences, prices and promotions, facial recognition, retail analytics – improving store layouts, assortment, opening checkout systems, indoor location, object recognition and asset tracking, product recognition and tracking); Security and Surveillance (with alarms promptly alerting authorities); Other.
SCC: Citizen engagement	Apps; Social media platforms; Websites; Quality of life (speech, music, or environmental noises, useful for voice assistants and security systems); Other.

continued on following page

Table 1. Continued

Key Parameters	Options
SCC: Smart agriculture	Robotics; Wildlife monitoring; Security systems; Environmental monitoring; Water supply chain; Product recognition and tracking; Monitor agricultural equipment and livestock locations.
SCC: Smart industry	Chemicals monitoring (Hazardous gases and chemicals); Robotics monitoring; Machines and equipment analysis and predictive maintainance (optimization processes and safety, reducing wear and tear); Human-machine interaction; Voice assistants; Industrial automation (machinery and workers movements monitoring, defects detection); Asset tracking; Security and surveillance (with alarms promptly alerting authorities); Other.
SCC: smart homes	Home systems (adjusting lighting, heating, cooling, entertainment systems); User experience personalization with domotics and automation; Sounds monitoring; Voice Assistants; Security systems; Wildlife monitoring in gardens and backyards; Activity recognition and healthcare monitoring; Security and surveillance (with alarms promptly alerting authorities); Object recognition and asset tracking.
Data processing AI algorithms	ANN; SVM; GA; LR; Others.
AI algorithms outputs	Predictive analytics; real-time descriptive analytics; Other.
Data visualization by users	Dashboards; Mobile apps; Interactive maps; Augmented reality / virtual reality devices; QR codes linked to platforms; Other.
Stakeholders engagement	Surveys; Feedback platforms; Community meetings; Gamification; Number of accesses to platforms and smart city data; Other.
Implementation	Pilot projects; Full-scale development; Public-private partnerships; Other.

One possible exploratory innovation idea based on this matrix could be a Smart Environmental Monitoring System, which leverages AI and IoT technologies to monitor and manage environmental conditions in urban areas. This system aims to enhance the quality of life by providing real-time data and predictive analytics on air quality, noise levels, and pollution. It has the characteristics highlighted in table 2.

Table 2. Smart Environmental Monitoring System options for each parameter considered

Key Parameters	Options
Data collection spaces	Data is collected both indoors and outdoors
Data collection modes	Mobile
Devices used to collect data	IoT devices and sensors
IoT sensor types	Ambient, acoustic, Chemical, Bio sensors
IoT sensor characteristics	Smart sensors
Data input types	Images, sounds, Geospatial and sensor data
Agents that collect the data	Local government and utility providers

continued on following page

Table 2. Continued

Key Parameters	Options
Network protocols	LoRaWAN and Wi-Fi
SCC: Environmental monitoring	Air Quality, Noise levels and pollution
Data processing AI algorithms	ANN and SVM
AI algorithm outputs	Predictive analytics and Real-time analytics
Data visualization by users	Dashboards and interactive maps
Stakeholders engagement	Surveys and Feedback platforms
Implementation	Pilot projects and public-private partnerships (with utility providers)

The potential benefits of these solutions are truly remarkable. By continuously monitoring environmental conditions, we can swiftly respond to adverse events as they happen. Advanced AI algorithms offer invaluable forecasts and trends, enabling proactive decision-making and well-informed policy formulation. Interactive platforms amplify public awareness and foster greater engagement in environmental conservation efforts. Additionally, improved air quality and noise management play a crucial role in enhancing health outcomes for residents.

The possibilities of morphological analysis matrix are endless. By combining various options and parameters, countless innovative ideas can be developed.

CONCLUSIONS

Theoretical Contributions

This study makes several significant contributions to the literature, despite its exploratory nature. In the Background section, the concept of smart cities was reviewed, along with its main objectives and indicators. The relationship between IoT devices and the possibilities for data utilization using AI algorithms was also highlighted. The methods for accessing information and using IoT data in smart cities were analyzed. Additionally, the conceptual model related to data acquisition, storage, processing, decision-making processes, and feedback loops in smart cities was identified and developed, with particular focus on IoT sensors, smart or edge sensors, and artificial intelligence algorithms.

In the research phase, a bibliometric study was conducted using a bibliographical coupling analysis, which identified ten research clusters and highlighted their main topics.

Finally, the use of mind maps and morphological analysis processes, carried out through two focus groups, parameters and their respective options were identified.

This allowed the generation of a matrix that combines various options within each parameter (or a subset of parameters), providing numerous possibilities for smart city management using AIoT devices and technologies.

The five formulated research questions and respective answers are highlighted in table 3.

Table 3. Research questions and main findings summary

Research questions (RQ)	Findings
RQ1) What are the main devices related to the IoT that can collect data for smart city management?	According to the biliometric study and content analysis of documents, and focus group analysis, the devices are: IoT devices and sensors, wearables, mobile apps, social media, aircraft systems, and satellite imagery.
RQ2) Who are the primary agents that can collect this data?	According to the biliometric study and content analysis of documents, and focus group analysis, the primary agents that can collect data are citizens, tourists, residents, local government, private sector organizations, non-government organizations, utility providers, transport agencies, financial institutions, among other interested stakeholders. It would be important to define the type of data that can be collected.
RQ3) How can AI algorithms utilize this data?	According to the biliometric study, the content analysis of documents, and focus group analysis, a non-exausthive collection of methods was highlighted in the Background scetion of this work. Some AI algorithms used are ANN, SVM, GA, LR, among others.
RQ4) What methods allow smart city stakeholders to access and use this data?	According to the biliometric study and content analysis of documents, and focus group analysis, the data visualization by users is based on Dashboards, Mobile apps, Interactive maps, Augmented reality / virtual reality devices, QR codes linked to platforms, among other possibilities. The stakeholders' engagement can be based on surveys, feedback platforms, community meetings, gamification, number of accesses to platforms and smart city data, among other possibilities.
RQ5) What innovative ideas can be developed for Smart City management using AIoT-driven solutions?	The possibilities are almost endless, according to the focus group conducted with the techniques of mind mapping and morphological analysis. An example of innovative idea was mentioned, as well as the parameters and options of a morphological analysis matrix, that allows users to develop multiple innovative ideas for Smart City management using AIoT-driven solutions.

An example of the morphological analysis demonstrates how readers can generate a large number of ideas, encouraging creativity among managers, consultants, and all stakeholders involved in a smart city.

Managerial Contributions

Leveraging morphological analysis and mind mapping through focus groups, this study systematically explores diverse parameters and options, offering a structured approach to innovation in urban management using AIoT. The resulting morphological analysis matrix is a powerful tool for generating innovative ideas. One key managerial contribution is its comprehensive data collection framework, detailing spaces (indoor, outdoor, both) and modes (static, mobile, satellite). Managers can design extensive data collection strategies, ensuring comprehensive urban coverage.

Another significant contribution is identifying devices used to collect data. Managers can leverage multiple devices and sources, enhancing the accuracy and reliability of data-driven insights. The matrix also outlines various data input types (images, sounds, videos, texts, graphs), enabling multi-modal data integration for richer insights and tailored solutions to urban challenges.

This research also details various IoT sensor types (e.g., presence, motion, hydraulic, acoustic) and characteristics (smart or edge sensors, non-smart sensors). This enables managers to select appropriate sensors for different applications, specifying real-time automation or centralized system needs.

Additionally, the research highlights network protocols (e.g., RFID, NFC, Bluetooth, Wi-Fi, LoRaWAN), facilitating interoperable systems. This standardization ensures seamless communication and data exchange within the smart city ecosystem.

The study underscores the importance of involving multiple stakeholders in smart city operationalization. By specifying different agents for data collection (citizens, tourists, government, private sector), the matrix encourages a collaborative approach. Managers can engage diverse stakeholders, fostering community involvement and ensuring inclusive and evaluated initiatives.

Furthermore, the research categorizes smart city components, helping managers identify specific AIoT application areas. This targeted approach allows efficient resource allocation and initiative prioritization. Finally, the matrix highlights various implementation options (pilot projects, full-scale development, and public-private partnerships). This flexibility provides strategic pathways for executing smart city projects, allowing iterative testing and scaling of solutions.

Limitations and Future Research Directions

While this research offers valuable insights into smart city management using AIoT devices through the innovative use of focus groups, mind maps, and morphological analysis, several limitations must be acknowledged.

Firstly, the sample representation is a concern. Focus groups are non-representative qualitative methods, which might bias the findings towards the views of participants, limiting the generalizability of the results.

Secondly, there is potential subjectivity in data interpretation. The use of mind maps and morphological analysis introduces a level of subjectivity, as researchers' biases may influence the categorization of parameters and options, affecting the objectivity of the ideas generated.

Thirdly, the scope of parameters and options is limited. Although the morphological analysis matrix provides a structured approach, it may not encompass all relevant factors for smart city management using AIoT, potentially overlooking other critical aspects or emerging technologies.

Fourthly, the research is subject to temporal and contextual variability. The findings are context-specific and may vary as new technologies emerge and urban dynamics evolve.

Lastly, the innovative ideas generated are conceptual and may face practical challenges during implementation. Factors such as technological feasibility, cost, regulatory constraints, and stakeholder acceptance could impact the successful deployment of AIoT solutions in real-world urban settings.

In terms of future research directions, the innovative possibilities generated through this research lay a robust foundation for future explorations. By employing focus groups, mind maps and morphological analysis, we delve into various parameters and options, providing a solid base for groundbreaking ideas in smart city management using AIoT. Although this research was exploratory in nature, it allows us to identify several promising directions for future studies.

One interesting avenue for future research is the detailed investigation of AIoT applications in predictive analytics for urban management. Predictive analytics, powered by AI algorithms, can foresee potential issues before they arise, such as traffic congestion, infrastructure deterioration, and public safety risks. By harnessing machine learning algorithms and big data analytics, AIoT systems can offer city planners and managers actionable insights, enabling proactive decision-making and efficient resource allocation.

Another critical research area involves enhancing the interoperability of AIoT devices and systems. Given the diverse nature of smart city ecosystems, seamless communication and data exchange between different devices and platforms are crucial. Developing standardized protocols and frameworks will ensure that various AIoT solutions can operate cohesively, creating an efficient urban management system. Exploring the potential of blockchain technology to facilitate secure and transparent data sharing among AIoT devices could be particularly advantageous.

Moreover, future research should thoroughly examine the ethical implications of deploying AIoT in smart cities. The focus groups highlighted concerns regarding data privacy, surveillance, and algorithmic biases. It is essential to establish ethical guidelines and regulatory frameworks to address these issues, ensuring that AIoT applications promote equity, inclusivity, and trust among urban residents. Investigating community-based participatory approaches to involve citizens in the decision-making process could enhance the legitimacy and acceptance of AIoT solutions.

The integration of AIoT in sustainable urban development also deserves further investigation. Smart cities must balance technological advancements with environmental stewardship. Future research should examine the potential of AIoT to optimize energy consumption, reduce carbon footprints, and manage natural resources efficiently. For instance, AIoT-enabled smart grids can dynamically adjust energy distribution based on real-time demand, while intelligent waste management systems can streamline recycling and waste reduction efforts.

Lastly, the focus groups identified a need for user-friendly interfaces and applications that cater to diverse demographics. Future research should prioritize the design and development of intuitive platforms that are accessible to all city residents, regardless of age, technical proficiency, or socio-economic background. Human-centered design principles should guide the creation of AIoT solutions, ensuring they are inclusive, adaptable, and responsive to the needs of the urban populace.

REFERENCES

Adi, E., Anwar, A., Baig, Z., & Zeadally, S. (2020). Machine learning and data analytics for the IoT. *Neural Computing & Applications, 32*(20), 16205–16233. DOI: 10.1007/s00521-020-04874-y

Almomani, A., & Al-Turjman, F. (2024). AI Based RSSI Algorithm for Localization in the IoT Era. Advances in Science [ASTI]. *Technology and Innovation*, •••, 63–69.

Álvarez, A., & Ritchey, T. (2015). Applications of general morphological analysis: From engineering design to policy analysis. *Acta Morphologica Generalis, 4*(2).

Arockia, M. P., Sharma, A., Dekka, S., Gowda, V. D., & Singh, M. (2024). Deep Learning Approaches for Real-Time Data Analytics in IoT Sensor Networks. *Lecture Notes in Networks and Systems, 1007*, 239–248. DOI: 10.1007/978-981-97-5146-4_21

Bhardwaj, V., Anooja, A., Vermani, L. S., Sunita, , & Dhaliwal, B. K. (2024). Smart cities and the IoT: An in-depth analysis of global research trends and future directions. *Discover Internet Things, 4*(1), 19. DOI: 10.1007/s43926-024-00076-3

Buzan, T. (2009). *The mind map book: Unlock Your Creativity, Boost Your Memory, Change Your Life*. Pearson Education Limited.

Chang, F.-J., & Chang, L.-C. (2022). Artificial Intelligence Techniques in Hydrology and Water Resources Management. [Special Issue]. *Water (Basel).*

Chen, S., Xiong, G., Xu, J., Han, S., Wang, F.-Y., & Wang, K. (2018). The smart street lighting system based on NB-IoT. In: *2018 Chinese Automation Congress (CAC)*. IEEE, 1196–1200. DOI: 10.1109/CAC.2018.8623281

IAEME Publication (2024). AI-Based Predictive Maintenance Strategies for Electrical Equipment and Power Networks. This publication explores AI-based predictive maintenance strategies tailored specifically for electrical equipment and power networks.

Jakubcinova, M., & Poruban, A. (2023). *The Concept of a Smart City Management in the Light of the Literature Review*. Zeszyty Naukowe Politechniki Częstochowskiej.

Kim, D., & Heo, T.-Y. (2022). Anomaly Detection with Feature Extraction Based on Machine Learning Using Hydraulic System IoT Sensor Data. *Sensors (Basel), 22*(7), 2479. DOI: 10.3390/s22072479 PMID: 35408096

Kumar, V., & Singh, P. (2024). Advancements in Smart City Technologies: Innovations and Future Directions. *Journal of Urban Technology, 31*(2), 102–128. DOI: 10.1080/10630732.2024.1145634

Matei, A., & Coco atu, M. (2024). Artificial Internet of Things, Sensor-Based Digital Twin Urban Computing Vision Algorithms, and Blockchain Cloud Networks in Sustainable Smart City Administration. *Sustainability (Basel), 16*(16), 6749. DOI: 10.3390/su16166749

Merenda, M., Porcaro, C., & Iero, D. (2020). Edge Machine Learning for AI-Enabled IoT Devices: A Review. *Sensors (Basel), 20*(9), 2533. DOI: 10.3390/s20092533 PMID: 32365645

Morais, C. M., Sadok, D., & Kelner, J. (2019). An IoT sensor and scenario survey for data researchers. *Journal of the Brazilian Computer Society, 25*(4), 2–17. DOI: 10.1186/s13173-019-0085-7

Moura, F. de Abreu e Silva, J. (2021). Smart Cities: Definitions, Evolution of the Concept, and Examples of Initiatives. In: Leal Filho, W., Azul, A.M., Brandli, L., Lange Salvia, A., Wall, T. (eds) Industry, Innovation and Infrastructure. Encyclopedia of the UN Sustainable Development Goals. Springer, Cham. https://doi.org/ DOI: 10.1007/978-3-319-95873-6_6

Myeong, S., Park, J., & Lee, M. (2022). Research Models and Methodologies on the Smart City: A Systematic Literature Review. *Sustainability (Basel), 14*(3), 1687. DOI: 10.3390/su14031687

Noh, D., & Oh, E. (2025). Chemical Detection Using Mobile Platforms and AI-Based Data Processing Technologies. *Journal of Sensing and Actuator Networks, 14*(1), 6. DOI: 10.3390/jsan14010006

Omrany, H., Al-Obaidi, K. M., Hossain, M., Alduais, N. A. M., Al-Duais, H. S., & Ghaffarianhoseini, A. (2024). IoT-enabled smart cities: A hybrid systematic analysis of key research areas, challenges, and recommendations for future direction. *Discover Cities, 1*(1), 2. DOI: 10.1007/s44327-024-00002-w

Panduman, Y. Y. F., Funabiki, N., Fajrianti, E. D., Fang, S., & Sukaridhoto, S. (2024). A Survey of AI Techniques in IoT Applications with Use Case Investigations in the Smart Environmental Monitoring and Analytics in Real-Time IoT Platform. *Information (Basel), 15*(3), 153. DOI: 10.3390/info15030153

Park, J. H., & Yen, N. Y. (2018). Advanced algorithms and applications based on IoT for the smart devices. *Journal of Ambient Intelligence and Humanized Computing, 9*(4), 1085–1087. DOI: 10.1007/s12652-018-0715-5

Popescu, S. M., Mansoor, S., Wani, O. A., Kumar, S. S., Sharma, V., Arya, V. M., Kirkham, M. B., Hou, D., Bolan, N., & Chung, Y. S. (2024). Artificial intelligence and IoT driven technologies for environmental pollution monitoring and management. *Frontiers in Environmental Science*, *12*, 1336088. DOI: 10.3389/fenvs.2024.1336088

Pratas, J., & Oliveira, Z. (2023). QR Codes Research in Marketing: A Bibliometric and Content Analysis. In Reis, J. L., Peter, M. K., Varela González, J. A., & Bogdanović, Z. (Eds.), *Marketing and Smart Technologies. Smart Innovation, Systems and Technologies* (Vol. 337). Springer., DOI: 10.1007/978-981-19-9099-1_19

Rao, A. N., Velivela, A., Reddy, M. S. R. L., Sagar, Y. A., Jyothi, N. J., & Shilpa, S. (2025). Machine Learning and Artificial Intelligence in IoT: Integration Techniques and Applications. Cognitive Science and Technology, 65-64.

Sehito, N., Yang, S., Larik, R. S. A., Kamal, M. M., Alwabli, A., & Ullah, I. (2024). Artificial Intelligence (AI) and Internet of Things (IoT) Applications in Sustainable Technology. Advanced Technologies and Societal Change, 227-246.

Shahbazian, R., Macrina, G., Scalzo, E., & Guerriero, F. (2023). Machine Learning Assists IoT Localization: A Review of Current Challenges and Future Trends. *Sensors (Basel)*, *23*(7), 3551. DOI: 10.3390/s23073551 PMID: 37050611

Shankar, A., & Zennaro, M. (2023). Efficient Data Interpretation and Artificial Intelligence Enabled IoT Based Smart Sensing System. *Artificial Intelligence Review*, *56*(12), 15053–15077. DOI: 10.1007/s10462-023-10519-y

Shirgir, B., Dimililer, K., & Asir, S. (2024). Applications of Artificial Intelligence in Biosensors. Smart Innovation. *Systems and Technologies*, *389*, 299–315.

Singh, Y. V., Khan, S., Singh, P., & Singh, R. S. (2022). *An Optimized Artificial Intelligence System Using IoT Biosensors Networking for Healthcare Problems*. Computational Intelligence and Neuroscience.

Soares, N., Monteiro, P., Duarte, F. J., & Machado, R. J. (2020). A Unified Reference Model for Smart Cities. In Santos, H., Pereira, G., Budde, M., Lopes, S., & Nikolic, P. (Eds.), *Science and Technologies for Smart Cities. SmartCity 360 2019. Lecture Notes of the Institute for Computer Sciences, Social Informatics and Telecommunications Engineering* (Vol. 323). Springer., DOI: 10.1007/978-3-030-51005-3_16

Stetter, J. R. (2012). Smart sensors and applications. In *Encyclopedia of Sensors* (Vol. 9, pp. 1–13). American Scientific Publishers.

Syed, A. S., Sierra-Sosa, D., Kumar, A., & Elmaghraby, A. (2021). IoT in Smart Cities: A Survey of Technologies, Practices and Challenges. *Smart Cities*, *4*(2), 429–475. DOI: 10.3390/smartcities4020024

Ullah, A., Anwar, S. M., Li, J., Nadeem, L., Mahmood, T., Rehman, A., & Saba, T. (2023). Smart cities: The role of Internet of Things and machine learning in realizing a data-centric smart environment. *Complex & Intelligent Systems, 10*(1), 1607–1637. DOI: 10.1007/s40747-023-01175-4

Wang, C., He, T., Zhou, H., Zhang, Z., & Lee, C. (2023). Artificial Intelligence Enhanced Sensors - Enabling Technologies to Next-Generation Healthcare and Biomedical Platform. *Bioelectronic Medicine*, *9*(1), 17. DOI: 10.1186/s42234-023-00118-1 PMID: 37528436

Wheeldon, J., & Ahlberg, M. (2019). Mind maps in qualitative research. In Creswell, K. A., & Creswell, S. D. (Eds.), *Handbook of qualitative research methods* (pp. 200–210). Sage Publications.

Wolniak, R., & Stecuła, K. (2024). Artificial Intelligence in Smart Cities—Applications, Barriers, and Future Directions: A Review. *Smart Cities*, *7*(3), 1346–1389. DOI: 10.3390/smartcities7030057

Yu, X., Ai, T., & Wang, K. (2024). Application of Nanogenerators in Acoustics Based on Artificial Intelligence and Machine Learning. *APL Materials*, *12*(2), 020602. DOI: 10.1063/5.0195399

Zaman, M., Puryear, N., Abdelwahed, S., & Zohrabi, N. (2024). A Review of IoT-Based Smart City Development and Management. *Smart Cities*, *7*(3), 1462–1501. DOI: 10.3390/smartcities7030061

Zennaro, M., & Manzoni, P. (2021). AI for IoT: Special Issue on AI for IoT. [Special Issue]. *Sensors (Basel).*

Zwicky, F. (1969). *Discovery, invention, research – Through the morphological approach*. Macmillan.

ADDITIONAL READING

Dias, T., Fonseca, T., Vitorino, J., Martins, A., Malpique, S., & Praça, I. (2023). From data to action: Exploring AI and IoT-driven solutions for smarter cities. arXiv preprint arXiv:2306.04653 DOI: 10.1007/978-3-031-38333-5_5

Hajek, P., Youssef, A., & Hajkova, V. (2022). Recent developments in smart city assessment: A bibliometric and content analysis-based literature review. *Cities (London, England)*, *126*, 103709. DOI: 10.1016/j.cities.2022.103709

Islam, M., Dukyil, A. S., Alyahya, S., & Habib, S. (2023). An IoT Enable Anomaly Detection System for Smart City Surveillance. *Sensors (Basel), 23*(4), 2358. DOI: 10.3390/s23042358 PMID: 36850955

Koca, G., Egilmez, O., & Akcakaya, O. (2021). Evaluation of the smart city: Applying the dematel technique. *Telematics and Informatics, 62*, 101625. DOI: 10.1016/j.tele.2021.101625

Kuguoglu, B. K., van der Voort, H., & Janssen, M. (2021). The giant leap for smart cities: Scaling up smart city artificial intelligence of things (AIoT) initiatives. *Sustainability (Basel), 13*(21), 12295. DOI: 10.3390/su132112295

Mishra, D., Vajire, S. L., Saxena, S., Gupta, P., Saini, D. K., Srivastava, A. K., & Rao, G. M. (2022). *GRUBin: Time-Series Forecasting-Based Efficient Garbage Monitoring and Management System for Smart Cities*. Hindawi Computational Intelligence and Neuroscience., DOI: 10.1155/2022/2538807

Saradopoulos, I., Potamitis, I., Ntalampiras, S., Konstantaras, A. I., & Antonidakis, E. N. (2022). Edge Computing for Vision-Based, Urban-Insects Traps in the Context of Smart Cities. *Sensors (Basel), 22*(5), 2006. DOI: 10.3390/s22052006 PMID: 35271153

Wu, C., Wang, Z., Hu, S., Lepine, J., Na, X., Ainalis, D., & Stettler, M. (2020). An automated machine-learning approach for road pothole detection using smartphone sensor data. *Sensors (Basel), 20*(19), 5564. Advance online publication. DOI: 10.3390/s20195564 PMID: 32998427

KEY TERMS AND DEFINITIONS

Algorithm: is a step-by-step guide designed to complete a task or solve a problem. It's a methodical blueprint for calculations, data processing, and automated decision-making. Algorithms simplify and automate processes by providing clear instructions for each step. They require some inputs to get started, produce results, and conclude after a specific number of steps. This methodical approach makes complex tasks manageable and efficient.

Artificial Intelligence (AI): refers to the simulation of human intelligence in machines that are programmed to think and learn like humans. These systems can perform tasks typically requiring human intelligence, such as understanding natural language, recognizing patterns, solving problems, and making decisions. Essentially, they mimic human cognitive functions, enabling them to carry out complex tasks with impressive efficiency and accuracy.

Artificial Intelligence of Things (AIoT): is the integration of Artificial Intelligence (AI) with the Internet of Things (IoT). By harnessing AI's power for data analysis, decision-making, and automation, AIoT transforms smart homes, cities, retail, industrial automation, healthcare, and transportation. It enables real-time decisions, operational optimization, and overall efficiency improvements.

Big Data analytics: involves analyzing large and diverse datasets, commonly known as "big data," to uncover hidden patterns, correlations, trends, and insights. These large volumes of data can originate from various sources such as sensors, transaction records, social media, and more. Through meticulous examination, valuable information is extracted to drive informed decision-making and innovative solutions.

Internet of Things (IoT): encompasses a network of physical devices, vehicles, appliances, and other items embedded with sensors, software, and connectivity features. These devices collect and exchange data with each other and with central systems over the internet. The goal of IoT is to create smarter, more efficient systems capable of monitoring, controlling, and optimizing various processes and activities.

Real-time Automation: refers to the use of technology to execute tasks and processes automatically and instantaneously as events unfold. Continuous monitoring and rapid data processing make this possible, enabling systems to respond immediately to changes or triggers in real-time. It encompasses continuous monitoring, instant processing, automated responses, and adaptive systems, ensuring seamless and efficient operations.

Smart Cities: are urban areas that use technology and data to boost public satisfaction, optimize service efficiency, and promote sustainability. By integrating advanced technologies like Internet-of-Things, big data analytics, and Artificial Intelligence, these cities strive to create more connected, efficient, and environmentally friendly urban environments.

Smart Infrastructure: involves integrating advanced technologies into physical structures and systems to boost efficiency, sustainability, and community responsiveness. By harnessing sensors, data analytics, and IoT for real-time monitoring and management, it fosters resilient urban environments. This technological fusion enhances public satisfaction while reducing environmental impact.

Chapter 10
Legal and Ethical Challenges in the Integration of AIoT in Retail:
Perspectives on Marketing and Consumer Behavior

David López Jiménez
https://orcid.org/0000-0002-7013-9556
EAE Business School, UNIE Universidad, Spain

Eduardo Carlos Dittmar
https://orcid.org/0000-0002-8087-2444
Universidad Rey Juan Carlos, Spain

Jenny Patricia Vargas Portillo
https://orcid.org/0000-0002-0226-3053
Universidad de Sevilla, Spain

ABSTRACT

This chapter addresses the growing need for a legal and ethical framework for implementing Artificial Intelligence (AI) and Internet of Things (IoT) technologies in the retail sector, with a specific focus on how these regulatory frameworks influence marketing strategies and consumer behavior. At the intersection of technological innovation and regulatory compliance, this chapter analyses how data privacy laws, regulations on the use of personal data, and ethical principles must progress to protect consumers while allowing retail companies to use AI and IoT to optimize

DOI: 10.4018/979-8-3693-8512-8.ch010

their marketing strategies. Through a qualitative research methodology involving literature review and case study analysis, this research examines the challenges and opportunities that arise when implementing AIoT in retail, providing insights for both academics and practitioners navigating this complex landscape.

INTRODUCTION

The convergence of Artificial Intelligence (AI) and the Internet of Things (IoT) has triggered an unprecedented transformation across various industries, with the retail sector being one of the most impacted by this technological synergy. As the boundaries between the physical and digital worlds blur, the integration of these technologies—known as Artificial Intelligence of Things (AIoT)—is redefining how retail companies interact with consumers, manage their operations, and design their marketing strategies. However, along with the immense opportunities AIoT offers, it also brings forth complex legal and ethical challenges that demand urgent and meticulous attention.

In a scenario where personal data has become the most valuable asset, the ability to collect, process, and analyze large volumes of information in real-time through connected devices raises fundamental questions about privacy, security, and consumer rights. The implementation of AIoT in retail enables companies to personalize offers, optimize inventory management, and improve customer experience on an unprecedented scale. Nevertheless, this capacity to influence consumer behavior, if not managed appropriately, can lead to manipulative or discriminatory practices, eroding public trust and triggering a negative response from both the legal and social spheres.

The current regulatory framework, with notable examples such as the General Data Protection Regulation (GDPR) in Europe and the California Consumer Privacy Act (CCPA) in the United States, establishes a set of strict rules on how companies must handle personal data (Veale & Zuiderveen Borgesius, 2021). These regulations reflect a global effort to balance technological innovation with the protection of individual rights. However, it is evident that these regulations need to address the new complexities that arise in this adaptive environment. The ability of algorithms to make autonomous decisions based on massive datasets poses new ethical and legal dilemmas that cannot be fully addressed by existing laws (Fatima et al., 2020).

Beyond regulatory compliance, there is a growing need to develop a robust ethical framework to guide the implementation of AIoT in retail. This framework must go beyond legal obligations, promoting practices that respect consumer autonomy, ensure transparency in data usage, and guarantee fairness in automated decisions. The responsibility of companies is to comply with the law and to adopt a proactive stance in protecting consumer rights, anticipating, and mitigating the risks that may arise from the exploitation of these technologies (Abungu, 2021).

This chapter deepens into the intersection of technological innovation and regulatory compliance, exploring how AIoT is transforming retail and its implications in legal and ethical terms. It thoroughly analyzes the challenges companies face in their attempt to fully harness the advantages of AIoT without compromising customer trust or violating existing regulations. Additionally, it examines the impact of these technologies on marketing strategies, considering how legal restrictions and ethical expectations influence the ability of companies to personalize and segment their offerings in an increasingly competitive and regulated environment.

Throughout this chapter, specific cases illustrating the tensions between technological innovation and the need for adequate control will be addressed. These examples underscore the best practices and approaches that companies can adopt to navigate this complex landscape. By providing an integral and critical overview of the legal and ethical aspects of AIoT in retail, this chapter aims to be an indispensable guide for academics, professionals, and policymakers interested in understanding the intersections between technology, law, and consumer behavior.

The research objectives of this chapter are threefold: first, to analyze the current state of AIoT implementation in retail and its implications for marketing and consumer behavior; second, to identify and evaluate the legal and ethical challenges associated with AIoT integration; and third, to propose a normative framework that can guide retailers in the responsible use of these technologies. Through a qualitative research methodology that combines a systematic literature review with case study analysis, this chapter aims to describe the current state of AIoT in retail and to inspire a broader debate on how we can build a future where technology serves humanity in a fair and equitable manner. The central question guiding this exploration is how we can ensure that the potential of AIoT is realized in a way that benefits both businesses and consumers without sacrificing the fundamental principles of ethics and legality.

This chapter investigates the multifaceted implications of integrating AIoT into the retail sector, with a particular focus on the legal and ethical dimensions of this technological convergence. To provide readers with a clear overview of the complex issues addressed in this research, Table 1 summarizes the key arguments and considerations that will be examined in depth throughout the subsequent sections. The table highlights the transformative potential of AIoT in retail, the regulatory frameworks governing its implementation, the ethical dilemmas it presents, and the proposed strategies for fostering responsible innovation. By outlining these central themes at the outset, we aim to facilitate an integral understanding of the challenges and opportunities that arise at the intersection of AIoT, retail, marketing, and consumer behavior.

Table 1. Key Arguments and Considerations in AIoT Integration in Retail

Dimension	Key Arguments	Implications
Technological Integration	• AIoT represents the convergence of AI and IoT technologies, creating smart retail environments. • Enables real-time data collection, analysis, and autonomous decision-making. • Facilitates unprecedented personalization and operational efficiency.	• Transformation of traditional retail operations and customer experiences. • Enhanced inventory management and supply chain optimization. • Creation of omnichannel shopping experiences.
Regulatory Landscape	• GDPR and CCPA establish strict requirements for data handling. • Fragmented global regulatory environment creates compliance challenges. • Emerging regulations in Asia, Latin America, and other regions add complexity.	• Need for robust data governance frameworks. • Challenges in cross-border data transfers. • Growing call for global harmonization of data protection standards.
Ethical Considerations	• Tension between personalization and manipulation of consumer behavior. • Risk of algorithmic bias and discrimination in AI-driven decisions. • Challenges in ensuring transparency and explainability of AIoT systems	• Importance of ethical guidelines for AIoT implementation. • Need for fairness and inclusivity in algorithmic design. • Balance between business interests and consumer welfare.
Consumer Rights and Trust	• Growing consumer awareness and concerns about data privacy. • Demand for greater control over personal information. • Importance of transparency in building consumer trust.	• Implementation of user-friendly consent mechanisms. • Development of privacy dashboards and preference management tools. • Shift toward ethical marketing practices that respect consumer autonomy.
Normative Framework	• Need for foundational principles of transparency and responsibility. • Importance of data minimization and purpose limitation. • Value of continuous monitoring and improvement of AIoT systems.	• Implementation of internal ethics committees. • Development of integral data management policies. • Regular audits and third-party certifications of ethical compliance.
Practical Implementation	• TechStyle case study demonstrates successful AIoT integration. • Balanced approach to innovation and ethical responsibility. • Focus on consumer trust as a competitive advantage.	• Strategies for implementing AIoT across operations and marketing. • Approaches to ensuring legal and ethical compliance. • Lessons learned and best practices for retailers.

CONCEPTUAL FRAMEWORK AND CONTEXT

The impact of the AIoT in the retail sector cannot be fully understood without a deep analysis of the concepts and context underlying this technological convergence. This section aims to provide a solid theoretical foundation to understand how the combination of AI and IoT is transforming the retail landscape. As companies adopt these technologies to optimize operations and improve consumer experience, there arises a need to study the conceptual roots of AIoT, its applications, and the historical and evolutionary context that has led to its integration in retail (Shekhawat, 2023). This analysis is essential for understanding the current benefits and challenges of AIoT, as well as anticipating its future developments and how these trends will impact market strategies, consumer behavior, and the legal and ethical frameworks regulating this transformation.

Definition of AIoT: Intersection of AI and IoT

The AIoT represents a powerful intersection between two of the most disruptive technologies of our time: AI and the IoT. To fully grasp the transformative potential of AIoT in the retail sector, it is essential first to clearly define these individual components and then study how their combination amplifies the capabilities and challenges associated with them.

AI refers to the ability of computational systems to perform tasks that would normally require human intelligence, such as decision-making, pattern recognition, and autonomous learning (Guha et al., 2021). In the context of retail, AI enables companies to analyze large volumes of data, automate processes, and predict consumer behavior with a high degree of accuracy (Fatima et al., 2020). Through advanced algorithms and deep learning techniques, AI can personalize shopping experiences, optimize inventory management, and improve operational efficiency across all levels of the supply chain (Kaplan, 2020).

On the other hand, the IoT refers to the interconnected network of physical devices that collect and share data via the Internet (Evans, 2011). These devices, ranging from sensors and cameras to smart appliances and mobile phones, are designed to interact with each other and with other systems through connectivity, enabling the continuous collection and transmission of information. In retail, IoT facilitates unprecedented real-time visibility into consumer behavior, inventory status, and in-store operations. The data generated by IoT devices provides valuable insights that can be used to optimize product placement, manage stock more efficiently, and personalize offers and promotions based on customer behavior (Calderaro & Blumfelde, 2022).

The fusion of these two technologies in AIoT creates an ecosystem where IoT devices collect data and process and analyze it using AI algorithms to make autonomous decisions and continuously improve processes (Anica-Popa et al., 2021; Ghosh et al., 2018). AIoT enables retail companies to create smart shopping environments where every consumer interaction is monitored and optimized in real-time. From inventory automation to personalized shopping experiences, AIoT has the potential to revolutionize every aspect of retail, offering companies a significant competitive advantage in an increasingly saturated and consumer-oriented market (Har, 2022).

A key aspect of AIoT in retail is its ability to generate and harness data on a massive scale. IoT devices, encompassing everything from security cameras to motion sensors and mobile devices, continuously collect information about consumer habits, store traffic patterns, and purchasing trends. This vast amount of data is then processed by AI systems that can identify patterns, predict trends, and make automated decisions that optimize consumer experience and improve operational efficiency (Liu & Lin, 2020).

For example, through AIoT, a retailer can personalize offers in real-time based on a consumer's previous behavior and their current interaction with products in the store. IoT sensors can detect when a customer picks up a product, and AI can use that information along with previous purchase data to offer personalized recommendations directly to the customer's mobile device or on in-store screens. This level of personalization improves the shopping experience and increases the likelihood of conversion, as consumers receive offers and recommendations that are highly relevant to their interests and needs.

Moreover, AIoT plays an important role in optimizing the supply chain in retail. IoT sensors installed in warehouses and distribution centers can monitor storage conditions, the movement of goods, and inventory in real-time, allowing AI systems to predict and respond to demand with greater accuracy. This allows for reduced operational costs by minimizing excess inventory or shortages and improves customer satisfaction by ensuring that products are available when and where they are needed (Taddeo & Floridi, 2018).

However, the implementation of AIoT in retail is not without challenges. The technical complexity of integrating multiple AI systems and IoT devices, managing large volumes of data, and the need to comply with strict regulations on data privacy and security are just some of the obstacles that companies must overcome. It is useful for companies to focus on immediate benefits and to consider the long-term implications, both in terms of technological sustainability and ethical and legal responsibility (Zhao, 2023).

AIoT represents a flexible intersection between AI and IoT that is transforming the retail sector by offering new ways to interact with consumers and manage operations. The combination of these technologies allows for an unprecedented level of personalization and efficiency but also poses significant challenges that require careful planning and a proactive approach to ensure that the benefits of AIoT are realized in an ethical and sustainable manner (Liu et al., 2021). As companies continue to adopt and adapt AIoT, it will be essential to maintain a balance between technological innovation and consumer rights protection, ensuring that this technological convergence is used for the benefit of both businesses and consumers (Sposato et al., 2025).

Evolution of AIoT in Retail

The journey of AIoT's evolution in retail is a testament to how rapidly technology can reshape an industry that, for decades, had remained relatively stable in its operational and consumer engagement strategies. The fusion of AI and the IoT began as two parallel advancements, each with its own set of promises and challenges, but it wasn't until their convergence that the full potential of digital transformation in retail was realized (Shekhawat, 2023). Understanding the evolution of AIoT within this sector requires a look at how each technology developed individually before merging into a cohesive and powerful toolset that now drives retail innovation (Gerlick & Liozu, 2020).

Initially, AI and IoT made progress separately, with distinct applications and objectives (Calderaro & Blumfelde, 2022). AI's roots in retail can be traced back to the early adoption of basic machine learning algorithms used for predictive analytics and customer segmentation (Guha et al., 2021). Retailers began using AI to analyze historical sales data, predict trends, and optimize supply chains (Anica-Popa et al., 2021). These early implementations were relatively simplistic, often limited by the computational power and data availability of the time. However, they laid the groundwork for more sophisticated AI applications by demonstrating that data-driven decision-making could raise operational efficiency and profitability (Kaplan, 2020).

Simultaneously, IoT was making its own strides, though initially focused more on improving logistics and inventory management using RFID (Radio Frequency Identification) tags and basic sensors (Veale & Zuiderveen Borgesius, 2021). These early IoT systems provided retailers with real-time data on stock levels and the movement of goods, reducing losses and improving the accuracy of inventory management. While these technologies were revolutionary, they operated in silos, and their true potential remained untapped until the integration of AI with IoT began to take shape (Har et al., 2022). Digital transformation was further accelerated by global events that forced rapid adaptation across sectors (Dittmar et al., 2025).

The convergence of AI and IoT into AIoT marked a significant shift in how retailers approached both technology and consumer interaction. This merger was driven by the realization that the massive amounts of data generated by IoT devices could be far more valuable when combined with AI's ability to analyze and derive insights from that data in real-time (Guha et al., 2021). The integration enabled a more flexible and responsive retail environment, where decisions could be made on the fly based on real-time data from interconnected devices. (Sposato, 2024).

An important aspect in this evolution was the increasing availability of cloud computing and big data technologies. These innovations provided the necessary infrastructure for storing and processing the vast amounts of data generated by IoT devices, making it feasible to apply AI models at scale (Lauterbach, 2019). Retailers began to deploy AIoT solutions that could automate everything from supply chain logistics to personalized marketing campaigns, all while learning and adapting continuously based on new data inputs (Kaplan, 2020).

Today, AIoT is at the forefront of retail innovation, driving a paradigm shift in how businesses operate and engage with consumers. The capabilities of AIoT have expanded far beyond the early predictive models and basic inventory management tools (Veale & Zuiderveen Borgesius, 2021). Modern AIoT systems are deeply integrated into every aspect of retail operations, offering a flawless blend of physical and digital experiences that were unimaginable just a decade ago.

In-store, AIoT powers everything from smart shelves that automatically restock themselves based on real-time sales data, to advanced customer service robots that assist shoppers and provide personalized recommendations. These technologies increase the efficiency of operations and also significantly improve the customer experience by offering more tailored and timely interactions (Gerlick & Liozu, 2020).

Moreover, AIoT is revolutionizing the concept of omnichannel retailing. Retailers can now offer a consistent and personalized shopping experience across all channels—whether online, in-store, or via mobile apps (Liu & Lin, 2020). For example, AIoT enables features like virtual fitting rooms, which use a combination of AI-driven image recognition and IoT sensors to recommend clothing sizes and styles based on a customer's previous purchases and preferences. This level of integration ensures that customers enjoy a cohesive and tailored experience, regardless of how they choose to shop.

Despite the impressive advancements, the evolution of AIoT in retail has not been without its challenges. As the technology progresses, concerns about data privacy, security, and ethical implications have grown. The vast amount of data collected by IoT devices—ranging from consumer behavior to personal information—has raised significant questions about how this data is stored, processed, and used.

Moreover, the reliance on AI-driven decision-making brings forth issues related to algorithmic bias and transparency (Veale & Zuiderveen Borgesius, 2021). Retailers must navigate these challenges carefully, ensuring that their AIoT systems are effective, fair and compliant with increasingly stringent data protection regulations. The evolution of AIoT in retail thus also includes the parallel development of best practices and regulatory frameworks that seek to protect consumer rights while enabling innovation (Kaplan, 2020).

As AIoT progresses, its role in retail is expected to grow even more sophisticated. The future may see the integration of AIoT with emerging technologies like blockchain for secure and transparent supply chains, or with augmented reality (AR) to create even more immersive shopping experiences (Fatima et al., 2020). Additionally, as consumer expectations continue to rise, AIoT systems will need to become more adaptive, harnessing advances in AI to predict and respond to customer needs with greater accuracy and speed.

The evolution of AIoT in retail is a flexible and ongoing process that has already reshaped the industry in profound ways. From its early beginnings as separate technologies to its current state as a powerful, integrated solution, AIoT continues to push the boundaries of what is possible in retail. As technology matures, retailers will need to stay ahead of the curve, covering both the opportunities and challenges that come with this next wave of digital transformation (Shekhawat, 2023).

REGULATION AND LEGAL COMPLIANCE IN THE USE OF AIoT

The integration of AIoT into the retail sector introduces significant legal and regulatory challenges. As these technologies become more pervasive, they raise complex questions about data privacy, consumer rights, and the ethical use of personal information. To navigate this changing landscape, it is useful for retailers to understand and comply with the various legal frameworks that govern the use of AIoT (Walters & Novak, 2021). This section analyses the international regulatory landscape, focusing on key regulations like the General Data Protection Regulation (GDPR), the California Consumer Privacy Act (CCPA), and emerging regulations in other regions.

International Regulatory Framework

The global nature of retail operations, especially in the digital age, necessitates a complete understanding of international regulatory frameworks. AIoT technologies do not operate within the confines of national borders; data collected from consumers can flow freely across the globe, making it essential for retailers to adhere to multiple, sometimes conflicting, legal standards. This section outlines the most influential regulations shaping the use of AIoT in retail, starting with the GDPR in Europe, followed by the CCPA in the United States, and concluding with an overview of emerging regulatory trends in other regions.

General Data Protection Regulation (GDPR)

The General Data Protection Regulation (GDPR), implemented by the European Union in May 2018, represents one of the most integral and stringent data protection laws globally (Huang et al., 2024). Its scope and impact have made it a cornerstone for data privacy regulations worldwide, influencing how AIoT technologies are implemented, especially in retail.

The GDPR's broad scope covers any organization that processes personal data of individuals within the EU, regardless of the organization's location. For retailers utilizing AIoT, this means that any data collected through IoT devices, such as customer behavior data, location tracking, or biometric information, must comply with GDPR standards.

One of the GDPR's most significant provisions is the requirement for explicit, informed consent from consumers before collecting and processing their data. This poses a challenge for AIoT systems, which often rely on continuous data collection from various devices. Retailers must ensure that they have robust consent mechanisms in place, providing clear and transparent information to consumers about what data is being collected, how it will be used, and for what purposes (Hermann, 2022).

Additionally, the GDPR introduces strict requirements for data minimization and purpose limitation, meaning that data collected through AIoT systems must be limited to what is necessary for the intended purpose and cannot be repurposed without additional consent (Kaplan, 2020). This regulation forces retailers to carefully design their AIoT systems to avoid excessive data collection and ensure compliance with the GDPR's principles.

The right to be forgotten, another element of the GDPR, allows consumers to request the deletion of their personal data. For AIoT systems, this can be particularly challenging, as data is often distributed across multiple devices and platforms. Retailers must develop mechanisms to ensure that they can efficiently locate and delete data upon request, which may require significant investment in data management infrastructure.

To comply with the GDPR, retailers must adopt a proactive approach to data protection (Lauterbach, 2019). This includes conducting Data Protection Impact Assessments (DPIAs) to identify and mitigate risks associated with AIoT technologies, implementing privacy by design principles, and ensuring that data protection is integrated into every stage of AIoT development and deployment.

Moreover, retailers should establish clear data governance frameworks that define roles and responsibilities for data protection, provide ongoing training for employees, and ensure that third-party vendors and partners also comply with GDPR standards. Regular audits and reviews of AIoT systems are essential to maintaining compliance and adapting to any changes in the regulatory environment.

California Consumer Privacy Act (CCPA)

The California Consumer Privacy Act (CCPA), enacted in January 2020, is another critical regulation that shapes the use of AIoT in retail, particularly for businesses operating in or serving customers in California (Wang et al., 2018). While the CCPA shares some similarities with the GDPR, it also introduces unique requirements that retailers must navigate.

The CCPA grants California residents several key rights concerning their personal data, including the right to know what personal information is being collected, the right to access and delete that information, and the right to opt out of the sale of their personal data (Gerlick & Liozu, 2020). For AIoT systems in retail, these provisions necessitate a high level of transparency and consumer control over data collection practices.

One of the defining features of the CCPA is its focus on data transparency. Retailers must provide clear and accessible privacy notices that inform consumers about the types of data being collected through AIoT devices, the purposes for which it is used, and whether it is shared with third parties. This is particularly relevant for AIoT systems that collect sensitive information, such as geolocation data or biometric identifiers, where the potential for misuse is high.

The CCPA also introduces the concept of "Do Not Sell My Personal Information," which requires retailers to offer consumers a simple way to opt out of the sale of their data (Huang et al., 2024). For AIoT systems that rely on data sharing with third-party service providers or advertisers, this opt-out mechanism can significantly impact how these systems are designed and implemented.

Retailers must ensure that their AIoT systems are capable of meeting the CCPA's transparency and consumer rights requirements. This includes developing processes for responding to consumer requests for data access, deletion, and opt-out, as well as implementing mechanisms to track and manage consumer consent across multiple platforms and devices.

Additionally, retailers should invest in technology solutions that allow for the secure and efficient management of personal data, such as data anonymization tools, consent management platforms, and automated systems for handling consumer requests. These tools can help ensure compliance with the CCPA while minimizing the operational burden on the business.

Given the CCPA's potential for significant financial penalties for non-compliance, it is useful for retailers to conduct regular audits of their AIoT systems and data practices, ensuring that they remain in line with regulatory requirements and can quickly adapt to any changes or updates to the law.

Emerging Regulations in Other Regions

Beyond the GDPR and CCPA, other regions are developing their own regulations to address the challenges posed by AIoT technologies. As AIoT continues to expand globally, retailers must stay informed about these emerging legal frameworks to ensure compliance and avoid potential legal pitfalls.

In the Asia-Pacific region, countries like Japan, South Korea, and Australia are at the forefront of developing complete data protection laws that address the unique challenges of AIoT (Fatima et al., 2020). Japan's Act on the Protection of Personal Information (APPI) has been revised to include stricter controls on data transfers, particularly for AIoT systems that operate across borders (Zhao, 2023). Similarly, South Korea's Personal Information Protection Act (PIPA) imposes rigorous requirements on data processing, with a strong accent on consumer rights and transparency (Du & Xie, 2021).

Australia's Privacy Act is also undergoing significant reforms, with proposed changes that would bring it more in line with the GDPR, including improved rights for consumers and stricter obligations for data controllers (Gerlick & Liozu, 2020). Retailers operating in these markets must adapt their AIoT systems to meet these new standards, particularly in areas related to cross-border data flows and consumer consent.

In Latin America, Brazil has introduced the General Data Protection Law (LGPD), which mirrors many aspects of the GDPR (Taddeo & Floridi, 2018). The LGPD applies to any company processing the data of Brazilian citizens, making it a critical regulation for retailers with AIoT systems in this market. The law stresses consumer rights, including the right to access, correct, and delete personal data, and mandates strict security measures to protect data from breaches (Guha et al., 2021).

Mexico is also looking into updates to its Federal Law on the Protection of Personal Data, aiming to strengthen protections for consumers considering new technological developments, including AIoT. Retailers in Latin America must keep abreast of these developments to ensure their AIoT systems are compliant with evolving legal standards.

In the Middle East, countries like the United Arab Emirates (UAE) and Saudi Arabia are beginning to develop data protection laws that address the specific challenges of AIoT (Taddeo & Floridi, 2018). The UAE has introduced the Federal Decree-Law on the Protection of Personal Data, which sets out integral requirements for data processing and consumer rights. Saudi Arabia's new data protection regulations, part of its Vision 2030 plan, also aim to regulate how personal data is collected and used, with a focus on transparency and consumer consent.

Africa is also seeing progress in data protection, with countries like South Africa implementing the Protection of Personal Information Act (POPIA), which governs the processing of personal data and stresses consumer rights. As AIoT adoption increases in these regions, retailers must ensure their systems comply with local laws and regulations (Gerlick & Liozu, 2020).

As AIoT technologies expand, there is a growing call for global harmonization of data protection regulations (Liu et al., 2021). The fragmented nature of current legal frameworks poses significant challenges for retailers operating across multiple jurisdictions, as they must navigate a complex web of differing regulations.

Some scholars and policymakers advocate for the development of international standards that could provide a consistent regulatory approach to AIoT. Such standards would help ensure that AIoT systems are developed and deployed in ways that respect consumer rights and promote trust, while also reducing the compliance burden on global businesses.

The international regulatory landscape for AIoT in retail is complex and rapidly evolving. Retailers must stay informed and agile, adapting their systems and practices to comply with the diverse and stringent legal requirements that govern the use of AIoT. By doing so, they can avoid legal risks, build consumer trust and drive long-term success in a highly competitive global market (López Jiménez et al., 2022).

ETHICAL DILEMMAS IN INFLUENCING PURCHASE DECISIONS

As AIoT technologies become increasingly sophisticated in their ability to influence consumer behavior, they bring with them significant ethical dilemmas. The power to shape and guide purchase decisions through data-driven insights and personalized experiences raises questions about the fine line between beneficial personalization and potential manipulation, as well as concerns about fairness and equity in algorithmic decision-making. This section considers these ethical challenges, focusing on the balance between manipulation and personalization, and the importance of justice and equity in the deployment of AI algorithms.

Manipulation vs. Personalization

One of the most pressing ethical dilemmas in the use of AIoT in retail is the tension between personalization and manipulation. While personalization is often understood as a key benefit of AIoT, offering consumers tailored experiences that raise convenience and satisfaction, there is a growing concern that these same technologies can be used to manipulate consumer behavior in ways that may not always be in their best interests (Guha et al., 2021).

Personalization is central to modern marketing strategies, enabled by AIoT's ability to gather and analyze vast amounts of consumer data. By understanding individual preferences, behaviors, and needs, retailers can create highly customized experiences that resonate with each consumer (Huang et al., 2024). This can range from personalized product recommendations and targeted discounts to tailored content that matches a consumer's specific interests.

From the consumer's perspective, personalization can be immensely valuable. It simplifies decision-making, improves the shopping experience, and often leads to greater satisfaction by presenting consumers with options that are more relevant to them. For retailers, personalization drives engagement, increases conversion rates, and facilitates brand loyalty.

However, the same technologies that enable personalization also have the potential to cross into the field of manipulation. Manipulation occurs when AIoT systems use consumer data to influence decisions in ways that benefit the retailer more than the consumer, often by exploiting psychological biases or vulnerabilities.

For example, AI-driven systems might deploy tactics like dynamic pricing, where prices are adjusted based on a consumer's perceived willingness to pay, or create urgency through scarcity messages that pressure consumers into making immediate purchases. While these strategies can increase sales, they raise ethical concerns about whether consumers are being nudged towards decisions that they might not otherwise make if they were fully informed or less susceptible to these tactics.

The ethical dilemma lies in the intent and transparency of these practices. When personalization is used to genuinely augment the consumer experience, it is generally seen as positive. But when it is used to manipulate consumer behavior—especially in ways that consumers are unaware of or cannot easily control—it can erode trust and lead to negative perceptions of the brand (Fatima et al., 2020; Martin & Murphy, 2017).

To navigate the balance between personalization and manipulation, retailers must adopt ethical guidelines that prioritize consumer welfare alongside business goals. This includes being transparent about how personalization algorithms work, offering consumers control over the degree of personalization they receive, and avoiding tactics that could be perceived as exploitative or deceptive (Du & Xie, 2021).

Retailers should also consider the long-term impact of their personalization strategies. While manipulation might yield short-term gains, it can lead to long-term damage to the brand if consumers feel that their trust has been violated. Ethical personalization should focus on empowering consumers, providing them with relevant choices that harmonize with their values and preferences, instead of subtly coercing them into decisions they might later regret.

Fairness and Equity in Algorithmic Decisions

Another critical ethical dilemma in the use of AIoT technologies is ensuring fairness and equity in algorithmic decision-making. As AI algorithms increasingly influence consumer interactions, from product recommendations to pricing and beyond, there is a risk that these systems may inadvertently perpetuate or even exacerbate existing biases, leading to unfair or discriminatory outcomes (Veale & Zuiderveen Borgesius, 2021).

Algorithmic bias occurs when AI systems reflect or amplify biases present in the data they are trained on. This can result in unequal treatment of different consumer groups, often along lines of race, gender, socioeconomic status, or other protected characteristics. In retail, this might manifest in biased product recommendations, differential pricing, or targeted advertising that excludes or unfairly targets certain groups.

For example, if an AIoT system is trained on data that reflects historical purchasing patterns, it might reinforce stereotypes by disproportionately recommending certain products to specific demographic groups. Similarly, dynamic pricing algorithms could result in consumers from lower-income areas being offered higher prices, based on assumptions about their purchasing power or perceived risk factors (Mittelstadt et al.,2016).

These biases are often unintentional, arising from the data or the design of the algorithms. However, the impact on consumers can be significant, leading to a loss of trust, legal challenges, and damage to the brand's reputation.

To address these challenges, retailers must take proactive steps to ensure that their AIoT systems are fair and equitable. This involves several key practices:

1. Bias Detection and Mitigation: Retailers should implement processes for detecting and mitigating bias in their AI systems (Veale & Zuiderveen Borgesius, 2021). This can include regular audits of algorithms to identify and correct any biases that may appear, as well as using diverse and representative data sets during the training phase to reduce the risk of biased outcomes.
2. Transparency and Explainability: It is useful that AI-driven decisions are transparent and explainable (Du & Xie, 2021). Consumers should be able to understand why a particular decision was made, whether it's a product recommendation, a price point, or an ad placement. Providing clear explanations can help build trust and allow consumers to challenge or question decisions that they perceive as unfair.
3. Inclusive Design: AIoT systems should be designed with inclusivity in mind, ensuring that they cater to the needs of a diverse consumer base (Kaplan, 2020). This includes considering how different groups might be affected by the tech-

nology and actively seeking to design systems that do not disadvantage any particular demographic.

4. Ethical AI Guidelines: Retailers should establish ethical guidelines for the use of AIoT, focusing on fairness, accountability, and transparency (Veale & Zuiderveen Borgesius, 2021). These guidelines should be embedded into the development and deployment processes, ensuring that ethical considerations are prioritized at every stage.

In an increasingly socially conscious market, demonstrating a commitment to fairness and equity can be a competitive advantage (Huang et al., 2024). Consumers are more likely to support brands that match their values, and ethical AI practices can differentiate a brand in a crowded marketplace (Du & Xie, 2021).

Moreover, regulators are paying closer attention to the ethical implications of AI, and ensuring fairness in algorithmic decision-making can help retailers avoid legal risks and adjust to emerging standards (Gerlick & Liozu, 2020). By taking a proactive approach to fairness and equity, retailers can protect their consumers and also position themselves as leaders in responsible AI use.

The ethical dilemmas surrounding the influence of AIoT on consumer purchase decisions are complex and multifaceted. The balance between personalization and manipulation, and the need for fairness and equity in algorithmic decisions, are central to the responsible use of these technologies. Retailers must navigate these challenges with care, adopting ethical practices that prioritize consumer trust and well-being while harnessing AIoT's potential to deliver innovative and personalized experiences.

By addressing these ethical dilemmas head-on, retailers can build stronger, more sustainable relationships with their customers, ensuring that AIoT technologies are used to increase the consumer experience. In a world where consumers are increasingly aware of and sensitive to the ethical implications of technology, those who lead with integrity and transparency will be best positioned to succeed.

CASE STUDY: IMPLEMENTATION OF AIoT IN A RETAIL COMPANY

The implementation of AIoT in the retail sector represents a significant shift in how companies operate and engage with consumers. By merging AI capabilities with IoT devices, retailers can achieve new levels of efficiency, personalization, and consumer insight. This case study analyses the successful integration of AIoT in a prominent retail company, examining both the context in which the implementation occurred and the specific ways in which AIoT technologies have been integrated into the company's operations and marketing strategies.

Description of the Context and Selected Company

The retail company selected for this case study is "TechStyle Fashion Group" (https://www.techstylefashiongroup.com), a multinational fashion retailer known for its innovative approach to combining technology with fashion retail. TechStyle operates both online and through a network of brick-and-mortar stores across several continents. The company is recognized for its strong accent on delivering personalized shopping experiences and staying ahead of technological trends to meet the evolving needs of its customer base.

TechStyle operates in a highly competitive retail environment where consumer expectations for personalized shopping experiences are at an all-time high. The rise of e-commerce, coupled with the increasing popularity of smart devices, has driven the company to study advanced technologies that can provide a competitive edge. The company's leadership recognized that integrating AIoT into its operations could increase customer experience and streamline backend processes, improve inventory management, and boost overall operational efficiency.

In the context of this digital transformation, TechStyle faced several challenges, including the need to differentiate itself in a crowded market, the demand for real-time data processing to support personalized marketing, and the imperative to maintain high levels of customer satisfaction and loyalty. These challenges created the perfect opportunity for TechStyle to take advantage of AIoT technologies to address these issues while simultaneously positioning itself as a leader in tech-driven retail.

TechStyle's vision for AIoT integration was driven by the desire to create a truly connected retail environment where data flows between online and offline touchpoints, providing a unified and personalized experience for every customer. The company aimed to use AIoT to improve its understanding of consumer behavior, optimize its supply chain, and deliver personalized marketing campaigns that resonate with individual shoppers.

To achieve this vision, TechStyle invested in state-of-the-art AIoT infrastructure, including IoT-enabled smart shelves, AI-powered customer analytics platforms, and connected devices that monitor and manage inventory in real-time. The company also committed to ensuring that its AIoT implementation would be ethically sound, with a strong focus on data privacy, transparency, and consumer trust.

Analysis of the Integration of AIoT in Operations and Marketing

The integration of AIoT into TechStyle's operations and marketing has had a profound impact on the company's ability to meet its strategic goals. This section provides an in-depth analysis of how AIoT has been deployed across various facets of the company's operations and marketing efforts.

Operations: Enhancing Efficiency and Responsiveness

One of the most significant areas where AIoT has transformed TechStyle's operations is in inventory management. The company implemented IoT-enabled smart shelves across its physical stores and warehouses, which are equipped with sensors that monitor stock levels in real-time. These smart shelves automatically alert the central inventory system when stock levels are low, triggering automatic reordering from suppliers or reallocation of inventory from other locations.

This real-time inventory tracking has enabled TechStyle to significantly reduce stockouts and overstock situations, leading to better inventory turnover and reduced storage costs. Additionally, the integration of AI with IoT has allowed the company to predict demand more accurately by analyzing historical sales data, current trends, and external factors such as weather patterns or local events. This predictive capability ensures that the right products are available at the right time, increasing customer satisfaction and driving sales.

Moreover, TechStyle has harnessed AIoT to optimize its supply chain logistics. IoT devices installed in delivery trucks and distribution centers monitor the condition and location of goods in transit, providing real-time updates to both the company and its customers. This visibility has improved the accuracy of delivery times, reduced the risk of product damage, and augmented overall supply chain efficiency.

Marketing: Personalization at Acale

On the marketing front, AIoT has empowered TechStyle to deliver highly personalized and context-aware marketing campaigns. By integrating AI-powered analytics with data from IoT devices, the company has been able to gain a deeper understanding of its customers' preferences, behaviors, and shopping habits.

For instance, TechStyle's mobile app, which is connected to IoT devices in-store, tracks customer movements and interactions with products. This data is then analyzed by AI algorithms to generate personalized product recommendations, targeted promotions, and customized content that is delivered directly to the customer's smartphone or displayed on in-store digital screens. The app also uses location-based data to offer promotions that are relevant to the customer's current shopping context, such as special discounts when they enter a specific store section or personalized offers based on their browsing history.

Additionally, AIoT has enabled TechStyle to implement dynamic pricing strategies that adjust prices in real-time based on demand, inventory levels, and customer segmentation. By analyzing data from IoT sensors and customer interactions, AI algorithms determine the optimal price for each product, maximizing profitability while ensuring that prices remain competitive and attractive to consumers.

TechStyle's marketing team has also used AIoT to improve customer engagement through personalized communication. The company's AI-driven CRM system integrates data from both online and offline touchpoints, enabling communication with customers across multiple channels. Whether through personalized emails, targeted social media ads, or push notifications, TechStyle ensures that its messaging is relevant, timely, and in line with each customer's unique preferences.

Ethical Considerations and Consumer Trust

Throughout its AIoT implementation, TechStyle has remained committed to maintaining high ethical standards, particularly regarding data privacy and consumer trust. The company has implemented stringent data protection measures, including encryption and anonymization of customer data, and has adopted a transparent approach to data usage. Customers are provided with clear information about how their data is collected and used, and they have full control over their data preferences through an intuitive privacy dashboard.

TechStyle's efforts to balance innovation with ethical responsibility have paid off, with the company reporting high levels of customer satisfaction and trust. By prioritizing transparency and consumer rights, TechStyle has managed to build a loyal customer base that values both the convenience of AIoT-driven services and the company's commitment to ethical practices.

The integration of AIoT into TechStyle's operations and marketing strategies has transformed the company's ability to deliver personalized, efficient, and responsive retail experiences. Through the use of smart shelves, predictive analytics, and personalized marketing campaigns, TechStyle has raised its operational efficiency, improved inventory management, and deepened customer engagement.

The company's success with AIoT serves as a model for other retailers looking to harness the power of these technologies while maintaining a strong commitment to ethical standards and consumer trust. By continuing to innovate and adapt its AIoT strategies, TechStyle is well-positioned to remain at the forefront of the retail industry, delivering value to both its customers and stakeholders in the years to come.

Evaluation of Legal and Ethical Compliance

As the retail industry increasingly takes advantage from AIoT technologies, ensuring that these implementations adhere to legal and ethical standards is instrumental. In the case of TechStyle, the company's commitment to compliance has been a foundational aspect of its AIoT strategy, guiding the development and deployment of its systems. This section evaluates how TechStyle has navigated the complex landscape of legal and ethical compliance, examining both the challenges it faced and the measures it implemented to meet regulatory requirements and uphold ethical standards.

Legal Compliance

TechStyle's AIoT initiatives operate within a global regulatory environment, where data privacy laws like the GDPR in Europe and the CCPA in California set stringent requirements for the collection, processing, and use of personal data. To ensure compliance with these regulations, TechStyle developed a complete legal compliance framework that is integrated into every stage of its AIoT operations.

One of the key elements of this framework is the company's approach to data minimization and purpose limitation. TechStyle has implemented strict data collection protocols that ensure only the data necessary for providing personalized services is collected. Additionally, the company adheres to the principle of purpose limitation, ensuring that data is used exclusively for the purposes for which it was collected, and any secondary use requires explicit consumer consent.

TechStyle also established robust mechanisms for obtaining and managing consumer consent, in line with GDPR and CCPA requirements. The company's consent management system is designed to be user-friendly, allowing consumers to easily understand what data is being collected and how it will be used. TechStyle provides clear options for consumers to opt in or out of specific data processing activities, ensuring that consent is informed and freely given.

Moreover, TechStyle has invested in advanced data security measures to protect consumer information from breaches and unauthorized access. These measures include encryption, multi-factor authentication, and regular security audits. The company also has a dedicated Data Protection Officer (DPO) who oversees compliance with data protection laws and serves as the point of contact for regulatory authorities.

Ethical Compliance

Beyond legal requirements, TechStyle has made ethical considerations a central part of its AIoT strategy. The company has established an internal ethics committee tasked with reviewing all AIoT initiatives to ensure they match the company's ethical principles, particularly in areas such as transparency, fairness, and consumer autonomy.

TechStyle has adopted a policy of algorithmic transparency, where the decision-making processes of its AI systems are made understandable to consumers. This includes providing explanations of how algorithms generate product recommendations, set prices, or personalize offers. By making these processes transparent, TechStyle empowers consumers to make informed decisions and promotes trust in the company's AIoT technologies.

Fairness and non-discrimination are also key ethical concerns addressed by TechStyle. The company conducts regular audits of its AI algorithms to identify and mitigate any biases that may result in unfair treatment of certain consumer groups. These audits are complemented by the use of diverse data sets during the training of AI models, ensuring that the systems are as inclusive and unbiased as possible.

To further enhance ethical compliance, TechStyle has implemented a system of ethical AI certification, seeking third-party validation of its AIoT practices. This certification process involves rigorous assessments of the company's data practices, algorithmic fairness, and consumer privacy protections. By obtaining ethical AI certification, TechStyle demonstrates its commitment to responsible innovation and sets a standard for ethical AIoT use in the retail industry.

Lessons Learned and Best Practices

TechStyle's journey with AIoT provides valuable insights into the successful implementation of these technologies in the retail sector. The company's experience highlights several key lessons and best practices that can serve as a guide for other retailers looking to integrate AIoT into their operations and marketing strategies.

Prioritize Transparency, Consumer Trust and Ethical AI Practices

One of the most important lessons from TechStyle's AIoT implementation is the critical role of transparency in building consumer trust. Consumers are increasingly concerned about how their data is being used, and companies that prioritize transparency are more likely to earn and retain their trust. TechStyle's commitment to providing clear, accessible information about its data practices and AI algorithms has been a key factor in its success.

Ethical considerations should be at the forefront of any AIoT initiative. TechStyle's focus on fairness, non-discrimination, and algorithmic transparency has helped the company avoid potential pitfalls and positioned it as a leader in ethical AI use. Retailers should establish internal ethics committees, conduct regular audits of AI systems, and seek third-party certifications to ensure their AIoT practices are put in line with ethical standards.

Harness Data for Personalization and Embrace Continuous Improvement

TechStyle's success with personalized marketing demonstrates the power of data-driven strategies in improving customer engagement. However, it is essential to balance personalization with respect for consumer autonomy. TechStyle has achieved this balance by giving consumers control over their data and ensuring that personalization is done transparently and ethically. Retailers should adopt similar practices, offering consumers clear choices and respecting their preferences.

The retail landscape is constantly evolving, and successful AIoT implementations require a commitment to continuous improvement. TechStyle's agile approach to marketing, where campaigns are continuously optimized based on real-time data, has allowed the company to stay ahead of the competition. Retailers should cover a mindset of continuous learning and adaptability, regularly reviewing and refining their AIoT strategies to ensure they remain effective and relevant.

PROPOSAL FOR AN ETHICAL AND NORMATIVE FRAMEWORK

The rapid integration of AIoT into the retail sector has brought forth transformative possibilities, from improved customer experiences to optimized supply chains. However, these advancements also introduce complex ethical and normative challenges that must be addressed to ensure that technology serves the interests of all stakeholders, particularly consumers. An ethical and normative framework is essential to guide the responsible deployment of AIoT in retail, balancing innovation with the protection of individual rights and societal values.

Ethical Foundations for the Integration of AIoT in Retail

The ethical integration of AIoT in retail requires a solid foundation that prioritizes the welfare of consumers and the broader community while encouraging innovation and economic growth. At the core of this foundation are the principles of transparency, responsibility, and respect for consumer rights. These principles should be embedded in the design, development, and deployment of AIoT technologies to create a retail environment that is both technologically advanced and ethically sound.

Transparency and Responsibility

Transparency and responsibility are critical to building trust between retailers and consumers. In the context of AIoT, transparency involves providing clear and accessible information about how data is collected, processed, and used (Kaplan, 2020). This is a legal requirement under regulations such as the GDPR and CCPA and an ethical imperative that ensures consumers are fully informed about the technologies that impact their lives.

Transparency should extend to all aspects of AIoT, including the functioning of algorithms, the criteria used for personalization, and the potential risks associated with data collection and usage (Veale & Zuiderveen Borgesius, 2021). Retailers should adopt a policy of "explainable AI," where the decisions made by AI systems are understandable and interpretable by consumers. This approach encourages trust and allows consumers to make informed choices about their interactions with AIoT systems.

Responsibility, on the other hand, refers to the obligation of retailers to act in the best interests of consumers and society. This involves taking proactive steps to ensure that AIoT systems do not cause harm, whether through data breaches, biased decision-making, or manipulation of consumer behavior. Retailers must be accountable for the outcomes of their AIoT systems, implementing robust governance structures that oversee the ethical use of these technologies.

One way to institutionalize responsibility is by establishing internal ethics committees or appointing data ethics officers who are tasked with evaluating the ethical implications of AIoT initiatives. These bodies should have the authority to review and approve AIoT projects, ensuring that they match the company's ethical standards and societal values.

Additionally, responsibility includes a commitment to continuous monitoring and improvement of AIoT systems. Retailers should regularly audit their AIoT technologies to identify and mitigate any potential ethical issues, such as algorithmic bias or unintended consequences (Belk, 2020). By adopting a proactive and transparent approach, retailers can demonstrate their commitment to ethical AIoT practices, building consumer trust and loyalty in the process.

Protection and Respect for Consumer Rights

Central to the ethical integration of AIoT in retail is the protection and respect of consumer rights (Huang et al., 2024). As AIoT systems increasingly collect and analyze personal data, it is imperative that retailers uphold the rights of consumers to privacy, autonomy, and control over their personal information (Zhao, 2023).

The right to privacy is a fundamental consumer right that must be rigorously protected in the AIoT era. Retailers should ensure that data collection practices are minimized and that only the necessary information is gathered to provide services. Moreover, consumers should have the ability to opt in or out of data collection and be fully informed about what data is being collected and how it will be used.

Respecting consumer autonomy involves empowering individuals to make informed decisions about their interactions with AIoT systems. This includes providing clear and accessible options for consumers to manage their data, such as privacy settings and consent management tools. Retailers should also respect the right of consumers to withdraw consent at any time and ensure that their data is promptly deleted or anonymized in accordance with their wishes (Wachter & Mittelstadt, 2018).

Another aspect of protecting consumer rights is ensuring the fairness and equity of AI-driven decisions (Calderaro & Blumfelde, 2022). Retailers must take active steps to prevent discrimination and bias in their AIoT systems, particularly in areas such as pricing, product recommendations, and targeted advertising (Gerlick & Liozu, 2020). This can be achieved through regular audits of AI algorithms, the use of diverse data sets, and the implementation of fairness checks during the development phase of AI models.

Moreover, retailers should commit to the principle of data sovereignty, where consumers retain full ownership and control over their personal information. This includes the right to access, correct, and delete their data, as well as the right to data portability, which allows consumers to transfer their data to another service provider if they choose. By respecting these rights, retailers can create a sense of trust and security among consumers, encouraging them to engage more openly with AIoT technologies.

Development of Internal Policies for Ethical Data Management

As the adoption of AIoT technologies continues to grow in the retail sector, it becomes increasingly important for companies to establish robust internal policies that govern the ethical management of data (Du & Xie, 2021). These policies are essential for ensuring that data collection, processing, and usage practices match ethical standards and legal requirements, while also promoting consumer trust. This section outlines the development of such policies, focusing on the establishment of responsible information use norms and the implementation of control and audit mechanisms.

Norms for Responsible Information Use, Data Minimization and Purpose Limitation

The foundation of any ethical data management policy lies in the establishment of clear norms for the responsible use of information (Kaplan, 2020). These norms should guide all data-related activities within the organization, from the initial collection of data through to its processing, storage, and eventual disposal. By setting these standards, retailers can ensure that their use of data is compliant with legal requirements and in line with broader ethical considerations (Veale & Zuiderveen Borgesius, 2021; López Jiménez et al., 2023).

One of the key principles of responsible information use is data minimization (Gerlick & Liozu, 2020). This principle dictates that only the data necessary for a specific purpose should be collected and processed, reducing the risk of data misuse and minimizing the impact on consumer privacy. Retailers should develop guidelines that specify the types of data that can be collected, the purposes for which it can be used, and the conditions under which it must be deleted or anonymized.

In addition to data minimization, purpose limitation is another critical norm. This principle ensures that data is used solely for the purposes for which it was collected and that any secondary use of the data requires explicit consumer consent. Retailers must establish clear procedures for obtaining consent and ensure that consumers are fully informed about how their data will be used (Huang et al., 2024). This includes providing transparency about any third-party data sharing arrangements and ensuring that these arrangements comply with the organization's ethical standards.

Implementation of Control, Audit Mechanisms and Internal Controls for Data Management

To ensure that the established norms for responsible information use are consistently followed, retailers must implement effective control and audit mechanisms. These mechanisms provide the necessary oversight to identify and mitigate risks, ensure compliance with internal policies and external regulations, and continuously improve data management practices (Wachter & Mittelstadt, 2018).

Internal controls are essential for maintaining the integrity and security of data within the organization. These controls should encompass all aspects of data management, including data access, processing, storage, and transfer. Retailers should establish a framework of controls that includes role-based access controls, encryption, data masking, and secure data storage solutions (Guha et al., 2021).

Role-based access controls ensure that only authorized personnel have access to sensitive data, reducing the risk of data breaches and unauthorized use (Fatima et al., 2020). Encryption and data masking further protect data by rendering it unreadable to anyone without the proper decryption keys or access rights (Liu & Lin, 2020). Secure data storage solutions, such as encrypted databases and cloud storage with robust security measures, are critical for protecting data from external threats (Kaplan, 2020).

In addition to these technical controls, retailers should establish clear policies for data retention and disposal. These policies should ensure that data is only retained for as long as necessary to fulfill its intended purpose and that it is securely deleted or anonymized when no longer needed (Du & Xie, 2021).

CONCLUSION

The integration of AIoT into the retail sector marks a pivotal moment in the evolution of consumer experience and business operations. As this technology continues to reshape the landscape, it brings both unprecedented opportunities and significant challenges that require careful navigation by retailers. Through this exploration, several key conclusions arise that highlight the transformative potential of AIoT, as well as the responsibilities that come with its adoption.

AIoT represents a convergence of AI and IoT technologies that allows retailers to deliver hyper-personalized, efficient, and responsive services to consumers. This integration has the potential to revolutionize every aspect of the retail experience—from dynamic pricing and personalized marketing to real-time inventory management and enhanced customer service. The ability to gather and analyze data at an unprecedented scale enables retailers to anticipate consumer needs, streamline operations, and ultimately drive greater customer satisfaction and business performance.

However, the true transformative power of AIoT lies not just in its technical capabilities but in how it can be used to create meaningful, value-driven relationships between brands and consumers. Retailers that benefit from AIoT to genuinely improve the consumer experience, while respecting privacy and ethical considerations, will be the ones that redefine the standards of retail in the digital age.

As AIoT technologies become more pervasive, the ethical implications of their use cannot be overlooked. The potential for misuse—whether through data privacy violations, algorithmic bias, or consumer manipulation—poses significant risks to individual consumers and to the broader reputation of the retail industry.

Retailers must prioritize ethical considerations in their AIoT strategies, embedding principles such as transparency, fairness, and accountability into the core of their operations. This involves complying with existing regulations and proactively addressing ethical dilemmas and setting higher standards for responsible AIoT use. By doing so, retailers can build and maintain the trust that is essential for long-term success in an increasingly privacy-conscious market.

The regulatory environment surrounding AIoT is rapidly changing, driven by growing concerns over data privacy, security, and the ethical use of technology. Retailers must stay ahead of these developments, adapting their strategies to ensure compliance with a complex and often fragmented set of laws and regulations.

While navigating this regulatory landscape presents challenges, it also offers opportunities for retailers to differentiate themselves through ethical leadership and best practices. Those that embrace regulatory compliance as a foundation for innovation and not a constraint, will be better positioned to thrive in a future where trust and transparency are very important.

The retail sector is undergoing a period of rapid transformation, driven by the adoption of AIoT and other advanced technologies. In this adaptive environment, continuous innovation and adaptability are key to staying competitive. Retailers must be willing to experiment with new AIoT applications, learn from both successes and failures, and quickly adapt to changing consumer expectations and market conditions.

This requires a culture of agility within retail organizations, where teams are empowered to survey new ideas, pivot when necessary, and encompass a mindset of continuous improvement. By encouraging such a culture, retailers can remain at the forefront of technological innovation, delivering cutting-edge experiences that resonate with consumers and set new industry standards.

Ultimately, the success of AIoT in retail hinges on the trust that consumers place in the technologies and the companies that deploy them. Building and maintaining this trust requires more than just compliance with laws and regulations, it demands a genuine commitment to respecting consumer rights safeguarding data privacy.

Retailers must engage with consumers transparently, providing them with clear information about how their data is used and giving them control over their interactions with AIoT systems. By putting consumers at the heart of their AIoT strategies, retailers can develop deep, lasting relationships that drive loyalty, advocacy, and long-term business success.

The journey of integrating AIoT into the retail sector is just beginning, and its full potential has yet to be realized. As retailers continue to expand the possibilities of AIoT, they will shape the future of retail and the broader relationship between technology and society. By embracing innovation with a strong ethical foundation, adapting to regulatory changes, and prioritizing consumer trust, retailers can harness the power of AIoT to create a retail landscape that is both technologically advanced and socially responsible.

AIoT offers a profound opportunity to transform the retail industry, but its successful implementation requires a careful balance of innovation, ethics, and consumer-centricity. As retailers navigate this new frontier, those who lead with integrity, transparency, and commitment to ethical practices will be best positioned to succeed in the evolving world of retail.

REFERENCES

Abungu, C. Y. (2021). Democratic Culture and the Development of Artificial Intelligence in the USA and China. *The Chinese Journal of Comparative Law*, *9*(1), 81–108. DOI: 10.1093/cjcl/cxaa032

Anica-Popa, I. F., Anica-Popa, L. E., Rădulescu, C., & Vrîncianu, M. (2021). The Integration of Artificial Intelligence in Retail: Benefits, Challenges and a Dedicated Conceptual Framework. *Amfiteatru Economic, 23*(56), 120-136. doi:: .DOI: 10.24818/EA/2021/56/120

Belk, R. (2020). Ethical issues in service robotics and artificial intelligence. *Service Industries Journal*, *41*(13–14), 860–876. DOI: 10.1080/02642069.2020.1727892

Calderaro, A., & Blumfelde, S. (2022). Artificial intelligence and EU security: The false promise of digital sovereignty. *European Security*, *31*(3), 415–434. DOI: 10.1080/09662839.2022.2101885

Dittmar, E. C., López Jiménez, D., & Vargas Portillo, J. P. (2025). COVID-19 and the new situation in higher education. *International Journal of Knowledge and Learning*, *18*(2), 204–214. DOI: 10.1504/IJKL.2025.145124

Du, S., & Xie, C. (2021). Paradoxes of artificial intelligence in consumer markets: Ethical challenges and opportunities. *Journal of Business Research*, *129*, 961–974. DOI: 10.1016/j.jbusres.2020.08.024

Evans, D. (2011). The internet of things. How the Next Evolution of the Internet is Changing Everything. *Whitepaper* [IBSG]. *Cisco Internet Business Solutions Group*, *1*, 1–12.

Fatima, S., Desouza, K. C., & Dawson, G. S. (2020). National strategic artificial intelligence plans: A multi-dimensional analysis. *Economic Analysis and Policy*, *67*, 178–194. DOI: 10.1016/j.eap.2020.07.008

Gerlick, J. A., & Liozu, S. M. (2020). Ethical and legal considerations of artificial intelligence and algorithmic decision-making in personalized pricing. *Journal of Revenue and Pricing Management*, *19*(2), 85–98. DOI: 10.1057/s41272-019-00225-2

Ghosh, A., Chakraborty, D., & Law, A. (2018). Artificial intelligence in Internet of things. *CAAI Transactions on Intelligence Technology*, *3*(4), 208–218. DOI: 10.1049/trit.2018.1008

Guha, A., Grewal, D., Kopalle, P. K., Haenlein, M., Schneider, M. J., Jung, H., Moustafa, R., Hegde, D. R., & Hawkins, G. (2021). How artificial intelligence will affect the future of retailing. *Journal of Retailing*, *97*(1), 28–41. DOI: 10.1016/j.jretai.2021.01.005

Har, L. L., Rashid, U. K., Te Chuan, L., Sen, S. C., & Xia, L. Y. (2022). Revolution of retail industry: From perspective of retail 1.0 to 4.0. *Procedia Computer Science*, *200*, 1615–1625. DOI: 10.1016/j.procs.2022.01.362

Hermann, E. (2022). Leveraging Artificial Intelligence in Marketing for Social Good—An Ethical Perspective. *Journal of Business Ethics*, *179*(1), 43–61. DOI: 10.1007/s10551-021-04843-y PMID: 34054170

Huang, K., Joshi, A., Dun, S., & Hamilton, N. (2024). AI Regulations. In Huang, K., Wang, Y., Goertzel, B., Li, Y., Wright, S., & Ponnapalli, J. (Eds.), *Generative AI Security. Future of Business and Finance* (pp. 61–98). Springer., DOI: 10.1007/978-3-031-54252-7_3

Kaplan, A. (2020). Retailing and the Ethical Challenges and Dilemmas Behind Artificial Intelligence. In Pantano, E. (Ed.), *Retail Futures* (pp. 181–191). Emerald Publishing Limited., DOI: 10.1108/978-1-83867-663-620201020

Lauterbach, A. (2019). Artificial intelligence and policy: Quo vadis? *Digital Policy. Regulation & Governance*, *21*(3), 238–263. DOI: 10.1108/DPRG-09-2018-0054

Liu, H. W., & Lin, C. F. (2020). Artificial Intelligence and Global Trade Governance: A Pluralist Agenda. *Harvard International Law Journal*, *61*(2). https://ssrn.com/abstract=3675505

Liu, N., Shapira, P., Yue, X., & Guan, J. (2021). Mapping technological innovation dynamics in artificial intelligence domains: Evidence from a global patent analysis. *PLoS One*, *16*(12), e0262050. DOI: 10.1371/journal.pone.0262050 PMID: 34972173

López Jiménez, D., Dittmar, E. C., & Vargas Portillo, J. P. (2022). Nuevas estrategias publicitarias con influencers: Un examen multidisciplinar. *Revista de Ciencias Sociales*, *28*(4), 63–78. DOI: 10.31876/rcs.v28i4.39117

López Jiménez, D., Dittmar, E. C., & Vargas Portillo, J. P. (2023). The Self-Regulating Jury in the Field of Interactive Advertising. *Revista de Direito. Estado e Telecomunicacoes*, *15*(1), 1–30. DOI: 10.26512/lstr.v15i1.42146

Martin, K. D., & Murphy, P. E. (2017). The role of data privacy in marketing. *Journal of the Academy of Marketing Science*, *45*(2), 135–155. DOI: 10.1007/s11747-016-0495-4

Mittelstadt, B. D., Allo, P., Taddeo, M., Wachter, S., & Floridi, L. (2016). The ethics of algorithms: Mapping the debate. *Big Data & Society*, *3*(2), 2053951716679679. Advance online publication. DOI: 10.1177/2053951716679679

Shekhawat, S. (2023). Smart retail: How AI and IoT are revolutionising the retail industry. *Journal of AI. Robotics & Workplace Automation*, *2*(2), 145–152. DOI: 10.69554/TCLG1264

Sposato, M. (2024). Leadership training and development in the age of artificial intelligence. *Development and Learning in Organizations*, *38*(4), 4–7. DOI: 10.1108/DLO-12-2023-0256

Sposato, M., Dittmar, E. C., & Vargas Portillo, J. P. (2025). New technologies in HR: Bridging efficiency and ethical considerations. *The International Journal of Organizational Analysis*. Advance online publication. DOI: 10.1108/IJOA-09-2024-4814

Taddeo, M., & Floridi, L. (2018). How AI can be a force for good. *Science*, *361*(6404), 751–752. DOI: 10.1126/science.aat5991 PMID: 30139858

Veale, M., & Zuiderveen Borgesius, F. (2021). - Demystifying the Draft EU Artificial Intelligence Act — Analysing the good, the bad, and the unclear elements of the proposed approach. *Computer Law Review International*, *22*(4), 97–112. DOI: 10.9785/cri-2021-220402

Wachter, S., & Mittelstadt, B. (2018). A Right to Reasonable Inferences: Re-Thinking Data Protection Law in the Age of Big Data and AI. *Columbia Business Law Review*, *2019*(2). Retrieved from: https://ssrn.com/abstract=3248829

Walters, R., & Novak, M. (2021). Artificial Intelligence and Law. In *Cyber Security, Artificial Intelligence, Data Protection & the Law*. Springer., DOI: 10.1007/978-981-16-1665-5_3

Wang, J., Yu, X., Li, J., & Jin, X. (2018). Artificial Intelligence and International Norms. In Jin, D. (Ed.), *Reconstructing Our Orders*. Springer., DOI: 10.1007/978-981-13-2209-9_7

Zhao, L. (2023). Artificial intelligence and law: emerging divergent national regulatory approaches in a changing landscape of fast-evolving AI technologies (369-399). In Collins, D., & Geist, M. (Eds.), *Research Handbook on Digital Trade* (pp. 369–399)., DOI: 10.4337/9781800884953.00033

Compilation of References

10. xDS Team (2023). *The Intelligent Warehouse: AI's Impact on Modern Inventory Strategies*. 13th December. 10xDS. Retrieved 25th November 2024 from https://10xds.com/blog/ai-impact-on-modern-inventory-strategies/

Aaron, S. (2024). *Blockchain in retail: Innovative use, cases, benefits and challenges*. Retrieved 3rd February 2025 from https://www.bitdegree.org/crypto/tutorials/blockchain-in-retail

Abungu, C. Y. (2021). Democratic Culture and the Development of Artificial Intelligence in the USA and China. *The Chinese Journal of Comparative Law*, *9*(1), 81–108. DOI: 10.1093/cjcl/cxaa032

Adamopoulou, E., & Moussiades, L. (2020). An overview of chatbot technology. In *IFIP international conference on artificial intelligence applications and innovations* (pp. 373–383). Springer.

Adi, E., Anwar, A., Baig, Z., & Zeadally, S. (2020). Machine learning and data analytics for the IoT. *Neural Computing & Applications*, *32*(20), 16205–16233. DOI: 10.1007/s00521-020-04874-y

Adler-Milstein, J., Aggarwal, N., Ahmed, M., Castner, J., Evans, B. J., Gonzalez, A. A., James, C. A., Lin, S., Mandl, K. D., Matheny, M. E., Sendak, M. P., Shachar, C., & Williams, A. (2022). Meeting the moment: Addressing barriers and facilitating clinical adoption of artificial intelligence in medical diagnosis. *NAM Perspectives*, *22*(9), 2022. DOI: 10.31478/202209c PMID: 36713769

Adli, H. K., Remli, M. A., Wan Salihin Wong, K. N. S., Ismail, N. A., González-Briones, A., Corchado, J. M., & Mohamad, M. S. (2023). Recent Advancements and Challenges of AIoT Application in Smart Agriculture: A Review. *Sensors (Basel)*, *23*(7), 3752. DOI: 10.3390/s23073752 PMID: 37050812

Adomavicius, G., & Kwon, Y. (2012). Multi-criteria recommender systems. *Computer Science Review*, *6*(4), 108–129.

Adomavicius, G., & Tuzhilin, A. (2005). Toward the next generation of recommender systems: A survey of the state-of-the-art and possible extensions. *IEEE Transactions on Knowledge and Data Engineering*, *17*(6), 734–749. DOI: 10.1109/TKDE.2005.99

Agarwal, P. (2014). Benefits and Issues Surrounding Data Mining and its Application in the Retail Industry. *International Journal of Scientific and Research Publications, 4 (7),* ISSN 2250-3153.

Agarwal, Y., Jain, M., Sinha, S., & Dhir, S. (2020). Delivering high-tech, AI-based health care at Apollo Hospitals. *Global Business and Organizational Excellence*, *39*(2), 20–30. DOI: 10.1002/joe.21981

Agrawal, R., & Srikant, R. (1994). Fast algorithms for mining association rules. *Proceedings of the 20th International Conference on Very Large Data Bases (VLDB '94)*, 487-499.

Ahmad, M., Naeem, M. K. H., Mobo, F. D., Tahir, M. W., & Akram, M. (2024). Navigating the Journey: How Chatbots Are Transforming Tourism and Hospitality. In *Design and Development of Emerging Chatbot Technology* (pp. 236-255). IGI Global.

Ahmed, A., Saleem, K., Khalid, O., & Rashid, U. (2021). On deep neural network for trust aware cross domain recommendations in E-commerce. *Expert Systems with Applications*, *174*, 114757. DOI: 10.1016/j.eswa.2021.114757

Ahmed, Z. (2024). Empowering Retailers With IoT: Opportunities, Benefits, And Challenges For Improved Customer Experience And Operational Efficiency. *International Journal of Creative Research Thoughts*, *12*(8), 453–461.

Ajayi, S., Loureiro, S. M. C., & Langaro, D. (2023). Internet of things and consumer engagement on retail: State-of-the-art and future directions. *EuroMed Journal of Business*, *18*(3), 397–423. DOI: 10.1108/EMJB-10-2021-0164

Al Kurdi, B., Alzoubi, H., Akour, I., & Alshurideh, M. (2022). The effect of blockchain and smart inventory system on supply chain performance: Empirical evidence from retail industry. *Uncertain Supply Chain Management*, *10*(4), 1111–1116. DOI: 10.5267/j.uscm.2022.9.001

Alaba, F. A., Oluwadare, A., Sani, U., Oriyomi, A. A., Lucy, A. O., & Najeem, O. (2024). Enabling Sustainable Transportation Through IoT and AIoT Innovations. In Misra, S., Siakas, K., & Lampropoulos, G. (Eds.), *Artificial Intelligence of Things for Achieving Sustainable Development Goals. Lecture Notes on Data Engineering and Communications Technologies* (Vol. 192). Springer., DOI: 10.1007/978-3-031-53433-1_14

Alamdari, P. M., Navimipour, N. J., Hosseinzadeh, M., Safaei, A. A., & Darwesh, A. (2020). A systematic study on the recommender systems in the E-commerce. *IEEE Access : Practical Innovations, Open Solutions*, *8*, 115694–115716. DOI: 10.1109/ACCESS.2020.3002803

Albayrak, Ö., Erkayman, B., & Usanmaz, B. (2023). Applications of Artificial Intelligence in Inventory Management: A Systematic Review of the Literature. *Archives of Computational Methods in Engineering*, *30*, 2605–2625. DOI: 10.1007/s11831-022-09879-5

Alduraywish, M., Unhelkar, B., Singh, S., & Prasad, M. (2021, October). Application of Artificial Intelligence in Recommendation Systems and Chatbots for Online Stores in Fast Fashion Industry. In *International Conference on Intelligent Vision and Computing* (pp. 558-567). Cham: Springer International Publishing.

Alenizi, A. S., & Al-Karawi, K. A. (2022). Internet of Things (IoT) Adoption: Challenges and Barriers. In: Yang, XS., Sherratt, S., Dey, N., Joshi, A. (eds) *Proceedings of Seventh International Congress on Information and Communication Technology. Lecture Notes in Networks and Systems,* 464. Springer. https://doi.org/ DOI: 10.1007/978-981-19-2394-4_20

Alfian, G., Octava, M. Q. H., Hilmy, F. M., Nurhaliza, R. A., Saputra, Y. M., Putri, D. G. P., Syahrian, F., Fitriyani, N. L., Atmaji, F., Farooq, U., Nguyen, D. T., & Syafrudin, M. (2023). Customer shopping behavior analysis using RFID and machine learning models. *Information (Basel)*, *14*(10), 551. Advance online publication. DOI: 10.3390/info14100551

Ali, A. (2024). *Revolutionizing Customer Support: The Impact of AI-Powered Chatbots and Virtual Assistants* (No. 12037). EasyChair.

Almomani, A., & Al-Turjman, F. (2024). AI Based RSSI Algorithm for Localization in the IoT Era. Advances in Science [ASTI]. *Technology and Innovation*, •••, 63–69.

Alsubari, S. N., Deshmukh, S. N., Al-Adhaileh, M. H., Alsaade, F. W., & Aldhyani, T. H. (2021). Development of integrated neural network model for identification of fake reviews in E-commerce using multidomain datasets. *Applied Bionics and Biomechanics*, *2021*, 2021. DOI: 10.1155/2021/5522574 PMID: 33953796

Alsubari, S. N., Deshmukh, S. N., Alqarni, A. A., Alsharif, N., Aldhyani, T. H., Alsaade, F. W., & Khalaf, O. I. (2022). Data analytics for the identification of fake reviews using supervised learning. *Computers, Materials & Continua*, *70*(2), 3189–3204. DOI: 10.32604/cmc.2022.019625

Álvarez, A., & Ritchey, T. (2015). Applications of general morphological analysis: From engineering design to policy analysis. *Acta Morphologica Generalis*, *4*(2).

Ameen, N., Tarhini, A., Reppel, A., & Anand, A. (2021). Customer experiences in the age of artificial intelligence. *Computers in Human Behavior*, *114*, 106548. DOI: 10.1016/j.chb.2020.106548 PMID: 32905175

Amrutha, R., Dhrishya, V., Gopika, J., & Biji, K. (2020). RFID based POS system. *International Research Journal of Engineering and Technology*, *7*(5), 716–721.

Anica-Popa, I., Anica-Popa, L., Rădulescu, C., & Vrîncianu, M. (2021). The Integration of Artificial Intelligence in Retail: Benefits, Challenges and a Dedicated Conceptual Article History. *Amfiteatru Economic*, *23*(56), 120–136. DOI: 10.24818/EA/2021/56/120

Ansari, S., & Gupta, S. (2021). Customer perception of the deceptiveness of online product reviews: A speech act theory perspective. *International Journal of Information Management*, *57*, 102286. DOI: 10.1016/j.ijinfomgt.2020.102286

Arif, F. V. (2021). The Future of Work: How Ai and Blockchain Technologies will impact HR and the Job Market.

Armenta, A. (2024). AI Applications in Warehouse and Inventory Management. 16th September 2024. Control. Retrieved 25th November 2024 from https://control.com/technical-articles/ai-applications-in-warehouse-and-inventory-management/

Arockia, M. P., Sharma, A., Dekka, S., Gowda, V. D., & Singh, M. (2024). Deep Learning Approaches for Real-Time Data Analytics in IoT Sensor Networks. *Lecture Notes in Networks and Systems*, *1007*, 239–248. DOI: 10.1007/978-981-97-5146-4_21

Aslam, F. (2023). The impact of artificial intelligence on chatbot technology: A study on the current advancements and leading innovations. *European Journal of Technology*, *7*(3), 62–72. DOI: 10.47672/ejt.1561

Assert, A. I. (2025). *Transforming Retail: The Game Changing Impact of Computer Vision.* Retrieved 3rd February 2025 from https://www.assertai.com/transforming-retail-the-game-changing-impact-of-computer-vision/

Atkinson, L. (2013). Smart shoppers? Using QR codes and "green" smartphone apps to mobilize sustainable consumption. *International Journal of Consumer Studies*, *37*(4), 387–393. DOI: 10.1111/ijcs.12025

Awaisi, K. S., Ye, Q., & Sampalli, S. (2024). A Survey of Industrial AIoT: Opportunities, Challenges, and Directions. *IEEE Access : Practical Innovations, Open Solutions*, *12*, 96946–96996. DOI: 10.1109/ACCESS.2024.3426279

Aw, E. C.-X., Tan, G. W.-H., Ooi, K.-B., & Hajli, N. (2024). Tap here to power up! Mobile augmented reality for consumer empowerment. *Internet Research*, *34*(3), 960–993. DOI: 10.1108/INTR-07-2021-0477

Badotra, S., & Sundas, A. (2021). A systematic review on security of E-commerce systems. *International Journal of Applied Science and Engineering*, *18*(2), 1–19.

Balagué, C., Martin-Fuentes, E., & Gómez, M. J. (2016). Fiabilidad de las críticas hoteleras autenticadas y no autenticadas: El caso de TripAdvisor y Booking.com. *Cuadernos de Turismo*, *38*(38), 67–86. DOI: 10.6018/turismo.38.271351

Barbado, R., Araque, O., & Iglesias, C. A. (2019). A framework for fake review detection in online consumer electronics retailers. *Information Processing & Management*, *56*(4), 1234–1244. DOI: 10.1016/j.ipm.2019.03.002

Bathla, G., Singh, P., Singh, R. K., Cambria, E., & Tiwari, R. (2022). Intelligent fake reviews detection based on aspect extraction and analysis using deep learning. *Neural Computing & Applications*, *34*(22), 20213–20229. DOI: 10.1007/s00521-022-07531-8

Bawack, R. E., Wamba, S. F., Carillo, K. D. A., & Akter, S. (2022). Artificial intelligence in E-Commerce: A bibliometric study and literature review. *Electronic Markets*, *32*(1), 297–338. DOI: 10.1007/s12525-022-00537-z PMID: 35600916

Beatty, P., Reay, I., Dick, S., & Miller, J. (2011). Consumer trust in e-commerce web sites: A meta-study. *ACM Computing Surveys*, *43*(3), 1–46. DOI: 10.1145/1922649.1922651

Belk, R. (2020). Ethical issues in service robotics and artificial intelligence. *Service Industries Journal*, *41*(13–14), 860–876. DOI: 10.1080/02642069.2020.1727892

Benlahbib, A., Boumhidi, A., & Nfaoui, E. H. (2022). Mining online reviews to support customers' decision-making process in e-commerce platforms: A narrative literature review. *Journal of Organizational Computing and Electronic Commerce*, *32*(1), 69–97. DOI: 10.1080/10919392.2022.2053454

Berning, S. C. (2021). Alibaba's International Digital Marketing Practices and Strategies. In *Advanced Digital Marketing Strategies in a Data-Driven Era* (pp. 80–98). IGI Global. DOI: 10.4018/978-1-7998-8003-5.ch005

Bhardwaj, V., Anooja, A., Vermani, L. S., Sunita, , & Dhaliwal, B. K. (2024). Smart cities and the IoT: An in-depth analysis of global research trends and future directions. *Discover Internet Things*, *4*(1), 19. DOI: 10.1007/s43926-024-00076-3

Bilgeri, N. (2020). *Artificial intelligence improving CRM, sales and customer experience: An analysis of an international B2B company* (Doctoral dissertation, FH Vorarlberg (Fachhochschule Vorarlberg)).

Bird, J. J. (2021). Improving customer service chatbots with attention-based transfer learning. *arXiv preprint arXiv:2111.14621.*

Birim, Ş. Ö., Kazancoglu, I., Mangla, S. K., Kahraman, A., Kumar, S., & Kazancoglu, Y. (2022). Detecting fake reviews through topic modelling. *Journal of Business Research, 149*, 884–900. DOI: 10.1016/j.jbusres.2022.05.081

Blei, D. M., Ng, A. Y., & Jordan, M. I. (2003). Latent Dirichlet Allocation. *Journal of Machine Learning Research, 3*, 993–1022.

Boesch (2024). *The 10 Top Applications of Computer Vision in Retail 2025.* 16th December 2024. Retrieved 3rd Febrauary 2025 from https://viso.ai/applications/computer-vision-in-retail/

Borrego, Á., & Comalat Navarra, M. (2021). What users say about public libraries: An analysis of Google Maps reviews. *Online Information Review, 45*(1), 84–98. DOI: 10.1108/OIR-09-2019-0291

Boto-García, D., Mariel, P., & Baños-Pino, J. F. (2023). Intra-household bargaining for a joint vacation. *Journal of Choice Modelling, 47*, 100408. Advance online publication. DOI: 10.1016/j.jocm.2023.100408

Bourechak, A., Zedadra, O., Kouahla, M. N., Guerrieri, A., Seridi, H., & Fortino, G. (2023). At the Confluence of Artificial Intelligence and Edge Computing in IoT-Based Applications: A Review and New Perspectives. *Sensors (Basel), 23*(3), 1639. DOI: 10.3390/s23031639 PMID: 36772680

BR. S. R. (2022). Information and Communication Technology Application in the Asian Tourism Industry. In *Handbook of Technology Application in Tourism in Asia* (pp. 19-48). Singapore: Springer Nature Singapore.

Bradlow, E. T., Gangwar, M., Kopalle, P., & Voleti, S. (2017). The Role of Big Data and Predictive Analytics in Retailing. *Journal of Retailing, 93*(1), 79–95. DOI: 10.1016/j.jretai.2016.12.004

Braun, S. (2015). *The History of Retail: A Timeline.* Retrieved 31th January 2025 from https://www.lightspeedhq.com/blog/the-history-of-retail-a-timeline/

Brown, C. (2024). *Walmart and Quantum Computing: Retail's Future. Augmented QuBit.* Retrieved 3rd February from https://augmentedqubit.com/walmart-and-quantum-computing-impact-to-retail-and-consumers/

Buhalis, D., Harwood, T., Bogicevic, V., Viglia, G., Beldona, S., & Hofacker, C. (2019). Technological disruptions in services: Lessons from tourism and hospitality. *Journal of Service Management, 30*(4), 484–506. DOI: 10.1108/JOSM-12-2018-0398

Burke, R. (2007). Hybrid recommender systems: Survey and experiments. *User Modeling and User-Adapted Interaction, 12*(4), 331–370. DOI: 10.1023/A:1021240730564

Burrows, L. (2021). *The present and future of AI. Finale Doshi-Velez on how AI is shaping our lives and how we can shape AI.* October, 19. Retrieved 23th November 2024 from https://seas.harvard.edu/news/2021/10/present-and-future-ai

Buzan, T. (2009). *The mind map book: Unlock Your Creativity, Boost Your Memory, Change Your Life*. Pearson Education Limited.

Byrum, J. (2022). AI in financial portfolio management: Practical considerations and use cases. *Innovative Technology at the Interface of Finance and Operations, I*, 249–270. DOI: 10.1007/978-3-030-75729-8_9

Calderaro, A., & Blumfelde, S. (2022). Artificial intelligence and EU security: The false promise of digital sovereignty. *European Security, 31*(3), 415–434. DOI: 10.1080/09662839.2022.2101885

Candes, E. J., & Recht, B. (2009). Exact matrix completion via convex optimization. *Foundations of Computational Mathematics, 9*(6), 717–772. DOI: 10.1007/s10208-009-9045-5

Cao, L. (2021). Artificial intelligence in retail: Applications and value creation logics. *International Journal of Retail & Distribution Management, 49*(7), 958–976. DOI: 10.1108/IJRDM-09-2020-0350

Carbonell, G., Barbu, C. M., Vorgerd, L., & Brand, M. (2019). The impact of emotionality and trust cues on the perceived trustworthiness of online reviews. *Cogent Business & Management, 6*(1), 1586062. DOI: 10.1080/23311975.2019.1586062

Chang, F.-J., & Chang, L.-C. (2022). Artificial Intelligence Techniques in Hydrology and Water Resources Management. [Special Issue]. *Water (Basel).*

Chang, Y. W., & Chen, J. (2021). What motivates customers to shop in smart shops? The impacts of smart technology and technology readiness. *Journal of Retailing and Consumer Services, 58*, 102325. DOI: 10.1016/j.jretconser.2020.102325

Chan, L., Hogaboam, L., & Cao, R. (2022). Artificial Intelligence in Fashion. In *Applied Artificial Intelligence in Business: Concepts and Cases* (pp. 325–334). Springer International Publishing. DOI: 10.1007/978-3-031-05740-3_21

Chatterjee, R. (2020). Digital Marketing Transformation of D2C Brands. *International Journal of Business and Management, 15*(4), 110–121.

Chaturvedi, R., & Verma, S. (2023). Opportunities and challenges of AI-driven customer service. *Artificial Intelligence in customer service: The next frontier for personalized engagement*, 33-71.

Chawla, N., & Kumar, B. (2022). E-commerce and consumer protection in India: The emerging trend. *Journal of Business Ethics, 180*(2), 581–604. DOI: 10.1007/s10551-021-04884-3 PMID: 34257470

Chehal, D., Gupta, P., & Gulati, P. (2021). Implementation and comparison of topic modeling techniques based on user reviews in e-commerce recommendations. *Journal of Ambient Intelligence and Humanized Computing, 12*(5), 5055–5070. DOI: 10.1007/s12652-020-01956-6

Chen, J., & Bell, D. R. (2020). Predictive Analytics for Direct-to-Consumer Retail. *Journal of Marketing Analytics, 8*(3), 134–145.

Chen, J., & Chang, Y. W. (2023). How smart technology empowers consumers in smart retail stores? The perspective of technology readiness and situational factors. *Electronic Markets, 33*(1), 1. Advance online publication. DOI: 10.1007/s12525-023-00635-6 PMID: 37035262

Chen, L., & Zhang, R. (2021). Real-Time Personalization with AI: Strategies and Outcomes. *International Journal of Market Research, 43*(4), 295–310. DOI: 10.1177/14707853211001234

Chen, S., Xiong, G., Xu, J., Han, S., Wang, F.-Y., & Wang, K. (2018). The smart street lighting system based on NB-IoT. In: *2018 Chinese Automation Congress (CAC)*. IEEE, 1196–1200. DOI: 10.1109/CAC.2018.8623281

Christiano, P. F., Leike, J., Brown, T., Martic, M., Legg, S., & Amodei, D. (2017). Deep reinforcement learning from human preferences. *Proceedings of the 31st International Conference on Neural Information Processing Systems (NeurIPS 2017)*, 1-9.

Climber. (2022). Qlik a leader in the 2022 Gartner Magic Quadrant. https://www.climber.eu/qlik-a-leader-in-the-2022-gartner-magic-quadrant/

Cogniteq (2023). *How IoT is Changing Advertising: Benefits and Use-Cases*. Retrieved 25th November 2024 from https://www.cogniteq.com/blog/how-iot-changing-advertising-new-possibilities-and-top-use-cases

Cummings, A. R. (2025). *How Machine Learning Transforms Retail: Benefits & Use Cases (2025).* Retrieved 30th January 2025 from https://www.shopify.com/retail/machine-learning-in-retail

Czerepicki, A. (2019). Study on effectiveness of using column-oriented databases in the processing of measurement characteristics of an electric vehicle. *Archives of Transport*, *51*(3), 77–84. DOI: 10.5604/01.3001.0013.6164

Daqar, M. A. A., & Smoudy, A. K. (2019). The role of artificial intelligence on enhancing customer experience. *International Review of Management and Marketing*, *9*(4), 22–31. DOI: 10.32479/irmm.8166

Daskalakis, E., Remoundou, K., Peppes, N., Alexakis, T., Demestichas, K., Adamopoulou, E., & Sykas, E. (2022). Applications of fusion techniques in e-commerce environments: A literature review. *Sensors (Basel)*, *22*(11), 3998. DOI: 10.3390/s22113998 PMID: 35684619

Das, R., Ahmed, W., Sharma, K., Hardey, M., Dwivedi, Y. K., Zhang, Z., Apostolidis, C., & Filieri, R. (2024). Towards the development of an explainable e-commerce fake review index: An attribute analytics approach. *European Journal of Operational Research*, *317*(2), 382–400. DOI: 10.1016/j.ejor.2024.03.008

Davenport, T. H. (2018). *The AI advantage: How to put the artificial intelligence revolution to work*. mit Press.

Davenport, T. H., & Miller, S. M. (2022). *Working with AI: real stories of human-machine collaboration*. MIT Press. DOI: 10.7551/mitpress/14453.001.0001

De Keyser, A., & Van Vaerenbergh, Y. (2024). Beyond the snafu: Research directions in customer experience-led business transformation. *AMS Review*, *14*(1-2), 1–14. DOI: 10.1007/s13162-024-00279-5

Dematis, I., Karapistoli, E., & Vakali, A. (2018). Fake review detection via exploitation of spam indicators and reviewer behavior characteristics. In SOFSEM 2018: Theory and Practice of Computer Science: 44th International Conference on Current Trends in Theory and Practice of Computer Science, Krems, Austria, January 29-February 2, 2018 [Springer International Publishing.]. *Proceedings*, *44*, 581–595.

Demir, I. B. (2023). Artificial Intelligence for predictive maintenance.

Deng, S., Zhao, H., Fang, W., Yin, J., Dustdar, S., & Zomaya, A. Y. (2020). Edge Intelligence: The confluence of Edge Computing and Artificial Intelligence. arXiv:1909.00560v2. https://arxiv.org/html/2407.04053v1

Dhaduk, H. (2024). *AI in Supply Chain: Top Use Cases and Applications With Examples.* 22th July 2024. Simform. Retrieved 25th November 2024 from https://www.simform.com/blog/ai-in-supply-chain/

Dijkman, R. M., Sprenkels, B., Peeters, T., & Janssen, A. (2015). Business models for the Internet of things. *International Journal of Information Management, 35*(6), 672–678. DOI: 10.1016/j.ijinfomgt.2015.07.008

Ding, H., Tian, J., Yu, W., Wilson, D. I., Young, B. R., Cui, X., Xin, X., Wang, Z., & Li, W. (2023). The Application of Artificial Intelligence and Big Data in the Food Industry. *Foods, 12*(24), 4511. DOI: 10.3390/foods12244511 PMID: 38137314

Dini, P., Diana, L., Elhanashi, A., & Saponara, S. (2024). Overview of AI-Models and Tools in Embedded IIoT Applications. *Electronics (Basel), 13*(12), 2322. DOI: 10.3390/electronics13122322

Dittmar, E. C., López Jiménez, D., & Vargas Portillo, J. P. (2025). COVID-19 and the new situation in higher education. *International Journal of Knowledge and Learning, 18*(2), 204–214. DOI: 10.1504/IJKL.2025.145124

Dunlea, J. (2024). *Machine Learning in Retail: Top Trends & Real Use cases.* 3rd January 2024. Retrieved from https://www.akkio.com/post/machine-learning-in-retail

Du, S., & Xie, C. (2021). Paradoxes of artificial intelligence in consumer markets: Ethical challenges and opportunities. *Journal of Business Research, 129*, 961–974. DOI: 10.1016/j.jbusres.2020.08.024

Edmondson, A. C. (2018). *The fearless organization: Creating psychological safety in the workplace for learning, innovation, and growth.* John Wiley & Sons.

El Bakkouri, B., Raki, S., & Belgnaoui, T. (2022). The role of chatbots in enhancing customer experience: Literature review. *Procedia Computer Science, 203*, 432–437. DOI: 10.1016/j.procs.2022.07.057

Elmurngi, E. I., & Gherbi, A. (2018). Unfair reviews detection on amazon reviews using Sentiment Analysis with supervised learning techniques. *Journal of Computational Science, 14*(5), 714–726. DOI: 10.3844/jcssp.2018.714.726

Enholm, I. M., Papagiannidis, E., Mikalef, P., & Krogstie, J. (2022). Artificial intelligence and business value: A literature review. *Information Systems Frontiers, 24*(5), 1709–1734. DOI: 10.1007/s10796-021-10186-w

Eurostat. (2008). NACE Rev. 2: Statistical classification of economic activities in the European Community. Office for Official Publications of the European Communities.

Evans, D. (2011). The internet of things. How the Next Evolution of the Internet is Changing Everything. *Whitepaper* [IBSG]. *Cisco Internet Business Solutions Group*, *1*, 1–12.

Eyada, B., & Ahmed, N. (2022). Effectiveness of CHATBOT Advertising on Consumer Buying Decision: An Analytical Study. *Journal of Design Sciences and Applied Arts*, *3*(2), 74–87. DOI: 10.21608/jdsaa.2022.121166.1158

Fang, B., Yu, J., Chen, Z., Osman, A. I., Farghali, M., Ihara, I., Hamza, E. H., Rooney, D. W., & Yap, P.-S. (2023). Artificial intelligence for waste management in smart cities: A review. *Environmental Chemistry Letters*, *21*(4), 1959–1989. DOI: 10.1007/s10311-023-01604-3 PMID: 37362015

Fares, O. H., Butt, I., & Lee, S. H. M. (2023). Utilization of artificial intelligence in the banking sector: A systematic literature review. *Journal of Financial Services Marketing*, *28*(2), 835–852. DOI: 10.1057/s41264-022-00176-7

Farina, M., Pedrycz, W., & Lavazza, A. (2024). Towards a mixed human-machine creativity. *Journal of Cultural Cognitive Science*, *8*(2), 151–165. DOI: 10.1007/s41809-024-00146-6

Fathia, A. (2024). Combining AI-Driven Knowledge Frameworks with ML for Real-Time Financial Decision Support and Automation.

Fatima, S., Desouza, K. C., & Dawson, G. S. (2020). National strategic artificial intelligence plans: A multi-dimensional analysis. *Economic Analysis and Policy*, *67*, 178–194. DOI: 10.1016/j.eap.2020.07.008

Flatirons (2024). AI in Transportation Industries: Use Cases and Benefits. 28th January. Flatirons. Retrieved 25th November 2024 from https://flatirons.com/blog/ai-in-transportation-industries/

Foltean, F. S., & van Bruggen, G. H. (2022). Digital Technologies, marketing agility, and Marketing Management Support Systems: How to remain competitive in changing markets. In *Organizational Innovation in the Digital Age* (pp. 1–38). Springer International Publishing. DOI: 10.1007/978-3-030-98183-9_1

Fosso Wamba, S., Gunasekaran, A., Papadopoulos, T., & Ngai, E. (2018). Big data analytics in logistics and supply chain management. *International Journal of Logistics Management*, *29*(2), 478–484. DOI: 10.1108/IJLM-02-2018-0026

Fragkiskaki, K. (2023). Big data and analytics in enhancing procurement and supply chain efficiency: a literature and empirical study.

Frank, E., & Henry, E. (2024). *AI-Driven Demand Forecasting for Optimized Inventory Management* (No. 13214). EasyChair.

Frey, M. (2021). *Netflix recommends: algorithms, film choice, and the history of taste*. Univ of California Press.

Fu, H.-P., Chang, T.-H., Lin, S.-W., Teng, Y.-H., & Huang, Y.-Z. (2023). Evaluation and adoption of artificial intelligence in the retail industry. *International Journal of Retail & Distribution Management, 51*(6), 773–790. DOI: 10.1108/IJRDM-12-2021-0610

Gauri, D. K., Jindal, R. P., Ratchford, B., Fox, E., Bhatnagar, A., Pandey, A., Navallo, J. R., Fogarty, J., Carr, S., & Howerton, E. (2021). Evolution of retail formats: Past, present, and future. *Journal of Retailing, 97*(1), 42–61. DOI: 10.1016/j.jretai.2020.11.002

Gerlick, J. A., & Liozu, S. M. (2020). Ethical and legal considerations of artificial intelligence and algorithmic decision-making in personalized pricing. *Journal of Revenue and Pricing Management, 19*(2), 85–98. DOI: 10.1057/s41272-019-00225-2

Ghosh, A., Chakraborty, D., & Law, A. (2018). Artificial intelligence in Internet of things. *CAAI Transactions on Intelligence Technology, 3*(4), 208–218. DOI: 10.1049/trit.2018.1008

Gielens, K., & Steenkamp, J. B. E. (2019). Branding in the Era of Digital. *Journal of Marketing*.

Gill, S. S., Golec, M., Hu, J., Xu, M., Du, J., Wu, H., Walia, G. K., Murugesan, S. S., Ali, B., Kumar, M., Ye, K., Verma, P., Kumar, S., Cuadrado, F., & Uhlig, S. (2024). *Edge AI: A Taxonomy, Systematic Review and Future Directions*. arXiv:2407.04053v1 04 Jul 2024. https://arxiv.org/html/2407.04053v1

Grewal, D., Motyka, S., & Levy, M. (2018). The Evolution and Future of Retailing and Retailing Education. *Journal of Marketing Education, 40*(1), 85–93. DOI: 10.1177/0273475318755838

Grewal, D., Noble, S. M., Roggeveen, A. L., & Nordfalt, J. (2020). The future of in-store technology. *Journal of the Academy of Marketing Science, 48*(1), 96–113. DOI: 10.1007/s11747-019-00697-z

Grewal, D., Roggeveen, A. L., & Nordfalt, J. (2017). The Future of Retailing. *Journal of Retailing, 93*(1), 1–6. DOI: 10.1016/j.jretai.2016.12.008

Grewal, D., Roggeveen, A. L., & Nordfält, J. (2023). Artificial intelligence applications in retailing. *Journal of Retailing, 99*(1), 13–27. DOI: 10.1016/j.jretai.2022.11.002

Guha, A., Grewal, D., Kopalle, P. K., Haenlein, M., Schneider, M. J., Jung, H., Moustafa, R., Hegde, D. R., & Hawkins, G. (2021). How artificial intelligence will affect the future of retailing. *Journal of Retailing*, *97*(1), 28–41. DOI: 10.1016/j.jretai.2021.01.005

Guo, X., Shen, Z., Zhang, Y., & Wu, T. (2019). Review on the Application of Artificial Intelligence in Smart Homes. *Smart Cities*, *2*(3), 402–420. DOI: 10.3390/smartcities2030025

Hajek, P., Hikkerova, L., & Sahut, J. M. (2023). Fake review detection in e-Commerce platforms using aspect-based Sentiment Analysis. *Journal of Business Research*, *167*, 114143. DOI: 10.1016/j.jbusres.2023.114143

Haleem, A., Javaid, M., Qadri, M. A., Singh, R. P., & Suman, R. (2022). Artificial intelligence (AI) applications for marketing: A literature-based study. *International Journal of Intelligent Networks*, *3*, 119–132. DOI: 10.1016/j.ijin.2022.08.005

Har, L. L., Rashid, U. K., Te Chuan, L., Sen, S. C., & Xia, L. Y. (2022). Revolution of retail industry: From perspective of retail 1.0 to 4.0. *Procedia Computer Science*, *200*, 1615–1625. DOI: 10.1016/j.procs.2022.01.362

Harrison, V. J. (2021). *Leveraging Pharma, Digital Innovation, and Partnerships to Increase Healthcare Access in China: A COVID-19 Case Study* (Doctoral dissertation, Harvard University).

Hasan, R., Thaichon, P., & Weaven, S. (2021). Are we already living with Skynet? Anthropomorphic artificial intelligence to enhance customer experience. In *Developing digital marketing* (pp. 103–134). Emerald Publishing Limited. DOI: 10.1108/978-1-80071-348-220211007

Hauser, J., Urban, G., Liberali, G., & Braun, M. (2021). Dynamic adaptation of scan rates for efficient and congestion-aware internet-wide scanning in IoT security. *JMR, Journal of Marketing Research*, *58*(2), 283–303. DOI: 10.1177/0022243720938837

Heins, C. (2023). Artificial intelligence in retail – a systematic literature review. *Foresight*, *25*(2), 264–286. DOI: 10.1108/FS-10-2021-0210

He, L., Liu, S., & Shen, Z. J. M. (2022). Smart urban transport and logistics: A business analytics perspective. *Production and Operations Management*, *31*(10), 3771–3787. DOI: 10.1111/poms.13775

Hermann, E. (2022). Leveraging Artificial Intelligence in Marketing for Social Good—An Ethical Perspective. *Journal of Business Ethics*, *179*(1), 43–61. DOI: 10.1007/s10551-021-04843-y PMID: 34054170

He, X., Liao, L., Zhang, H., Nie, L., Hu, X., & Chua, T. S. (2017). Neural collaborative filtering. *Proceedings of the 26th International Conference on World Wide Web (WWW '17)*, 173-182. DOI: 10.1145/3038912.3052569

Hossain, M. S., Chisty, N. M. A., Hargrove, D. L., & Amin, R. (2021). Role of Internet of Things (IoT) in Retail Business and Enabling Smart Retailing Experiences. *Asian Business Review*, *11*(2), 75–80. DOI: 10.18034/abr.v11i2.579

Howson, C. (2013). Successful business intelligence (2nd ed.): Unlock the value of BI & big data. McGraw-Hill Professional.

Hoyer, H. D., Kroschke, M., Schmitt, B., Kraume, K., & Shankar, V. (2020). Transforming the Customer Experience Through New Technologies. *Journal of Interactive Marketing*, *51*(1), 57–71. DOI: 10.1016/j.intmar.2020.04.001

Huang, A. (2018). A risk detection system of e-commerce: Researches based on soft information extracted by affective computing web texts. *Electronic Commerce Research*, *18*(1), 143–157. DOI: 10.1007/s10660-017-9262-y

Huang, H., Asemi, A., & Mustafa, M. B. (2023). Sentiment analysis in e-commerce platforms: A review of current techniques and future directions. *IEEE Access : Practical Innovations, Open Solutions*, *11*, 90367–90382. DOI: 10.1109/ACCESS.2023.3307308

Huang, K., Joshi, A., Dun, S., & Hamilton, N. (2024). AI Regulations. In Huang, K., Wang, Y., Goertzel, B., Li, Y., Wright, S., & Ponnapalli, J. (Eds.), *Generative AI Security. Future of Business and Finance* (pp. 61–98). Springer., DOI: 10.1007/978-3-031-54252-7_3

Huang, M. H., & Rust, R. T. (2021). A strategic framework for artificial intelligence in marketing. *Journal of the Academy of Marketing Science*, *49*(1), 30–50. DOI: 10.1007/s11747-020-00749-9

Hughes-Castleberry, K. (2023). *Inside Quantum Technology's "Inside Scoop:" Quantum and the Retail Industry.* Retrieved 3rd February from https://www.insidequantumtechnology.com/news-archive/inside-quantum-technologys-inside-scoop-quantum-and-the-retail-industry/

Hui, S. K., Bradlow, E. T., & Fader, P. S. (2009). Testing behavioral hypotheses using an integrated model of grocery store shopping path and purchase behavior. *The Journal of Consumer Research*, *36*(3), 478–493. DOI: 10.1086/599046

Hunt, W., & Rolf, S. (2022). *Artificial Intelligence and automation in Retail: benefits, challenges and applications (a union perspective).* UNI Global Union. Friedrich Ebert Stiftung. Retieved 24 th November from https://library.fes.de/pdf-files/bueros/bruessel/19054.pdf

Hunt, W., & Rolf, S. (2022). *Artificial Intelligence and Automation in Retail: Benefits, challenges and implications (a union perspective).* Friedrich Ebert Stiftung. Retrieved from https://library.fes.de/pdf-files/bueros/bruessel/19054.pdf

Hussain, N., Turab Mirza, H., Rasool, G., Hussain, I., & Kaleem, M. (2019). Spam review detection techniques: A systematic literature review. *Applied Sciences (Basel, Switzerland), 9*(5), 987. DOI: 10.3390/app9050987

IAEME Publication (2024). AI-Based Predictive Maintenance Strategies for Electrical Equipment and Power Networks. This publication explores AI-based predictive maintenance strategies tailored specifically for electrical equipment and power networks.

Insider, R. (2024). *The Retail benefits of Quantum AI.* Retrieved 3rd February 2025 from https://retail-insider.com/articles/2024/01/the-retail-benefits-of-quantum-ai/

Intuz (2022). *AI-enabled IoT Smart Parking Management System.* Intuz. Retrieved 24th November 2024 from https://www.intuz.com/blog/iot-in-smart-parking-management-benefits-challenges

Intuz (2024). 9 Most Practical Applications of AI in Transportation. Intuz. Retrieved 25th November 2024 from https://www.intuz.com/blog/use-cases-of-ai-in-transportation

IoT World Magazine. (2024). *15 Examples of Digital Healthcare Solutions with AI, IoT, and Blockchain in 2024.* Retrieved 25th November 2024 from https://iotworldmagazine.com/2024/03/29/2198/15-examples-of-digital-healthcare-solutions-with-ai-iot-and-blockchain-in-2024

Jachimowski, R., Gołębiowski, P., Izdebski, M., Pyza, D., & Szczepański, E. (2017). Designing and efficiency of database for simulation of processes in systems: Case study for the simulation of warehouse processes. *Archives of Transport, 41*(1), 31–42. DOI: 10.5604/01.3001.0009.7380

Jacyna, M., Semenov, I., & Trojanowski, P. (2015). The research directions of increase effectiveness of the functioning of the RSA with regard to specialized transport. *Archives of Transport, 35*(3), 27–39. DOI: 10.5604/08669546.1185181

Jain, A. K., Murty, M. N., & Flynn, P. J. (1999). Data clustering: A review. *ACM Computing Surveys, 31*(3), 264–323. DOI: 10.1145/331499.331504

Jakubcinova, M., & Poruban, A. (2023). *The Concept of a Smart City Management in the Light of the Literature Review*. Zeszyty Naukowe Politechniki Częstochowskiej.

Jarrahi, M. H., Askay, D., Eshraghi, A., & Smith, P. (2023). Artificial intelligence and knowledge management: A partnership between human and AI. *Business Horizons*, *66*(1), 87–99. DOI: 10.1016/j.bushor.2022.03.002

Jayakrishnan, S. (2022). Artificial Intelligence (AI) in Retailing - A Systematic Review and Research Agenda. *Contemporary Research in Management: Volume XI - SDM Research Centre for Management Studies.* DOI: 10.2139/ssrn.4134959

Jordan, M. I. (2004). Graphical models. *Statistical Science*, *19*(1), 140–155. DOI: 10.1214/088342304000000026

Jordanous, A., & Keller, B. (2016). Modelling Creativity: Identifying Key Components through a Corpus-Based Approach. *PLoS One*, *11*(10), e0162959. DOI: 10.1371/journal.pone.0162959 PMID: 27706185

Joyia, G. J., Liaqat, R. M., Farooq, A., & Rehman, S. (2017). Internet of Medical Things (IOMT): Applications benefits and future challenges in healthcare domain. *Journal of Communication*, *12*(4), 240–247.

Ju, L., Wu, J., Lin, H., Tan, Q., Li, G., Tan, Z., & Li, J. (2020). Robust purchase and sale transactions optimization strategy for electricity retailers with energy storage system considering two-stage demand response. *Applied Energy*, *271*, 115155. Advance online publication. DOI: 10.1016/j.apenergy.2020.115155

Kakkad, J., Macon-Cooney, B., Northend, J., Phillips, J., Rajkumar, N., Stanley, L., & Westgarth, T. (2023). *A New National Purpose: Innovation Can Power the Future of Britain*. Tony Blair Institute for Global Change.

Kamaruddin, N. (2021). Comparative Study on Sentiment Analysis Approach for Online Shopping Review. [TURCOMAT]. *Turkish Journal of Computer and Mathematics Education*, *12*(3), 1358–1370.

Kaneko, Y., & Yada, K. (2016a). A deep learning approach for the prediction of retail store sales. In 2016 IEEE 16th International Conference on Data Mining Workshops (ICDMW) (pp. 531–537). IEEE. DOI: 10.1109/ICDMW.2016.0082

Kaneko, Y., & Yada, K. (2016b). Fractal dimension of shopping path: Influence on purchase behavior in a supermarket. *Procedia Computer Science*, *96*, 1764–1771. DOI: 10.1016/j.procs.2016.08.225

Kang, J. W., & Namkung, Y. (2019). The role of personalization on continuance intention in food service mobile apps: A privacy calculus perspective. *International Journal of Contemporary Hospitality Management, 31*(2), 734–752. DOI: 10.1108/IJCHM-12-2017-0783

Kaplan, A. (2020). Retailing and the Ethical Challenges and Dilemmas Behind Artificial Intelligence. In Pantano, E. (Ed.), *Retail Futures* (pp. 181–191). Emerald Publishing Limited., DOI: 10.1108/978-1-83867-663-620201020

Kaplan, A., & Haenlein, M. (2019). Siri, Siri, in my hand: Who's the fairest in the land? On the interpretations, illustrations, and implications of artificial intelligence. *Business Horizons, 62*(1), 15–25. DOI: 10.1016/j.bushor.2018.08.004

Kasturi, S. (2023). Evolving consumer expectations and the future of digital banking. *Journal of Digital Banking, 8*(1), 37–48. DOI: 10.69554/LURA3454

Kauffmann, E., Peral, J., Gil, D., Ferrández, A., Sellers, R., & Mora, H. (2020). A framework for big data analytics in commercial social networks: A case study on Sentiment Analysis and fake review detection for marketing decision-making. *Industrial Marketing Management, 90*, 523–537. DOI: 10.1016/j.indmarman.2019.08.003

Kazagli, E., & de Lapparent, M. (2023). A discrete choice modeling framework of heterogenous decision rules accounting for non-trading behavior. *Journal of Choice Modelling, 48*, 100413. Advance online publication. DOI: 10.1016/j.jocm.2023.100413

Khadam, U., Davidsson, P., & Spalazzese, R. (2024). Exploring the Role of Artificial Intelligence in Internet of Things Systems: A Systematic Mapping Study. *Sensors (Basel), 24*(20), 6511. DOI: 10.3390/s24206511 PMID: 39459993

Khan, M. S. U., Hasan, M. F., Islam, M. S., & Hassan, S. T. (2021). Artificial intelligenc e in the banking sector of Bangladesh: Applicability and the challenges. *Roundtabl e discussion series-2021. Keynote Paper of Roundtable Discussion of BIBM, 6*(2).

Khan, S., Khari, M., & Azrour, M. (2023). IoT in retail and e-commerce. *Electronic Commerce Research*. Advance online publication. DOI: 10.1007/s10660-023-09785-3

Kholod, M., Golubtsov, P., Varlamov, A., Filatov, S., & Yada, K. (2019). Modeling customers speed of movement from POS- and RFID-data. In Smart Innovation, Systems and Technologies (Vol. 143, pp. 151–160). Springer. DOI: 10.1007/978-981-13-8260-4_15

Kholod, M., Lyandau, Y., Maslennikov, V., Kalinina, I., & Mrochkovskiy, N. (2019). Upper level processes and projects model building. In Smart Innovation, Systems and Technologies (Vol. 143, pp. 267–276). Springer. DOI: 10.1007/978-981-13-8303-8_24

Kim, D., & Heo, T.-Y. (2022). Anomaly Detection with Feature Extraction Based on Machine Learning Using Hydraulic System IoT Sensor Data. *Sensors (Basel), 22*(7), 2479. DOI: 10.3390/s22072479 PMID: 35408096

Kim, W. (2007). Online call quality monitoring for automating agent-based call centers. In *Proceedings of Interspeech 2007* (pp. 130–133). ISCA. DOI: 10.21437/Interspeech.2007-56

Klaus, P., Weijters, G., & Verhoef, P. C. (2022). Voice assistants, mobile AR, and digital transformation in retail. *Journal of Retailing and Consumer Services*, *60*, 102–110. DOI: 10.1016/j.jretconser.2022.102110

Koren, Y., Bell, R., & Volinsky, C. (2009). Matrix factorization techniques for recommender systems. *Computer*, *42*(8), 30–37. DOI: 10.1109/MC.2009.263

Krishnaiah, K. R. (2023). Predicting Fake Online Reviews: A Comprehensive Study of Supervised and Semi-Supervised Learning Models. [TURCOMAT]. *Turkish Journal of Computer and Mathematics Education*, *14*(03), 392–399.

Kubina, M., Koman, G., & Kubinova, I. (2015). Possibility of improving efficiency within business intelligence systems in companies. *Procedia Economics and Finance*, *26*, 300–305. DOI: 10.1016/S2212-5671(15)00856-4

Kulkarni, P. M., Gokhale, P. P., & Dandannavar, P. (2022). Internet of Things (IoT) Adoption: Challenges among small and medium scale enterprises (SMEs). In: Haldorai, A., Ramu, A., Mohanram, S. & Zgheib, R. (eds) *4th EAI International Conference on Big Data Innovation for Sustainable Cognitive Computing*. EAI/Springer. https://doi.org/DOI: 10.1007/978-3-031-07654-1_9

Kumar, A., Gopal, R. D., Shankar, R., & Tan, K. H. (2022). Fraudulent review detection model focusing on emotional expressions and explicit aspects: Investigating the potential of feature engineering. *Decision Support Systems*, *155*, 113728. DOI: 10.1016/j.dss.2021.113728

Kumar, N., Venugopal, D., Qiu, L., & Kumar, S. (2018). Detecting review manipulation on online platforms with hierarchical supervised learning. *Journal of Management Information Systems*, *35*(1), 350–380. DOI: 10.1080/07421222.2018.1440758

Kumar, S., Talukder, M. B., & Tyagi, P. K. (2024). The Impact of Artificial Intelligence on Improving Efficiency in Service and Implementing Best Practices in Service Marketing. In *AI Innovations in Service and Tourism Marketing* (pp. 57–79). IGI Global. DOI: 10.4018/979-8-3693-7909-7.ch004

Kumar, V., & Singh, P. (2024). Advancements in Smart City Technologies: Innovations and Future Directions. *Journal of Urban Technology*, *31*(2), 102–128. DOI: 10.1080/10630732.2024.1145634

Kunnathuvalappil Hariharan, N. (2018). Artificial Intelligence and human collaboration in financial planning.

Kushwaha, A. K., Kumar, P., & Kar, A. K. (2021). What impacts customer experience for B2B enterprises on using AI-enabled chatbots? Insights from Big data analytics. *Industrial Marketing Management*, *98*, 207–221. DOI: 10.1016/j.indmarman.2021.08.011

Larson, J. S., Bradlow, E. T., & Fader, P. S. (2005). An exploratory look at supermarket shopping paths. *International Journal of Research in Marketing*, *22*(4), 395–414. DOI: 10.1016/j.ijresmar.2005.09.005

Lau, R. Y., Liao, S. Y., Kwok, R. C. W., Xu, K., Xia, Y., & Li, Y. (2012). Text mining and probabilistic language modeling for online review spam detection. [TMIS]. *ACM Transactions on Management Information Systems*, *2*(4), 1–30. DOI: 10.1145/2070710.2070716

Lauterbach, A. (2019). Artificial intelligence and policy: Quo vadis? *Digital Policy. Regulation & Governance*, *21*(3), 238–263. DOI: 10.1108/DPRG-09-2018-0054

Lazaris, C., & Vrechopoulos, A. (2014). From Multichannel to "Omnichannel" Retailing: Review of the Literature and Calls for Research. *2nd International Conference on Contemporary Marketing Issues, (ICCMI), 18-20 June 2014At: Athens, Greece.* https://doi.org/DOI: 10.13140/2.1.1802.4967

Lee, S. M., & Lee, D. (2020). "Untact": A new customer service strategy in the digital age. *Service Business*, *14*(1), 1–22. DOI: 10.1007/s11628-019-00408-2

Lemon, K. N., & Verhoef, P. C. (2016). Understanding Customer Experience Throughout the Customer Journey. *Journal of Marketing*, *80*(6), 69–96. DOI: 10.1509/jm.15.0420

Liang, W., Tadesse, G. A., Ho, D., Fei-Fei, L., Zaharia, M., Zhang, C., & Zou, J. (2022). Advances, challenges and opportunities in creating data for trustworthy AI. *Nature Machine Intelligence*, *4*(8), 669–677. DOI: 10.1038/s42256-022-00516-1

Liu, H. W., & Lin, C. F. (2020). Artificial Intelligence and Global Trade Governance: A Pluralist Agenda. *Harvard International Law Journal, 61*(2). https://ssrn.com/abstract=3675505

Liu, N., Shapira, P., Yue, X., & Guan, J. (2021). Mapping technological innovation dynamics in artificial intelligence domains: Evidence from a global patent analysis. *PLoS One, 16*(12), e0262050. DOI: 10.1371/journal.pone.0262050 PMID: 34972173

Loideain, N. N., & Adams, R. (2020). From Alexa to Siri and the GDPR: The gendering of virtual personal assistants and the role of data protection impact assessments. *Computer Law & Security Review, 36*, 105366. DOI: 10.1016/j.clsr.2019.105366

Lokman, A. S., & Aberdeen, M. A. (2019). Modern chatbot systems: A technical review. In K. Arai, R. Bhatia, & S. Kapoor (Eds.), Proceedings of the Future Technologies Conference (FTC) 2018 (pp. 1012–1023). Springer International Publishing. DOI: 10.1007/978-3-030-02683-7_75

López Jiménez, D., Dittmar, E. C., & Vargas Portillo, J. P. (2022). Nuevas estrategias publicitarias con influencers: Un examen multidisciplinar. *Revista de Ciencias Sociales, 28*(4), 63–78. DOI: 10.31876/rcs.v28i4.39117

López Jiménez, D., Dittmar, E. C., & Vargas Portillo, J. P. (2023). The Self-Regulating Jury in the Field of Interactive Advertising. *Revista de Direito. Estado e Telecomunicacoes, 15*(1), 1–30. DOI: 10.26512/lstr.v15i1.42146

Lops, P., De Gemmis, M., & Semeraro, G. (2011). Content-based recommender systems: State of the art and trends. *Recommender Systems Handbook*, 73-105.

Loshin, D. (2003). *Business intelligence: The savvy manager's guide, getting onboard with emerging IT*. Morgan Kaufmann. DOI: 10.1016/B978-155860916-7/50003-8

Lu, L., Zhang, H., & Song, Y. (2023). AI-driven personalized services in retail: Impacts on customer experience. *Journal of Business Research, 145*, 712–721. DOI: 10.1016/j.jbusres.2022.10.014

Lu, Y. (2019). Artificial intelligence: A survey on evolution, models, applications and future trends. *Journal of Management Analytics, 6*(1), 1–29. DOI: 10.1080/23270012.2019.1570365

Lynn, T., Endo, P. T., Ribeiro, A. M. N. C., Barbosa, G. B. N., & Rosati, P. (2020). The Internet of Things: Definitions, Key Concepts, and Reference Architectures. In Lynn, T., Mooney, J., Lee, B., & Endo, P. (Eds.), *The Cloud-to-Thing Continuum. Palgrave Studies in Digital Business & Enabling Technologies*. Palgrave Macmillan., DOI: 10.1007/978-3-030-41110-7_1

Lyyra, A., Koskinen, K., Sørensen, C., & Marion, T. (2023). Tethered Architectures in Cyber-Physical System Development: The Case of Tesla's Autopilot System. *Available at SSRN* 4515061. DOI: 10.2139/ssrn.4515061

Ma, T-J., Lee, G-G., Liu, J.S., Lan, R., & Weng, J-H. (2022). Bibliographic coupling: a main path analysis from 1963 to 2020. *Information Research,* 27 (1), paper 918. https://doi.org/DOI: 10.47989/irpaper918

MacGregor, J. N., & Chu, Y. (2011). Human performance on the traveling salesman and related problems: A review. *The Journal of Problem Solving*, *3*(2), 2. Advance online publication. DOI: 10.7771/1932-6246.1090

Ma, L., Cheng, S., & Shi, Y. (2021). Enhancing learning efficiency of brain storm optimization via orthogonal learning design. *IEEE Transactions on Systems, Man, and Cybernetics. Systems*, *51*(11), 6723–6742. DOI: 10.1109/TSMC.2020.2963943

Ma, L., Huang, M., Yang, S., Wang, R., & Wang, X. (2022). An adaptive localized decision variable analysis approach to large-scale multiobjective and many-objective optimization. *IEEE Transactions on Cybernetics*, *52*(7), 6684–6696. DOI: 10.1109/TCYB.2020.3041212 PMID: 33476273

Manta, A. G., Bădîrcea, R. M., Doran, N. M., Badareu, G., Gher escu, C., & Popescu, J. (2024). Industry 4.0 Transformation: Analysing the Impact of Artificial Intelligence on the Banking Sector through Bibliometric Trends. *Electronics (Basel)*, *13*(9), 1693. DOI: 10.3390/electronics13091693

Maria, K., Drigas, A., & Skianis, C. (2022). Chatbots as cognitive, educational, advisory & coaching systems. *Technium Soc. Sci. J.*, *30*, 109.

MarketsandMarkets. (2024, October 2). Business intelligence market worth $33.3 billion by 2025. https://www.marketsandmarkets.com/PressReleases/social-business-intelligence-bi.asp

Martin-Fuentes, E., Mateu, C., & Fernandez, C. (2020). The more the merrier? Number of reviews versus score on TripAdvisor and Booking.com. *International Journal of Hospitality & Tourism Administration*, *21*(4), 1–14. DOI: 10.1080/15256480.2018.1429337

Martin, K. D., & Murphy, P. E. (2017). The role of data privacy in marketing. *Journal of the Academy of Marketing Science*, *45*(2), 135–155. DOI: 10.1007/s11747-016-0495-4

Matei, A., & Coco atu, M. (2024). Artificial Internet of Things, Sensor-Based Digital Twin Urban Computing Vision Algorithms, and Blockchain Cloud Networks in Sustainable Smart City Administration. *Sustainability (Basel)*, *16*(16), 6749. DOI: 10.3390/su16166749

Mathew, S. M. (2023). Banking 4.0-AI Driven Chatbots-Sun Setting of the Traditional Banking. *Innovatus: An Ivanian Journal of Economics and Business Studies*, 8-16.

Matthews, K. (2020). *5 applications of AIoT in the retail industry*. 19th February. IoT Times. Retrieved 24th November 2024 from https://iot.eetimes.com/5-applications-of-aiot-in-the-retail-industry/

Mavani, N. R., Ali, J. M., Othman, S., Hussain, M. A., Hashim, H., & Rahman, N. (2022). Application of Artificial Intelligence in Food Industry - A Guideline. *Food Engineering Reviews*, *14*(1), 134–175. DOI: 10.1007/s12393-021-09290-z PMID: 40477643

McAdams, R. M., Kaur, R., Sun, Y., Bindra, H., Cho, S. J., & Singh, H. (2022). Predicting clinical outcomes using artificial intelligence and machine learning in neonatal intensive care units: A systematic review. *Journal of Perinatology*, *42*(12), 1561–1575. DOI: 10.1038/s41372-022-01392-8 PMID: 35562414

McBride, N. (2014). Business intelligence in magazine distribution. *International Journal of Information Management*, *34*(1), 58–62. DOI: 10.1016/j.ijinfomgt.2013.09.006

McCarthy, M. L., Ding, R., Pines, J. M., & Zeger, S. L. (2011). Comparison of methods for measuring crowding and its effects on length of stay in the emergency department. *Academic Emergency Medicine*, *18*(12), 1269–1277. DOI: 10.1111/j.1553-2712.2011.01232.x PMID: 22168190

Medwave (2024). *How AI is Transforming Healthcare: 12 Real-World Use Cases.* Retrieved 24th November 2024 from https://medwave.io/2024/01/how-ai-is-transforming-healthcare-12-real-world-use-cases/

Merenda, M., Porcaro, C., & Iero, D. (2020). Edge Machine Learning for AI-Enabled IoT Devices: A Review. *Sensors (Basel)*, *20*(9), 2533. DOI: 10.3390/s20092533 PMID: 32365645

Mewada, A., & Dewang, R. K. (2022). Research on False Review Detection Methods: A state-of-the-art review. *Journal of King Saud University. Computer and Information Sciences*, *34*(9), 7530–7546. DOI: 10.1016/j.jksuci.2021.07.021

Mijwil, M. M., & Abttan, R. A. (2021). Artificial Intelligence: A Survey on Evolution and Future Trends. *Asian Journal of Applied Sciences*, *9*(2). Advance online publication. DOI: 10.24203/ajas.v9i2.6589

Mitchell, W. D. (2020). *Proactive Predictive Analytics Within the Customer Lifecycle to Prevent Customer Churn*. Northcentral University.

Mittal, A. (2024). *AI in Food Industry: Benefits, Use Cases, and Trends in 2025.* Rerieved 25th November 2024 from https://www.ongraph.com/ai-in-food-industry/

Mittelstadt, B. D., Allo, P., Taddeo, M., Wachter, S., & Floridi, L. (2016). The ethics of algorithms: Mapping the debate. *Big Data & Society*, *3*(2), 2053951716679679. Advance online publication. DOI: 10.1177/2053951716679679

Mohammed, S., Bealer, R., & Cohen, J. (2021). Embracing advanced AI/ML to help investors achieve success: Vanguard Reinforcement Learning for Financial Goal Planning. *arXiv preprint arXiv:2110.12003*.

Mohanty, B., & Mishra, S. (2023). Role of Artificial Intelligence in Financial Fraud Detection. *Academy of Marketing Studies Journal*, *27*(S4).

Mohawesh, R., Tran, S., Ollington, R., & Xu, S. (2021). Analysis of concept drift in fake reviews detection. *Expert Systems with Applications*, *169*, 114318. DOI: 10.1016/j.eswa.2020.114318

Mohawesh, R., Xu, S., Tran, S. N., Ollington, R., Springer, M., Jararweh, Y., & Maqsood, S. (2021). Fake reviews detection: A survey. *IEEE Access : Practical Innovations, Open Solutions*, *9*, 65771–65802. DOI: 10.1109/ACCESS.2021.3075573

Moon, S., Kim, M. Y., & Iacobucci, D. (2021). Content analysis of fake consumer reviews by survey-based text categorization. *International Journal of Research in Marketing*, *38*(2), 343–364. DOI: 10.1016/j.ijresmar.2020.08.001

Morais, C. M., Sadok, D., & Kelner, J. (2019). An IoT sensor and scenario survey for data researchers. *Journal of the Brazilian Computer Society*, *25*(4), 2–17. DOI: 10.1186/s13173-019-0085-7

Morid, M. A., & Shajari, M. (2012). An enhanced e-commerce trust model for community based centralized systems. *Electronic Commerce Research*, *12*(4), 409–427. DOI: 10.1007/s10660-012-9099-3

Moura, F. de Abreu e Silva, J. (2021). Smart Cities: Definitions, Evolution of the Concept, and Examples of Initiatives. In: Leal Filho, W., Azul, A.M., Brandli, L., Lange Salvia, A., Wall, T. (eds) Industry, Innovation and Infrastructure. Encyclopedia of the UN Sustainable Development Goals. Springer, Cham. https://doi.org/ DOI: 10.1007/978-3-319-95873-6_6

Mulè, L. (2024). *Revolutionizing waste management: the role of AI in building sustainable practices.* Retrieved 25th November from https://aiforgood.itu.int/revolutionizing-waste-management-the-role-of-ai-in-building-sustainable-practices/

Myeong, S., Park, J., & Lee, M. (2022). Research Models and Methodologies on the Smart City: A Systematic Literature Review. *Sustainability (Basel)*, *14*(3), 1687. DOI: 10.3390/su14031687

Naim, I., Rajuddin, W. O. N., & Ansyori, A. (2024). Customer Relationship Management In The Digital Era To Enhance Customer Experience Through Technology. *Transforma Jurnal Manajemen*, *2*(2), 77–85. DOI: 10.56457/tjm.v2i2.131

Naslednikov, M. (2024). The Impact of Artificial Intelligence on Customer Relationship Management (CRM). *Strategies (La Jolla, Calif.).*

Nazir, H., & Fan, J. (2024). Revolutionizing Retail: Examining the Influence of Blockchain-Enabled IoT Capabilities on Sustainable Firm Performance. *Sustainability (Basel)*, *16*(9), 3534. DOI: 10.3390/su16093534

Ng, K. (2019). IoT in Retail: Enhancing Operational Efficiency and Customer Experience. *Journal of Retail Technology*, 15 (3), 45-58. Retrieved 3rd February from www.gsma.com

Nguyen, B., Simkin, L., & Canhoto, A. (2021). The Dark Side of AI in Customer Experience. *Journal of Services Marketing.*

Ninkov, A., Frank, J. R., & Maggio, L. A. (2022). Bibliometrics: Methods for studying academic publishing. *Perspectives on Medical Education*, *11*(3), 173–176. DOI: 10.1007/S40037-021-00695-4 PMID: 34914027

Nirala, K. K., Singh, N. K., & Purani, V. S. (2022). A survey on providing customer and public administration based services using AI: Chatbot. *Multimedia Tools and Applications*, *81*(16), 22215–22246. DOI: 10.1007/s11042-021-11458-y PMID: 35002470

Noble, S. M., & Mende, M. (2023). The future of artificial intelligence and robotics in the retail and service sector: Sketching the field of consumer-robot-experiences. *Journal of the Academy of Marketing Science*, *51*(4), 747–756. DOI: 10.1007/s11747-023-00948-0 PMID: 37359262

Noh, D., & Oh, E. (2025). Chemical Detection Using Mobile Platforms and AI-Based Data Processing Technologies. *Journal of Sensing and Actuator Networks, 14*(1), 6. DOI: 10.3390/jsan14010006

Nozari, H., Szmelter-Jarosz, A., & Ghahremani-Nahr, J. (2022). *Analysis of the Challenges of Artificial Intelligence of Things (AIoT) for the Smart Supply Chain (Case Study: FMCG Industries). Sensors (Basel), 22*(8), 2931–2945. DOI: 10.3390/s22082931 PMID: 35458916

Nujic, L., & Ambrusec, M. (2021). Influencer marketing in the tourism sector: A company's perspective. In *Proceedings of the Interdisciplinary Management Research*. Opatija, Croatia.

Ogunbiyi, V.O., Bala, G.G. & George, A.C. (2023). Exploring Artificial Intelligence Application and Implication: Evidence From The UK Retail Industry. *IOSR Journal of Business and Management (IOSR-JBM)*, 25 (9), 1-10. https://doi.org/ DOI: 10.9790/487X-2509050110

Ogunjimi, I., Kavak, B., & Seyrek, I. H. (2021). Smart mirrors in retail: Enhancing customer experience with augmented reality. *International Journal of Retail & Distribution Management, 49*(3), 369–383. DOI: 10.1108/IJRDM-12-2020-0465

Olateju, O., Okon, S. U., Olaniyi, O. O., Samuel-Okon, A. D., & Asonze, C. U. (2024). Exploring the concept of explainable AI and developing information governance standards for enhancing trust and transparency in handling customer data. *Available at SSRN*. DOI: 10.2139/ssrn.4879025

Olsen, T. L., & Tomlin, B. (2020). Industry 4.0: Opportunities and Challenges for Operations Management. *Manufacturing & Service Operations Management, 22*(1), 113–122. Advance online publication. DOI: 10.1287/msom.2019.0796

Omrany, H., Al-Obaidi, K. M., Hossain, M., Alduais, N. A. M., Al-Duais, H. S., & Ghaffarianhoseini, A. (2024). IoT-enabled smart cities: A hybrid systematic analysis of key research areas, challenges, and recommendations for future direction. *Discover Cities, 1*(1), 2. DOI: 10.1007/s44327-024-00002-w

Oosthuizen, K., Botha, E., Robertson, J., & Montecchi, M. (2020). Artificial Intelligence in Retail: The AI-Enabled Value Chain. [AMJ]. *Australasian Marketing Journal, 29*(3), 264–273. DOI: 10.1016/j.ausmj.2020.07.007

Ordr (2024). *10 Internet of Things (IoT) Healthcare Examples*. Retrieved 24th November 2024 from https://ordr.net/article/iot-healthcare-examples

Panduman, Y. Y. F., Funabiki, N., Fajrianti, E. D., Fang, S., & Sukaridhoto, S. (2024). A Survey of AI Techniques in IoT Applications with Use Case Investigations in the Smart Environmental Monitoring and Analytics in Real-Time IoT Platform. *Information (Basel)*, *15*(3), 153. DOI: 10.3390/info15030153

Panfilov, P., Suleykin, A., ElDarawany, A., & Elpashev, D. (2021b). Open-source digital infrastructure capacity prediction system for production company. In 2021 3rd International Conference on Control Systems, Mathematical Modeling, Automation and Energy Efficiency (SUMMA) (pp. 915–920). IEEE. DOI: 10.1109/SUMMA53307.2021.9632166

Panfilov, P., Suleykin, A., & ElDarawany, A. (2021a). Digital ecosystem-based KPI-driven railway communication network reporting system. In *MEDES '21: Proceedings of the 13th International Conference on Management of Digital EcoSystems* (pp. 163–166). Association for Computing Machinery. DOI: 10.1145/3444757.3485173

Pantano, E., & Dennis, C. (2019). *Smart Retailing: Technologies and Strategies*. Palgrave Macmillan., DOI: 10.1007/978-3-030-12608-7

Pantano, E., & Timmermans, H. (2014). What is Smart for Retailing? *Procedia Environmental Sciences*, *22*, 101–107. DOI: 10.1016/j.proenv.2014.11.010

Parking Telecom. (2022). AI-based Smart Parking Solutions. Retrieved 24th November 2024 from https://parkingtelecom.com/en/ai-based-smart-parking-solutions/

Park, J. H., & Yen, N. Y. (2018). Advanced algorithms and applications based on IoT for the smart devices. *Journal of Ambient Intelligence and Humanized Computing*, *9*(4), 1085–1087. DOI: 10.1007/s12652-018-0715-5

Passas, I. (2024). Bibliometric Analysis: The Main Steps. *Encyclopedia*, *4*(2), 1014–1025. DOI: 10.3390/encyclopedia4020065

Patil, K., & Kulkarni, M. S. (2019). Artificial intelligence in financial services: Customer chatbot advisor adoption. *International Journal of Innovative Technology and Exploring Engineering*, *9*(1), 4296–4303. DOI: 10.35940/ijitee.A4928.119119

Paul, H., & Nikolaev, A. (2021). Fake review detection on online E-commerce platforms: A systematic literature review. *Data Mining and Knowledge Discovery*, *35*(5), 1830–1881. DOI: 10.1007/s10618-021-00772-6

Peruchini, M., da Silva, G. M., & Teixeira, J. M. (2024). Between artificial intelligence and customer experience: A literature review on the intersection. *Discover Artificial Intelligence*, *4*(4), 4. Advance online publication. DOI: 10.1007/s44163-024-00105-8

Petrescu, M., & Krishen, A. S. (2023). Hybrid intelligence: human–AI collaboration in marketing analytics. *Journal of Marketing Analytics*, *11*(3), 263–274. DOI: 10.1057/s41270-023-00245-3

Picareta, G., Weissheim, E., & Klöhn, M. (2021). Intelligent applications in the modern sales organization. In *The Machine Age of Customer Insight* (pp. 19–35). Emerald Publishing Limited. DOI: 10.1108/978-1-83909-694-520211003

Policarpo, L. M., da Silveira, D. E., da Rosa Righi, R., Stoffel, R. A., da Costa, C. A., Barbosa, J. L. V., & Arcot, T. (2021). Machine learning through the lens of e-commerce initiatives: An up-to-date systematic literature review. *Computer Science Review*, *41*, 100414. DOI: 10.1016/j.cosrev.2021.100414

Polireddi, N. S. A. (2024). Artificial intelligence in banking and financial services. *Research Advances in Intelligent Computing*, *2*, 139–152. DOI: 10.1201/9781003433941-9

Popescu, S. M., Mansoor, S., Wani, O. A., Kumar, S. S., Sharma, V., Arya, V. M., Kirkham, M. B., Hou, D., Bolan, N., & Chung, Y. S. (2024). Artificial intelligence and IoT driven technologies for environmental pollution monitoring and management. *Frontiers in Environmental Science*, *12*, 1336088. DOI: 10.3389/fenvs.2024.1336088

Pratas, J., Amorim, C., & Reis, J. L. (2023). Measuring the Impacts of Smart Retailing Technologies Pilot Implementation – Proposal Framework. *CAPSI 2023 Proceedings. 4.* https://aisel.aisnet.org/capsi2023/4

Pratas, J., Rodrigues, M. A., & Carvalho, M. A. (2024). *Unraveling Managerial Resistance: An Analysis of the reasons of Non-Investment in Cutting-Edge Digital Technologies*. ISPGAYA International Congress 2024 – Business and Sustainability. Vila Nova de Gaia, Portugal.

Pratas, J., Amorim, C., & Reis, J. L. (2024). Subscription Retailing Research Evolution Analysis Using Bibliometric Indicators and Content Analysis. In Reis, J. L., Del Rio Araujo, M., Reis, L. P., & dos Santos, J. P. M. (Eds.), *Marketing and Smart Technologies. ICMarkTech 2022. Smart Innovation, Systems and Technologies* (Vol. 344). Springer., DOI: 10.1007/978-981-99-0333-7_10

Pratas, J., & Brito, P. (2019). *Distribuição - Gestão de pontos de venda e de retalho - Gestão eficiente do negócio*. Actual Editora.

Pratas, J., & Oliveira, Z. (2023). QR Codes Research in Marketing: A Bibliometric and Content Analysis. In Reis, J. L., Peter, M. K., Varela González, J. A., & Bogdanović, Z. (Eds.), *Marketing and Smart Technologies. Smart Innovation, Systems and Technologies* (Vol. 337). Springer., DOI: 10.1007/978-981-19-9099-1_19

ProvenRobotics. (2024 a). *Robots for Retail Stores: Driving Sales & Customer Satisfaction*. 3rd April, Retrieved from https://provenrobotics.ai/robots-for-retail-stores/

ProvenRobotics. (2024 b). *What robots can do for retail: 30 applications*. 27th May, Retrieved from https://provenrobotics.ai/what-robots-can-do-for-retail/

Pyarelal, S., & Das, A. K. (2018). Automating the design of user interfaces using artificial intelligence. *DS 91: Proceedings of NordDesign 2018,* Linköping, Sweden, 14th-17th August 2018.

Quinlan, J. R. (1986). Induction of decision trees. *Machine Learning*, *1*(1), 81–106. DOI: 10.1023/A:1022643204877

Raj, R., Kumar, K., Prakash, A., Kumar, A., Kumari, S., & Kumar, G. (2024, May). Enhancing E-Commerce Engagement: Exploring AR and VR-Based Marketing Strategies. In *2024 International Conference on Computational Intelligence and Computing Applications (ICCICA)* (Vol. 1, pp. 448-453). IEEE. DOI: 10.1109/ICCICA60014.2024.10585182

Rameshkumar, P. M., & Shanthi, R. (2017). Internet of Things (IoT's) in Retail Industry - A Study to Trace the Feasible Business Model. *International Journal of Advance Research in Science and Engineering*, *6*(1), 288–292.

Rao, A. N., Velivela, A., Reddy, M. S. R. L., Sagar, Y. A., Jyothi, N. J., & Shilpa, S. (2025). Machine Learning and Artificial Intelligence in IoT: Integration Techniques and Applications. Cognitive Science and Technology, 65-64.

Rao, P. H. N., Vihari, N. S., & Jabeen, S. S. (2021). Reimagining the Fashion Retail Industry Through the Implications of COVID-19 in the Gulf Cooperation Council (GCC) Countries. *FIIB Business Review*, *10*(4), 327–338. DOI: 10.1177/23197145211039580

Rawas, S. (2024). AI: The future of humanity. *Discover Artificial Intelligence*, *4*(1), 25. DOI: 10.1007/s44163-024-00118-3

Reddy, S. R. B. (2022). Enhancing Customer Experience through AI-Powered Marketing Automation: Strategies and Best Practices for Industry 4.0. *Journal of Artificial Intelligence Research*, *2*(1), 36–46.

Reinartz, W., Wiegand, N., & Imschloss, M. (2019). The impact of digital transformation on the retailing value chain. *International Journal of Research in Marketing*, *36*(3), 350–366. DOI: 10.1016/j.ijresmar.2018.12.002

Rendle, S. (2012). Factorization machines. *Proceedings of the 10th IEEE International Conference on Data Mining (ICDM 2012)*, 995-1000.

Revilla, E., Saenz, M. J., Seifert, M., & Ma, Y. (2023). Human–Artificial Intelligence Collaboration in Prediction: A Field Experiment in the Retail Industry. *Journal of Management Information Systems*, *40*(4), 1071–1098. DOI: 10.1080/07421222.2023.2267317

Reyes-Menendez, A., Saura, J. R., & Filipe, F. (2019). The importance of behavioral data to identify online fake reviews for tourism businesses: A systematic review. *PeerJ. Computer Science*, *5*, e219. DOI: 10.7717/peerj-cs.219 PMID: 33816872

Ricci, F., Rokach, L., & Shapira, B. (2015). *Recommender Systems Handbook*. Springer. DOI: 10.1007/978-1-4899-7637-6

Rivera, R., Amorim, M., & Reis, J. (2021). Technological Evolution in Grocery Retail: A systematic literature review. *16th Iberian Conference on Information Systems and Technologies (CISTI)*, 23 – 26 June 2021, Chaves, Portugal ISBN: 978-989-54659-1-0 DOI: 10.23919/CISTI52073.2021.9476598

Rizzoli, A. (2021). *AI in Transportation: 9 Disruptive Use Cases [2024 Update]*. V7 Labs. Retrieved 23th November 2024 from https://www.v7labs.com/blog/ai-in-transportation

Roe, M., Spanaki, K., Ioannou, A., Zamani, E., & Giannakis, M. (2022). Drivers and challenges of internet of things diffusion in smart stores: A field exploration. *Technological Forecasting and Social Change*, *178*, 121593. DOI: 10.1016/j.techfore.2022.121593

Rogers, A., Foxall, G. R., & Morgan, P. H. (2017). Building consumer understanding by utilizing a Bayesian hierarchical structure within the behavioral perspective model. *The Behavior Analyst*, *40*(2), 419–437. DOI: 10.1007/s40614-017-0120-y PMID: 31976948

Roggeveen, A., & Sethuraman, R. (2020). Customer-interfacing retail technologies in 2020 & beyond: An integrative framework and research directions. *Journal of Retailing*, *96*(3), 299–309. DOI: 10.1016/j.jretai.2020.08.001

Rohden, S. F., & Espartel, L. B. (2024). Consumer Reactions to Technology in Retail: Choice Uncertainty and Reduced Perceived Control in Decisions Assisted by Recommendation Agents. *Electronic Commerce Research*, *24*(2), 901–923. DOI: 10.1007/s10660-024-09808-7

Roy, S. K., Balaji, M. S., & Quazi, A. (2020). Consumer-computer interaction and in-store smart technology (IST) in the retail industry: The role of motivation, opportunity, and ability. *Journal of Marketing Management*, *36*(5-6), 517–548. DOI: 10.1080/0267257X.2020.1736130

Roy, S. K., Balaji, M. S., Quazi, A., & Quaddus, M. (2018). Predictors of customer acceptance of and resistance to smart technologies in the retail sector. *Journal of Retailing and Consumer Services, 42*, 147–160. DOI: 10.1016/j.jretconser.2018.02.005

Sagar, S. (2024). The Impact Of Digital Transformation On Retail Management And Consumer Behavior. *IOSR Journal of Business and Management, 26 (1),* 06-14. https://doi.org/DOI: 10.9790/487X-2601010614

Salminen, J., Kandpal, C., Kamel, A. M., Jung, S. G., & Jansen, B. J. (2022). Creating and detecting fake reviews of online products. *Journal of Retailing and Consumer Services, 64*, 102771. DOI: 10.1016/j.jretconser.2021.102771

Sano, N., & Yada, K. (2015). The influence of sales areas and bargain sales on customer behavior in a grocery store. *Neural Computing & Applications, 26*(2), 355–361. DOI: 10.1007/s00521-014-1619-8

Sari, P. K., Alamsyah, A., & Wibowo, S. (2018, March). Measuring e-Commerce service quality from online customer review using Sentiment Analysis. []. IOP Publishing.]. *Journal of Physics: Conference Series, 971*, 012053. DOI: 10.1088/1742-6596/971/1/012053

Sarwar, B. M., Karypis, G., Konstan, J. A., & Riedl, J. (2001). Item-based collaborative filtering recommendation algorithms. *Proceedings of the 10th International Conference on World Wide Web (WWW 2001)*, 285-295. DOI: 10.1145/371920.372071

Schafer, J. B., Konstan, J. A., & Riedl, J. (2001). E-commerce recommendation applications. *Data Mining and Knowledge Discovery, 5*(1-2), 115–153. DOI: 10.1023/A:1009804230409

Schwartz, S. A., & Mahnke, M. S. (2021). Facebook use as a communicative relation: Exploring the relation between Facebook users and the algorithmic news feed. *Information Communication and Society, 24*(7), 1041–1056. DOI: 10.1080/1369118X.2020.1718179

Sehito, N., Yang, S., Larik, R. S. A., Kamal, M. M., Alwabli, A., & Ullah, I. (2024). Artificial Intelligence (AI) and Internet of Things (IoT) Applications in Sustainable Technology. Advanced Technologies and Societal Change, 227-246.

Selamat, M. A., & Windasari, N. A. (2021). Chatbot for SMEs: Integrating customer and business owner perspectives. *Technology in Society, 66*, 101685. DOI: 10.1016/j.techsoc.2021.101685

Sepasgozar, S., Karimi, R., Farahzadi, L., Moezzi, F., Shirowzhan, S. M., Ebrahimzadeh, S., Hui, F., & Aye, L. (2020). A Systematic Content Review of Artificial Intelligence and the Internet of Things Applications in Smart Home. *Applied Sciences (Basel, Switzerland)*, *10*(9), 3074. DOI: 10.3390/app10093074

Shah, H. (2024). *AI in Transportation Industry: Use Cases, Benefits, Applications and Real World Examples.* 9th October 2024. Prismetric. Retrieved 25th november 2024 from https://www.prismetric.com/ai-in-transportation/

Shahbazian, R., Macrina, G., Scalzo, E., & Guerriero, F. (2023). Machine Learning Assists IoT Localization: A Review of Current Challenges and Future Trends. *Sensors (Basel)*, *23*(7), 3551. DOI: 10.3390/s23073551 PMID: 37050611

Shankar, A., & Zennaro, M. (2023). Efficient Data Interpretation and Artificial Intelligence Enabled IoT Based Smart Sensing System. *Artificial Intelligence Review*, *56*(12), 15053–15077. DOI: 10.1007/s10462-023-10519-y

Shankara, P., Mahanta, P., Arora, E., & Srinivasamurthy, G. (2015). Impact of Internet of Things in the Retail Industry. In Ciuciu, I. (Eds.), Lecture Notes in Computer Science: Vol. 9416. *On the Move to Meaningful Internet Systems: OTM 2015 Workshops. OTM 2015*. Springer., DOI: 10.1007/978-3-319-26138-6_9

Shankar, K., Kalyanam, K., Setia, P., Golmohammadi, A., Tirunillai, S., Douglass, T., Hennessey, J., Bull, J. S., & Waddoups, R. (2021). How technology is changing retail. *Journal of Retailing*, *97*(1), 13–27. DOI: 10.1016/j.jretai.2020.10.006

Shankar, V.. (2021). How Artificial Intelligence is Reshaping Retailing. *Journal of Retailing*.

Shankar, V., & Balasubramanian, S. (2009). Mobile Marketing: A Synthesis and Prognosis. *Journal of Interactive Marketing*, *23*(2), 118–129. DOI: 10.1016/j.intmar.2009.02.002

Sharma, I., & Aggarwal, A. (2024). Revolutionizing Creative Tourism: Integrating AI in Marketing for Immersive Travel Experiences. *Innovative Technologies for Increasing Service Productivity*, 179-197.

Sharma, R. (2023). Leveraging AI and IoT for Sustainable Waste Management. In Whig, P., Silva, N., Elngar, A. A., Aneja, N., & Sharma, P. (Eds.), *Sustainable Development through Machine Learning, AI and IoT. ICSD 2023. Communications in Computer and Information Science* (Vol. 1939). Springer., DOI: 10.1007/978-3-031-47055-4_12

Shekhawat, S. (2023). Smart retail: How AI and IoT are revolutionising the retail industry. *Journal of AI. Robotics & Workplace Automation*, *2*(2), 145–152. DOI: 10.69554/TCLG1264

Shin, D. (2014). A Socio-technical Framework for Internet-of-Things Design: A Human-Centered Design for the Internet of Things. *Telematics and Informatics*, *31*(4), 519–531. DOI: 10.1016/j.tele.2014.02.003

Shirgir, B., Dimililer, K., & Asir, S. (2024). Applications of Artificial Intelligence in Biosensors. Smart Innovation. *Systems and Technologies*, *389*, 299–315.

Shneiderman, B. (2020). Bridging the gap between ethics and practice: Guidelines for reliable, safe, and trustworthy human-centered AI systems. [TiiS]. *ACM Transactions on Interactive Intelligent Systems*, *10*(4), 1–31. DOI: 10.1145/3419764

Singh, S. (2020). AI and IoT in Retail: Its impact on retail value chain & shoppers' behaviour. [IJARET]. *International Journal of Advanced Research in Engineering and Technology*, *11*(7), 766–777. DOI: 10.34218/IJARET.11.7.2020.075

Singh, Y. V., Khan, S., Singh, P., & Singh, R. S. (2022). *An Optimized Artificial Intelligence System Using IoT Biosensors Networking for Healthcare Problems*. Computational Intelligence and Neuroscience.

Sjodin, D., Parida, V., Kohtamaki, M., & Wincent, J. (2020). An agile co-creation process for digital servitization: A micro-service innovation approach. *Journal of Business Research*, *112*, 478–491. DOI: 10.1016/j.jbusres.2020.01.009

Skutle, M. (2022). *Discovering music in the streaming era: How online recommendation engines and application design influence users' habits and discoveries in online music streaming services* (Master's thesis, The University of Bergen).

Soares, N., Monteiro, P., Duarte, F. J., & Machado, R. J. (2020). A Unified Reference Model for Smart Cities. In Santos, H., Pereira, G., Budde, M., Lopes, S., & Nikolic, P. (Eds.), *Science and Technologies for Smart Cities. SmartCity 360 2019. Lecture Notes of the Institute for Computer Sciences, Social Informatics and Telecommunications Engineering* (Vol. 323). Springer., DOI: 10.1007/978-3-030-51005-3_16

Sorensen, H. (2009). *Inside the mind of the shopper*. Pearson Education.

Sposato, M. (2024). Leadership training and development in the age of artificial intelligence. *Development and Learning in Organizations*, *38*(4), 4–7. DOI: 10.1108/DLO-12-2023-0256

Sposato, M., Dittmar, E. C., & Vargas Portillo, J. P. (2025). New technologies in HR: Bridging efficiency and ethical considerations. *The International Journal of Organizational Analysis*. Advance online publication. DOI: 10.1108/IJOA-09-2024-4814

Srivastava, V., Kishore, S., & Dhingra, D. (2021). Technology and the future of customer experience. In *Crafting customer experience strategy* (pp. 91–116). Emerald Publishing Limited. DOI: 10.1108/978-1-83909-710-220211006

StarUs Insights. (2025). *IoT in Retail: Discover Top 9 Ways it is Reshaping the Industry.* Retrieved 14th February from https://www.startus-insights.com/innovators-guide/iot-in-retail/

Stetter, J. R. (2012). Smart sensors and applications. In *Encyclopedia of Sensors* (Vol. 9, pp. 1–13). American Scientific Publishers.

Štofková, K. R., Bajza, F., Janošková, P., & Kováčiková, M. (2024). Proposal of innovative smart solutions for retail store in order to support competitiveness and sustainable development. *Frontiers of Computer Science*, *6*, 1328913. DOI: 10.3389/fcomp.2024.1328913

Stone, D., & Heen, S. (2014). *Thanks for the feedback: The science and art of receiving feedback well.* Penguin.

Stoyanov, D. (2021). The role of vending channels in marketing: A systematic review and taxonomy of studies. *The Journal of Consumer Affairs*, *55*(2), 654–679. DOI: 10.1111/joca.12362

Strom, R., Vendel, M., & Bredican, J. (2014). Mobile marketing: A literature review on its value for consumers and retailers. *Journal of Retailing and Consumer Services*, *21*(6), 1001–1012. DOI: 10.1016/j.jretconser.2013.12.003

Subramanian, N., Chaudhuri, A., & Kayıkcı, Y. (2020). Blockchain Applications in Retail Supply Chain. In *Blockchain and Supply Chain Logistics*. Palgrave Pivot., DOI: 10.1007/978-3-030-47531-4_6

Sulastri, L. (2023). The Role of Artificial Intelligence in Enhancing Customer Experience: A Case Study of Global E-commerce Platforms. *The International Journal of Science in Society*, *5*(3), 451–469. DOI: 10.54783/ijsoc.v5i3.1257

Sutton, R. S., & Barto, A. G. (2018). *Reinforcement learning: An introduction.* MIT Press.

Swani, K., & Milne, G. (2017). Evaluating Facebook brand content popularity for service versus goods offerings. *Journal of Business Research*, *79*, 123–133. DOI: 10.1016/j.jbusres.2017.06.003

Syed, A. S., Sierra-Sosa, D., Kumar, A., & Elmaghraby, A. (2021). IoT in Smart Cities: A Survey of Technologies, Practices and Challenges. *Smart Cities*, *4*(2), 429–475. DOI: 10.3390/smartcities4020024

Szabo-Szentgroti, G., Gyenge, B., & Papp, B. (2023). The rise of cashierless stores: Implications for the retail industry. *Technological Forecasting and Social Change*, *182*, 121855. DOI: 10.1016/j.techfore.2022.121855

Taddeo, M., & Floridi, L. (2018). How AI can be a force for good. *Science*, *361*(6404), 751–752. DOI: 10.1126/science.aat5991 PMID: 30139858

Takai, K., & Yada, K. (2013). A framework for analysis of the effect of time on shopping behavior. *Journal of Intelligent Information Systems*, *41*(1), 91–107. DOI: 10.1007/s10844-012-0223-6

Tamura, T., Inaba, T., Nakamura, O., Kokuryo, J., & Murai, J. (2010). *A proposal on RFID data analytics methods. In 2010 Internet of Things (IOT)*. IEEE., DOI: 10.1109/IOT.2010.5678448

Tan, F. T. C., Guo, Z., Cahalane, M., & Cheng, D. (2016). Developing business analytic capabilities for combating e-commerce identity fraud: A study of Trustev's digital verification solution. *Information & Management*, *53*(7), 878–891. DOI: 10.1016/j.im.2016.07.002

Tan, L., Ren, C., Zhan, Y., Chang, Y. W., Chen, J., & Hsu, M. C. (2024). Exploring consumers' adoption and recommendation in smart retailing: A cognitive absorption perspective. *Current Psychology (New Brunswick, N.J.)*, *43*(26), 22560–22577. DOI: 10.1007/s12144-024-06042-0

Thirunarayan, K., Anantharam, P., Henson, C., & Sheth, A. (2014). Comparative trust management with applications: Bayesian approaches emphasis. *Future Generation Computer Systems*, *31*, 182–199. DOI: 10.1016/j.future.2013.05.006

Thomas, M. (2022). *14 Key IoT In Retail Examples You Need to Know*. 28th September. Built In. Retrieved 24th November from https://builtin.com/articles/iot-in-retail-tech-applications

Thomas-Francois, K., & Somogyi, S. (2023). Self-Checkout Behaviours at Supermarkets: Does the Technological Acceptance Model (TAM) Predict Smart Grocery Shopping Adoption? *International Review of Retail, Distribution and Consumer Research*, *33*(1), 44–66. DOI: 10.1080/09593969.2022.2051195

Ullah, A., Anwar, S. M., Li, J., Nadeem, L., Mahmood, T., Rehman, A., & Saba, T. (2023). Smart cities: The role of Internet of Things and machine learning in realizing a data-centric smart environment. *Complex & Intelligent Systems, 10*(1), 1607–1637. DOI: 10.1007/s40747-023-01175-4

Underhill, P. (2009). *Why we buy: The science of shopping*. Simon & Schuster.

Van de Sanden, S., Willems, K., & Brengman, M. (2019). In-store location-based marketing with beacons: From inflated expectations to smart use in retailing. *Journal of Marketing Management, 35*(15-16), 1514–1541. DOI: 10.1080/0267257X.2019.1689154

Van Es, K. (2023). Netflix & big data: The strategic ambivalence of an entertainment company. *Television & New Media, 24*(6), 656–672. DOI: 10.1177/15274764221125745

Vapnik, V. (1995). *The Nature of Statistical Learning Theory*. Springer. DOI: 10.1007/978-1-4757-2440-0

Vashishth, T. K., Sharma, V., Sharma, K. K., Kumar, B., Kumar, A., & Panwar, R. (2024). Artificial Intelligence (AI)–Powered Chatbots: Providing Instant Support and Personalized Recommendations to Guests 24/7. In *Technology and Luxury Hospitality* (pp. 211-236). Routledge.

Veale, M., & Zuiderveen Borgesius, F. (2021). - Demystifying the Draft EU Artificial Intelligence Act — Analysing the good, the bad, and the unclear elements of the proposed approach. *Computer Law Review International, 22*(4), 97–112. DOI: 10.9785/cri-2021-220402

Velosiot (2024). *Top IoT Use Cases in Retail with Real-Life Examples*. 20th February. Retrieved 25th November 2024 from https://blog.velosiot.com/top-iot-use-cases-in-retail-with-real-life-examples

Vidanagama, D. U., Silva, T. P., & Karunananda, A. S. (2020). Deceptive consumer review detection: A survey. *Artificial Intelligence Review, 53*(2), 1323–1352. DOI: 10.1007/s10462-019-09697-5

Villar, E., Martín Toral, I., Calvo, I., Barambones, O., & Fernández-Bustamante, P. (2024). Architectures for Industrial AIoT Applications. *Sensors (Basel), 24*(15), 4929. DOI: 10.3390/s24154929 PMID: 39123976

Viswanadha, V., Pavan Kumar, P., & Chiranjeevi Reddy, S. (2018). Smart shopping cart. In *2018 International Conference on Circuits and Systems in Digital Enterprise Technology (ICCSDET)* (pp. 1–4). IEEE. DOI: 10.1109/ICCSDET.2018.8821165

Wachter, S., & Mittelstadt, B. (2018). A Right to Reasonable Inferences: Re-Thinking Data Protection Law in the Age of Big Data and AI. *Columbia Business Law Review, 2019*(2). Retrieved from: https://ssrn.com/abstract=3248829

Wakefield, L. (2024). *Understanding the adoption and application of AI in Digital Advertising*. IAB Europe and Microsoft, 30th April 2024. Retrieved 25th November 2024 from https://iabeurope.eu/knowledge_hub/iab-europe-and-microsofts-understanding-the-adoption-and-application-of-ai-in-digital-advertising-report/

Walters, R., & Novak, M. (2021). Artificial Intelligence and Law. In *Cyber Security, Artificial Intelligence, Data Protection & the Law*. Springer., DOI: 10.1007/978-981-16-1665-5_3

Wang, C., He, T., Zhou, H., Zhang, Z., & Lee, C. (2023). Artificial Intelligence Enhanced Sensors - Enabling Technologies to Next-Generation Healthcare and Biomedical Platform. *Bioelectronic Medicine*, *9*(1), 17. DOI: 10.1186/s42234-023-00118-1 PMID: 37528436

Wang, G., Xie, S., Liu, B., & Yu, P. S. (2012). Identify online store review spammers via social review graph. [TIST]. *ACM Transactions on Intelligent Systems and Technology*, *3*(4), 1–21. DOI: 10.1145/2337542.2337546

Wang, J., Yu, X., Li, J., & Jin, X. (2018). Artificial Intelligence and International Norms. In Jin, D. (Ed.), *Reconstructing Our Orders*. Springer., DOI: 10.1007/978-981-13-2209-9_7

Wang, Q., Zhang, W., Li, J., Mai, F., & Ma, Z. (2022). Effect of online review sentiment on product sales: The moderating role of review credibility perception. *Computers in Human Behavior*, *133*, 107272. DOI: 10.1016/j.chb.2022.107272

Warner, K. S. R., & Wäger, M. (2019). Building dynamic capabilities for digital transformation: An ongoing process of strategic renewal. *Long Range Planning*, *52*(3), 326–349. DOI: 10.1016/j.lrp.2018.12.001

Watson, H. J., & Wixom, B. H. (2007). The current state of business intelligence. *Computer*, *40*(9), 96–99. DOI: 10.1109/MC.2007.331

Wei, L., & Xia, Z. (2022). Big Data-Driven Personalization in E-Commerce: Algorithms, Privacy Concerns, and Consumer Behavior Implications. *International Journal of Applied Machine Learning and Computational Intelligence*, *12*(4).

Westerlund, M. (2019). The Emergence of Deepfake Technology: A Review. *Technology Innovation Management Review*, *9*(11), 39–52. DOI: 10.22215/timreview/1282

Wheeldon, J., & Ahlberg, M. (2019). Mind maps in qualitative research. In Creswell, K. A., & Creswell, S. D. (Eds.), *Handbook of qualitative research methods* (pp. 200–210). Sage Publications.

Wheeler, J. (2023). *The Digital-First Customer Experience: Seven Design Strategies from the World's Leading Brands*. Kogan Page Publishers.

Whittlestone, J., Nyrup, R., Alexandrova, A., Dihal, K., & Cave, S. (2019). *Ethical and societal implications of algorithms, data, and artificial intelligence: a roadmap for research*. Nuffield Foundation.

Willems, K., Smolders, A., Brengman, M., Luyten, K., & Schöning, J. (2017). The path-to-purchase is paved with digital opportunities: An inventory of shopper-oriented retail technologies. *Journal of Retailing and Consumer Services*, *39*, 229–238. DOI: 10.1016/j.jretconser.2017.07.009

Wolniak, R., & Stecuła, K. (2024). Artificial Intelligence in Smart Cities—Applications, Barriers, and Future Directions: A Review. *Smart Cities*, *7*(3), 1346–1389. DOI: 10.3390/smartcities7030057

Wolpert, R., & Roth, A. (2020). Development of a classification framework for retail technologies. *Journal of Retailing and Consumer Services*, *57*, 102–110. DOI: 10.1016/j.jretconser.2020.102110

Wu, Y., Ngai, E. W., Wu, P., & Wu, C. (2020). Fake online reviews: Literature review, synthesis, and directions for future research. *Decision Support Systems*, *132*, 113280. DOI: 10.1016/j.dss.2020.113280

Yada, K. (2011). String analysis technique for shopping path in a supermarket. *Journal of Intelligent Information Systems*, *36*(3), 385–402. DOI: 10.1007/s10844-009-0113-8

Yada, K., Ishibashi, K., Ohashi, T., Wang, D., & Tsumoto, S. (2020). How shoppers walk and shop in a supermarket. In *2020 International Conference on Data Mining Workshops (ICDMW)* (pp. 114–118). IEEE. DOI: 10.1109/ICDMW51313.2020.00025

Yao, L., Zhang, F., & Zhang, D. (2019). Deep learning for recommender systems. *Proceedings of the 28th International Joint Conference on Artificial Intelligence (IJCAI-19)*, 3202-3208.

Yasar, K., Gillis, A. S., & Christensen, G. (2023). *Artificial intelligence of things (AIoT)*. Retrieved 22th November 2024 from https://www.techtarget.com/iotagenda/definition/Artificial-Intelligence-of-Things-AIoT

Yin, H., Zhang, Z. P., & Liu, Y. Y. (2024). The Exploration of Integrating the Midjourney Artificial Intelligence Generated Content Tool into Design Systems to Direct Designers towards Future-Oriented Innovation. *Systems*, *11*(12), 566. Advance online publication. DOI: 10.3390/systems11120566

Yongho Hyun, M., Kim, H.-C., & O'Keefe, R. M. (2014). Inter-satisfaction between website and automated call distribution (ACD) systems. *Journal of Travel & Tourism Marketing*, *31*(8), 1039–1056. DOI: 10.1080/10548408.2014.892467

Yu, X., Ai, T., & Wang, K. (2024). Application of Nanogenerators in Acoustics Based on Artificial Intelligence and Machine Learning. *APL Materials*, *12*(2), 020602. DOI: 10.1063/5.0195399

Zahara, A. N., Rini, E. S., & Sembiring, B. K. F. (2021). The Influence of Seller Reputation and Online Customer Reviews towards Purchase Decisions through Consumer Trust from C2C E-Commerce Platform Users in Medan, North Sumatera, Indonesia. *International Journal of Research and Review*, *8*(2), 422–438.

Zaman, M., Puryear, N., Abdelwahed, S., & Zohrabi, N. (2024). A Review of IoT-Based Smart City Development and Management. *Smart Cities*, *7*(3), 1462–1501. DOI: 10.3390/smartcities7030061

Zapier. (2021). The 9 best free form builders and survey tools in 2021. https://zapier.com/blog/best-free-survey-tool-form-app/

Zeng, J., Lu, Y., & Huang, Y. (2022). Algorithmic Bias in Marketing AI. *Journal of Business Research*, *145*, 678–689.

Zennaro, M., & Manzoni, P. (2021). AI for IoT: Special Issue on AI for IoT. [Special Issue]. *Sensors (Basel)*.

Zhang, L., Wu, M., & Lu, W. (2015). Collaborative filtering with matrix factorization and KNN., *1*(1), 81-106.

Zhang, S. (2024). The role of Artificial Intelligence in enhancing online sales and the customer experience.

Zhang, G., Li, Z., Huang, J., Wu, J., Zhou, C., Yang, J., & Gao, J. (2022). efraudcom: An e-commerce fraud detection system via competitive graph neural networks. [TOIS]. *ACM Transactions on Information Systems*, *40*(3), 1–29. DOI: 10.1145/3474379

Zhang, X., Guo, F., Chen, T., Pan, L., Beliakov, G., & Wu, J. (2023). A Brief Survey of Machine Learning and Deep Learning Techniques for E-Commerce Research. *Journal of Theoretical and Applied Electronic Commerce Research*, *18*(4), 2188–2216. DOI: 10.3390/jtaer18040110

Zhang, Y., Bian, J., & Zhu, W. (2013). Trust fraud: A crucial challenge for China's e-commerce market. *Electronic Commerce Research and Applications, 12*(5), 299–308. DOI: 10.1016/j.elerap.2012.11.005

Zhao, L. (2023). Artificial intelligence and law: emerging divergent national regulatory approaches in a changing landscape of fast-evolving AI technologies (369-399). In Collins, D., & Geist, M. (Eds.), *Research Handbook on Digital Trade* (pp. 369–399)., DOI: 10.4337/9781800884953.00033

Zhao, L., Zuo, Y., & Yada, K. (2023). Sequential classification of customer behavior based on sequence-to-sequence learning with gated-attention neural networks. *Advances in Data Analysis and Classification, 17*(3), 549–581. DOI: 10.1007/s11634-022-00517-3

Zheng, X., Zhu, S., & Lin, Z. (2013). Capturing the essence of word-of-mouth for social commerce: Assessing the quality of online e-commerce reviews by a semi-supervised approach. *Decision Support Systems, 56*, 211–222. DOI: 10.1016/j.dss.2013.06.002

Zulfan, G., Kee, D. M. H., Khor, T. W., Lee, S. Y., Ali, H. J., Hanan, A., & Akansha, V. (2020). The Influence of Organizational Culture on Employee Retention: A Case of Google. *Journal of the community development in Asia, 3*(1), 25-32.

Zuo, Y., & Yada, K. (2015). Using statistical learning theory for purchase behavior prediction via direct observation of in-store behavior. In 2015 2nd Asia-Pacific World Congress on Computer Science and Engineering (APWC on CSE) (pp. 1–6). IEEE. DOI: 10.1109/APWCCSE.2015.7476215

Zuo, Y., Yada, K., & Ali, A. B. M. S. (2016). Prediction of consumer purchasing in a grocery store using machine learning techniques. In 2016 Asia-Pacific World Congress on Computer Science and Engineering and Asia-Pacific World Congress on Engineering (APWC on CSE) (pp. 18–25). IEEE. DOI: 10.1109/APWC-on-CSE.2016.015

Zuo, Y., Shawkat Ali, A. B. M., & Yada, K. (2014). Consumer purchasing behavior extraction using statistical learning theory. *Procedia Computer Science, 35*, 1464–1473. DOI: 10.1016/j.procs.2014.08.209

Zwicky, F. (1969). *Discovery, invention, research – Through the morphological approach.* Macmillan.

About the Contributors

Joaquim Pratas holds a PhD and Master's degree in Business and Management Studies, with a specialization in Marketing and Strategy, and a Bachelor's degree in Economics from the University of Porto. He is a lecturer at Polytechnic of Porto and regularly teaches postgraduated courses at Porto Business School. He is a researcher at CEOS.PP at Polytechnic of Porto and GOVCOPP at University of Aveiro. His main areas of interest involve Retail, Marketing, Communication, Tourism, Sales, E-Business and Artificial intelligence. He published a book, several chapters in books edited by IGI, and articles in the International Journal of Retail and Distribution Management, Tourism Management and Anatolia: an International Journal of Tourism and Hospitality Research. He has also contributed to several conference proceedings and has served as a reviewer for various journals and conferences. Before entering the academia, he worked in one of the largest retail companies in Portugal.

Maria Antónia Gonçalves Rodrigues has a PhD in Communication/Marketing, from the University of Vigo, a Master in Marketing, from the University of Porto, a Bachelor's degree in Marketing (2002), and a Bachelor's degree in International Trade, both from the Polytechnic of Porto. She is a senior lecturer, a council member, and a Director of Marketing Bachelor's degree at the Management School of the Polytechnic of Porto. She is a researcher at CEOS.PP and SIIS. She has published several papers and 3 books, with IGI Global (2 are SCOPUS Indexing). She has organized 1 scientific event and participated in several scientific events. She supervised several MSc dissertation(s). She has received 2 awards/honors. She works in the area of Social Sciences with an emphasis on business and marketing management. Her research topics are consumer behavior, customer experience; business models, marketing services; digital marketing, tourism, and customer experience with technology (SST, AI, VR, AR, metaverse).

Maria Amélia Machado Carvalho is a PhD in Business and Management Studies, with a specialization in Marketing and Strategy, from the Faculty of Economics (FEP) at the University of Porto, in 2017. In 2012, completed a Master's degree in Economics and Management of Cities and graduated in Economics in 2010. Both academic degrees were obtained from the Faculty of Economics (FEP) at the University of Porto. Invited Assistant Professor at ISCAP since 2018. Her main areas of research relate to brands and consumer behavior, having published articles in the Journal of Marketing Theory and Practice, International Journal of Tourism Cities, Tourism Recreation Research, among others. She has also published two books with IGI Global (both indexed in Scopus) and reviewed several articles for IGI Global and other publications. She is a researcher at CEOS.PP. and is specific interests in city branding, customer engagement, consumer experience, city marketing, service marketing, and tourism marketing.

***

Monica Bhutani is a distinguished academician and researcher in Electronics & Communications Engineering and Computer Science. She serves as an Associate Professor at Bharati Vidyapeeth's College of Engineering (BVCOE), New Delhi, and as a Postdoctoral Researcher and Research Associate at Lincoln University College, Malaysia. She is Editor-in-Chief of the Scienxt Journal of Electrical & Electronics Communication and on the editorial board of Wireless and Communication Letters (Bentham Science). She earned her Ph.D. from IIT Delhi on MAC layer issues in Optical Wireless Communication. With 18+ years of academic experience, her research spans Optical Wireless Communication, VLC, Li-Fi, WSNs, Zigbee, IEEE 802.15.x, Computer Networks, and Machine Learning for IoT. She leads the IEEE BVCOE Student Chapter and has published 85+ papers, chaired 50+ conferences, authored books, and holds two patents.

Eduardo Carlos Dittmar is an economist holding a PhD in Economic and Business Sciences. He brings extensive teaching expertise at both undergraduate and graduate levels. His scholarly work encompasses fundamental and applied research, resulting in a contribution of over 50 peer-reviewed publications and book chapters. Throughout his career, he has maintained active involvement in various research groups and served on editorial boards of multiple academic journals. His research interests focus on new technologies, corporate social responsibility, strategic marketing, and business ethics.

David López Jiménez obtained his Law degree from the Complutense University of Madrid. He obtained one PhD (with European mention) from the

Seville University and another PhD from the Rey Juan Carlos University. He has an Extraordinary Doctoral Award. He has leaded research stays in different European countries. He is the author of several monographs, some of them published by the prestigious publisher Thomson Reuters and Marcial Pons, as well as more than 200 publications in various scientific journals, book chapters, book reviews, and comments about national and international law.

Kamalendu Pal is with the Department of Computer Science, School of Mathematics, Computer Science and Engineering, City University London. Kamalendu received his BSc (Hons) degree in Physics from Calcutta University, India, Postgraduate Diploma in Computer Science from Pune, India; MSc degree in Software Systems Technology from Sheffield University, Postgraduate Diploma in Artificial Intelligence from Kingston University, MPhil degree in Computer Science from University College London, and MBA degree from University of Hull, United Kingdom. He has published dozens of research papers in international journals and conferences. His research interests include knowledge-based systems, decision support systems, computer integrated design, software engineering, and service oriented computing. He is a member of the British Computer Society, the Institution of Engineering and Technology, and the IEEE Computer Society.

Jenny Patricia Vargas Portillo is a PhD with the highest qualification, three master's degrees, an Advanced Studies Diploma and numerous specialization courses. The research carried out involves both basic and applied exploration. The lines she has been working involves, among others, Consumer Behavior, Marketing and New Technologies (Interactive Advertising and Electronic Commerce). She has been teaching and doing research in different countries of the world. She has been a professor at undergraduate and graduate levels. Likewise, she has directed a significant number of Bachelor and Master theses.

Index

T

U

V

www.ingramcontent.com/pod-product-compliance
Lightning Source LLC
LaVergne TN
LVHW080601300926
849162LV00005B/1014